A REBEL WAR CLERK'S DIARY AT THE CONFEDERATE STATES CAPITAL.

BY

J. B. JONES,

CLERK IN THE WAR DEPARTMENT OF THE CONFEDERATE STATES GOVERNMENT;
AUTHOR OF "WILD WESTERN SCENES," ETC. ETC.

VOL. I.

PHILADELPHIA:
J. B. LIPPINCOTT & CO.
1866.

PREFACE.

THIS DIARY was written with the knowledge of the President and the Secretary of War. I informed them of it by note. They did not deprecate criticism on their official conduct; for they allowed me still to execute the functions of a very important position in the Government until the end of its career.

My discriminating friends will understand why I accepted the poor title of a clerkship, after having declined the *Chargéship* to Naples, tendered by Mr. Calhoun during the administration of President Polk.

J. B. J.

ONANCOCK, Accomac Co., Va.,
March, 1866.

CONTENTS.

VOLUME I.

CHAPTER XVI.

CHAPTER XVII.

CHAPTER XVIII.

CHAPTER XIX.

CHAPTER XX.

CHAPTER XXVI.

CHAPTER XXVII.

CHAPTER XXVIII.

VOLUME II.

CHAPTER XXIX.

CHAPTER XXX.

CHAPTER XXXI.

CHAPTER XXXII.

CHAPTER XXXIII.

CHAPTER XXXIV.

A REBEL WAR CLERK'S DIARY.

CHAPTER I.

My flight from the North and escape into Virginia.—Revolutionary scene at Richmond.—The Union Convention passes the Ordinance of Secession.—Great excitement prevails in the South.

April 8th, 1861. Burlington, New Jersey.—The expedition sails to-day from New York. Its purpose is to reduce Fort Moultrie, Charleston harbor, and relieve Fort Sumter, invested by the Confederate forces. Southern born, and editor of the *Southern Monitor*, there seems to be no alternative but to depart immediately. For years the *Southern Monitor*, Philadelphia, whose motto was "The Union as it was, the Constitution as it is," has foreseen and foretold the resistance of the Southern States, in the event of the success of a sectional party inimical to the institution of African slavery, upon which the welfare and existence of the Southern people seem to depend. And I must depart immediately; for I well know that the first gun fired at Fort Sumter will be the signal for an outburst of ungovernable fury, and I should be seized and thrown into prison.

I must leave my family—my property—everything. My family cannot go with me—but they may follow. The storm will not break in its fury for a month or so. Only the most obnoxious persons, deemed dangerous, will be molested immediately.

8 o'clock p.m.—My wife and children have been busy packing my trunk, and making other preparations for my departure. They are cheerful. They deem the rupture of the States a *fait accompli*, but reck not of the horrors of war. They have contrived to pack up, with other things, my fine old portrait of Calhoun, by Jarvis. But I must leave my papers, the accumulation of twenty-

five years, comprising thousands of letters from predestined rebels. My wife opposes my suggestion that they be burned. Among them are some of the veto messages of President Tyler, and many letters from him, Governor Wise, etc. With the latter I had a correspondence in 1856, showing that this blow would probably have been struck then, if Fremont had been elected.

APRIL 9TH.—My adieus over, I set out in the broad light of day. When the cars arrived at Camden, I proceeded, with the rest of the *through* passengers, in the boat to the navy yard, without going ashore in the city. The passengers were strangers to me. Many could be easily recognized as Southern men; but quite as many were going only as far as Washington, for their reward. They were bold denouncers of the rebellion; the others were silent, thoughtful, but in earnest.

The first thing which attracted my attention, as the cars left the Delaware depot, was a sign-board on my left, inscribed in large letters, "UNION CEMETERY." My gaze attracted the notice of others. A mocking *bon-mot* was uttered by a Yankee wit, which was followed by laughter.

For many hours I was plunged in the deepest abstraction, and spoke not a word until we were entering the depot at Washington, just as the veil of night was falling over the scene.

Then I was aroused by the announcement of a conductor that, failing to have my trunk rechecked at Baltimore, it had been left in that city! Determined not to lose it, I took the return train to Baltimore, and put up at Barnum's Hotel. Here I met with Mr. Abell, publisher of the Baltimore *Sun*, an old acquaintance. Somewhat contrary to my expectations, knowing him to be a native of the North, I found him an ardent secessionist. So enthusiastic was he in the cause, that he denounced both Maryland and Virginia for their hesitancy in following the example of the Cotton States; and he invited me to furnish his paper with correspondence from Montgomery, or any places in the South where I might be a sojourner.

APRIL 10TH.—Making an early start this morning, I once more arrived at Washington City. I saw no evidences of a military force in the city, and supposed the little army to be encamped at the west end of the Avenue, guarding the Executive Mansion.

We took an omnibus without delay and proceeded to the

steamer. As soon as we left the shore, I fancied I saw many of the passengers breathing easier and more deeply. Certainly there was more vivacity, since we were relieved of the presence of Republicans. And at the breakfast table there was a freer flow of speech, and a very decided manifestation of secession proclivities.

Among the passengers was Major Holmes, who had just resigned his commission in the U. S. army. He had been ordered to proceed with the expedition against Charleston; but declined the honor of fighting against his native land. The major is a little deaf, but has an intellectual face, the predominant expression indicating the discretion and prudence so necessary for success in a large field of operations. In reply to a question concerning the military qualities of Beauregard and Bragg, he said they were the flower of the young officers of the U. S. army. The first had great genius, and was perhaps the most dashing and brilliant officer in the country; the other, more sedate, nevertheless possessed military capacities of a very high order. President Davis, in his opinion, had made most excellent selections in the appointment of his first generals. The major, however, was very sad at the prospect before us; and regarded the tenders of pecuniary aid to the U. S. by the Wall Street capitalists as ominous of a desperate, if not a prolonged struggle. At this time the major's own State, North Carolina, like Virginia, Tennessee, Kentucky, Arkansas, and Missouri, yet remains in the Union.

We were delayed several hours at Aquia Creek, awaiting the arrival of the cars, which were detained in consequence of a great storm and flood that had occurred the night before.

April 10th and 11th.—These two days were mainly lost by delays, the floods having swept away many bridges, which had not yet been repaired. As we approached Richmond, it was observed that the people were more and more excited, and seemed to be pretty nearly unanimous for the immediate secession of the State. Everywhere the Convention then in session was denounced with bitterness, for its adherence to the Union; and Gov. Letcher was almost universally execrated for the chocks he had thrown under the car of secession and Southern independence. I heard very many who had voted for him, regret that they had ever supported the clique of politicians who managed to secure his nomination.

And now I learned that a People's Spontaneous Convention would assemble in Richmond on the 16th of the month, when, if the other body persisted in its opposition to the popular will, the most startling revolutionary measures would be adopted, involving, perhaps, arrests and executions. Several of the members of this body with whom I conversed bore arms upon their persons.

APRIL 12TH.—To-day I beheld the first secession flag that had met my vision. It was at Polecat Station, Caroline County, and it was greeted with enthusiasm by all but the two or three Yankees in the train. One of these, named Tupps, had been questioned so closely, and his presence and nativity had become so well known, that he became alarmed for his safety, although no one menaced him. He could not sit still a moment, nor keep silence. He had been speculating in North Carolina the year before, and left some property there, which, of course, he must save, if needs be, at the risk of his life. But *he* cared nothing for slavery, and would never bear arms against the South, if she saw fit to "set up Government business for herself." He rather guessed war was a speculation that wouldn't pay. His volubility increased with his perturbation, and then he drank excessively and sang Dixie. When we reached Richmond, he was beastly drunk.

Arrived at the Exchange Hotel, Richmond. A storm rages above, and below in the minds of men; but the commotion of the elements above attracts less attention than the tempest of excitement agitating the human breast. The news-boys are rushing in all directions with extras announcing the bombardment of Fort Sumter! This is the irrevocable blow! Every reflecting mind here should know that the only alternatives now are successful revolution or abject subjugation. But they do not lack for the want of information of the state of public sentiment in the North. It is in vain that the laggards are assured by persons just from the North, that the Republican leaders now composing the cabinet at Washington were prepared to hail the event at Charleston as the most auspicious that could have happened for the accomplishment of their designs; and that their purpose is the extinction of slavery, at least in the border States; the confiscation of the estates of rebels to reimburse the Federal Government for the expenses of the war which had been deliberately resolved on; and to gratify the cupidity of the "Wide-Awakes," and to give employment to foreign mercenaries.

But it is not doubtful which course the current of feeling is rapidly taking. Even in this hitherto Union city, secession demonstrations are prevalent; and the very men who two days ago upheld Gov. Letcher in his *conservatism*, are now stricken dumb amid the popular clamor for immediate action. I am now resolved to remain in Richmond for a season.

After tea I called upon Gov. Wise, who occupied lodgings at the same hotel. He was worn out, and prostrated by a distressing cough which threatened pneumonia. But ever and anon his eagle eye assumed its wonted brilliancy. He was surrounded by a number of his devoted friends, who listened with rapt attention to his surpassing eloquence. A test question, indicative of the purpose of the Convention to adjourn without action, had that day been carried by a decided majority. The governor once rose from his recumbent position on the sofa and said, whatever the majority of Union men in the Convention might do, or leave undone, Virginia must array herself on one side or the other. She must fight either Lincoln or Davis. If the latter, he would renounce her, and tender his sword and his life to the Southern Confederacy. And although it was apparent that his *physique* was reduced, as he said, to a mere "bag of bones," yet it was evident that his spirit yet struggled with all its native fire and animation.

Soon after President Tyler came in. I had not seen him for several years, and was surprised to find him, under the weight of so many years, unchanged in activity and energy of body and mind. He was quite as ardent in his advocacy of prompt State action as Wise. Having recently abandoned the presidency of the Peace Congress at Washington, in despair of obtaining concessions or guarantees of safety from the rampant powers then in the ascendency, he nevertheless believed, as did a majority of the statesmen of the South, that, even then, in the event of the secession of all the Southern States, presenting thus a united front, no war of great magnitude would ensue. I know better, from my residence in the North, and from the confessions of the Republicans with whom I have been thrown in contact; but I will not dissent voluntarily from the opinions of such statesmen. I can only, when my opinion is desired, intimate my conviction that a great war of the sections might have been averted, if the South had made an adequate *coup d'état* before the inauguration of Lincoln, and while the Democratic party everywhere was yet writhing under the sting and mortification of defeat. *Then* the arm of the Republican party would have been paralyzed, for the attitude of the Democratic party would at least have been a menacing one; but *now*, the Government has been suffered to fall into the possession of the enemy, the sword and the purse have been seized, and it is *too late* to dream of peace—in or out of the Union. Submission will be dishonor. Secession can only be death, which is preferable.

Gov. Wise, smiling, rose again and walked to a corner of the room where I had noticed a bright musket with a sword-bayonet attached. He took it up and criticised the sword as inferior to the *knife*. Our men would require long drilling to become expert with the former, like the French Zouaves; but they instinctively knew how to wield the bowie-knife. The conversation turning upon the probable deficiency of a supply of improved arms in the South, if a great war should ensue, the governor said, with one of his inevitable expressions of feeling, that it was not the improved *arm*, but the improved *man*, which would win the day. Let brave men advance with flint locks and old-fashioned bayonets, on the popinjays of the Northern cities—advance on, and on, under the fire, reckless of the slain, and he would answer for it with his life, that the Yankees would break and run. But, in the event of the Convention adjourning without decisive action, he apprehended the first conflict would be with *Virginians*—the Union men of Virginia. He evidently despaired, under repeated defeats, of seeing an ordinance of secession passed immediately, and would have preferred "resistance" to "secession."

April 13th.—After breakfast I accompanied Gov. Wise to his room. He advised me to remain a few days before proceeding elsewhere. He still doubted, however, whether Virginia would move before autumn. He said there was a majority of 500 Union men then in the city. But the *other* Convention, to meet on the 16th, might do something. He recommended me to a friend of his who distributed the tickets, who gave me a card of admission.

April 14th.—Wrote all day for several journals.

April 15th.—Great demonstrations made throughout the day, and hundreds of secession flags are flying in all parts of the city.

At night, while sitting with Captain O. Jennings Wise in the editorial room of the *Enquirer*, I learned from the Northern exchange papers, which still came to hand, that my office in Philadelphia, "*The Southern Monitor*," had been sacked by the mob. It was said ten thousand had visited my office, displaying a rope with which to hang me. Finding their victim had escaped, they vented their fury in sacking the place. I have not ascertained the extent of the injury done; but if they injured the building, it belonged to H. B., a rich Republican. They tore down the signs (it was a corner house east of the Exchange), and split them up, putting the splinters in their hats, and wearing them as trophies. They next visited the mansion of Gen. P., who had made his fortune dealing in cotton, and had been a bold Northern champion of Southern rights. But the general flinched on this trying occasion. He displayed the stars and stripes, and pledged "the boys" to lead them in battle against the secessionists.

During the evening, a procession with banners and torch-lights came up the street and paused before the *Enquirer* office. They called for Captain Wise, and I accompanied him to the iron balcony, where he made them a soul-stirring speech. At its conclusion, he seized me by the arm and introduced me to the crowd. He informed them of the recent proceedings in Philadelphia, etc., and then ceased speaking, leaving me to tell my own story to the listening multitude. That was not my fault; I had never attempted to make a public speech in my life; and I felt that I was in a predicament. Wise knew it, and enjoyed my embarrassment. I contrived, however, to say to the people that the time for speaking had gone by, and there was no time left for listening. They proceeded up the street, growing like a snow-ball as they rolled onward. At every corner there were cheers uttered for Davis, and groans for Lincoln.

Upon returning to my boarding-house (the hotel being found too expensive), kept by Mrs. Samuels, and her sister, Miss Long, I found the ladies making secession flags. Indeed, the ladies everywhere seem imbued with the spirit of patriotism, and never fail to exert their influence in behalf of Southern independence.

April 15th.—To-day the secession fires assumed a whiter heat. In the Convention the Union men no longer utter denunciations against the disunionists. They merely resort to pretexts and quibbles to stave off the inevitable ordinance. They had sent a deputation to Washington to make a final appeal to Seward and Lincoln to vouchsafe them such guarantees as would enable them to keep Virginia to her moorings. But in vain. They could not obtain even a promise of concession. And now the Union members as they walk the streets, and even Gov. Letcher himself, hear the indignant mutterings of the impassioned storm which threatens every hour to sweep them from existence. Business is generally suspended, and men run together in great crowds to listen to the news from the North, where it is said many outrages are committed on Southern men and those who sympathize with them. Many arrests are made, and the victims thrown into Fort Lafayette. These crowds are addressed by the most inflamed members of the Convention, and never did I hear more hearty responses from the people.

April 16th.—This day the Spontaneous People's Convention met and organized in Metropolitan Hall. The door-keeper stood with a drawn sword in his hand. But the scene was orderly. The assembly was full, nearly every county being represented, and the members were the representatives of the most ancient and respectable families in the State. David Chalmers, of Halifax County, I believe, was the President, and Willoughby Newton, a life-long Whig, among the Vice-Presidents. P. H. Aylett, a grandson of Patrick Henry, was the first speaker. And his eloquence indicated that the spirit of his ancestor survived in him. But he was for moderation and delay, still hoping that the other Convention would yield to the pressure of public sentiment, and place the State in the attitude now manifestly desired by an overwhelming majority of the people. He was answered by the gallant Capt. Wise, who thrilled every breast with his intrepid bearing and electric bursts of oratory. He advocated action, without reference to the other Convention, as the best means of bringing the Unionists to their senses. And the so-called Demosthenean Seddon, and G. W. Randolph (grandson of Thomas Jefferson), Lieut.-Gov. Montague, James Lyons, Judge Robertson, etc., were there. Never, never did I hear more exalted and effective bursts of oratory. And it was apparent that messages were constantly received from the other Convention. What they were, I did not learn at the moment; but it was evident that the Unionists were shaking in their shoes, and they certainly begged one—just one—day's delay, which was accorded them. The People's Convention agreed to adjourn till 10 o'clock A.M. the next day. But before we separated a commotion was observed on the stage, and the next moment a Mr. P., from Gov. Wise's old district, rushed forward and announced that he had just arrived from Norfolk, where, under instructions, and *with the acquiescence of Gov. Letcher*, he had succeeded in blocking the channel of the river; and this would either secure to us, or render useless to the United States, certain ships of the navy, stores, armament, etc., of the value of millions of dollars. This announcement was received with the wildest shouts of joy. Young men threw up their hats, and old men buttoned their coats and clapped their hands most vigorously. It was next hinted by some one who seemed to know something of the matter, that before another day elapsed, Harper's Ferry would fall into the hands of the secessionists.

At night the enthusiasm increases in intensity, and no further opposition is to be apprehended from the influence of Tim Rives, Baldwin, Clemens, etc. etc. It was quite apparent, indeed, that if an ordinance of secession were passed by the new Convention, its validity would be recognized and acted upon by the majority of the people. But this would be a complication of the civil war, now the decree of fate.

Perhaps the occurrence which has attracted most attention is the raising of the Southern flag on the capitol. It was hailed with the most deafening shouts of applause. But at a quiet hour of the night, the governor had it taken down, for the Convention had not yet passed the ordinance of secession. Yet the stars and stripes did not float in its stead; it was replaced by the flag of Virginia.

April 17th.—This was a memorable day. When we assembled at Metropolitan Hall, it could be easily perceived that we were on the threshold of momentous events. All other subjects, except that of a new political organization of the State, seemed to be momentarily delayed, as if awaiting action elsewhere. And this plan of political organization filled me with alarm, for I apprehended it would result in a new conflict between the old parties—Whig and Democrat. The ingenious discussion of this subject was probably a device of the Unionists, two or three of them having obtained seats in the Revolutionary Convention. I knew the ineradicable instincts of Virginia politicians, and their inveterate habit of public speaking, and knew there were well-grounded fears that we should be launched and lost in an illimitable sea of argument, when the business was Revolution, and death to the coming invader. Besides, I saw no hope of unanimity if the old party distinctions and designations were not submerged forever.

These fears, however, were groundless. The Union had received its *blessure mortelle*, and no power this side of the Potomac could save it. During a pause in the proceedings, one of the leading members arose and announced that he had information that the vote was about being taken in the other Convention on the ordinance of secession. "Very well!" cried another member, "we will give them another chance to save themselves. But it is the last!" This was concurred in by a vast majority. Not long after, Lieut.-Gov. Montague came in and announced the passage of the ordinance by the other Convention! This was succeeded by a moment too thrilling for utterance, but was followed by tears of gladness and rapturous applause. Soon after, President Tyler and Gov. Wise were conducted arm-in-arm, and bare-headed, down the center aisle amid a din of cheers, while every member rose to his feet. They were led to the platform, and called upon to address the Convention. The venerable ex-President of the United States first rose responsive to the call, but remarked that the exhaustion incident to his recent incessant labors, and the nature of his emotions at such a momentous crisis, superadded to the feebleness of age, rendered him physically unable to utter what he felt and thought on such an occasion. Nevertheless, he seemed to acquire supernatural strength as he proceeded, and he spoke most effectively for the space of fifteen minutes. He gave a brief history of all the struggles of our race for freedom, from *Magna Charta* to the present day; and he concluded with a solemn declaration that at no period of our history were we engaged in a more just and holy effort for the maintenance of liberty and independence than at the present moment. The career of the dominant party at the North was but a series of aggressions, which fully warranted the steps we were taking for resistance and eternal separation; and if we performed our whole duty as Christians and patriots, the same benign Providence which favored the cause of our forefathers in the Revolution of 1776, would again crown our efforts with similar success. He said he might not survive to witness the consummation of the work begun that day; but generations yet unborn would bless those who had the high privilege of being participators in it.

He was succeeded by Gov. Wise, who, for a quarter of an hour, electrified the assembly by a burst of eloquence, perhaps never surpassed by mortal orator. During his pauses a silence reigned, pending which the slightest breathing could be distinctly heard, while every eye was bathed in tears. At times the vast assembly rose involuntarily to their feet, and every emotion and expression of feature seemed responsive to his own. During his speech he alluded to the reports of the press that the oppressors of the North had probably seized one of his children sojourning in their midst. "But," said he, "if they suppose hostages of my own heart's blood will stay my hand in a contest for the maintenance of sacred rights, they are mistaken. Affection for kindred, property, and life itself sink into insignificance in comparison with the overwhelming importance of public duty in such a crisis as this." He lamented the blindness which had prevented Virginia from seizing Washington before the Republican hordes got possession of it—but, said he, we must do our best under the circumstances. It was now Independence or Death—although he had preferred fighting in the Union—and when the mind was made up to die rather than fail, success was certain. For himself, he was eager to meet the ordeal, and he doubted not every Southern heart pulsated in unison with his own.

Hon. J. M. Mason, and many other of Virginia's distinguished sons were called upon, and delivered patriotic speeches. And finally, *Gov. Letcher* appeared upon the stage. He was loudly cheered by the very men who, two days before, would gladly have witnessed his execution. The governor spoke very briefly, merely declaring his concurrence in the important step that had been taken, and his honest purpose, under the circumstances, to discharge his whole duty as Executive of the State, in conformity to the will of the people and the provisions of the Constitution.

Before the *sine die* adjournment, it was suggested that inasmuch as the ordinance had been passed in secret session, and it was desirable that the enemy should not know it before certain preparations could be made to avert sudden injury on the border, etc., that the fact should not be divulged at present.

April 18th.—In spite of every precaution, it is currently whispered in the streets to-day that Virginia has seceded from the Union; and that the act is to be submitted to the people for ratification a month hence. This is perhaps a blunder. If the Southern States are to adhere to the old distinct sovereignty doctrine, God help them one and all to achieve their independence of the United States. Many are inclined to think the safest plan would be to obliterate State lines, and merge them all into an indivisible nation or empire, else there may be incessant conflicts between the different sovereignties themselves, and between them and the General Government. I doubt our ability to maintain the old cumbrous, complicated, and expensive form of government. A national executive and Congress will be sufficiently burdensome to the people without the additional expense of governors, lieutenant-governors, a dozen secretaries of State, as many legislatures, etc. etc. It is true, State rights gave the States the right to secede. But what is in a name? Secession by any other name would smell as sweet. For my part, I like the name of Revolution, or even Rebellion, better, for they are sanctified by the example of Washington and his compeers. And separations of communities are like the separations of bees when they cannot live in peace in the same hive. The time had come apparently for us to set up for ourselves, and we should have done it if there had been no such thing as State sovereignty. It is true, the Constitution adopted at Montgomery virtually acknowledges the right of any State to secede from the Confederacy; but that was necessary in vindication of the action of its fathers. That Constitution, and the *permanent* one to succeed it, will, perhaps, never do. They too much resemble the governmental organization of the Yankees, to whom we have bid adieu forever in disgust.

April 19th.—Dispatches from Montgomery indicate that President Davis is as firm a States right man as any other, perfectly content to bear the burdens of government six years, and hence I apprehend he will not budge in the business of guarding Virginia until after the ratification of the secession ordinance. Thus a month's precious time will be lost; and the scene of conflict, instead of being in Pennsylvania, near Philadelphia, will be in Virginia. From the ardor of the volunteers already beginning to pour into the city, I believe 25,000 men could be collected and armed in a week, and in another they might sweep the whole Abolition concern beyond the Susquehanna, and afterward easily keep them there. But this will not be attempted, nor permitted, by the Convention, so recently composed mostly of Union men.

To-night we have rumors of a collision in Baltimore. A regiment of Northern troops has been assailed by the mob. No good can come of mob assaults in a great revolution.

Wrote my wife to make preparations with all expedition to escape into Virginia. Women and children will not be molested for some weeks yet; but I see they have begun to ransack their baggage. Mrs. Semple, daughter of President Tyler, I am informed, had her plate taken from her in an attempt to get it away from New York.

April 20th.—The news has been confirmed. It was a brick-bat "Plug Ugly" fight—the result of animal, and not intellectual or patriotic instincts. Baltimore has better men for the strife than bar-room champions. The absence of dignity in this assault will be productive of evil rather than good. Maryland is probably lost—for her fetters will be riveted before the secession of Virginia will be communicated by the senseless form of ratification a month hence. Woe, woe to the politicians of Virginia who have wrought this delay! It is now understood that the very day before the ordinance was passed, the members were gravely splitting hairs over proposed amendments to the Federal Constitution!

Guns are being fired on Capitol Hill in commemoration of secession, and the Confederate flag now floats unmolested from the summit of the capitol. I think they had better save the powder, etc.

At night. We have a gay illumination. This too is wrong. We had better save the candles.

April 21st.—Received several letters to-day which had been delayed in their transmission, and were doubtless opened on the way. One was from my wife, informing me of the illness of Custis, my eldest son, and of the equivocal conduct of some of the neighbors. The Rev. Mr. D., son of the late B——p, raised the flag of the Union on his church.

The telegraphic wires are still in operation.

APRIL 22D.—Early a few mornings since, I called on Gov. Wise, and informed him that Lincoln had called out 70,000 men. He opened his eyes very widely and said, emphatically, "I don't believe it." The greatest statesmen of the South have no conception of the real purposes of the men now in power in the United States. They cannot be made to believe that the Government at Washington are going to wage war immediately. But when I placed the President's proclamation in his hand, he read it with deep emotion, and uttered a fierce "Hah!" Nevertheless, when I told him that these 70,000 were designed to be merely the videttes and outposts of an army of 700,000, he was quite incredulous. He had not witnessed the Wide-Awake gatherings the preceding fall, as I had done, and listened to the pledges they made to subjugate the South, free the negroes, and hang Gov. Wise. I next told him they would blockade our ports, and endeavor to cut off our supplies. To this he uttered a most positive negative. He said it would be contrary to the laws of nations, as had been decided often in the Courts of Admiralty, and would be moreover a violation of the Constitution. Of course I admitted all this; but maintained that such was the intention of the Washington Cabinet. Laws and Courts and Constitutions would not be impediments in the way of Yankees resolved upon our subjugation. Presuming upon their superior numbers, and under the pretext of saving the Union and annihilating slavery, they would invade us like the army-worm, which enters the green fields in countless numbers. The real object was to enjoy our soil and climate by means of confiscation. He poohed me into silence with an indignant frown. He had no idea that the Yankees would *dare* to enter upon such enterprises in the face of an enlightened world. But I know them better. And it will be found that they will learn how to fight, and will not be afraid to fight.

APRIL 23D.—Several prominent citizens telegraphed President Davis to-day to hasten to Virginia with as many troops as he can catch up, assuring him that his army will grow like a snow-ball as it progresses. I have no doubt it would. I think it would swell to 50,000 before reaching Washington, and that the people on the route would supply the quartermaster's stores, and improvise an adequate commissariat. I believe he could drive the Abolitionists out of Washington even yet, if he would make a bold dash, and that there would be a universal uprising in all the border States this side of the Susquehanna. But he does not respond. Virginia was too late moving, and North Carolina, Tennessee, Arkansas, Kentucky, and Missouri have not seceded yet—though all of them will soon follow Virginia. Besides, the vote on the ratification in this State is to take place a month hence. It would be an infringement of State rights, and would be construed as an *invasion of Virginia!* Could the Union men in the Convention, after being forced to pass the ordinance, have dealt a more fatal blow to their country? But that is not all. The governor is appointing his Union partisans to military positions. Nevertheless, as time rolls on, and eternal separation is pronounced by the events that must be developed, they may prove true to the best interests of their native land.

Every hour there are fresh arrivals of organized companies from the country, tendering their services to the governor; and nearly all the young men in the city are drilling. The cadets of the Military Institute are rendering good service now, and Professor Jackson is truly a benefactor. I hope he will take the field himself; and if he does, I predict for him a successful career.

April 24th.—Martial music is heard everywhere, day and night, and all the trappings and paraphernalia of war's decorations are in great demand. The ladies are sewing everywhere, even in the churches. But the gay uniforms we see to-day will change their hue before the advent of another year. All history shows that fighting is not only the most perilous pursuit in the world, but the *hardest* and the roughest work one can engage in. And many a young man bred in luxury, will be killed by exposure in the night air, lying on the damp ground, before meeting the enemy. But the same thing may be said of the Northmen. And the arbitrament of war, and war's desolation, is a foregone conclusion. How much better it would have been if the North had permitted the South to depart in peace! With political separation, there might still have remained commercial union. But they would not.

April 25th.—Ex-President Tyler and Vice-President Stephens are negotiating a treaty which is to ally Virginia to the Confederate States.

April 26th.—To-day I recognize Northern merchants and

Jews in the streets, busy in collecting the debts due them. The Convention has thrown some impediments in the way; but I hear on every hand that Southern merchants, in the absence of legal obligations, recognize the demands of honor, and are sending money North, even if it be used against us. This will not last long.

APRIL 27TH.—We have had a terrible alarm. The tocsin was sounded in the public square, and thousands have been running hither and thither to know its meaning. Dispatches have been posted about the city, purporting to have been received by the governor, with the startling information that the U. S. war steamer Pawnee is coming up the James River for the purpose of shelling the city!

All the soldiery, numbering some thousands, are marching down to Rocketts, and forming in line of battle on the heights commanding the approaches. The howitzers are there, frowning defiance; and two long French bronze guns are slowly passing through Main Street in the same direction. One of them has just broken down, and lies abandoned in front of the Post-Office. Even civilians, by hundreds, are hurrying with shot-guns and pistols to the scene of action, and field officers are galloping through the streets. Although much apprehension is apparent on many faces, it is but just to say that the population generally are resolved to make a determined defense. There is no fear of personal danger; it is only the destruction of property that is dreaded. But, in my opinion, the Pawnee is about as likely to attempt the navigation of the River Styx, as to run up this river within shelling distance of the city.

I walked down to the lower bridge, without even taking a pocket-pistol, and saw the troops drawn up in line of battle awaiting the enemy. Toward evening the howitzers engaged in some unprofitable practice, shelling the trees on the opposite side.

It was a false alarm, if not something worse. I fear it is an invention of the enemy to divert us from the generally conceived policy of attacking Washington, and rousing up Maryland in the rear of Lincoln.

Met with, and was introduced to, Gov. Letcher, in the evening, at the *Enquirer* office. He was revising one of his many proclamations; and is now undoubtedly as zealous an advocate of secession as any man. He said he would be ready to fight in *three or four days;* and that he would soon have arrangements completed to blockade the Potomac by means of formidable batteries.

APRIL 28TH.—Saw Judge Scarburg, who has resigned his seat in the Court of Claims at Washington. I believe he brought his family, and abandoned his furniture, etc. Also Dr. Garnett, who left most of his effects in the hands of the enemy. He was a marked man, being the son-in-law of Gov. Wise.

Many clerks are passing through the city on their way to Montgomery, where they are sure to find employment. Lucky men, some of them! They have eaten Lincoln bread for more than a month, and most of them would have been turned out of office if there had been no secession. And I observe among them some who have left their wives behind *to take care of their homes.*

APRIL 29TH.—I wrote to my agent on the Eastern Shore to send me the last year's rent due on the farm. But I learn that the cruisers in the bay are intercepting the communications, and I fear remittances will be impracticable. I hope my family are ready by this to leave Burlington. Women and children have not yet been interfered with. What if they should be compelled to abandon our property there? Mrs. Semple had her plate seized at New York.

At fifty-one, I can hardly follow the pursuit of arms; but I will write and preserve a DIARY of the revolution. I never held or sought office in my life; but now President Tyler and Gov. Wise say I will find employment at Montgomery. The latter will prepare a letter to President Davis, and the former says he will draw up a paper in my behalf, and take it through the Convention himself for signatures. I shall be sufficiently credentialed, at all events—provided old partisan considerations are banished from the new confederacy. To make my DIARY full and complete as possible, is now my business. And,

> "When the hurly-burly's done,
> When the battle's lost and won,"

if the South wins it, I shall be content to retire to my farm, provided it falls on the Southern side of the line, and enjoy sweet repose "under my own vine and fig-tree."

APRIL 30TH.—Gen. Kearney has been brought here, having been taken on his way to Washington from Missouri. He manifested surprise at his captivity, and says that he is no enemy; being, I believe, Southern born. I learn it is the purpose of the governor to release him. And this may be a blunder. I fear about as much from ill-timed Southern magnanimity as from Northern malignity.

The Pawnee "scare" turned out just as I thought it would. She merely turned her nose up the river, and then put about and steamed away again. It may do good, however, if it stimulates the authorities to due preparation against future assaults from that quarter.

CHAPTER II.

Depart for Montgomery.—Interview with President Davis.—My position in the Government.—Government removed to Richmond.—My family.

MAY 1ST.—Troops are coming in from all directions, cavalry and infantry; but I learn that none scarcely are accepted by the State. This is great political economy, with a vengeance! How is Gov. Letcher to be ready to fight in a few days? Oh, perhaps he thinks the army will spontaneously spring into existence, march without transportation, and fight without rations or pay! But the Convention has passed an act authorizing the enlistment of a regular army of 12,000 men. If I am not mistaken, Virginia will have to put in the field ten times that number, and the confederacy will have to maintain 500,000 in Virginia, or lose the border States. And if the border States be subjugated, Mr. Seward probably would grant a respite to the rest *for a season.*

But by the terms of the (Tyler and Stephens) treaty, the Confederate States will reimburse Virginia for all her expenses; and therefore I see no good reason why this State, of all others, being the most exposed, should not muster into service every well-armed company that presents itself. There are arms enough for 25,000 men now, and that number, if it be too late to take Washington, might at all events hold this side of the Potomac, and keep the Yankees off the soil of Virginia.

MAY 2D.—There are vague rumors of lawless outrages committed on Southern men in Philadelphia and New York; but they are not well authenticated, and I do not believe them. The Yankees are not yet ready for retaliation. They know that game wouldn't pay. No—they desire time to get their money out of the South; and they would be perfectly willing that trade should go on, even during the war, for they would be the greatest gainers by the information derived from spies and emissaries. I see, too, their papers have extravagant accounts of imprisonments and summary executions here. Not a man has yet been molested. It is true, we have taken Norfolk, without a battle; but the enemy did all the burning and sinking.

MAY 3D.—No letters from my wife. Probably she has taken the children to the Eastern Shore. Her farm is there, and she has many friends in the county. On that narrow peninsula it is hardly to be supposed the Yankees will send any troops. With the broad Atlantic on one side and the Chesapeake Bay on the other, it is to be presumed there will be no military demonstration by the inhabitants, for they could neither escape nor receive reinforcements from the mainland. In the war of the first Revolution, and the subsequent one with Great Britain, this peninsula escaped the ravages of the enemy, although the people were as loyal to the government of the United States as any; but the Yankees are more enterprising than the British, and may have an eye to "truck farms" in that fruitful region.

MAY 4TH.—Met Wm. H. B. Custis, Esq., to-day in the square, and had a long conversation with him. He has made up his mind to sign the ordinance. He thinks secession might have been averted with honor, if our politicians at Washington had not been ambitious to figure as leaders in a new revolution. Custis was always a Democrat, and supported Douglas on the ground that he was the regular nominee. He said his negro property a month before was worth, perhaps, fifty thousand dollars; now his slaves would not bring probably more than five thousand; and that would be the fate of many slaveowners in Virginia.

MAY 5TH.—President Tyler has placed in my hands a memorial to President Davis, signed by himself and many of the members of the Convention, asking appropriate civil employment for me in the new government. I shall be content to obtain the necessary position to make a full and authentic Diary of the transactions of the government. I could not hope for any commission as a civil officer, since the leaders who have secured possession of the government know very well that, as editor, I never advocated the pretensions of any of them for the Presidency of the United States. Some of them I fear are unfit for the positions they occupy. But the cause in which we are embarked will require, to be successful, the efforts of every man. Those capable of performing military duty, must perform it; and those physically incapable of wielding the bayonet and the sword, must wield the pen. It is no time to stand on ceremony or antecedents. The post of duty is the post of honor. In the mighty winnowing we must go through, the wheat will be separated from the chaff. And many a true man who this day stands forth as a private, will end as a general. And the efficient subordinate in the departments may be likewise exalted if he deserves it, provided the people have rule in the new confederacy. If we are to have a monarchy for the sake of economy and stability, I shall submit to it in preference to the domination of the Northern radicals.

MAY 6TH.—To-day a Yankee was caught in the street questioning some negroes as to which side they would fight on, slavery or freedom. He was merely rebuked and ordered out of the country. Another instance of Southern magnanimity! It will only embolden the insidious enemy.

MAY 7TH.—Col. R. E. Lee, lately of the United States army, has been appointed major-general, and commander-in-chief of the army in Virginia. He is the son of "Light Horse Harry" of the Revolution. The North can boast no such historic names as we, in its army. Gov. Wise is sick at home, in Princess Ann County, but has sent me a strong letter to President Davis. I fear the governor will not survive many months.

MAY 8TH.—The Convention has appointed five members of Congress to go to Montgomery: Messrs. Hunter, Rives, Brockenborough, Staples, and ——. I have not yet seen Mr. Hunter; he has made no speeches, but no doubt he has done all in his power to secure the passage of the ordinance, in his quiet but effective way. To-day President Tyler remarked that the politicians in the Convention had appointed a majority of the members from the old opposition party. The President would certainly have been appointed, if it had not been understood he did not desire it. Debilitated from a protracted participation in the exciting scenes of the Convention, he could not bear the fatigue of so long a journey at this season of the year.

MAY 9TH.—The *Examiner* still fires shot and shell at Gov. Letcher and the dominant majority in the Convention, on account of recent appointments. It is furious over the selection of Mr. Baldwin, recently a leading Union man, for inspector-general; and seems to apprehend bad results from thrusting Union men forward in the coming struggle. The *Enquirer* is moderate, and kind to Gov. Letcher, whose nomination and subsequent course were so long the theme of bitter denunciation. It is politic. The *Whig* now goes into the secession movement with all its might. Mr. Mosely has resumed the helm; and he was, I believe, a secessionist many years ago. The *Dispatch*, not long since neutral and conservative, throws all its powers, with its large circulation, into the cause. So we have perfect unanimity in the press. *Per contra*, the New York *Herald* has turned about and leap-frogged over the head of the *Tribune* into the front ranks of the Republicans. No doubt, when we win the day, the *Herald* will leap back again.

MAY 10TH.—The ladies are postponing all engagements until their lovers have fought the Yankees. Their influence is great. Day after day they go in crowds to the Fair ground where the 1st S. C. Vols. are encamped, showering upon them their smiles, and all the delicacies the city affords. They wine them and cake them—and they deserve it. They are just from taking Fort Sumter, and have won historic distinction. I was introduced to several of the privates by their captain, who told me they were worth from $100,000 to half a million dollars each. The *Tribune* thought all these men would want to be captains! But that is not the only hallucination the North labors under, judging from present appearances; by closing our ports it is thought we can be subdued by the want of accustomed luxuries. These rich young men were dressed in coarse gray homespun! We have the best horsemen and the best marksmen in the world, and these are the qualities that will tell before the end of the war. We fight for existence—the enemy for Union and the freedom of the slave. Well, let the Yankees see if this "new thing" will pay.

MAY 11TH.—Robert Tyler has arrived, after wonderful risks

and difficulties. When I left Mr. Tyler in the North, the people were talking about electing him their representative in Congress. They tempted him every way, by threats and by promises, to make them a speech under the folds of the "star spangled banner" erected near his house. But in vain. No doubt they would have elected him to Congress, and perhaps have made him a general, if he had fallen down and worshiped their Republican idol, and fought against his father.

MAY 12TH.—To-day I set out for Montgomery. The weather was bright and pleasant. It is Sunday. In the cars are many passengers going to tender their services, and all imbued with the same inflexible purpose. The corn in the fields of Virginia is just becoming visible; and the trees are beginning to disclose their foliage.

MAY 13TH.—We traveled all night, and reached Wilmington, N. C., early in the morning. There I saw a Northern steamer which had been seized in retaliation for some of the seizures of the New Yorkers. And there was a considerable amount of ordnance and shot and shell on the bank of the river. The people everywhere on the road are for irremediable, eternal separation. Never were men more unanimous. And North Carolina has passed the ordinance, I understand, without a dissenting voice. Better still, it is not to be left to a useless vote of the people. The work is finished, and the State is out of the Union without contingency or qualification. I saw one man, though, at Goldsborough, who looked very much like a Yankee, and his enthusiasm seemed more simulated than real; and some of his words were equivocal. His name was Dibble.

To-day I saw rice and cotton growing, the latter only an inch or so high. The pine woods in some places have a desolate appearance; and whole forests are dead. I thought it was caused by the scarifications for turpentine; but was told by an intelligent traveler that the devastation was produced by an insect or worm that cut the inner bark.

The first part of South Carolina we touched was not inviting. Swamps, with cane, and cypress knees, and occasionally a plunging aligator met the vision. Here, I thought the Yankees, if they should carry the war into the far south, would fare worse than Napoleon's army of invasion in Russia.

But railroads seldom run through the fairest and richest portions of the country. They must take the route where there is the least grading. We soon emerged, however, from the marshy district, and then beheld the vast cotton-fields, now mostly planted in corn. A good idea. And the grain crops look well. The corn, in one day, seems to have grown ten inches.

In the afternoon we were whisked into Georgia, and the face of the country, as well as the color of the soil, reminded me of some parts of France between Dieppe and Rouen. No doubt the grape could be profitably cultivated here. The corn seems to have grown a *foot* since morning.

MAY 14TH.—The weather is very warm. Day before yesterday the wheat was only six or eight inches high. To-day it is two or three feet in height, headed, and almost ripe for the scythe.

At every station [where I can write a little] we see crowds of men, and women, and boys; and during our pauses some of the passengers, often clergymen, and not unfrequently Northern born, address them in soul-stirring strains of patriotic eloquence. If Uncle Abe don't find subjugation of this country, and of such a people as this, is truly a "big job" on his hands, I am much mistaken.

Passed the Stone Mountain at 11 o'clock A.M. It appears at a distance like a vast artificial formation, resembling the pictures of the pyramids.

Arrived at Montgomery 10 o'clock P.M., and put up at the Montgomery House. The mosquitoes bled me all night. Mosquitoes in the middle of May! And as they never cease to bite till killed by the frost, the pest here is perennial.

MAY 15TH.—From my window at the top of the house, I see corn in silk and tassel. Three days ago the corn I saw was not three inches high. And blackberries are in season. Strawberries and peas are gone.

This city is mostly situated in a bottom on the Alabama River.

Being fatigued I did not visit the departments to-day, but employed myself in securing lodgings at a boarding-house. Here I met, the first time, with my friend Dr. W. T. Sawyer, of Hollow Square, Alabama. A skillful surgeon and Christian gentleman, his mission on earth seems to be one of pure beneficence. He had known me before we met, it appears; and I must say he did me many kind offices.

In the afternoon I walked to the capitol, a fine structure with massive columns, on a beautiful elevation, where I delivered several letters to the Virginia delegation in Congress. They were exceedingly kind to me, and proffered their services very freely.

MAY 16TH.—Met John Tyler, Jr., to-day, who, with his native cordiality, proffered his services with zeal and earnestness. He introduced me at once to Hon. L. P. Walker, Secretary of War, and insisted upon presenting me to the President the next day. Major Tyler had recently been commissioned in the army, but is now detailed to assist the Secretary of War in his correspondence. The major is favorably known in the South as the author of several Southern essays of much power that have been published in a Review, signed "Python."

The principal hotel is the Exchange, as in Richmond; the entrance to the bar, reading-room, etc. is by a flight of stairs from the street to the second story, with stores underneath. Here there is an incessant influx of strangers coming from all directions on business with the new government. But the prevalent belief is that the government itself will soon travel to Richmond. The buildings here will be insufficient in magnitude for the transaction of the rapidly increasing business.

MAY 17TH.—Was introduced to the President to-day. He was overwhelmed with papers, and retained a number in his left hand, probably of more importance than the rest. He received me with urbanity, and while he read the papers I had given him, as I had never seen him before, I endeavored to scrutinize his features, as one would naturally do, for the purpose of forming a vague estimate of the character and capabilities of the man destined to perform the leading part in a revolution which must occupy a large space in the world's history. His stature is tall, nearly six feet; his frame is very slight and seemingly frail; but when he throws back his shoulders he is as straight as an Indian chief. The features of his face are distinctly marked with character; and no one gazing at his profile would doubt for a moment that he beheld more than an ordinary man. His face is handsome, and his thin lip often basks a pleasant smile. There is nothing sinister or repulsive in his manners or appearance; and if there are no special indications of great grasp of intellectual power on his forehead and on his sharply defined nose and chin, neither is there any evidence of weakness, or that he could be easily moved from any settled purpose. I think he has a clear perception of matters demanding his cognizance, and a nice discrimination of details. As a politician he attaches the utmost importance to *consistency*—and here I differ with him. I think that to be consistent as a politician, is to change with the circumstances of the case. When Calhoun and Webster first met in Congress, the first advocated a protective tariff and the last opposed it. This was told me by Mr. Webster himself, in 1842, when he was Secretary of State; and it was confirmed by Mr. Calhoun in 1844, then Secretary of State himself. Statesmen are the physicians of the public weal; and what doctor hesitates to vary his remedies with the new phases of disease?

When the President had completed the reading of my papers, and during the perusal I observed him make several emphatic nods, he asked me what I wanted. I told him I wanted employment with my pen, perhaps only temporary employment. I thought the correspondence of the Secretary of War would increase in volume, and another assistant besides Major Tyler would be required in his office. He smiled and shook his head, saying that such work would be only temporary indeed; which I construed to mean that even *he* did not then suppose the war was to assume colossal proportions.

May 18th.—To-day I had another interview with the President. He advised me to see the Secretary of the Treasury without delay; but the Treasury would not answer so well for my Diary.

May 19th.—The Secretary of War sent for me this morning, and said he required more assistance in his correspondence, then increasing daily; but the act of Congress limiting salaries would prevent him from offering me an adequate compensation. He could only name some ten or twelve hundred dollars. I told him my great desire was employment, and facilities to preserve interesting facts for future publication. I was installed at once, with Major Tyler, in the Secretary's own office. It was my duty to open and read the letters, noting briefly their contents on the back. The Secretary would then indicate in pencil marks the answers to be written, which the major and I prepared. These were signed by the Secretary, copied in another room, and mailed. I was happy in the discharge of these duties, and worked assiduously day and night.

4

May 20th.—Mr. Walker, the Secretary of War, is some forty-seven or eight years of age, tall, thin, and a little bent; not by age, but by study and bad health. He was a successful lawyer, and having never been in governmental employment, is fast working himself down. He has not yet learned how to avoid unnecessary labor; being a man of the finest sensibilities, and exacting with the utmost nicety all due deference to the dignity of his official position. He stands somewhat on ceremony with his brother officials, and accords and exacts the etiquette natural to a sensitive gentleman who has never been broken on the wheel of office. I predict for him a short career. The only hope for his continuance in office is unconditional submission to the President, who, being once Secretary of War of the United States, is familiar with all the wheels of the department. But soon, if I err not, the President will be too much absorbed in the fluctuations of momentous campaigns, to give much of his attention to any one of the departments. Nevertheless Mr. Walker, if he be an apt scholar, may learn much before that day; and Congress may simplify his duties by enacting a uniform mode of filling the offices in the field. The applications now give the greatest trouble; and the disappointed class give rise to many vexations.

May 21st.—Being in the same room with the Secretary, and seen by all his visitors, I am necessarily making many new acquaintances; and quite a number recognize me by my books which they have read. Among this class is Mr. Benjamin, the Minister of Justice, who, to-day, informed me that he and Senator Bayard had been interested, at Washington, in my "Story of Disunion." Mr. Benjamin is of course a Jew, of French lineage, born I believe in Louisiana, a lawyer and politician. His age may be sixty, and yet one might suppose him to be less than forty. His hair and eyes are black, his forehead capacious, his face round and as intellectual as one of that shape can be; and Mr. B. is certainly a man of intellect, education, and extensive reading, combined with natural abilities of a tolerably high order. Upon his lip there seems to bask an eternal smile; but if it be studied, it is not a smile—yet it bears no unpleasing aspect.

May 22d.—To-day I had, in our office, a specimen of Mr. Memminger's oratory. He was pleading for an installment of the claims of South Carolina on the Confederacy; and Mr. Walker, always hesitating, argued the other side, merely for delay. Both are fine speakers, with most distinct enunciation and musical voices. The demand was audited and paid, amounting, I believe, to several hundred thousand dollars.

And I heard and saw Mr. Toombs to-day, the Secretary of State. He is a portly gentleman, but with the pale face of the student and the marks of a deep thinker. To gaze at him in repose, the casual spectator would suppose, from his neglect of dress, that he was a planter in moderate circumstances, and of course not gifted with extraordinary powers of intellect; but let him open his mouth, and the delusion vanishes. At the time alluded to he was surrounded by the rest of the cabinet, in our office, and the topic was the policy of the war. He was for taking the initiative, and carrying the war into the enemy's country. And as he warmed with the subject, the *man* seemed to vanish, and the *genius* alone was visible. He was most emphatic in the advocacy of his policy, and bold almost to rashness in his denunciations of the merely defensive idea. He was opposed to all delays, as fraught with danger; the enemy were in the field, and their purposes were pronounced. Why wait to see what they meant to do? If we did that, they would not only invade us, but get a permanent foothold on our soil. We must invade or be invaded; and he was for making the war as terrible as possible from the beginning. It was to be no child's play; and nothing could be gained by reliance upon the blunders and forbearance of the Yankees. News had been received of the occupation of Alexandria and Arlington Heights, in Virginia; and if we permitted them to build fortifications there, we should not be able to expel them. He denounced with bitterness the neglect of the authorities in Virginia. The enemy should not have been permitted to cross the Potomac. During the month which had elapsed since the passage of the ordinance in Virginia, nothing had been done, nothing attempted. It was true, the vote on ratification had not been taken; and although that fact might shield the provisional government from responsibility, yet the delay to act was fraught with danger and perhaps irreparable injury. Virginia alone could have raised and thrown across the Potomac 25,000 men, and driven the Yankees beyond the Susquehanna. But she, to avoid responsibility, had been telegraphing Davis to come to the rescue; and if he (Toombs) had been in Davis's place, he would have taken the responsibility.

The Secretary of War well knew how to parry these thrusts; he was not responsible. He was as ultra a man as any; and all he could do was to organize and arm the troops authorized by Congress. Some thirty odd thousand were mustered in already; and at least five thousand volunteers were offering daily. Mr. Toombs said five hundred thousand volunteers ought to be accepted and for the war. We wanted no six or twelve months' men. To this the Secretary replied that the Executive could not transcend the limits prescribed by Congress.

These little discussions were of frequent occurrence; and it soon became apparent that the Secretary of War was destined to be the most important man among the cabinet ministers. His position afforded the best prospect of future distinction—always provided he should be equal to the position, and his administration attended with success. I felt convinced that Toombs would not be long chafing in the cabinet, but that he would seize the first opportunity to repair to the field.

MAY 23D.—To-day the President took the cars for Pensacola, where it had been said everything was in readiness for an assault on Fort Pickens. Military men said it could be taken, and Toombs, I think, said it ought to be taken. It would cost, perhaps, a thousand lives; but is it not the business of war to consume human life? Napoleon counted men as so much powder to be consumed; and he consumed millions in his career of conquest. But still he conquered, which he could not have done without the consumption of life. And is it not better to consume life rapidly, and attain results quickly, than to await events, when all history shows that a protracted war, of immobile armies, always engulfs more men in the grave from camp fevers than usually fall in battle during the most active operations in the field?

To-day I saw Col. Bartow, who has the bearing and eye of a gallant officer. He was attended by a young man named Lamar, of fine open countenance, whom he desired to have as his aid; but the regulations forbid any one acting in that capacity who was not a lieutenant; and Lamar not being old enough to have a commission, he said he would attend the colonel as a volunteer aid till he attained the prescribed age. I saw Ben McCulloch, also—an unassuming but elastic and brave man. He will make his mark. Also Capt. McIntosh, who goes to the West. I think I saw him in 1846, in Paris, at the table of Mr. King, our Minister; but I had no opportunity to ask him. He is all enthusiasm, and will rise with honor or fall with glory. And here I beheld for the first time Wade Hampton, resolved to abandon all the comforts of his great wealth, and encounter the privations of the tented field in behalf of his menaced country.

Arkansas and Tennessee, as I predicted, have followed the example of Virginia and North Carolina; and I see evidence daily in the mass of correspondence, that Missouri and Kentucky will follow in good time.

MAY 24TH.—Congress passed, in secret session, a resolution to remove the seat of government to Richmond; but I learn it has been vetoed by the President. There is a strong feeling against going thither among some of the secessionists in the Cotton States. Those who do not think there will be a great deal of fighting, have apprehensions that the border States, so tardy in the secession movement, will strive to monopolize the best positions and patronage of the new government. Indeed, if it were quite certain that there is to be no war for existence—as if a nation could be free without itself striking the blow for freedom—I think there would be a party—among the politicians, not the people—opposed to confederating with the border slave States.

Some of his fellow-members tell many jokes on Mr. Hunter. They say every time he passes the marble-yards going up to the capitol, and surveys the tomb-stones, he groans in agony, and predicts that he will get sick and die here. If this be true, I predict that he will get the seat of government moved to Richmond, a more congenial climate. He has a way of moving large bodies, which has rarely failed him; and some of his friends at the hotels, already begin to hint that he is the proper man to be the first President of the *permanent* government. I think he will be President some day. He would be a safe one. But this whisper at the hotel has produced no little commotion. Some propose making him Secretary of War, as a sure means of killing him off. I know a better way than that, but I wouldn't suggest it for the world. I like him very much.

To-day the Secretary placed in my hands for examination and report, a very long document, written by a deposed or resigned Roman priest. He urged a plan to avert the horrors of war. He had been to see Lincoln, Gov. Letcher, etc., and finally obtained an interview on "important business" with President Davis. The President, not having leisure even to listen to his exordium, requested him to make his communication briefly in writing. And this was *it*—about twenty pages of foolscap. It consisted chiefly of evidences of the exceeding wickedness of war, and suggestions that if both belligerents would *only forbear to take up arms*, the peace might be preserved, and God would mediate between them. Of course I could only indorse on the back "demented." But the old man hung round the department for a week afterward, and then departed, I know not whither. I forget his name, but his paper is in the archives of the government. I have always differed with the preachers in politics and war, except the Southern preachers who are now in arms against the invader. I think war is one of the providences of God, and certainly no book chronicles so much fighting as the Bible. It may be to the human race what pruning is to vegetation, a necessary process for the general benefit.

MAY 25TH.—There is to be no fight—no assault on Pickens. But we are beginning to send troops forward in the right direction—to Virginia. Virginia herself ought to have kept the invader from her soil. Was she reluctant to break the peace? And is it nothing to have her soil polluted by the martial tramp of the Yankees at Alexandria and Arlington Heights? But the wrath of the Southern chivalry will some day burst forth on the ensanguined plain, and then let the presumptuous foemen of the North beware of the fiery ordeal they have invoked. The men I see daily keeping time to the music of revolution are fighting men, men who will conquer or die, and who prefer death to subjugation. But the Yankee has no such motive to fight for, no thought of serious wounds and death. He can go back to his own country; our men have no other country to go to.

MAY 26TH.—Was called on by the Episcopal minister to-day, Dr. Sawyer having informed him that I was a member of the church—the doctor being one also. He is an enthusiastic young man, and though a native of the North, seems to sympathize with us very heartily. He prays for the President of the Confederate States. The President himself attends very regularly, and some intimate that he intends to become a candidate for membership.

I have not learned whether he has been baptized. Gen. Cooper, the first on our list of generals in the regular army, is a member of the church. The general was, I think, adjutant-general at Washington. He is Northern born. Major Gorgas is likewise a native of the North. He is Chief of the Bureau of Ordnance. The Quartermaster-General, Major Myers, is said to be a Jew; while the Commissary-General is almost a Jesuit, so zealous is he in the advocacy of the Pope.

Mr. Mallory, the Secretary of the Navy, I have seen but once; but I have heard him soundly abused for not accepting some propositions and plans from Mobile and elsewhere, to build iron-clad steam rams to sink the enemy's navy. Some say Mr. M. is an Irishman born. He was in the United States Senate, and embraced secession with the rest of the "conspirators" at Washington.

I saw the Vice-President to-day. I first saw Mr. Stephens at Washington in 1843. I was behind him as he sat in the House of Representatives, and thought him a boy, for he was sitting beside large members. But when I got in front of him, it was apparent he was a man—every inch a man.

There is some excitement in official circles here against Mr. Browne, the Assistant Secretary of State, on the ground that he interfered in behalf of a Mr. Hurlbut, a Northern man (probably arrested), a writer in the English Reviews against slavery in the South, and a correspondent for the New York Tribune. Mr. B. is an Englishman, who came from Washington on the invitation of Mr. Toombs, and through his influence was appointed Assistant Secretary of State, and the Southern gorge rises at it. I doubt whether he will be molested.

I saw Major Tochman to-day, also a foreigner. He is authorized to enlist a regiment or two of Polanders in New Orleans, where I am told there are none.

And there are several Northern men here wanting to be generals. This does not look much like Southern homogeneity. God save us, if we are not to save ourselves!

How hot it is! But I like hot weather better than cold, and would soon become accustomed to this climate. This morning Mr. Hunter really seemed distressed; but he has four inches on his ribs, and I not the eighth of an inch.

Since writing the foregoing, I have seen Mr. Hunter again, and although there is no diminution of heat, he is quite cheerful. Congress has again passed the resolution to remove the seat of government to Richmond, and it is said the President will not veto it this time. The President himself came into our office to-day and sat some time conversing with Secretary Walker. He did not appear vexed at the determination of Congress, which he must have been apprised of.

MAY 26TH.—The President is sick to-day—having a chill, I believe. Adjutant-General Cooper was in, comparing notes with the Secretary as to the number of regiments in the field. The Secretary has a most astonishing memory, and could easily number the forces without referring to his notes. The amount is not large, it is true; but, from the eagerness to volunteer, I believe if we had the arms there might soon be organized an army of three or four hundred thousand men. And yet it would seem that no one dreams of armies of such magnitude. Wait till we sleep a little longer! A great many separate companies are accepted; all indeed that offer for three years or the war, provided they have arms—even double-barreled shot-guns and hunting rifles. What a deal of annoyance and labor it will be to organize these into battalions, regiments, brigades, and divisions! And then comes the appointment of staff and field officers. This will be labor for the President. But he works incessantly, sick or well.

We have an agent in Europe purchasing arms. This was well thought on. And Capt. Huse is thought to be a good selection. It will be impossible for Lincoln to keep all our ports hermetically sealed. Hitherto improvident, it is to be hoped the South will now go to work upon her own resources. We have plunged into the sea of revolution, and must, unaided, sink or swim. The Yankees say they are going to subdue us in six months. What fools!

I tasted green corn to-day, and, although very fond of it, I touched it lightly, because it seemed so much out of season. The country around is beautiful, and the birds are singing as merrily as if we were about to enter upon a perennial Sabbath-day, instead of a desolating war. But the gunpowder will be used to destroy the destroyer, man, and why should not the birds sing? The china-trees are beautiful, and abundant about the dwellings.

May 27th.—We leave Montgomery day after to-morrow. The President goes to-day—but quietly—no one, not connected with the Government, to have information of the fact until his arrival in Richmond. It is understood that the Minister of Justice (Attorney-General) accompanies him. There are a great number of spies and emissaries in the country—sufficient, if it were known when the train would pass, to throw it off the track. This precaution is taken by the friends of the President.

The day is pretty much occupied in the packing of boxes. It is astonishing how vast a volume of papers accumulates in a short space of time—but when we consider the number of applications for office, the wonder ceases.

May 28th.—Little or no business was done this day. The Secretary announced that no more communications would be considered by him in Montgomery. He placed in my charge a great many unopened letters, and a special list of candidates for office, with annotations. These I packed in my trunk.

As I was to precede the Secretary, and having some knowledge of the capacity of the public buildings in Richmond, I was charged with the duty of securing, if possible, suitable offices for the Department of War. I made hasty preparations for departure.

Before starting, something prompted me to call once more at the post-office, where, to my surprise and delight, I found a letter from my wife. She was in Richmond, with all the children, *Tabby* and the parrot. She had left Burlington about the same time I had left Richmond. At Havre-de-Grace, on the Susquehanna, which they crossed in the night, my youngest daughter was compelled with difficulty to stride over the sleeping bodies of Yankee soldiers. She writes that she deposited, very carefully, our plate in the bank! The idea that all might have been brought off if she had only known it, is the source of her wretchedness. She writes that she had been materially assisted by Mr. Grubb and his lady, prompted by personal friendship, by humanity, and by those generous instincts of the true nobility of heart imparted by the Creator. Mr. G. is true to the Constitution and the Government under which he lives—and would doubtless never consent to a rupture of the Union under any circumstances. He has a son in the army against us. And Col. Wall, another personal friend, boldly shook hands with my family at parting, while the Wide-Awake file leaders stood scowling by. I hope he may not suffer for his temerity.

These things occupied my thoughts during a sleepless night in the cars. My abode in New Jersey had been a pleasant one. I had a fine yard and garden, and many agreeable neighbors. I loved my garden, and cultivated my own grapes, pears, peaches, apples, raspberries, currants, and strawberries. I had fruits and vegetables in the greatest profusion. And the thrushes and other migratory birds had come to know me well, and sang me to sleep at night, and awakened me with their strains in the morning. They built their nests near the windows, for the house was embowered in trees, and half covered with ivy. Even my cats, for every living thing was a pet to some one of the family,—when I think of them now, wandering about unprotected, give rise to painful emotions. But even my youngest child was willing to make any sacrifice for the sake of her country. The South is our only home—we have been only temporary sojourners elsewhere.

MAY 29TH AND 30TH.—The remainder of the journey was without interest, until we arrived at Wythville, Va., where it was discovered Gen. Floyd was in the cars. He was called out and made a speech in vindication of his conduct at Washington, as Secretary of War, wherein he had caused the transfer of arms, etc. from the North to the South. He was then organizing a brigade for the field, having been commissioned a brigadier-general by the President.

MAY 31ST.—I arrived in Richmond about 1 o'clock P.M. The meeting with my family was a joyful scene. All were well.

I lost no time in securing rooms for the department in the new custom-house. Mr. Giles had been employed in this business by the Congressional Committee, and I found him every way accommodating. I succeeded without difficulty in convincing him that the War Department was the most important one, and hence entitled to the first choice of rooms. I therefore selected the entire suites on both sides of the hall on the lower floor. The Treasury, the Executive office, Cabinet chamber, and Departments of Justice and the Navy were located on the floor above. This arrangement, however, was understood to be but a temporary one; Mechanics Hall was leased for future purposes; and I was consulted on the plan of converting it into suites of offices.

CHAPTER III.

Troops pour into Richmond.—Beginning of hostilities.—Gen. Lee made a full general.—Major-Gen. Polk.—A battle expected at Manassas.

JUNE 1ST.—In the absence of the Secretary, I arranged the furniture as well as I could, and took possession of the five offices I had selected. But no business, of course, could be done before his arrival. Yet an immense mass of business was accumulating—letters by the hundreds were demanding attention.

And I soon found, as the other Secretaries came in, that some dissatisfaction was likely to grow out of the appropriation by the Secretary of War of the best offices. Mr. Toombs said the "war office" might do in any ordinary building; but that the Treasury should appropriately occupy the custom-house, which was fire-proof. For his own department, he said he should be satisfied with a room or two anywhere. But my arrangement was not countermanded by the President, to whom I referred all objectors. His decision was to be final—and he did not decide against it. I had given him excellent quarters; and I knew he was in the habit of having frequent interviews both with the Secretary of War and the Adjutant-General, and this would be inconvenient if they were in different buildings.

JUNE 2D.—My wife had a little gold among her straightened finances; and having occasion to purchase some article of dress, she obtained seven and a half per cent. premium. The goods began to go up in price, as paper money fell in value. At Montgomery I bought a pair of fine French boots for $10 in gold—but packed my old ones in the top of my trunk. I was under the necessity, likewise, of buying a linen coat, which cost only $3.50. What will be the price of such commodities a year hence if the blockade continues? It is fearful to contemplate! And yet it ought to be considered. Boarding is rising rapidly, and so are the blood-thirsty insects at the Carleton House.

JUNE 3D.—The Secretary arrived to-day, sick; and was accompanied by Major Tyler, himself unwell. And troops are beginning to arrive in considerable numbers. The precincts of the city will soon be a series of encampments. The regiments are drilled here, and these mostly forwarded to Manassas, where a battle must soon occur, if the enemy, now in overwhelming numbers, should advance. The Northern papers say the Yankee army will celebrate the 4th of July in Richmond. *Nous verrons.* But no doubt hostilities have commenced. We have accounts of frightful massacres in Missouri, by German mercenaries. Hampton has been occupied by the enemy, a detachment having been sent from Fortress Monroe for that purpose. They also hold Newport News on the Peninsula. There are rumors of a fight at Philippi. One Col. Potterfield was *surprised.* If this be so, there is no excuse for him. I think the President will make short work of incompetent commanders. Now a blunder is worse than a crime.

JUNE 4TH.—The Secretary is still sick. Having nothing better to do, and seeing that eight-tenths of the letters received are merely applications for commissions in the regular army—an organization without men—and none being granted from civil life, I employed myself writing certain articles for the press, hoping by this means to relieve the Secretary of the useless and painful labor of dictating negative replies to numberless communications. This had the sanction of both the President and the Secretary, and produced, in some measure, the desired relief.

JUNE 5TH.—There are rumors of a fight down at Pig's Point to-day; and it is said our battery has torn the farthingale of the Harriet Lane pretty extensively. The cannon was heard by persons not many miles east of the city. These are the mutterings of the storm. It will burst some of these days.

JUNE 6TH.—We have hard work at the War Department, and some confusion owing to the loss of a box of papers in transitu from Montgomery. I am not a betting man, but I would wager a trifle that the contents of the box are in the hands of some correspondent of the New York *Herald* or *Tribune.* Our careless people think that valor alone will win the day. The Yankees desire, above all things, *information* of our condition and movements, of which they will take advantage. We must learn by dear-bought experience.

JUNE 7TH.—We have a Chief of the Bureau of War, a special favorite, it is said, of Mr. Davis. I went into the Secretary's room (I now occupy one adjoining), and found a portly gentleman in a white vest sitting alone. The Secretary was out, and had not instructed the new officer what to do. He introduced himself to me, and admitted that the Secretary had not assigned him to duty. I saw at a glance how the land lay. It was Col. A. T. Bledsoe, lately of the University of Virginia; and he had been appointed by the President, *not* upon the recommendation of the Secretary. Here was a muss not larger than a mustard-seed; but it might *grow*, for I knew well how sensitive was the nature of the Secretary; and he had not been consulted. And so I took it upon myself to be cicerone to the stranger. He was very grateful,—for a long time. Col. B. had graduated at West Point in the same class with the President and Bishop Polk, and subsequently, after following various pursuits, being once, I believe, a preacher, became settled as a teacher of mathematics at the University of Virginia. The colonel stayed near me, aiding in the work of answering letters; but after sitting an hour, and groaning repeatedly when gazing at the mass of papers constantly accumulating before us, he said he believed he would take a number of them to his lodging and answer them there. I saw nothing more of him during the day. And once or twice, when the Secretary came in, he looked around for him, but said nothing. Finally I informed him what I had done; and, without signifying an assent, he merely remarked that there was no room in his office for him.

JUNE 8TH.—This morning Col. Bledsoe came in with his letters, some fifty in number, looking haggard and worn. It was, indeed, a vast number. But with one of his humorous smiles, he said they were short. He asked me to look over them, and I found them mainly appropriate responses to the letters marked for answer, and pretty closely in accordance with the Secretary's dictation. In one or two instances, however, he had been unable to decipher the Secretary's most difficult chirography—for he had no idea of punctuation. In these instances he had wholly misconceived the meaning, and the replies were exactly the reverse of what they were intended to be. These he tore up, and wrote others before submitting any to the Secretary.

I had only written some thirty letters; but mine were longer—longer than there was any necessity for. I told the colonel that the Secretary had a partiality for "full" letters, especially when addressing any of his friends; and that Major Tyler, who had returned, and was then sitting with the Secretary, rarely dismissed one from his pen under less than three pages. The colonel smiled, and said when there was nothing further to say, it was economy to say nothing. He then carried his letters into the Secretary's office, clearing his throat according to custom on passing a door. I trembled for him; for I knew Mr. Walker had an aversion to signing his name to letters of merely two or three lines. He returned again immediately, saying the Secretary was busy. He left the letters, however.

Presently Major Tyler came out of the Secretary's room with several voluminous letters in his own handwriting, duly signed. The major greeted the colonel most cordially; and in truth his manners of a gentleman are so innate that I believe it would be utterly impossible for him to be clownish or rude in his address, if he were to make a serious effort to be so.

The major soon left us and re-entered the Secretary's office; but returned immediately bearing the colonel's fifty letters, which he placed before him and then retired. The very first one the colonel's eye rested upon, brought the color to his face. Every line in it had been effaced, and quite a different answer substituted in pencil marks between the lines! "I wrote that," said the colonel, "according to his own dictation." And as every letter carried in its fold the one to which it was a reply, he exhibited the Secretary's words in pencil marks. The colonel was right. The Secretary had omitted the little word "not"; and hence the colonel had written to the Georgian: "Your company of cavalry *is* accepted." The Secretary refused almost uniformly to accept cavalry, and particularly Georgia cavalry. I took blame to myself for not discovering this blunder previously. But the colonel, with his rapid pen, soon wrote another answer. About one-half the letters had to be written over again; and the colonel, smiling, and groaning, and perspiring so extravagantly that he threw off his coat, and occupied himself several hours in preparing the answers in accordance with the Secretary's corrections. And when they were done, Mr. S. S. Scott, who was to copy them in the letter-book, complimented the colonel on their brevity. In response to this, the colonel said, unfortunately, he wished he, Scott, were the secretary. Scott abused every one who wrote a long letter.

JUNE 9TH.—To-day the Secretary refused to sign the colonel's letters, telling him to sign them himself—"by order of the Secretary of War."

JUNE 10TH.—Yesterday the colonel did not take so many letters to answer; and to-day he looked about him for other duties more congenial to his nature.

JUNE 11TH.—It is coming in earnest! The supposed thunder, heard down the river yesterday, turns out to have been artillery. A fight has occurred at Bethel, and blood—Yankee blood—has flowed pretty freely. Magruder was assailed by some five thousand Yankees at Bethel, on the Peninsula. His force was about nine hundred; but he was behind intrenchments. We lost but one man killed and five wounded. The enemy's loss is several hundred. That road to Richmond is a hard one to travel! But I learn there is a panic about Williamsburg. Several young men from that vicinity have shouldered their *pens* and are applying for clerkships in the departments. But most of the men of proper age in the literary institutions are volunteering in defense of their native land.

JUNE 12TH.—Gen. Lee has been or is to be created a full general in the Confederate army, and will be assigned to duty here. He is third on the list, Sydney Johnston being second. From all I can see and infer, we shall make no attempt this year to invade the enemy's country. Our policy is to be defensive, and it will be severely criticised, for a vast majority of our people are for "carrying the war into Africa" without a moment's delay. The sequel will show which is right, the government or the people. At all events, the government will rule.

JUNE 13TH.—Only one of the Williamsburg volunteers came into the department proper; and he will make his way, for he is a flatterer. He told me he had read my "Wild Western Scenes" twice, and never was so much entertained by any other book. He went to work with hearty good-will.

JUNE 14TH.—Col. Bledsoe has given up writing almost entirely, but he groans as much as ever. He is like a fish out of water, and unfit for office.

JUNE 15TH.—Another clerk has been appointed; a sedate one, by the name of Shepherd, and a former pupil of the colonel's.

I received several hints that the Chief of the Bureau was not at all a favorite with the Secretary, who considered him utterly unfit for the position; and that it could hardly be *good policy* for me to be on terms of such intimacy with him. Policy! A word I never appreciated, a thing I never knew. All I know is that Col. Bledsoe has been appointed by the President to fill an important position; and the same power appoints the secretaries, and can unmake them. Under these circumstances I find him permitted to sit for hours and days in the department with no one to inform him of the condition of the business or to facilitate him in the performance of his official duties. Not for any partiality in his behalf, or prejudice against the Secretary, I step forward and endeavor to discharge my own duty. I strive to serve the cause, whatsoever may be the consequences to my personal interests.

JUNE 16TH.—To-day, receiving dispatches from General Floyd, in Western Virginia, that ten thousand Yankees were advancing through Fayette County, and might intercept railroad communication between Richmond and Chattanooga—the Secretary got me to send a telegraphic dispatch to his family to repair hither without delay, for *military* reasons. About this time the Secretary's health gave way again, and Major Tyler had another fit of indisposition totally disqualifying him for business. Hence I have nearly all the correspondence of the department on my hands, since Col. Bledsoe has ceased to write.

JUNE 17TH.—To-day there was a rumor in the streets that Harper's Ferry had been evacuated by Gen. Joseph E. Johnston, and, for the first time, I heard murmurs against the government. So far, perhaps, no Executive had ever such cordial and unanimous support of the people as President Davis. I knew the motive of the evacuation, and prepared a short editorial for one of the papers, suggesting good reasons for the retrograde movement; and instancing the fact that when Napoleon's capital was surrounded and taken, he had nearly 200,000 men in garrison in the countries he had conquered, which would have been ample for the defense of France. This I carried to the Secretary at his lodgings, and he was so well pleased with it he wanted me to accompany him to the lodgings of the President, in the same hotel, and show it to him.

This I declined, alleging it might be too late for the press. He laughed at my diffidence, and disinclination on such occasions to approach the President. I told him my desire was to serve the *cause*, and not myself. I suppose he was incredulous.

JUNE 18TH.—The city is content at the evacuation. The people have unbounded confidence in the wisdom of the administration, and the ability of our generals. Beauregard is the especial favorite. The soldiers, now arming daily, are eager for the fray; and it is understood a great battle must come off before many weeks; as it is the determination of the enemy to advance from the vicinity of Washington, where they are rapidly concentrating. But our people must curb their impatience. And yet we dare not make known the condition of the army,—the awful fact which may be stated here—and will not be known until after-years,—that we have not enough ammunition at Manassas to fight a battle. *There are not percussion caps enough in our army for a serious skirmish.* It will be obviated in a few weeks; and until then I pray there may be no battle. But if the enemy advance, our brave men will give them the cold steel. We *must* win the first battle at all hazards, and at any cost; and, after that,—how long after? —we must win the last!

JUNE 19TH.—Yesterday I saw Colonel Bartow, still accompanied by young Lamar, his aid. I wish all our officers were inspired by the same zeal and determination that they are. And are they not?

JUNE 20TH.—Gov. Wise has been appointed brigadier-general, of a subsequent date to General Floyd's commission. He goes to the West, where laurels grow; but I think it will be difficult to win them by any one acting in a subordinate capacity, and especially by generals appointed from civil life. They are the aversion of the West Pointers at the heads of bureaus.

JUNE 21ST.—A large, well-proportioned gentleman with florid complexion and intellectual face, who has been whispering with Col. Bledsoe several times during the last week, attracted my attention to-day. And when he retired, Colonel B. informed me it was Bishop Polk, a classmate of his and the President's at West Point. He had just been appointed a *major*-general, and assigned to duty in the West, where he would rank Gen. Pillow, who was exceedingly unpopular in Adjutant-Gen. Cooper's office. I presume this arose solely from mistrust of his military abilities; for he had certainly manifested much enthusiasm in the cause, and was constantly urging the propriety of aggressive movements with his command. All his purposed advances were countermanded. The policy of the government is to be economical of the men. We have but a limited, the enemy an inexhaustible number.

JUNE 22D.—The Convention has appointed ten additional members to the Provisional Congress—President Tyler among them. It will be observed that my Diary goes on, including every day. Fighting for our homes and holy altars, there is no intermission on Sunday. It is true, Mr. Memminger came in the other day with a proposition to cease from labor on Sunday, but our Secretary made war on it. The President, however, goes to church very regularly—St. Paul's.

On last Sunday the President surprised me. It was before church time, and I was working alone. No one else was in the large room, and the Secretary himself had gone home, quite ill. I thought I heard some one approaching lightly from behind, but wrote on without looking up; even when he had been standing some time at the back of my chair. At length I turned my head, and beheld the President not three feet from me. He smiled, and said he was looking for a certain letter referred by him to the Secretary. I asked the name of the writer, which he told me. I said I had a distinct recollection of it, and had taken it into the Secretary with other papers that morning. But the Secretary was gone. We then proceeded into the Secretary's office in search of it. The Secretary's habit was to take the papers from his table, and after marking on them with his pencil the disposition he wished made of them, he threw them helter-skelter into a large arm-chair. This chair now contained half a bushel; and the President and I set to work in quest of the letter. We removed them one by one; and as we progressed, he said with an impatient smile, "it is always sure to be the last one." And so it was. Having found it, he departed immediately; and soon after I saw him on his way to church.

JUNE 23D.—Every day as soon as the first press of business is over, the Secretary comes out of his office and taps me on the shoulder, and invites me to ride with him in quest of a house. We go to those offered for rent; but he cannot be suited.

JUNE 24TH.—To-day I was startled by the announcement from Col. Bledsoe that he would resign soon, and that it was his purpose to ask the President to appoint *me* chief of the bureau in his place. I said I preferred a less conspicuous position—and less labor—but thanked him. He said he had no influence with the Secretary — an incontrovertible fact; and that he thought he should return to the University. While we were speaking, the President's messenger came in with a note to the colonel; I did not learn the purport of it, but it put the colonel in a good humor. He showed me the two first words: "Dear Bledsoe." He said nothing more about resigning.

I must get more lucrative employment, or find something for my son to do. The boarding of my family, alone, comes to more than my salary; and the cost of everything is increasing.

JUNE 25TH.—More accounts of battles and massacres in Missouri and Kansas. I never thought the Yankees would be permitted to ascend the Missouri River. What has become of the marksmen and deer hunters of Missouri? There has been also a fight at Leesburg, and one near Romney, Va. Blood has been shed in all of them. These are the pattering drops that must inevitably be succeeded by a torrent of blood!

JUNE 26TH.—The President revised one of my articles for the press to-day, suggesting some slight modifications, which, perhaps, improved it. It was not a political article; but designed exclusively to advance the cause by inciting the people of Virginia and elsewhere to volunteer *for the war*. Such volunteers are accepted, and ordered into active service at once; whereas six and twelve months' men, unless they furnish their own arms, are not accepted.

It is certain the United States intend to raise a grand army, to serve for three years or the war. Short enlistments constituted the bane of Washington's army; and this fact is reiterated a thousand times in his extant letters.

There are a great many applications for clerkships in the departments by teachers who have not *followed* their *pupils* to the army. Army and naval officers, coming over at this late day, are commissioned in our service. In regard to this matter, the President is supposed to know best.

JUNE 27TH.—We have, I think, some 40,000 pretty well armed

men in Virginia, sent hither from other States. Virginia has—I know not how many; but she should have at least 40,000 in the field. This will enable us to cope with the Federal army of 70,000 volunteers, and the regular forces they may hurl against us. But so far as this department is aware, Virginia has not yet *two* regiments in the service for three years, or the war. And here the war will be sure to rage till the end!

JUNE 28TH.—We have a flaming comet in the sky. It comes unannounced, and takes a northwestern course. I dreamed last night that I saw a great black ball moving in the heavens, and it obscured the moon. The stars were in motion, visibly, and for a time afforded the only light. Then a brilliant halo illuminated the zenith like the quick-shooting irradiations of the aurora borealis. And men ran in different directions, uttering cries of agony. These cries, I remember distinctly, came from *men*. As I gazed upon the fading and dissolving moon, I thought of the war brought upon us, and the end of the United States Government. My family were near, all of them, and none seemed alarmed or distressed. I experienced no perturbation; but I awoke. I felt curious to prolong the vision, but sleep had fled. I was gratified, however, to be conscious of the fact that in this illusory view of the end of all things sublunary, I endured no pangs of remorse or misgivings of the new existence it seemed we were about to enter upon.

JUNE 29TH.—I cannot support my family here, on the salary I receive from the government; and so they leave me in a few days to accept the tendered hospitality of Dr. Custis, of Newbern, N. C., my wife's cousin.

JUNE 30TH.—My family engaged packing trunks. They leave immediately.

CHAPTER IV.

My family in North Carolina.—Volunteers daily rejected.—Gen. Winder appears upon the stage.—Toombs commissioned.—Hunter Secretary of State.—Duel prevented.—Col B. Secretary for a few hours.—Gen. Garnett killed.—Battle of Manassas.—Great excitement.—Col. Bartow.

JULY 1ST.—My family are gone. We have moved the department to Mechanics' Hall, which will be known hereafter as the War Department. In an evil hour, I selected a room to write my letters in, quite remote from the Secretary's office. I thought Mr. Walker resented this. He had likewise been piqued at the effect produced by an article I had written on the subject of the difficulty of getting arms from Georgia with the volunteers from that State. One of the spunky Governor's organs had replied with acerbity, not only defending the Governor, but striking at the Secretary himself, to whom the authorship was ascribed. My article had been read and approved by the Secretary before its insertion; nevertheless he now regretted it had been written—not that there was anything improper in it, but that it should have been couched in words that suggested the idea to the Southern editor that the Secretary might be its author. I resolved to meddle with edged tools no more; for I remembered that Gil Blas had done the same thing for the Duke of Lerma. Hereafter I shall study Gil Blas for the express purpose of being his antithesis. But I shall never rise until the day of doom brings us all to our feet again.

JULY 2D.—There has been some brilliant fighting by several brothers named Ashby, who led a mounted company near Romney. One of the brothers, Richard, was slain. Turner Ashby put half a dozen Yankees *hors du combat* with his own arm. He will make a name. We have accounts of an extraordinary exploit of Col. Thomas, of Maryland. Disguised as a French lady, he took passage on the steamer St. Nicholas at Baltimore en route for Washington. During the voyage he threw off his disguise, and in company with his accomplices, seized the steamer. Coming down the Bay, he captured three prizes, and took the whole fleet into Fredericksburg in triumph. Lieut. Minor, C. S. N., participated in this achievement. Gen. Patterson, who conciliated the mob in Philadelphia, which had intended to hang me, seems to be true to his pledge to fight the Southern people. He is now advancing into Virginia at the head of a brigade.

JULY 3D.—The Secretary said to me to-day that he desired my young friend, the classical teacher, to assist me in writing letters. I told him I needed assistance, and Mr. Jacques was qualified. Major Tyler's ill health keeps him absent half the time. There was abundance of work for both of us. Mr. J. is an agreeable companion, and omitted no opportunity to oblige me. But he trenches on the major's manor, and can write as long letters as any one. I would never write them, unless the subject-matter demanded it; and so, all the answers marked "full" by the Secretary, when the sum and substance is to be merely an affirmative or a negative, will fall to my co-laborer's share.

JULY 4TH.—These simple things provoked some remarks from the young gentlemen in the department, and gave rise to predictions that he would soon supplant us all in the affections of the Secretary. And he is nimble of foot too, and enters the Secretary's room twice to Col. B.'s or Major T.'s once. I go not thither unless sent for; for in a cause like this, personal advancement, when it involves catering to the caprices of functionaries dressed in a little brief authority, should be spurned with contempt. But Col. Bledsoe is shocked, and renews his threats of resignation. Major Tyler is eager to abandon the pen for the sword; but Congress has not acted on his nomination; and the West Pointers, many of them indebted to his father for their present positions, are inimical to his confirmation.

JULY 5TH.—We have news of a fight at Gainesville between Gen. Patterson and Col. Jackson; the latter, being opposed by overwhelming numbers, fell back after punishing the Philadelphia general so severely that he will not be likely to have any more stomach for fighting during the remainder of the campaign.

JULY 6TH.—Col. Bledsoe complains that the Secretary still has quite as little intercourse with him, personal and official, as possible. The consequence is that the Chief of the Bureau is drawing a fine salary and performing no service. Still, it is not without the sweat of his brow, and many groans.

JULY 7TH.—Major Tyler's health has improved, but I do not perceive a resumption of his old intimate relations with the Secretary. Yet he is doing the heavy epistolary work, being a lawyer; and the correspondence sometimes embracing diverse legal points. My intimacy with the colonel continues. It seems he would do anything in the world for me. He has put Mr. Shepherd to issuing passports to the camps, etc.—the form being dictated by the Secretary. These are the first passports issued by the government. I suggested that they should be granted by and in the name of the Chief of the Bureau of War—and a few were so issued—but the Secretary arrested the proceeding. The Secretary was right, probably, in this matter.

The President is appointing generals enough, one would suppose. I hope we shall have men for them. From five to ten thousand volunteers are daily offered—but not two thousand are accepted. Some have no arms; and others propose to serve only for six or twelve months. Infantry will not fight with hunting rifles or shot-guns; and the department will not accept mounted men, on account of the expense of transportation, etc. Oh, that I had power but for a week! There should then be accepted fifty regiments of cavalry. These are the troops for quick marches, surprises, and captures. And our people, even down to the little boys, are expert riders. If it were to be a short war—or if it were to be a war of invasion on our part—it might be good policy, economically, to discourage cavalry organizations. But we shall want all our men; and many a man would fight in the saddle who could not or would not march in the infantry. And mounted men are content to use the double-barreled shot-gun—one barrel for ball, the other for buck-shot and close quarters.

JULY 8TH.—There is a stout gray-haired old man here from Maryland applying to be made a general. It is Major J. H. Winder, a graduate of West Point, I believe; and I think he will be successful. He is the son, I believe, of the Gen. Winder whose command in the last war with England unfortunately permitted the City of Washington to fall into the hands of the enemy. I have almost a superstitious faith in *lucky* generals, and a corresponding prejudice against unlucky ones, and their progeny. But I cannot suppose the President will order this general into the field. He may take the prisoners into his custody—and do other jobs as a sort of head of military police; and this is what I learn he proposes. And the French Prince, Polignac, has been made a colonel; and a great nephew of Kosciusko has been commissioned a lieutenant in the regular army. Well, Washington had his Lafayette—and I like the nativity of these officers better than that of the Northern men, still applying for commissions.

JULY 9TH.—Mr. Toombs is to be a brigadier-general. That is what I looked for. The two brothers Cobb are to be colonels; and Orr is to have a regiment.

Mr. Hunter succeeds Toombs in the State Department—and that disposes of him, if he will stay there. It is to be an obscure place; and if he were indolent, without ambition, it would be the very place for him. Wise is done for. He has had several fights, always drawing blood; but when he gets ready to make a great fight, he is ordered back for fear of his "rashness." Exacting obedience in his own subordinates, of course he will obey the orders of Adjt.-Gen. Cooper. In this manner I apprehend that the three giants of Virginia, Wise, Hunter, and Floyd, will be neutralized and dwarfed at the behest of West Point. Napoleon's marshals were privates once—ours—but perhaps West Point may be killed off in the end, since they rush in so eagerly at the beginning of the war.

JULY 10TH.—There are indications of military operations on a large scale on the Potomac. We have intelligence that McDowell is making preparations to advance against our forces at Manassas. Gen. Johnston is expected to be there in time; and for that purpose is manœuvring Gen. Patterson out of the way. Our men have *caps* now—and will be found in readiness. They have short-commons under the Commissary Department; but even with empty stomachs, they can beat the Yankees at the ordeal of dying. Fighting is a sport our men always have an appetite for.

JULY 11TH.—The colonel tried his hand to-day at dictating answers to certain letters. Together we pitched upon the proper replies, which, after being marked with his pencil, I elaborated with the pen. These were first approved by the Secretary, then signed by the Chief of the Bureau, and copied by Mr. Scott.

To-day the colonel essayed a flight with his own plumage. I followed his dictation substantially in the answers. But the moment the Secretary's eyes rested upon them, they were promptly *reversed.* The Secretary himself, suspecting how it was, indeed he saw the colonel's pencil marks, brought them to me, while a humorous smile played upon his usually not very expressive lip. When the colonel came in, and beheld what had been done, he groaned, and requested me to write the proper answers. From that day he ceased to have anything more to do with the correspondence than to sign his name to the letters I prepared for him. He remarked to-day that if he was to have nothing to do, he would do nothing.

JULY 12TH.—The colonel's temper is as variable as an April day—now all smiles and sunshine, but by-and-by a cloud takes all away. He becomes impatient with a long-winded story, told by some business applicant—and *storms* whenever any one asks him if the Secretary is in.

To-day, for the first time, I detected a smile on the lip of Col. Myers, the Quartermaster-General, as he passed through the office. A moment after, Gen. Walker, of Georgia, came in, and addressed the colonel thus:

"Is the Secretary in?"

Col. (*with a stare*). I don't know.

Gen. W. (returning the stare). Could you not ascertain for me? I have important business with him; and am here by appointment.

Col. B. You can ascertain for yourself. I am not his doorkeeper. There is his door.

Gen. W. (after a moment's reflection). I asked you a civil question in a courteous manner, and have not deserved this harshness, and will not submit to it.

Col. B. It is not courteous to presume I am acting in the capacity of a messenger or door-keeper.

Just then the Secretary appeared at the door, having heard the loud language, and Gen. W. immediately entered his office.

Afterward the colonel fumed and fretted like an angry volcano. He disliked Col. Myers, and believed he had sent the general in under prompting to annoy him about the Secretary, whom he (Myers) really hated.

JULY 13TH.—The Secretary made peace yesterday between the general and the colonel, or a duel might have transpired.

To-day the colonel carried into the Secretary a number of applications for commissions as surgeons. Among the applicants were some of the colonel's friends. He returned soon after in a rage, slamming the door after him, and then throwing down the papers violently on the floor. He picked them up the next moment, however, and sitting down beside me, became instantaneously as gentle as a dove. He said the men of science were thrust aside to give way to quacks; but, laughing, he remarked that the quacks would do well enough for the wounded ——. *Our* men would have too much sense to submit to their malpractice.

JULY 14TH.—The Secretary is sick again. He has been recommended by his physician to spend some days in the country; and to-morrow he will leave with his family. What will be the consequence?

JULY 15TH.—Early this morning, Major Tyler was seated in the Secretary's chair, prepared to receive the visitors. This, I suppose, was of course in pursuance of the Secretary's request; and accordingly the door-keeper ushered in the people. But not long after Col. Bledsoe arrived, and exhibited to me an order from the President for him to act as Secretary of War *pro tem.* The colonel was in high spirits, and full dress; and seemed in no measure piqued at Major Tyler for occupying the Secretary's chair. The Secretary must have been aware that the colonel was to *act* during his absence—but, probably, supposed it proper that the major, from his suavity of manners, was best qualified for the reception of the visitors. He had been longer in the department, and was more familiar with the routine of business. Yet the colonel was not satisfied; and accordingly requested me to intimate the fact to Major Tyler, of which, it seemed, he had no previous information, that the President had appointed Col. Bledsoe to act as Secretary of War during the absence of Mr. Walker. The major retired from the office immediately, relinquishing his post with grace.

JULY 16TH.—The Secretary was back again this evening. He could not procure comfortable quarters in the country. He seemed vexed, but from what cause, I did not learn. The colonel, however, had *rushed the appointments*. He was determined to be *quick*, because Mr. W. was known to be slow and hesitating.

JULY 17TH.—The news is not so good to-day. Gen. Garnett's small command has been defeated by the superior numbers of Gen. McClellan. But the general himself was killed, fighting in the rear of his retreating men. His example will not be without its effect. Our generals will resolve never to survive a defeat. This will embolden the enemy to attack us at Manassas, where their suddenly acquired confidence will be snuffed out, or I am mistaken.

JULY 18TH.—The major is sick again, and Jacques is away; therefore I have too much work, and the colonel groans for me. He is proud of the appointments he made with such rapidity, and has been complimented. And in truth there is no reason why the thousands of applications should not be acted on promptly; and there are many against delay. A large army must be organized immediately, and it will be necessary to appoint thousands of field and staff officers—unless all the governors are permitted to do as Gov. Brown desires to do. The Secretary is in better health, and quite condescending. My work pleases him; and I shouldn't be astonished if he resented the sudden absence of Mr. Jacques. But he should consider that Mr. J. is only an amateur clerk getting no pay, rich, and independent of the government.

JULY 19TH.—We had fighting yesterday in earnest, at Bull Run! Several brigades were engaged, and the enemy were repulsed with the loss of several hundred left dead and wounded on the field. That *was* fighting, and we shall soon have more of it.

Brig.-Gen. Holmes, my friend and fellow-fugitive, now stationed near Fredericksburg, has been ordered by Gen. Beauregard to be ready to march at an hour's notice. And Col. Northrop's chin and nose have become suddenly sharper. He is to send up fighting rations for three days, and discerns the approach of sanguinary events.

Mr. Hunter calls every evening, just as the dusky shades of eve descend, to inquire if we have any news.

JULY 20TH.—The Secretary works too much—or rather does not economize his labor. He procrastinates final action; and hence his work, never being disposed of, is always increasing in volume. *Why* does he procrastinate? Can it be that his hesitation is caused by the advice of the President, in his great solicitude to make the best appointments? We have talent enough in the South to officer millions of men. Mr. Walker is a man of capacity, and has a most extraordinary recollection of details. But I fear his nerves are too finely strung for the official treadmill. I heard him say yesterday, with a sigh, that no *gentleman* can be fit for office. Well, Mr. Walker *is* a gentleman by education and instincts; and is fastidiously tenacious of what is due a gentleman. Will his official life be a long one? I know one thing—there are several aspiring dignitaries waiting impatiently for his shoes. But those who expect to reach the Presidency by a successful administration of any of the departments, or by the bestowal of patronage, are laboring under an egregious error. None but generals will get the Imperial purple for the next twenty years—if indeed the prematurely made "*permanent*" government should be permanent.

JULY 21ST.—The President left the city this morning for Manassas, and we look for a battle immediately. I have always thought he would avail himself of his prerogative as commander-in-chief, and direct in person the most important operations in the field; and, indeed, I have always supposed he was selected to be the Chief of the Confederacy, mainly with a view to this object, as it was generally believed he possessed military genius of a high order. In revolutions like the present, the chief executive occupies a most perilous and precarious position, if he be not a military chieftain, and present on every battle-field of great magnitude. I have faith in President Davis, and believe he will gain great glory in this first mighty conflict.

Early in the evening Secretary Walker returned from tea in great excitement. He strode to and fro in the room where we were sitting, d——g his office. He said a great battle was then going on, and he wished himself present participating in its perils. Again he denounced the office he filled—and seemed, for a time, almost frantic with anxiety. He said all young men ought to be in the field, and this was understood by those present, who had merely shouldered their pens.

Before long the hall of the department was filled with people eager to hear the news; and as successive dispatches were received, the excitement increased. All the cabinet were in our office;

and Hon. Howell Cobb, President of Congress, making deductions from the dispatches, announced his belief that it was a drawn battle. This moved the wrath of Col. Bledsoe, and he denounced Cobb. Mr. Hunter did nothing but listen. It was night, now. Finally, Mr. Benjamin, who had gone to the Spottswood Hotel, where Mrs. Davis resided, returned with news that stopped every detracting tongue. Mrs. D. had just got a dispatch from the President announcing a dearly-bought but glorious victory. Some of the editors of the papers being present, and applying to me for a copy of the dispatch, Mr. Benjamin said he could repeat it from memory, which he did, and I wrote it down for the press. Then joy ruled the hour! The city seemed lifted up, and every one appeared to walk on air. Mr. Hunter's face grew shorter; Mr. Reagan's eyes subsided into their natural size; and Mr. Benjamin's glowed something like Daniel Webster's after taking a pint of brandy. The men in place felt that now they held their offices for life, as the *permanent* government would soon be ratified by the people, and that the Rubicon had been passed in earnest. We had gained a great victory; and no doubt existed that it would be followed up the next day. If so, the Federal city would inevitably fall into our hands; and this would soon be followed by the expulsion of the enemy from Southern soil. All men seemed to think that the tide of war would roll from that day northward into the enemy's country, until we should win a glorious peace.

July 22d.—Both Col. B. and I were in a passion this morning upon finding that the papers had published a dispatch from their own agent at Manassas, stating that the President did not arrive upon the field until the victory was won; and therefore did not participate in the battle at all. From the President's own dispatch, and other circumstances, we had conceived the idea that he was not only present, but had directed the principal operations in the field. The colonel intimated that another paper ought to be established in Richmond, that would do justice to the President; and it was conjectured by some that a scheme was on foot to elect some other man to the Presidency of the permanent government in the autumn. Nevertheless, we learned soon after that the abused correspondent had been pretty nearly correct in his statement. The battle had been won, and the enemy were flying from the field before the President appeared upon it. It had been won by

Beauregard, who, however, was materially assisted by his superior in command, Gen. Joseph E. Johnston. Gen. J. remained in the rear, and brought up the reinforcements which gained the day. Beauregard is, to-day, the most popular general in the service. Besides some 500 prisoners, the enemy, it is said, had 4500 killed and wounded. The casualties would have been much greater, if the enemy had not broken and fled. We lost some 2000 men, killed and wounded.

The President returned to-day and made a speech at the Spottswood Hotel, wherein he uttered the famous words: "Never be haughty to the humble, or humble to the haughty." And he said that no doubt the Confederate flag then floated over Fairfax C. H., and would soon be raised at Alexandria, etc. etc. Never heard I more hearty cheering. Every one believed our banners would wave in the streets of Washington in a few days; that the enemy would be expelled from the District and from Maryland, and that a peace would be consummated on the banks of the Susquehanna or the Schuylkill. The President had pledged himself, on one occasion, to carry the war into the enemy's country, if they would not let us go in peace. Now, in that belief, the people were well pleased with their President.

JULY 23D.—Jacques is back and as busy as a bee; and, in truth, there is work enough for all.

JULY 24TH.—Yesterday we received a letter from Col. Bartow, written just before the battle (in which he fell, his letter being received after the announcement of his death), urging the appointment of his gallant young friend Lamar to a lieutenancy. I noted these facts on the back of his letter, with the Secretary's approbation, and also that the request had been granted, and placed the letter, perhaps the last he ever wrote, in the archives for preservation.

JULY 25TH.—Bartow's body has arrived, and lies in state at the Capitol. Among the chief mourners was his young friend Barton, who loved him as a son loves his father. From Lamar I learned some interesting particulars of the battle. He said when Bartow's horse was killed, he, Lamar, was sent to another part of the field for another, and also to order up certain regiments, Bartow then being in command of a brigade. Lamar galloped through a hot cross-fire to the regiments and delivered the order, but got no horse. He galloped back, however, through the terrible fire, with the intention of giving his own horse to Bartow, if none other could be had. On his return he encountered Col. Jones, of the 4th Alabama, wounded, his arms being around the necks of two friends, who were endeavoring to support him in a standing attitude. One of these called to Lamar, and asked for his horse, hoping that Col. Jones might be able to ride (his thigh-bone was terribly shattered), and thus get off the field. Lamar paused, and promised as soon as he could report to Bartow he would return with that or another horse. Col. Jones thanked him kindly, but cautioned him against any neglect of Bartow's orders, saying he probably could not ride. Lamar promised to return immediately; and putting spurs to his noble steed, started off in a gallop. He had not gone fifty yards before his horse fell, throwing him over his head. He saw that the noble animal had been pierced by as many as eight balls, from a single volley. He paused a moment and turned away, when the poor horse endeavored to rise and follow, but could not. He returned and patted the groaning and tearful steed on his neck; and, while doing this, *five more* balls struck him, and he died instantly. Lamar then proceeded on foot through a storm of bullets, and, untouched, rejoined Bartow in time to witness his fall.

Our prisons are filled with Yankees, and Brig.-Gen. Winder has employment. There is a great pressure for passports to visit the battle-field. At my suggestion, all physicians taking amputating instruments, and relatives of the wounded and slain, have been permitted by the Secretary to go thither.

JULY 26TH.—Many amusing scenes occur daily between the Chief of the Bureau and applicants for passports. Those not included specially in the Secretary's instructions, are referred to the Chief of the Bureau; and Col. Bledsoe cannot bear importunity. Sometimes he becomes so very boisterous that the poor applicants are frightened out of the office.

JULY 27TH.—A large number of new arrivals are announced from the North. Clerks resigned at Washington, and embryo heroes having military educations, are presenting themselves daily, and applying for positions here. They represent the panic in the North as awful, and ours is decidedly the winning side. These gentry somehow succeed in getting appointments.

Our army *does not advance.* It is said both Beauregard and Johnston are anxious to cross the Potomac; but what is *said* is not always true. The capabilities of our army to cross the Potomac are not known; and the policy of doing so if it were practicable, is to be determined by the responsible authority. Of one thing I am convinced: the North, so far from desisting from the execution of its settled purpose, even under this disagreeable reverse, will be stimulated to renewed preparations on a scale of greater magnitude than ever.

JULY 28TH.—We have taken two prisoners in civilian's dress, Harris and ——, on the field, who came over from Washington in quest of the remains of Col. Cameron, brother of the Yankee Secretary of War. They claim a release on the ground that they are non-combatants, but admit they were sent to the field by the Yankee Secretary. Mr. Benjamin came to the department last night with a message for Secretary Walker, on the subject. The Secretary being absent, he left it with me to deliver. It was that the prisoners were not to be liberated without the concurrence of the President. There was no danger of Secretary Walker releasing them; for I had heard him say the authorities might have obtained the remains, if they had sent a flag of truce. Disdaining to condescend thus far toward a recognition of us as belligerents, they abandoned their dead and wounded; and he, Walker, would see the prisoners, thus surreptitiously sent on the field, in a very hot place before he would sign an order for their release. I was gratified to see Mr. Benjamin so zealous in the matter.

JULY 29TH.—To-day quite a number of our wounded men on crutches, and with arms in splints, made their appearance in the streets, and created a sensation. A year hence, and we shall be accustomed to such spectacles.

JULY 30TH.—Nothing of importance to-day.

JULY 31ST.—Nothing worthy of note.

CHAPTER V.

My son Custis appointed clerk in the War Department.—N. Y. Herald contains a pretty correct army list of the C. S.—Appearance of "Plug Uglies."—President's rupture with Beauregard.—President sick.—Alien enemies ordered away.—Brief interview with the President.—"Immediate."—Large numbers of cavalry offering.—Great preparations in the North.

AUGUST 1ST.—Col. Bledsoe again threatens to resign, and again declares he will get the President to appoint me to his place. It would not suit me.

AUGUST 2D.—After some brilliant and successful fights, we have a dispatch to-day stating that Gen. Wise has fallen back in Western Virginia, obeying peremptory orders.

AUGUST 3D.—Conversed with some Yankees to-day who are to be released to-morrow. It appears that when young Lamar lost his horse on the plains of Manassas, the 4th Alabama Regiment had to fall back a few hundred yards, and it was impossible to bear Col. Jones, wounded, from the field, as he was large and unwieldy. When the enemy came up, some half dozen of their men volunteered to convey him to a house in the vicinity. They were permitted to do this, and to remain with him as a guard. Soon after our line advanced, and with such impetuosity as to sweep everything before it. Col. Jones was rescued, and his guard made prisoners. But, for their attention to him, he asked their release, which was granted. They say their curiosity to see a battle-field has been gratified, and they shall be contented to remain at home in safety hereafter. They regarded us as rebels, and believed us divided among ourselves. If this should be true, the rebellion would yet be crushed; but if we were unanimous and continued to fight as we did at Manassas, it would be revolution, and our independence must some day be acknowledged by the United States. But, they say, a great many Northern men remain to be gratified as they had been; and the war will be a terrible one before they can be convinced that a reduction of the rebellion is not a practicable thing.

AUGUST 4TH.—To-day Mr. Walker inquired where my son Custis was. I told him he was with his mother at Newbern, N. C. He authorized me to telegraph him to return, and he should be appointed to a clerkship.

AUGUST 5TH.—Col. Bledsoe has a job directly from the President: which is to adapt the volume of U. S. Army Regulations to the service of the Confederate States. It is only to strike out U. S. and insert C. S., and yet the colonel groans over it.

AUGUST 6TH.—Custis arrived and entered upon the discharge of his duties.

AUGUST 7TH.—Saw Col. Pendleton to-day, but it was not the first time. I have seen him in the pulpit, and heard him preach good sermons. He is an Episcopal minister. He it was that plowed such destruction through the ranks of the invaders at Manassas. At first the battery did no execution; perceiving this, he sighted the guns himself and fixed the range. Then exclaiming, "Fire, boys! and may God have mercy on their guilty souls!" he beheld the lanes made through the regiments of the enemy. Since then he has been made a colonel, and will some day be a general; for he was a fellow-cadet at West Point with the President and Bishop Polk.

A tremendous excitement! The New York *Herald* has been received, containing a pretty accurate list of our military forces in the different camps of the Confederate States, with names and grades of the general officers. The Secretary told me that if he had required such a list, a more correct one could not have been furnished him. Who is the traitor? Is he in the Adjutant-General's office? Many suppose so; and some accuse Gen. Cooper, simply because he is a Northern man by birth. But the same information might be supplied by the Quartermaster's or Commissary-General's office; and perhaps by the Ordnance Bureau; for all these must necessarily be in communication with the different organizations in the field. Congress was about to order an investigation; but it is understood the department suggested that the matter could be best searched into by the Executive. For my part, I have no doubt there are many Federal spies in the departments. Too many clerks were imported from Washington. And yet I doubt if any one in a subordinate position, without assistance from higher authority, could have prepared the list published in the *Herald*

AUGUST 8TH.—For some time past (but since the battle at Manassas) quite a number of Northern and Baltimore policemen have made their appearance in Richmond. Some of these, if not indeed all of them, have been employed by Gen. Winder. These men, by their own confessions, have been heretofore in Baltimore, Philadelphia, and New York, merely petty larceny detectives, dwelling in bar-rooms, ten-pin alleys, and such places. How can they detect political offenders, when they are too ignorant to comprehend what constitutes a political offense? They are illiterate men, of low instincts and desperate characters. But their low cunning will serve them here among unsuspecting men. They will, if necessary, give information to the enemy themselves, for the purpose of convincing the authorities that a detective police is indispensable; and it is probable a number of them will be, all the time, on the pay-rolls of Lincoln.

AUGUST 9TH.—Gen. Magruder commands on the Peninsula. President Tyler had a villa near Hampton, which the Yankees despoiled in a barbarous manner. They cut his carpets, defaced the pictures, broke the statues, and made kindling wood of the piano, sofas, etc.

AUGUST 10TH.—Mr. Benjamin is a frequent visitor at the department, and is very sociable: some intimations have been thrown out that he aspires to become, some day, Secretary of War. Mr. Benjamin, unquestionably, will have great influence with the President, for he has studied his character most carefully. He will be familiar not only with his "likes," but especially with his "dislikes." It is said the means used by Mr. Blair to hold Gen. Jackson, consisted not so much in a facility of attaching strong men to him as his friends, but in aiming fatal blows at the great leaders who had incurred the enmity of the President. Thus Calhoun was incessantly pursued.

AUGUST 11TH.—There is a whisper that something like a rupture has occurred between the President and Gen. Beauregard; and I am amazed to learn that Mr. Benjamin is inimical to Gen. B. I know nothing of the foundation for the report; but it is said that Beauregard was eager to pass with his army into Maryland, immediately after the battle, and was prevented. It is now quite apparent, from developments, that a small force would have sufficed to take Washington, a few days or weeks after the battle. But was Beauregard aware of the fact, before the opportunity ceased to exist? It is too late now!

AUGUST 12TH.—There is trouble with Mr. Tochman, who was authorized to raise a regiment or so of foreigners in Louisiana. These troops were called (by whom?) the Polish Brigade, though, perhaps, not one hundred Polanders were on the muster-rolls; Major Tochman being styled *General* Tochman by "everybody," he has intimated to the President his expectation of being commissioned a brigadier. The President, on his part, has promptly and emphatically, as is sometimes his wont, declared his purpose to give him no such commission. He never, for a moment, thought of making him more than a colonel. To this the major demurs, and furnishes a voluminous correspondence to prove that his claims for the position of brigadier-general had been recognized by the Secretary of War.

AUGUST 13TH.—The President sent to the department an interesting letter from Mr. Zollicoffer, in Tennessee, relating to the exposed condition of the country, and its capacities for defense.

AUGUST 14TH.—Zollicoffer has been appointed a brigadier-general; and although not a military man by education, I think he will make a good officer.

AUGUST 15TH.—No clew yet to the spies in office who furnish the Northern press with information. The matter will pass uninvestigated. Such is our indifference to everything but desperate fighting. The enemy will make good use of this species of information.

AUGUST 16TH.—The President is sick, and goes to the country. I did not know until to-day that he is blind of an eye. I think an operation was performed once in Washington.

AUGUST 17TH.—Some apprehension is felt concerning the President's health. If he were to die, what would be the consequences? I should stand by the Vice-President, of course, because "it is so nominated in the bond," and because I think he would make as efficient an Executive as any other man in the Confederacy. But others think differently; and there might be trouble.

The President has issued a proclamation, in pursuance of the act of Congress passed on the 8th instant, commanding all alien enemies to leave in forty days; and the Secretary of War has indicated Nashville as the place of exit. This produces but little excitement, except among the Jews, some of whom are converting their effects into gold and departing.

Col. Bledsoe's ankles are much too weak for his weighty body, but he can shuffle along quite briskly when in pursuit of a refractory clerk; and when he catches him, if he resists, the colonel is sure to leave him.

August 18th.—Nothing worthy of note.

August 19th.—The Secretary has gone to Orange C. H., to see Col. Jones, of the 4th Alabama, wounded at Manassas, and now in a dying condition.

Meeting with Mr. Benjamin this morning, near the Secretary's door, I asked him if he did not think some one should act as Secretary during Mr. Walker's absence. He replied quickly, and with interest, in the affirmative. There was much pressing business every hour; and it was uncertain when the Secretary would return. I asked him if he would not speak to the President on the subject. He assented; but, hesitating a moment, said he thought it would be better for me to see him. I reminded him of my uniform reluctance to approach the Chief Executive, and he smiled. He then urged me to go to the presidential mansion, and in his, Mr. B.'s name, request the President to appoint a Secretary *ad interim.* I did so, for the President was in the city that day, and fast recovering from his recent attack of ague.

Arrived at the mansion in Clay Street, I asked the servant if I could see the President. He did not know me, and asked my name, saying the President had not yet left his chamber. I wrote my business on a card with a pencil, not omitting to use the name of Mr. Benjamin, and sent it up. A moment after the President came down, shook hands with me, and, in his quick and rather pettish manner, said "send me the order." I retired immediately, and finding Mr. Benjamin still in the hall of the department, informed him of my success. Then, in conformity with his suggestion, I repaired to Adjutant-General Cooper, who wrote the order that A. T. Bledsoe discharge the duties of Secretary of War during the absence of Mr. Walker. This I sent by a messenger to the President, who signed it.

Then I informed Col. Bledsoe of what had been done, and he proceeded without delay to the Secretary's office. It was not long before I perceived the part Mr. Benjamin and I had acted was likely to breed a storm; for several of the employees, supposed to be in the confidence of Mr. Walker, designated the proceeding as an "outrage;" and some went so far as to intimate that Mr. Benjamin's motive was to have some of his partisans appointed to lucrative places in the army during the absence of the Secretary. I know not how that was; but I am sure I had no thought but for the public service. The Secretary *ad in.* made but few appointments this time, and performed the functions quietly and with all the dignity of which he was capable.

AUGUST 20TH.—Secretary Walker returned last night, having heard of the death of Col. Jones before reaching his destination. I doubt whether the Secretary would have thought a second time of what had been done in his absence, if some of his friends had not fixed his attention upon it. He shut himself up pretty closely, and none of us could see or hear whether he was angry. But calling me into his room in the afternoon to write a dispatch which he dictated, I saw, lying on his table, an envelope directed in his own hand to the President. Hints had been circulated by some that it was his purpose to resign. Could this communication be his resignation? It was placed so conspicuously before me where I sat that it was impossible not to see it. It was marked, too, "*immediate.*"

AUGUST 21ST.—Called in again by the Secretary to-day, I find the ominous communication to the President still there, although marked "*immediate.*" And there are no indications of Mr. Walker's quitting office that I can see.

AUGUST 22D.—"*Immediate*" is still there; but the Secretary has not yet been to the council board, though yesterday was cabinet day. Yet the President sends Capt. Josselyn regularly with the papers referred to the Secretary. These are always given to me, and after they are "briefed," delivered to the Secretary. Among these I see some pretty *sharp* pencil marks. Among the rest, the whole batch of Tochman papers being returned unread, with the injunction that "when papers of such volume are sent to him for perusal, it is the business of the Secretary to see that a brief abstract of their contents accompany them."

August 23d.—No arms yet of any amount from Europe; though our agent writes that he has a number of manufactories at work. The U. S. agent has engaged the rest. All the world seems to be in the market buying arms. Mr. Dayton, U. S. Minister in Paris, has bought 30,000 flint-locks in France; and our agent wants authority to buy some too. He says the French statisticians allege that no greater mortality in battle occurs from the use of the percussion and the rifled musket than from the old smooth-bore flint-lock musket. This may be owing to the fact that a shorter range is sought with the latter.

August 24th.—We are resting on our oars after the victory at Manassas, while the enemy is drilling and equipping 500,000 or 600,000 men. I hope we may not soon be floating down stream! We know the enemy is, besides, building iron-clad steamers—and yet we are not even erecting casemate batteries! We are losing precious time, and, perhaps, the government is saving money!

August 25th.—I believe the Secretary will resign; but "*immediate*" still lies on his table.

News of a battle near Springfield, Mo. McCulloch and Price defeat the Federals, killing and wounding thousands. Gen. Lyon killed.

August 26th.—What a number of cavalry companies are daily tendered in the letters received at this department. Almost invariably they are refused; and really it is painful to me to write these letters. This government must be aware, from the statistics of the census, that the South has quite as many horses as the North, and twice as many good riders. But for infantry, the North can put three men in the field to our one. Ten thousand mounted men, on the border of the enemy's country, would be equal to 30,000 of the enemy's infantry; not in combat: but that number would be required to watch and guard against the inroads of 10,000 cavalry. It seems to me that we are declining the only proper means of equalizing the war. But it is my duty to obey, and not to deliberate.

August 27th.—We have news of a fight at Hawk's Nest, Western Virginia. Wise whipped the Yankees there quite handsomely.

August 28th.—Beauregard offers battle again on the plains of Manassas; but it is declined by the enemy, who retire behind their fortifications. Our banners are advanced to Munson's Hill, in sight of Washington. The Northern President and his cabinet may see our army, with good glasses, from the roof of the White House. It is said they sleep in their boots; and that some of them leave the city every night, for fear of being captured before morning.

Generals Johnston, Wise, and Floyd are sending here, daily, the Union traitors they discover to be in communication with the enemy. We have a Yankee member of Congress, Ely, taken at Manassas; he rode out to witness the sport of killing rebels as terriers kill rats, but was caught in the trap himself. He says his people were badly whipped; and he hopes they will give up the job of subjugation as a speculation that won't pay. Most of the prisoners speak thus while in confinement.

August 29th.—We have intelligence from the North that immense preparations are being made for our destruction; and some of our people begin to say, that inasmuch as we did not follow up the victory at Manassas, it was worse than a barren one, having only *exasperated* the enemy, and stimulated the Abolitionists to renewed efforts. I suppose these critics would have us forbear to injure the invader, for fear of maddening him. *They* are making this war; *we* must make it *terrible*. With them war is a *new thing*, and they will not cease from it till the novelty wears off, and all their fighting men are sated with blood and bullets. It must run its course, like the measles. We must both bleed them and deplete their pockets.

August 30th.—Gen. Floyd has had a fight in the West, and defeated an Ohio regiment. I trust they were of the Puritan stock, and not the descendants of Virginians.

August 31st.—We have bad news to-day. My wife and children are the bearers of it. They returned to the city with the tidings that all the women and children were ordered to leave Newbern. The enemy have attacked and taken Fort Hatteras, making many prisoners, and threaten Newbern next. This is the second time my family have been compelled to fly. But they are well.

CHAPTER VI.

Four hundred thousand troops to be raised.—Want of arms.—Yankees offer to sell them to us.—Walker resigns.—Benjamin succeeds.—Col. J. A. Washington killed.—Assigned, temporarily, to the head of the passport office.

September 1st.—The press and congressional critics are opening their batteries on the Secretary of War, for incompetency. He is not to blame. A month ago, Capt. Lee, son of the general, and a good engineer, was sent to the coast of North Carolina to inspect the defenses. His report was well executed; and the recommendations therein attended to with all possible expedition. It is now asserted that the garrison was deficient in ammunition. This was not the case. The position was simply not tenable under the fire of the U. S. ships of war.

September 2d.—I voluntarily hunted up Capt. Lee's report, and prepared an article for the press based on its statements.

September 3d.—My article on the defenses of North Carolina seems to have silenced the censures of the cavilers.

September 4th.—J. R. Anderson, proprietor of the iron-works here, has been appointed brigadier-general by the President. He, too, was a West Pointer; but does not look like a military genius. He is assigned to duty on the coast of North Carolina.

September 5th.—Our Congress has authorized the raising and organizing of four hundred regiments. The Yankee Congress, 500,000 men. The enemy will get their's first; and it is said that between 600,000 and 700,000, for three years or the war, have already been accepted by the U. S. Government. Their papers boast that nearly a million volunteers were tendered. This means mischief. How many will rush forward a year hence to volunteer their services on the plains of the South? Full many ensanguined plains will greet the horrific vision before this time next year; and many a venal wretch coming to possess our land, will occupy till the day of final doom a tract of six feet by two in some desolate and unfrequented swamp. The toad will croak his requiem, and the viper will coil beneath the thistle growing over his head.

SEPTEMBER 6TH.—We are not increasing our forces as rapidly as might be desired, for the want of arms. We had some 150,000 stand of small arms, at the beginning of the war, taken from the arsenals; and the States owned probably 100,000 more. Half of these were flint-locks, which are being altered. None have been imported yet. Occasionally a letter reaches the department from Nashville, offering improved arms at a high price, *for gold.* These are Yankees. I am instructed by the Secretary to say they will be paid for in gold on delivery to an agent in Nashville. The number likely to be obtained in this manner, however, must be small; for the Yankee Government is exercising much vigilance. Is not this a fair specimen of Yankee cupidity and character? The New England manufacturers are furnishing us, with whom they are at war, with arms to fight with, provided we agree to pay them a higher price than is offered by their own Government! The philosophical conclusion is, that this war will end when it ceases to be a pecuniary speculation.

SEPTEMBER 7TH.—The Jews are at work. Having no nationality, all wars are harvests for them. It has been so from the day of their dispersion. Now they are scouring the country in all directions, buying all the goods they can find in the distant cities, and even from the country stores. These they will *keep,* until the process of consumption shall raise a greedy demand for all descriptions of merchandise.

Col. Bledsoe *has resigned,* but says nothing now about getting me appointed in his place. That matter rests with the President, and I shall not be an applicant.

SEPTEMBER 8TH.—Major Tyler has been appointed *acting* Chief of the Bureau of War.

SEPTEMBER 9TH.—Matters in *statu quo,* and Major Tyler still acting chief of the bureau.

SEPTEMBER 10TH.—Col. Bledsoe is back again! He says the President refuses to accept his resignation; and tells me in confidence, not to be revealed for a few days, that Mr. Walker has tendered his resignation, *and that it will be accepted.*

SEPTEMBER 11TH.—The colonel enjoys a joke. He whispered me to-day, as he beheld Major Tyler doing the honors of his office, that I might just hint at the possibility of his resumption soon of the functions of chief of the bureau. But he said he wanted a few days holiday.

SEPTEMBER 12TH.—Gen. Pillow has advanced, and occupied Columbus, Ky. He was ordered, by telegraph, to abandon the town and return to his former position. Then the order was countermanded, and he remains. The authorities have learned that the enemy occupies Paducah.

SEPTEMBER 13TH.—The Secretary, after writing and tendering his resignation, appointed my young friend Jaques a special clerk with $2000 salary. This was allowed by a recent act.

SEPTEMBER 14TH.—Some of Mr. Walker's clerks must know that he intends giving up the seals of office soon, for they are engaged day and night, and all night, *copying* the entire letter-book, which is itself but a copy of the letters I and others have written, with Mr. Walker's name appended to them. Long may they be a monument of his epistolary administrative ability, and profound statesmanship!

SEPTEMBER 15TH.—And, just as I expected, Mr. Benjamin is to be Mr. Walker's successor. Col. Bledsoe is back again; and it devolved on me to inform Major Tyler that the *old* chief of the bureau was now the *new* chief. Of course he resigned the seals of office with the grace and courtesy of which he is so capable. And then he informed me (in confidence) that the Secretary had resigned, and would be appointed a brigadier-general in the army of the Southwest; and that he would accompany him as his adjutant-general.

SEPTEMBER 16TH.—Mr. Benjamin's hitherto perennial smile faded almost away as he realized the fact that he was now the most important member of the cabinet. He well knew how arduous the duties were; but then he was robust in health, and capable of any amount of labor.

It seems, after all, that Mr. Benjamin is only *acting* Secretary of War, until the President can fix upon another. Can that be the reason his smile has faded almost away? But the President will appoint him. Mr. Benjamin will please him; he knows how to do it.

SEPTEMBER 17TH.—A man from Washington came into my office to-day, saying he had important information from Washington.

I went into the Secretary's room, and found Mr. Benjamin surrounded by a large circle of visitors, all standing hat in hand, and quite silent. I asked him if he would see the gentleman from Washington. He said he "*didn't know who to see.*" This produced a smile. He seemed to be standing there waiting for some one to speak, and they seemed to be waiting an invitation from him to speak. I withdrew from the embarrassing scene, remarking that my gentleman would call some other time. Meanwhile I wrote down the information, and sent it to the President.

SEPTEMBER 18TH.—Gen. Floyd has been attacked at Gauley, by greatly superior numbers. But he was intrenched, and slew hundreds of the enemy before he retreated, which was effected without loss.

SEPTEMBER 19TH.—We hear of several splendid dashes of cavalry near Manassas, under Col. Stuart; and Wise's cavalry in the West are doing good service.

SEPTEMBER 20TH.—Col. J. A. Washington has been killed in a skirmish. He inherited Mount Vernon. This reminds me that Edward Everett is urging on the war against us. The universal education, so much boasted of in New England, like their religion, is merely a humbug, or worse than a humbug, the fruitful source of crime. I shall doubt hereafter whether superior intelligence is promotive of superior virtue. The serpent is wiser than the dove, but never so harmless. Ignorance is bliss in comparison with Yankee wisdom.

SEPTEMBER 21ST.—The Secretary has authorized me to sign passports "for the Secretary of War." My son attends to his letters. I have now an opportunity of *seeing* more. I have authority to order transportation for the parents of soldiers, and for goods and provisions taken to the camps.

SEPTEMBER 22D.—Harris and Magraw, who were taken on the field of Manassas, looking for the remains of Col. Cameron, have been liberated by Gen. Winder, on the order of the acting Secretary of War. This is startling; for Mr. Benjamin was the most decided man, at the time of their capture, against their liberation. *Per contra,* a Mr. G., a rich New York merchant, and Mr. R., a wealthy railroad contractor, whom I feared would break through the meshes of the law, with the large sums realized by them here, have been arrested by the Secretary's order, on the ground that they have no right to transfer the sinews of war to the North, to be used against us.

SEPTEMBER 23D.—Thousands of dollars worth of clothing and provisions, voluntary and patriotic contributions to the army, are arriving daily.

SEPTEMBER 24TH.—The time is up for the departure of alien enemies. This is the last day, according to the President's proclamation. We have had no success lately, and never can have success, while the enemy know all our plans and dispositions. Keep them in total ignorance of our condition and movements, and they will no more invade us than they would explore a vast cave, in which thousands of rattlesnakes can be heard, without lights. Their spies and emissaries here are so many torch-bearers for them.

SEPTEMBER 25TH.—Mr. Benjamin and Gen. Winder, after granting a special interview to Messrs. G. and R., have concluded to let them depart for Pennsylvania and New York! Nor is this all. *I have an order from Mr. Benjamin to give passports*, until further orders, *to leave the country to all persons who avow themselves alien enemies, whether in person or by letter*, provided they take no wealth with them. This may be a fatal policy, or it may be a *trap*.

SEPTEMBER 26TH.—Had a conversation with the Secretary to-day, on the policy of sending Union men out of the Confederacy. I told him we had 15,000 sick in the hospitals at Manassas, and this intelligence might embolden the enemy to advance, capture the hospitals, and make our sick men prisoners. He said such prisoners would be a burden to them, and a relief to us. I remarked that they would count as prisoners in making exchanges; and to abandon them in that manner, would have a discouraging effect on our troops. He said that sending unfriendly persons out of the country was in conformity with the spirit of the act of Congress, and recommended me to reperuse it and make explanations to the people, who were becoming clamorous for some restriction on the egress of spies.

SEPTEMBER 27TH.—To-day I prepared a leading editorial article for the *Enquirer*, taking ground directly opposite to that advocated by Mr. Benjamin. It was written with the law before me, which gave no warrant, as I could perceive, for the assumption of the Secretary.

SEPTEMBER 28TH.—I sent the paper containing my article to J. R. Davis, Esq., nephew of the President, avowing its authorship, and requesting him to ask the President's attention to the subject.

SEPTEMBER 29TH.—To-day Mr. Benjamin issued several passports himself, and sent several others to me with peremptory orders for granting them.

SEPTEMBER 30TH.—A pretty general jail delivery is now taking place. Gen. Winder, acting I suppose, of course, under the instructions of the Secretary of War—and Mr. Benjamin is now Secretary indeed—is discharging from the prisons the disloyal prisoners sent hither during the last month by Gens. Johnston, Floyd, and Wise. Not only liberating them, but giving them transportation to their homes, mostly within the enemy's lines. Surely if the enemy reciprocates such magnanimous courtesy, the war will be merely child's play, and we shall be spared the usual horrors of civil war. We shall see how the Yankees will appreciate this kindness.

CHAPTER VII.

An order for the publication of the names of alien enemies.—Some excitement.—Efforts to secure property.—G. A. Myers, lawyer, actively engaged.—Gen. Price gains a victory in Missouri.—Billy Wilson's cut-throats cut to pieces at Fort Pickens.—A female spy arrives from Washington.—Great success at Leesburg or Ball's Bluff.

OCTOBER 1ST.—I find that only a few hundred alien enemies departed from the country under the President's proclamation, allowing them forty days, from the 16th of August, to make their arrangements; but under the recent order of Mr. Benjamin, if I may judge from the daily applications, there will be a large emigration. The persons now going belong to a different class of people: half of them avowing themselves friendly to our cause, and desiring egress through our lines on the Potomac, or in the West, to avoid being published as alien enemies going under flag of truce *via* Norfolk and Fortress Monroe. Many of them declare a purpose to return.

OCTOBER 2D.—A day or two ago Col. Bledsoe, who visits me now very seldom, sent an order by Mr. Brooks for me to furnish a list of the names of alien enemies for publication. This was complied with cheerfully; and these publications have produced some excitement in the community.

OCTOBER 3D.—The President not having taken any steps in the matter, I have no alternative but to execute the order of the Secretary.

OCTOBER 4TH.—Sundry applications were made to-day to leave the country under flag of truce, *provided I would not permit the names to be published.* The reason for this request is that these persons have connections here who might be *compromised.* I refused compliance. In one or two instances they intimated that they would not have their names published for *thousands of dollars.* My response to this was such as to cause them to withdraw their applications.

OCTOBER 5TH.—To-day several Southern-born gentlemen, who have lived long in the North, and have their fortunes and families there, applied for passports. They came hither to save the investments of their parents in Northern securities, by having them transferred to their children. This seems legitimate, and some of the parties are old and valued friends of mine. I know their sympathies are with their native land. Yet why are they so late in coming? I know not. It is for me to send them out of the country, for such is the order of the Secretary of War. The loyalty of the connections of these gentlemen is vouched for in a note (on file) written by Mr. Hunter, Secretary of State. Their names must be published as alien enemies. They will take no part in the war.

OCTOBER 6TH.—Nothing of importance.

OCTOBER 7TH.—Nothing of note.

OCTOBER 8TH.—Mr. Gustavus Myers, a lawyer of this city, seems to take an active interest in behalf of parties largely engaged in business at Baltimore. And he has influence with the Secretary, for he generally carries his points over my head. The parties he engineers beyond our lines may possibly do us no harm; but I learn they certainly do themselves much *good* by their successful speculations. And do they not take gold and other property to the North, and thereby defeat the object of the sequestration act? The means thus abstracted from the South will certainly be taxed by the North to make war on us.

OCTOBER 9TH.—Contributions of clothing, provisions, etc. are coming in large quantities; sometimes to the amount of $20,000 in a single day.

Never was there such a patriotic *people* as ours! Their blood and their wealth are laid upon the altar of their country with enthusiasm.

I must say here that the South Carolinians are the *gentlest* people I ever met with. They accede to every requisition with cheerfulness; and never have I known an instance where any one of them has used subterfuge to evade a rule, however hard it might bear upon them. They are the soul of honor, truth, and patriotism.

OCTOBER 10TH.—A victory—but not in the East. I expect none here while there is such a stream of travel flowing Northward. It was in Missouri, at Lexington. Gen. Price has captured the town and made several thousand prisoners, whom he dismissed on parole.

OCTOBER 11TH.—And Wise has had bloody fighting with Rosecrans in Western Virginia. He can beat the enemy at fighting; but they beat him at manœuvring, with the use of the guides Gen. Winder has sent them from our prisons here.

OCTOBER 12TH.—Col. Wright has had a race with the Yankees on the North Carolina coast. They fled to their works before his single regiment with such precipitation as to leave many of their arms and men behind. We lost but one man: and he was fat, broke his wind, and died in the pursuit.

OCTOBER 13TH.—Another little success, but not in this vicinity. Gen. Anderson, of South Carolina, in the night crossed to Santa Rosa Island and cut up Billy Wilson's regiment of New York cutthroats and thieves, under the very guns of Fort Pickens.

OCTOBER 14TH.—Kissing goes by favor! Col. M——r, of Maryland, whose published letter of objuration of the United States Government attracted much attention some time since, is under the ban. He came hither and tendered his services to this government, but failed to get the employment applied for, though his application was urged by Mr. Hunter, the Secretary of State, who is his relative. After remaining here for a long time, vainly hoping our army would cross the Potomac and deliver his native State, and finding his finances diminishing, he sought permission of the Secretary to return temporarily to his family in Maryland, expecting to get them away and to save some portion of his effects. His fidelity was vouched for in strong language by Mr. Hunter, and yet the application has been refused! I infer from this that Mr. Benjamin is omnipotent in the cabinet, and that Mr. Hunter cannot remain long in it.

OCTOBER 15TH.—I have been requested by Gen. Winder to-day to refuse a passport to Col. M——r to leave the city in any direction. So the colonel is within bounds! I learn that he differed with Gen. Winder (both from Maryland) in politics. But if he was a Whig, so was Mr. Benjamin. Again, I hear that Col. M. had some difficulty with Col. Northrop, Commissary-General, and challenged him. This is a horse of another color. Col. N. is one of the special favorites of the President.

OCTOBER 16TH.—Col. M. applied to me to-day for a passport to Maryland, bringing a strong letter from Mr. Hunter, and also a note from Col. Bledsoe, Chief of the Bureau of War. He seemed thunderstruck when I informed him that Gen. Winder had obtained an order from the Secretary of War to detain him. A few moments after Gen. Winder came with a couple of his detectives (all from Baltimore) and arrested him. Subsequently he was released on parole of honor, not to leave the city without Gen. Winder's permission. I apprehend bad consequences from this proceeding. It may prevent other high-toned Marylanders from espousing our side of this contest.

OCTOBER 17TH.—Hurlbut has been released from prison. Mr. Hunter has a letter (intercepted) from Raymond, editor of the New York *Times*, addressed to him since the battle of Manassas.

OCTOBER 18TH.—I cannot perceive that our army increases much in strength, particularly in Virginia. The enemy have now over 660,000 in the field in various places, and seem to be preparing for a simultaneous advance.

It is said *millions* of securities, the property of the enemy, are transferred to the United States. It is even intimated that the men engaged in this business have the protection of men in high positions *on both sides.* Can it be possible that *we* have men in power who are capable of taking bribes from the enemy? If so, God help the country!

October 19th.—Col. Ashby with 600 men routed a force of 1000 Yankees, the other day, near Harper's Ferry. That is the cavalry again! The spies here cannot inform the enemy of the movements of our mounted men, which are always made with celerity.

October 20th.—A lady, just from Washington, after striving in vain to procure an interview with the Secretary of War, left with me the programme of the enemy's contemplated movements. She was present with the family of Gen. Dix at a party, and heard their purposes disclosed. They meditate an advance immediately, with 200,000 men. The head of Banks's column is to cross near Leesburg; and when over, a movement upon our flank is intended from the vicinity of Arlington Heights. This is truly a formidable enterprise, if true. We have not 70,000 effective men in Northern Virginia. The lady is in earnest—and remains here.

I wrote down the above information and sent it to the President; and understood that dispatches were transmitted immediately to Gen. Johnston, by telegraph.

The lady likewise spoke of a contemplated movement by sea with gun-boats, to be commanded by Burnside, Butler, etc.

In the evening I met Mr. Hunter, and told him the substance of the information brought by the lady. He seemed much interested, for he knows the calm we have been enjoying bodes no good; and he apprehends that evil will grow out of the order of the Secretary of War, permitting all who choose to call themselves alien enemies to leave the Confederacy. While we were speaking (in the street) Mr. Benjamin came up, and told me he had seen the letter I sent to the President. He said, moreover, that he did not doubt the enemy intended to advance as set forth in the programme.

October 21st.—The enemy's papers represent that we have some 80,000 men in Kentucky, and this lulls us from vigilance and effort in Virginia. The Secretary of War knows very well that we have not 30,000 there, and that we are not likely to have more. We supposed Kentucky would rise. The enemy knows this fact as well as we do; nevertheless, it has been his practice from the beginning to exaggerate our numbers. It lulls us into fancied security.

OCTOBER 22D.—We have news of a victory at Leesburg. It appears that the head of one of the enemy's columns, 8000 strong, attempted a passage of the Potomac yesterday, at that point pursuant to the programme furnished by the lady from Washington. That point had been selected by the enemy because the spies had reported that there were only three Confederate regiments there. But crossing a river in boats in the face of a few Southern regiments, is no easy matter. And this being the *People's War*, although Gen. Evans, in command, had received orders to fall back if the enemy came in force, our troops decided for themselves to fight before retreating. Therefore, when seven or eight regiments of Yankees landed on this side of the river, two or three of our regiments advanced and fired into them with terrible effect. Then they charged; and ere long such a panic was produced that the enemy rushed in disorder into the river, crowding their boats so much that several went to the bottom, carrying down hundreds. The result was that the head of the serpent received a tremendous bruising, and the whole body recoiled from the scene of disaster. We had only some 1500 men engaged, and yet captured 1600 muskets; and the enemy's loss, in killed, wounded, and prisoners, amounted to 2000 men. This battle was fought, in some respects, by the privates alone—much of the time without orders, and often without officers.

OCTOBER 23D.—The President is highly delighted at the result of the battle of Leesburg; and yet some of the red-tape West Point gentry are indignant at Gen. Evans for not obeying orders, and falling back. There is some talk of a court-martial; for it is maintained that no commander, according to strict military rules, should have offered battle against such superior numbers. They may disgrace Gen. Evans; but I trust our *soldiers* will repeat the experiment on every similar occasion.

OCTOBER 24TH.—We made a narrow escape; at least, we have a respite. If the Yankee army had advanced with its 200,000 men, they would not have encountered more than 70,000 fighting Confederate soldiers between the Potomac and Richmond. It was our soldiers (neither the officers nor the government) that saved us; and they fought contrary to rule, and even in opposition to orders. Of course our officers at Leesburg did their duty manfully; nevertheless, the soldiers had determined to fight, officers or no officers.

But as the man in the play said, "it will suffice." The Yankees are a calculating people: and if 1500 Mississippians and Virginians at Leesburg were too many for 8000 Yankees, what could 200,000 Yankees do against 70,000 Southern soldiers? It made them pause, and give up the idea of taking Richmond this year. But the enemy will fight better every successive year; and this should not be lost sight of. They, too, are Anglo-Saxons.

OCTOBER 25TH.—Gen. Price, of Missouri, is too popular, and there is a determination on the part of the West Pointers to "kill him off." I fear he will gain no more victories.

OCTOBER 26TH.—Immense amounts of patriotic contributions, in clothing and provisions, are daily registered.

OCTOBER 27TH.—Still the Jews are going out of the country and returning at pleasure. They deplete the Confederacy of coin, and sell their goods at 500 per cent. profit. They pay no duty; and Mr. Memminger has lost hundreds of thousands of dollars in this way.

The press everywhere is thundering against the insane policy of permitting all who avow themselves enemies to return to the North; and I think Mr. B. is beginning to wince under it. I tremble when I reflect that those who made the present government, and the one to succeed it, did not represent one-third of the people composing the inhabitants of the Confederate States.

OCTOBER 28TH.—The most gigantic naval preparations have been made by the enemy; and they must strike many blows on the coast this fall and winter. They are building great numbers of gun-boats, some of them iron-clad, both for the coast and for the Western rivers. If they get possession of the Mississippi River, it will be a sad day for the Confederacy. And what are we doing? We have many difficulties to contend against; and there is a deficiency in artisans and material. Nevertheless, the government is constructing a monster at Norfolk, and several similar floating batteries in the West. But we neglect to construct casemated batteries! Our fortifications, without them, must fall before the iron ships of the enemy. The battle of Manassas has given us a long exemption from the fatigues and horrors of war; but this calm will be succeeded by a storm.

OCTOBER 29TH.—The election to take place during the ensuing month creates no excitement. There will be less than a moiety of the whole vote cast; and Davis and Stephens will be elected without opposition. No disasters have occurred yet to affect the popularity of any of the great politicians; and it seems no risks will be run. The battle of Manassas made everybody popular—and especially Gen. Beauregard. If he were a candidate, I am pretty certain he would be elected.

OCTOBER 30TH.—I understand a dreadful quarrel is brewing between Mr. Benjamin and Gen. Beauregard. Gen. B. being the only individual ever hinted at as an opponent of Mr. Davis for the Presidency, the Secretary of War fights him on vantage-ground, and likewise commends himself to the President. Van Buren was a good politician in his day, and so is Mr. Benjamin in *his* way. I hope these dissensions may expend themselves without injury to the country.

OCTOBER 31ST.—Mr. Benjamin, it is understood, will be a candidate for a seat in the C. S. Senate. And I have learned from several members of the Louisiana legislature that he will be defeated. They charge him with hob-nobbing too much with Northern friends; and say that he still retains membership in several clubs in New York and Boston.

CHAPTER VIII.

Quarrel between Gen. Beauregard and Mr. Benjamin.—Great Naval preparations in the North.—The loss of Port Royal, S. C., takes some prestige. —The affair at Belmont does not compensate for it.—The enemy kills an old hare.—Missouri secedes.—Mason and Slidell captured.—French Consul and the actresses.—The lieutenant in disguise.—Eastern Shore of Virginia invaded.—Messrs. Breckinridge and Marshall in Richmond.

NOVEMBER 1ST.—There is an outcry against the appointment of two major-generals, recommended, perhaps, by Mr. Benjamin, Gustavus W. Smith and Gen. Lovell, both recently from New York. They came over since the battle of Manassas. Mr. Benjamin is perfectly indifferent to the criticisms and censures of the people and the press. He knows his own ground; and since he is sustained by the President, we must suppose he knows his own footing in the government. If defeated in the legislature, he may have a six years' tenure in the cabinet.

NOVEMBER 2D.—It has culminated. Mr. Benjamin's quarrel with Beauregard is openly avowed. Mr. Benjamin spoke to me about it to-day, and convinced me at the time that Gen. B. was really in the wrong. He said the general had sent in his report of the battle of Manassas, in which he stated that he had submitted a plan to the department for the invasion of Maryland; and no such plan having been received, as Mr. B. says, and the matter being foreign to the business in hand, the department had seen proper to withhold the report from publication. But this did not concern him, Mr. B., because he was not the Secretary of War when the alleged plan had been sent to Richmond. But his difference with the general grew out of an attempt of the latter to organize troops and confer commands without the sanction of the department. He had rebuked the general, he said; and then the general had appealed to the President, who sustained the Secretary. Mr. B. said that Gen. B. had ascertained who was *strongest* with the President.

NOVEMBER 3D.—From this day forth, I hope Mr. Benjamin and I will be of better accord. I have an official order, directed by him and written by Col. Bledsoe, to the effect that no more alien enemies are to have passports. On the contrary, when any one avows himself an alien enemy, and applies for permission to leave the country, Gen. Winder is to take him in charge.

NOVEMBER 4TH.—Several were arrested yesterday. Still I doubt whether we are dealing fairly, even with enemies. They have been *encouraged* to come into and go out of the country by the facilities afforded them; and now, without any sort of notification whatever, they are to be arrested when they present themselves. I hate all traps and stratagems for the purpose of stimulating one to commit a wrong; and hence this business, although it seems to afford employment, if not delight, to Gen. Winder and his Baltimore detectives, is rather distasteful to me. And when I reflect upon it, I cannot imagine how Mr. Benjamin may adjust the matter with his conscience. It will soon cure itself, however; a few arrests will alarm them all.

NOVEMBER 5TH.—To my amazement, a man came to me to-day for a passport to Norfolk, saying he had one from the Secretary to pass by flag of truce to Fortress Monroe, etc. He wished me to give him one to show at the cars, not desiring to exhibit the other, as it might subject him to annoying looks and remarks.

NOVEMBER 6TH.—All accounts from the North indicate that great preparations are being made to crush us on the coast this winter. I see no corresponding preparations on our side.

NOVEMBER 7TH.—We hear of the resignation of Gen. Scott, as Commander-in-Chief of the U. S. forces.

NOVEMBER 8TH.—There are many applications for passports to leave the country. I have declared my purpose to sign no more for the Secretary without his official order. But he is signing them himself, as I find out by the parties desiring the usual passports from me to leave the city. They, like guilty men, dislike to exhibit their permits to leave the country at the depots. And the Northern press bears testimony of the fact that the spies in our midst are still at work, and from this I apprehend the worst consequences. Why did Mr. Benjamin send the order for every man to be arrested who applied for permission to leave the country? Was it merely to deceive *me*, knowing that I had some influence with certain leading journals? I am told he says, "no one leaves the country now."

NOVEMBER 9TH.—Gen. Winder and all his police and Plug Ugly gang have their friends or agents, whom they continually desire to send to Maryland. And often there comes a request from Gen. Huger, at Norfolk, for passports to be granted certain parties to go out under flag of truce. I suppose he can send whom he pleases.

We have news of a bloody battle in the West, at Belmont. Gen. Pillow and Bishop Polk defeated the enemy, it is said, killing and wounding 1000. Our loss, some 500.

Port Royal, on the coast of South Carolina, has been taken by the enemy's fleet. We had no casemated batteries. Here the Yankees will intrench themselves, and cannot be dislodged. They will take negroes and cotton, and menace both Savannah and Charleston.

NOVEMBER 10TH.—A gentleman from Urbana, on the Rappahannock, informs me that he witnessed the shelling of that village a few days ago. There are so few houses that the enemy did not strike any of them. The only blood shed was that of an old *hare*, that had taken refuge in a hollow stump.

NOVEMBER 11TH.—Bad news. The Unionists in East Tennessee have burnt several of the railroad bridges between this and Chattanooga. This is one of the effects of the discharge of spies captured in Western Virginia and East Tennessee. A military police, if properly directed, composed of honest men, true Southern men, might do much good, or prevent much evil; but I must not criticise Gen. Winder's inefficiency, for he acts under the instructions of Mr. Benjamin.

The burning of these bridges not only prevents the arrival of an immense amount of clothing and provisions for the army, contributed by the patriotic people, but it will embarrass the government in the transmission of men and muniments of war, which an emergency may demand at any moment. Until the avenues by which the enemy derives information from our country are closed, I shall look for a series of disasters.

NOVEMBER 12TH.—We have news of the enemy's gun-boats penetrating the rivers of South Carolina. It is said they got some cotton. Why was it not burnt?

NOVEMBER 13TH.—Dry goods have risen more than a hundred per cent. since spring, and rents and boarding are advancing in the same ratio.

NOVEMBER 14TH.—The enemy, knowing our destitution of gunboats, and well apprised of the paucity of our garrisons, are sending expeditions southward to devastate the coast. They say New Orleans will be taken before spring, and communication be opened with Cairo, at the mouth of the Ohio. They will not succeed so soon; but success is certain ultimately, if Mr. Benjamin, Gen. Winder, and Gen. Huger do not cease to pass Federal spies out of the country.

NOVEMBER 15TH.—We have intelligence that Missouri has joined the Confederacy. She will be scourged by the vengeful enemy; but will rise some day and put her foot on the neck of the oppressor. Missouri is a giant.

NOVEMBER 16TH.—It is sickening to behold the corruption of the commercial men, which so much wounds our afflicted country. There are large merchants here who come over from Baltimore breathing vengeance against the Northern "despots," and to make a show of patriotism they subscribed liberally to equip some volunteer companies in the city; but now they are sending their agents North and importing large amounts of merchandise, which they sell to the government and the people at most fabulous prices. I am informed that some of them realize $50,000 per month profit! And this after paying officials on both sides bonuses to wink at their operations.

After the order of Mr. Benjamin for applicants for passports to leave the country to be arrested, some of these men applied to me, and I reported the facts to Gen. Winder; but they were not molested. Indeed, they came to me subsequently and exhibited passports they had obtained from the Secretary himself.

NOVEMBER 17TH.—There are also quite a number of *letter-carriers* obtaining special passports to leave the Confederacy. They charge $1.50 postage to Washington and Maryland, and as much coming hither. They take on the average three hundred letters, and bring as many, besides diverse articles they sell at enormously high prices. Thus they realize $1000 per trip, and make two each month. They furnish the press with Northern journals; but they give no valuable information: at least I have not conversed with any who could furnish it. They seem particularly ignorant of the plans and forces of the enemy. It is my belief that they render as much service to the enemy as to us; and they certainly do obtain passports on the other side.

Gen. Winder and his *alien* detectives seem to be on peculiar terms of intimacy with some of these men; for they tell me they convey letters for them to Maryland, and deliver them to their families. This is an equivocal business. Why did they not bring their families away before the storm burst upon them?

NOVEMBER 18TH.—To-day the Secretary told me, in reply to my question, that he had authentic information of the seizure of Messrs. Slidell and Mason, our commissioners to Europe, by Capt. Wilkes, of the U. S. Navy, and while on board the steamer Trent, a British vessel, at sea. *I said I was glad of it.* He asked why, in surprise. I remarked that it would bring the Eagle cowering to the feet of the Lion. He smiled, and said it was, perhaps, the best thing that could have happened. And he cautions me against giving passports to *French* subjects even to visit Norfolk or any of our fortified cities, for it was understood that foreigners at Norfolk were contriving somehow to get on board the ships of their respective nations.

NOVEMBER 19TH.—To-day Monsieur Paul, French Consul, applied in person for passports on behalf, I believe, of some French players (Zouaves) to Norfolk. Of course I declined granting them. He grew enthusiastic, and alleged that British subjects had enjoyed the privilege. He said he cared nothing for the parties applying in this instance; but he argued vehemently against British subjects being favored over French subjects. I sent a note concerning our interview to the Secretary; and while Monsieur Paul still sat in the office, the following reply came in from the Secretary: "All you need do is to say to the French Consul, when he calls, that you obey your instructions, and have no authority to discuss with him the rights of French subjects. J. P. B." Monsieur Paul departed with "a flea in his ear." But he received an invitation to dine with the Secretary to-day.

NOVEMBER 20TH.—I had a protracted and interesting interview to-day with a gaudily dressed and rather diminutive lieutenant, who applied for a passport to the Mississippi River, *via* Chattanooga, and insisted upon my giving him transportation also. This demand led to interrogatories, and it appeared that he was not going under special orders of the adjutant-general. It was unusual for officers, on leave, to apply for transportation, and my curiosity was excited. I asked to see his furlough. This was refused; but he told me to what company he belonged, and I knew there was such a company in Bishop or Gen. Polk's command. Finally he escaped further interrogatories by snatching up the passport I had signed and departing hastily. But instead of the usual military salute at parting, he *courtesied.* This, when I reflected on the fineness of his speech, the fullness of his breast, his attitudes and his short steps, led me to believe the person was a woman instead of a lieutenant. Gen. Winder coming in shortly after, upon hearing my description of the stranger, said he would ascertain all about the sex.

NOVEMBER 21ST.—My mysterious lieutenant was arrested this morning, on the western route, and proved, as I suspected, to be a woman. But Gen. Winder was ordered by the Secretary to have her released.

NOVEMBER 22D.—We have information that the enemy have invaded and taken possession of the Eastern Shore of Virginia, Accomac and Northampton Counties. They invaded the two counties with a force of 8000 men, and we had only 800 to oppose them. Of course there could be no contest against such odds. They carried my tenant to Drummondtown, the county seat, and made him (I suppose) assist in raising the United States flag over the court-house.

NOVEMBER 23D.—J. C. Breckinridge and Humphrey Marshall, of Kentucky, have been here; and both have been made brigadier-generals, and assigned to duty in the West. Although the former retained his seat in the Senate of the United States for many months after the war began, no one doubts that he is now with us, and will do good service.

NOVEMBER 24TH.—Gen. Floyd has retreated from Cotton Hill, and the enemy threatens our western communications. Gen. Lee has been sent to Western Virginia, but it is not an adequate field for him. He should have command of the largest army in the service, for his is one of the most capacious minds we have.

NOVEMBER 25TH.—Yesterday Fort Pickens opened fire on our batteries at Pensacola, but without effect. One of their ships was badly crippled.

NOVEMBER 26TH.—The enemy occupy Tybee Island, and threaten Savannah. Vice-President Stephens was in my office to-day, and he too deprecates the passage of so many people to the North, who, from the admission of the journals there, give them information of the condition of our defenses. He thinks our affairs are not now in a prosperous condition, and has serious apprehensions for the fate of Savannah.

NOVEMBER 27TH.—Saw President Tyler to-day. He augurs the worst effects from the policy of permitting almost unrestricted intercourse with the enemy's country in time of war.

NOVEMBER 28TH.—Nothing of importance to-day. There will be no such quiet time after this year.

NOVEMBER 29TH.—Gen. Sydney Johnston has command of the army in Tennessee and Kentucky. I wish it were only as strong as the wily enemy is in the habit of representing it!

NOVEMBER 30TH.—Mr. Benjamin has been defeated for the C. S. Senate. Mr. Hunter has been named as a candidate for the

C. S. Senate from Virginia. I thought he would not remain in the cabinet, after his relative was arrested (with no reason assigned) by order of Mr. Benjamin. Besides, the office is a sinecure, and may remain so for a long time, if the powers at Washington should "stint, and say aye" to the demands of England.

CHAPTER IX.

Gen. Lee ordered South.—Gen. Stuart ambuscaded at Drainsville.—W. H. B. Custis returns to the Eastern Shore.—Winder's detectives.—Kentucky secedes.—Judge Perkins's resolution.—Dibble goes North.—Waiting for Great Britain to do something.—Mr. Ely, the Yankee M. C.

DECEMBER 1ST.—The people here begin to murmur at the idea that they are questioned about their loyalty, and often arrested, by Baltimore petty larceny detectives, who, if they were patriotic themselves (as they are all able-bodied men), would be in the army, fighting for the redemption of Maryland.

DECEMBER 2D.—Gen. Lee has now been ordered South for the defense of Charleston and Savannah, and those cities are safe! Give a great man a field worthy of his powers, and he can demonstrate the extent of his abilities; but dwarf him in an insignificant position, and the veriest fool will look upon him with contempt. Gen. Lee in the streets here bore the aspect of a discontented man, for he saw that everything was going wrong; but now his eye flashes with zeal and hope. Give him time and opportunity, and he will hurl back the invader from his native land; yes, and he will commend the chalice of invasion to the lips of the North; but not this year—it is too late for that.

DECEMBER 3D.—Several members of Congress came into my office and denounced the policy which the government seemed to have adopted of permitting Yankees, and those who sympathize with them, to be continually running over to the enemy with information of our condition, and thus inviting attacks and raids at points where we are utterly defenseless. They seemed surprised when I told them that I not only agreed with them entirely, but that I had really written most of the articles they had read in the press denunciatory of the policy they condemned. I informed them, moreover, that I had long since refused to sign any such passports as they alluded to, at the risk of being removed. They said they believed the President, in his multiplicity of employments, was not aware of the extent of the practice, and the evil effects it was certain to entail on the country; and it was their purpose to wait upon him and remonstrate against the pernicious practice of Mr. Benjamin.

DECEMBER 4TH.—We are now tasting the bitter fruits of a too indulgent treatment of our enemies. Yesterday Gen. Stuart's cavalry and the 6th Regiment S. C. volunteers met with a bloody disaster at Drainsville. It appears that several of the traitors arrested and sent hither by Gen. Johnston were subsequently discharged by Gen. Winder, under the instructions of Mr. Benjamin, and sent to their homes, in the vicinity of Drainsville, at the expense of the government. These men, with revenge rankling in their breasts, reported to Gen. Stuart that a large amount of forage might be obtained in the vicinity of Drainsville, and that but a few companies of the enemy were in the neighborhood. The general believing these men to be loyal, since they seemed to have the confidence of the War Department, resolved to get the forage; and for that purpose started some 80 wagons early the next morning, escorted by several regiments of infantry and 1000 cavalry, hoping to capture any forces of the enemy in the vicinity. Meantime the Drainsville traitors had returned to their homes the preceding evening, and sent off intelligence to the headquarters of the enemy of the purpose of Gen. Stuart to send out in that direction, early the next day, a foraging party consisting of so many wagons, and small forces of infantry, artillery, and cavalry.

The enemy hastened away to Drainsville an overwhelming force, and ambuscaded the road, where it entered the woods, with artillery and men of all arms. Their line was the shape of a horseshoe, and completely concealed from view.

Gen. Stuart had not entered far into the jaws of this trap, before some of his trusty scouts reported the presence of the enemy. Believing it to be only the pickets of the few companies previously reported, the general advanced still farther; but at the same time ordering the wagons to retire. He was soon undeceived by a simultaneous and concentric fire of artillery and musketry, which brought down many of his men. Nevertheless, he charged through the lines in one or two places, and brought his guns to bear with effect on such portions of the enemy's line as were not wholly protected by the inequalities of the ground and the dense growth of woods. He quickly ascertained, however, that he was contending against vastly superior numbers, and drew off his forces in good order, protecting his wagons. The enemy did not pursue, for Stuart had rather more men than the informers reported to the enemy. But we lost 200 men, while the enemy sustained but little injury; their killed and wounded not exceeding 30.

This is the first serious wound inflicted on the country by Mr. Benjamin's policy.

DECEMBER 5TH.—The account of the Drainsville massacre was furnished me by an officer of the 6th S. C. Regiment, which suffered severely. The newspaper accounts of the occurrence, upon which, perhaps, the history of this war will be founded, give a different version of the matter. And hence, although not so designed at first, this Diary will furnish more authentic data of many of the events of the war than the grave histories that will be written. Still, I do not aspire to be the Froissart of these interesting times: but intend merely to furnish my children, and such others as may read them, with reliable chronicles of the events passing under my own observation.

DECEMBER 6TH.—It is rumored to-day, I know not on what authority, that the President mentioned the matter of the Drainsville disaster to the Secretary of War, and intimated that it was attributed to the machinations of the Union men discharged from prison here. It is said Mr. Benjamin denied it—denied that any such men had been discharged by Gen. Winder, or had been concerned in the affair at all. Of course the President had no alternative but to credit the solemn assertions of his confidential adviser. But my books, and the register of the prisons, would show that the Drainsville prisoners sent hither by Gen. Joseph E. Johnston were discharged by Gen. Winder, and that their expenses home were paid by the government; and officers of unimpeachable veracity are ready to testify that Gen. Stuart was misled by these very men.

DECEMBER 7TH.—Quite a commotion has been experienced in

official circles by the departure of Mr. W. H. B. Custis, late Union member of the Virginia Convention, without obtaining a passport to leave the city. Some of his secession constituents being in the city, reported that they knew it was his purpose to return to the Eastern Shore of Virginia, and avow his adherence to the United States authorities, alleging that he had signed the ordinance of secession under some species of duress, or instruction. Under these representations, it seems Gen. Winder telegraphed to Norfolk, whither it was understood Custis had gone, to have him arrested. This was done; and it is said he had passports from Gen. Huger to cross the Chesapeake Bay. I must doubt this. What right has a military commander to grant such passports?

DECEMBER 8TH.—I saw Mr. Benjamin to-day, and asked him what disposition he intended to make of Mr. Custis. He was excited, and said with emphasis that he was investigating the case. He seemed offended at the action of Gen. Winder, and thought it was a dangerous exercise of military power to arrest persons of such high standing, without the clearest evidence of guilt. Mr. Custis had signed the ordinance of secession, and that ought to be sufficient evidence of his loyalty.

DECEMBER 9TH.—Gen. Winder informed me to-day that he had been ordered to release Mr. Custis; and I learned that the Secretary of War had transmitted orders to Gen. Huger to permit him to pass over the bay.

DECEMBER 10TH.—Nothing new.

DECEMBER 11TH.—Several of Gen. Winder's detectives came to me with a man named Webster, who, it appears, has been going between Richmond and Baltimore, conveying letters, money, etc. I refused him a passport. He said he could get it from the Secretary himself, but that it was sometimes difficult in gaining access to him. I told him to get it, then; I would give him none.

DECEMBER 12TH.—More of Gen. Winder's men came with a Mr. Stone, whom they knew and vouched for, and who wanted a passport merely to Norfolk. I asked if it was not his design to go farther. They said yes, but that Gen. Winder would write to Gen. Huger to let him pass by way of Fortress Monroe. I refused, and great indignation was manifested.

DECEMBER 13TH.—One of the papers has a short account of the application of Stone in its columns this morning. One of the reporters was present at the interview. The article bore pretty severely upon the assumption of power by the military commander of the department. Gen. Winder came in during the day, and denied having promised to procure a passport for Stone from Gen. Huger.

DECEMBER 14TH.—Nothing.

DECEMBER 15TH.—The President's private secretary, Capt. Josselyn, was in to-day. He had no news.

DECEMBER 16TH.—We hear to-day that the loyal men of Kentucky have met in convention and adopted an ordinance of secession and union with our Confederacy.

DECEMBER 17TH.—Bravo, Col. Edward Johnson! He was attacked by 5000 Yankees on the Alleghany Mountains, and he has beaten them with 1200 men. They say Johnson is an energetic man, and swears like a trooper; and instead of a sword, he goes into battle with a stout cane in his hand, with which he belabors any skulking miscreant found dodging in the hour of danger.

DECEMBER 18TH.—Men escaped from the Eastern Shore of Virginia report that Mr. Custis had landed there, and remains quiet.

DECEMBER 19TH.—Judge Perkins came in to-day and denounced in bitter terms the insane policy of granting passports to spies and others to leave the country, when every Northern paper bore testimony that we were betrayed by these people. He asked me how many had been permitted to go North by Mr. Benjamin since the expiration of the time named in the President's proclamation. This I could not answer: but suggested that a resolution of inquiry might elicit the information. He desired me to write such a resolution. I did so, and he departed with it. An hour afterward, I learned it had been passed unanimously.

DECEMBER 20TH.—A man by the name of *Dibble*, the identical one I passed on my way to Montgomery last spring, and whom I then thought acted and spoke like a Yankee, is here seeking permission to go North; he *says* to Halifax. He confesses that he is a Yankee born; but has lived in North Carolina for many years, and has amassed a fortune. He declares the South does not contain a truer Southern man than himself; and he says he is going to the British Provinces to purchase supplies for the Confederacy. He brought me an order from Mr. Benjamin, indorsed on the back of a letter, for a passport. I declined to give it; and he departed in anger, saying the Secretary would grant it. He knew this, for he said the Secretary had promised him one.

DECEMBER 21ST.—Col. Bledsoe was in to-day. I had not seen him for a long time. He had not been sitting in the office two minutes before he uttered one of his familiar groans. Instantly we were on the old footing again. He said Secretary Benjamin had never treated him as Chief of the Bureau, any more than Walker.

DECEMBER 22D.—Dibble has succeeded in obtaining a passport from the Secretary himself.

DECEMBER 23D.—Gen. T. J. Jackson has destroyed a principal dam on the Chesapeake and Ohio Canal. That will give the enemy abundance of trouble. This Gen. Jackson is always doing something to vex the enemy; and I think he is destined to annoy them more.

It is with much apprehension that I see something like a general relaxation of preparation to hurl back the invader. It seems as if the government were waiting for England to do it; and after all, the capture of Slidell and Mason may be the very worst thing that could have happened. Mr. Benjamin, I learn, feels very confident that a rupture between the United States and Great Britain is inevitable. War with England is not to be thought of by Mr. Seward at this juncture, and he will not have it. And we should not rely upon the happening of any such contingency. Some of our officials go so far as to hint that in the event of a war between the United States and Great Britain, and our recognition by the former, it might be good policy for us to stand neutral. The war would certainly be waged on our account, and it would not be consistent with Southern honor and chivalry to retire from the field and leave the friend who interfered in our behalf to fight it out alone. The principal members of our government should possess the highest stamp of character, for never did there exist a purer people.

DECEMBER 24TH.—I am at work on the resolution passed by Congress. The Secretary sent it to me, with an order to prepare the list of names, and saying that he would explain the *grounds* upon which they were permitted to depart. I can only give the number registered in this office.

DECEMBER 25TH.—Mr. Ely, the Yankee member of Congress, who has been in confinement here since the battle of Manassas, has been exchanged for Mr. Faulkner, late Minister to France, who was captured on his return from Europe. Mr. Ely smiled at the brown paper on which I had written his passport. I told him it was Southern manufacture, and although at present in a crude condition, it was in the process of improvement, and that "necessity was the mother of invention." The necessity imposed on us by the blockade would ultimately redound to our advantage, and might injure the country inflicting it by diminishing its own products. He smiled again, and said he had no doubt we should rise to the dignity of *white paper*.

DECEMBER 26TH.—I have been requested by several members of Congress to prepare a bill, establishing a passport office by law. I will attempt it; but it cannot pass, unless it be done in spite of the opposition of the Secretary, who knows how to use his patronage so as to bind members to his interest. He learned that at Washington.

DECEMBER 27TH.—Notwithstanding the severe strictures, and the resolution of Congress, there is an increase rather than a diminution of the number of persons going North. Some of our officials seem to think the war is over, or that England will do the balance of our fighting!

DECEMBER 28TH.—The fathers and mothers and sisters of our brave soldiers continue to send their clothing and provisions. *They* do not relax in the work of independence.

DECEMBER 29TH.—Persons are coming here from that portion of Western Virginia held by the enemy, with passports from Gen. Cox, the Yankee commander. They applied to me to-day for passports to return to Kanawha, which I refused. They obtained them from the Assistant Secretary of War, Mr. Ould.

DECEMBER 30TH.—Some of our officers on furlough complain of the dullness of the war. The second year will be different.

DECEMBER 31ST.—Northern papers, received in this city, show very conclusively that the enemy are pretty accurately informed of the condition of our defenses and the paucity of the numbers in our regiments.

CHAPTER X.

Seward gives up Mason and Slidell.—Great preparations of the enemy.—Gen. Jackson betrayed.—Mr. Memminger's blunders.—Exaggerated reports of our troops in Kentucky and Tennessee.

JANUARY 1ST, 1862.—Seward has cowered beneath the roar of the British Lion, and surrendered Mason and Slidell, who have been permitted to go on their errand to England. Now we must depend upon our own strong arms and stout hearts for defense.

JANUARY 2D.—The enemy are making preparations to assail us everywhere. Roanoke Island, Norfolk, Beaufort, and Newbern; Charleston, Savannah, Mobile, Pensacola, and New Orleans are all menaced by numerous fleets on the sea-board, and in the West great numbers of iron-clad floating batteries threaten to force a passage down the Mississippi, while monster armies are concentrating for the invasion of Tennessee and the Cotton States. Will Virginia escape the scourge? Not she; here is the bull's-eye of the mark they aim at.

JANUARY 3D.—The enemy have in the field, according to their official reports, some three-quarters of a million of men; we, about 250,000, or one-quarter of a million. This might answer for defense if we could only know where their blows will fall; but then they have a strong navy and thousands of transports, and we have next to nothing afloat to oppose to them. And there is no *entente cordiale* between Mr. Benjamin and any of our best generals.

JANUARY 4TH.—It is just as I feared. Gen. T. J. Jackson, supposing his project to be a profound secret, marched on the 1st instant from Winchester, intending to surprise a force of the enemy at Romney. But he had not proceeded half the distance before he found a printed account of his intended expedition in a Baltimore paper at an inn on the roadside. This was treason of the blackest dye, and will cost us a thousand men. The enemy, of course, escaped, and our poor soldiers, frost-bitten and famished, must painfully retrace all steps of this fruitless march.

JANUARY 5TH.—There are rumors of a court-martial, and I fear the enterprising Jackson will be made to suffer for the crime of others. That men sympathizing with the Union cause were daily leaving Richmond for Baltimore was known to all, but how they gained intelligence of the contemplated movement of Jackson is the mystery.

JANUARY 6TH.—No news.

JANUARY 7TH.—Brig-Gen. Wise is to command on Roanoke Island. It is not far from Princess Ann County, where his place of residence is. If they give him men enough, say half as many as the enemy, he *will* defend it.

JANUARY 8TH.—Dearth of news.

JANUARY 9TH.—Butter is 50 cts. per pound, bacon 25 cts., beef has risen from 13 cts. to 30 cts., wood is selling for $8 per cord, but flour is abundant, and cheap enough to keep us from starving.

JANUARY 10TH.—The President is rarely seen in the streets now, and it is complained that he is not so accessible as formerly in his office. I do not know what foundation there is for these reports, and see no reason to credit them. I know he rides out in the afternoon, if the weather be fair, after the labors of the day, and he is a regular attendant at St. Paul's Church. I am rather inclined to credit the rumor that he intends to join the church. All his messages and proclamations indicate that he is looking to a mightier power than England for assistance. There is a general desire to have the cabinet modified and Christianized upon the inauguration of the permanent government.

JANUARY 11TH.—We have three candidates in the field in this district for Congress: President Tyler, James Lyons, and Wm. H. McFarland. The first will, of course, walk over the track.

JANUARY 12TH.—Gen. Wise, whose headquarters are to be fixed at Nag's Head on the beach near Roanoke Island, reports that the force he commands is altogether inadequate to defend the position. Burnside is said to have 20,000 men, besides a numerous fleet of gun-boats; and Gen. Wise has but 3000 effective men.

JANUARY 13TH.—The department leaves Gen. Wise to his superior officer, Gen. Huger, at Norfolk, who has 15,000 men. But I understand that Huger says Wise has ample means for the defense of the island, and refuses to let him have more men. This looks like a man-trap of the "Red-tapers" to get rid of a popular leader. I hope the President will interfere.

JANUARY 14TH.—All calm and quiet to-day.

JANUARY 15TH.—I forgot to mention the fact that some weeks ago I received a work in manuscript from London, sent thither before the war, and brought by a bearer of dispatches from our Commissioner, Hon. Ambrose Dudley Mann, to whom I had written on the subject. I owe him a debt of gratitude for this kindness. When peace is restored, I shall have in readiness some contributions to the literature of the South, and my family, if I should not survive, may derive pecuniary benefit from them. I look for a long war, unless a Napoleon springs up among us, a thing not at all probable, for I believe there are those who are constantly on the watch for such dangerous characters, and they may possess the power to nip all embryo emperors in the bud.

Some of our functionaries are not justly entitled to the great positions they occupy. They attained them by a species of *snap-judgment*, from which there may be an appeal hereafter. It is very certain that many of our *best* men have no adequate positions, and revolutions are mutable things.

JANUARY 16TH.—To-day, Mr. Benjamin, whom I met in the hall of the department, said, "I don't grant any passports to leave the country, except to a few men on business for the government. I have ceased to grant any for some time past." I merely remarked that I was glad to hear it.

Immediately on returning to my office I referred to my book, and counted the names of fifty persons to whom the Secretary had granted passports within thirty days; and these were not all agents of the government. Mr. Benjamin reminded me of Daniel Webster, when he used to make solemn declarations that his friends in office were likewise the partisans of President Tyler.

JANUARY 17TH.—A Mr. O. Hendricks, very lately of the U. S. Coast Survey, has returned from a tour of the coast of North Carolina, and has been commissioned a lieutenant by the Secretary of War. He says Burnside will take Roanoke Island, and that Wise and all his men wlll be captured. It is a *man-trap*.

JANUARY 18TH.—Gen. L. P. Walker, the first Secretary of War, is assigned to duty in the Southwest under Gen. Bragg. How can he obey the orders of one who was so recently under his command? I think it probable he will resign again before the end of the campaign.

JANUARY 19TH.—There has been a storm on the coast, sinking some of the enemy's ships. Col. Allen, of New Jersey, was lost. He was once at my house in Burlington, and professed to be friendly to the Southern cause. I think he said he owned land and slaves in Texas.

JANUARY 20TH.—Mr. Memminger advertises to pay interest on certain government bonds in *specie.* That won't last long. He is paying 50 per cent. premium in treasury notes for the specie, and the bonds are given for treasury notes. What sort of financiering is this?

JANUARY 21ST.—A great number of Germans and others are going to Norfolk, thinking, as one remarked, if they can't go to the United States the United States will soon come to them. Many believe that Burnside will get Norfolk. I think differently, but I may be mistaken.

JANUARY 22D.—Some of the letter-carriers' passports from Mr. Benjamin, which have the countenance of Gen. Winder, are now going into Tennessee. What is this for? We shall see.

JANUARY 23D.—Again the Northern papers give the most extravagant numbers to our army in Kentucky. Some estimates are as high as 150,000. I know, and Mr. Benjamin knows, that Gen. Johnston has not exceeding 29,000 effective men. And the Secretary knows that Gen. J. has given him timely notice of the inadequacy of his force to hold the position at Bowling Green. The Yankees are well aware of our weakness, but they intend to claim the astounding feat of routing 150,000 men with 100,000! And they suppose that by giving us credit for such a vast army, we shall not deem it necessary to send reinforcements. Well, *reinforcements are not sent.*

JANUARY 24TH.—Beauregard has been ordered to the West. I knew the doom was upon him! But he will make his mark even at Columbus, though the place seems to me to be altogether untenable and of no practicable importance, since the enemy may attack both in front and rear. It would seem that some of the jealous functionaries would submit to any misfortune which would destroy Beauregard's popularity. But these are exceptions: they are few and far between, thank Heaven!

JANUARY 25TH.—The French players have been permitted by the Secretary to leave the country. But *British* subjects are now refused passports.

JANUARY 26TH.—President Tyler has been elected to Congress by an overwhelming majority.

JANUARY 27TH.—The Secretary of War has issued such a peremptory order to Gen. Wise, that the latter has no alternative but to attempt the defense of Roanoke Island with 3000 men against 15,000 and a fleet of gun-boats. The general is quite sick, but he will fight. His son, Capt. O. Jennings Wise, who has been under fire many times already, commands a company on the island. He will *deserve* promotion. The government seems to have proscribed the great men of the past and their families, as if *this government was the property of the few men who happen to wield power at the present moment.* Arrogance and presumption in the South must, sooner or later, have a fall. The great men who were the leaders of this revolution may be ignored, but they cannot be kept down by the smaller fry who aspire to wield the destinies of a great and patriotic people. Smith and Lovell, New York politicians and Street Commissioners, have been made *major-generals*, while Wise and Breckinridge are brigadiers.

JANUARY 28TH.—There must soon be collisions in the West on a large scale; but the system of lying, in vogue among the Yankees, most effectually defeats all attempts at reliable computation of numbers. They say we have 150,000 men in Tennessee and Kentucky, whereas we have not 60,000. Their own numbers they represent to be not exceeding 50,000, but I suspect they have three times that number. The shadows of events are crowding thickly upon us, and the events will speak for themselves—and that speedily.

JANUARY 29TH.—What we want is a military man capable of directing operations in the field everywhere. I think Lee is such a man. But can he, a modest man and a Christian, aspire to such a position? Would not Mr. Benjamin throw his influence against such a suggestion? I trust the President will see through the mist generated around him.

JANUARY 30TH.—Some of the mysterious letter-carriers, who have just returned from their jaunt into Tennessee, are applying again for passports to Baltimore, Washington, etc. I refuse them, though they are recommended by Gen. Winder's men; but they will obtain what they want from the Secretary himself, or his Assistant Secretary.

JANUARY 31ST.—What if these men (they have passports) should be going to Washington to report the result of their reconnoissances in Tennessee? The Tennessee River is high, and we have no casemated batteries, or batteries of any sort, on it above Fort Henry.

CHAPTER XI.

Fall of Fort Henry.—Of Fort Donelson.—Lugubrious Inauguration of the President in the Permanent Government.—Loss of Roanoke Island.

FEBRUARY 1ST.—We had a startling rumor yesterday that New Orleans had been taken by the enemy, without firing a gun. I hastened to the Secretary and asked him if it could be true. He had not heard of it, and turned pale. But a moment after, recollecting the day on which it was said the city had fallen, he seized a New Orleans paper of a subsequent date, and said the news could not be true, since the paper made no mention of it.

FEBRUARY 2D.—The rumor of yesterday originated in the assertion of a Yankee paper that New Orleans *would* be taken without firing a gun. Some of our people fear it may be so, since Mr. Benjamin's friend, Gen. Lovell, who came from New York since the battle of Manassas, is charged with the defense of the city. He delivered lectures, it is said, last summer on the defenses of New York—*in that city.* Have we not Southern men of sufficient genius to make generals of, for the defense of the South, without sending to New York for military commanders?

FEBRUARY 3D.—We have intelligence of the sailing of an expedition from Cairo for the reduction of Fort Henry on the Tennessee River.

FEBRUARY 4TH.—Burnside has entered the Sound at Hatteras with his fleet of gun-boats and transports. The work will soon begin.

FEBRUARY 5TH.—I am sorry to hear that Gen. Wise is quite ill. But, on his back, as on his feet, he will direct operations, and the enemy will be punished whenever he comes in reach of him.

FEBRUARY 6TH.—The President is preparing his Inaugural Message for the 22d, when he is to begin his new administration of six years. He is to read it from the Washington Monument in Capitol Square.

FEBRUARY 7TH.—We have vague rumors of fighting at Roanoke. Nothing reliable.

FEBRUARY 8-20TH.—Such astounding events have occurred since the 8th instant, such an excitement has prevailed, and so incessant have been my duties, that I have not kept a regular journal. I give a running account of them.

Roanoke has fallen before superior numbers, although we had 15,000 idle troops at Norfolk within hearing of the battle. The government would not interfere, and Gen. Huger refused to allow the use of a few thousand of his troops.

But Gen. Wise is safe; Providence willed that he should escape the "man-trap." When the enemy were about to open fire on his headquarters at Nag's Head, knowing him to be prostrated with illness (for the island had then been surrendered after a heroic defense), Lieutenants Bagly and Wise bore the general away in a blanket to a distance of ten or fifteen miles. The Yankees would have gladly exchanged all their prisoners for Gen. Wise, who is ever a terror to the North.

Capt. O. Jennings Wise fell, while gallantly cheering his men, in the heat of the battle. A thousand of the enemy fell before a few hundred of our brave soldiers. We lost some 2500 men, for there was no alternative but to surrender.

Capt. Wise told the Yankee officers, who persisted in forcing themselves in his presence during his dying moments, that the South could never be subjugated. They might exterminate us, but every man, woman, and child would prefer death to abject subjugation. And he died with a sweet smile on his lip, eliciting the profound respect of his most embittered enemies.

The enemy paroled our men taken on the island; and we recovered the remains of the heroic Capt. Wise. His funeral here was most impressive, and saddened the countenances of thousands who witnessed the pageant. None of the members of the government were present; but the ladies threw flowers and evergreens upon his bier. He is dead—but history will do him justice; and his example will inspire others with the spirit of true heroism.

And President Tyler is no more on earth. He died after a very brief illness. There was a grand funeral, Mr. Hunter and others delivering orations. They came to me, supposing I had written one of the several biographies of the deceased which have appeared during the last twenty years. But I had written none—and none published were worthy of the subject. I could only refer them to the bound volumes of the MADISONIAN in the State library for his messages and other State papers. The originals are among my papers in the hands of the enemy. His history is yet to be written—and it will be read centuries hence.

Fort Henry has fallen. Would that were all! The catalogue of disasters I feared and foretold, under the policy adopted by the War Department, may be a long and a terrible one.

The mission of the spies to East Tennessee is now apparent. Three of the enemy's gun-boats have ascended the Tennessee River to the very head of navigation, while the women and children on its banks could do nothing more than gaze in mute despair. No batteries, no men were there. The absence of these is what the traitors, running from here to Washington, have been reporting to the enemy. Their boats would no more have ventured up that river without the previous exploration of spies, than Mr. Lincoln would dare to penetrate a cavern without torch-bearers, in which the rattle of venomous snakes could be heard. They have ascended to Florence, and may get footing in Alabama and Mississippi!

And Fort Donelson has been attacked by an immensely superior force. We have 15,000 men there to resist, perhaps, 75,000! Was ever such management known before? Who is responsible for it? If Donelson falls, what becomes of the ten or twelve thousand men at Bowling Green?

FEBRUARY 21ST.—All our garrison in Fort Henry, with Gen. Tilghman, surrendered. I think we had only 1500 men there. Guns, ammunition, and stores, all gone.

No news from Donelson—and that is *bad* news. Benjamin says he has no definite information. But prisoners taken say the enemy have been reinforced, and are hurling 80,000 against our 15,000.

FEBRUARY 22D.—Such a day! The heavens weep incessantly. Capitol Square is black with umbrellas; and a shelter has been erected for the President to stand under.

I walked up to the monument and heard the Inaugural read by the President. He read it well, and seemed self-poised in the midst of disasters, which he acknowledged had befallen us. And he admitted that there had been errors in our war policy. We had attempted operations on too extensive a scale, thus diffusing our powers which should have been concentrated. I like these candid confessions. They augur a different policy hereafter, and we may hope for better results in the future. We must all stand up for our country.

Mr. Hunter has resigned, and taken his place in the Senate.

FEBRUARY 23D.—At last we have the astounding tidings that Donelson has fallen, and Buckner, and 9000 men, arms, stores, everything are in possession of the enemy! Did the President know it yesterday? Or did the Secretary keep it back till the new government (permanent) was launched into existence? Wherefore? The Southern *people* cannot be daunted by calamity!

Last night it was still raining—and it rained all night. It was a lugubrious reception at the President's mansion. But the President himself was calm, and Mrs. Davis seemed in spirits. For a long time I feared the bad weather would keep the people away; and the thought struck me when I entered, that if there were a Lincoln spy present, we should have more ridicule in the Yankee presses on the paucity of numbers attending the reception. But the crowd came at last, and filled the ample rooms. The permanent government had its birth in storm, but it may yet flourish in sunshine. For my own part, however, I think a provisional government of few men, should have been adopted "for the war."

FEBRUARY 24TH.—Gen. Sydney Johnston has evacuated Bowling Green with his *ten* or *twelve* thousand men! Where is his mighty army now? It never did exist!

FEBRUARY 25TH.—And Nashville must fall—although no one seems to anticipate such calamity. We must run the career of disasters allotted us, and await the turning of the tide.

FEBRUARY 26TH.—Congress, in secret session, has authorized

the declaration of martial law in this city, and at some few other places. This might be well under other circumstances; but it will not be well if the old general in command should be clothed with powers which he has no qualifications to wield advantageously. The facile old man will do *anything* the Secretary advises.

Our army is to fall back from Manassas! The Rappahannock is not to be our line of *defense*. Of course the enemy will soon strike at Richmond from some direction. I have given great offense to some of our people by saying the policy of permitting men to go North at will, will bring the enemy to the gates of the city in ninety days. Several have told me that the prediction has been marked in the Secretary's tablets, and that I am marked for destruction if it be not verified. I reply that I would rather be destroyed than that it should be fulfilled.

FEBRUARY 27TH.—Columbus is to be evacuated. Beauregard sees that it is untenable with Forts Henry and Donelson in possession of the enemy. He will not be caught in such a trap as that. But he is erecting a battery at Island No. 10 that will give the Yankees trouble. I hope it may stay the catalogue of disasters.

FEBRUARY 28TH.—These calamities may be a wholesome chastening for us. We shall now go to work and raise troops enough to defend the country. Congress will certainly pass the Conscription Act recommended by the President.

CHAPTER XII.

Nashville evacuated.—Martial law.—Passports.—Com. Buchanan's naval engagement.—Gen. Winder's blunders.—Mr. Benjamin Secretary of State.—Lee commander-in-chief.—Mr. G. W. Randolph Secretary of War.

MARCH 1ST.—It is certain that the City of Nashville has been evacuated, and will, of course, be occupied by the enemy. Gen. Johnston, with the remnant of his army, has fallen down to Murfreesborough, and as that is not a point of military importance, will in turn be abandoned, and the enemy will drop out of the State into Alabama or Mississippi.

MARCH 2D.—Gen. Jos. E. Johnston has certainly made a skill-ful retrograde movement in the face of the enemy at Manassas. He has been keeping McClellan and his 210,000 men at bay for a long time with about 40,000. After the abandonment of his works it was a long time before the enemy knew he had retrograded. They approached very cautiously, and found that they had been awed by a few *Quaker guns—logs of wood* in position, and so painted as to resemble cannon. Lord, how the Yankee press will quiz McClellan!

MARCH 3D.—But McClellan would not advance. He could not drag his artillery at this season of the year; and so he is embark-ing his army, or the greater portion of it, for the Peninsula.

MARCH 4TH.—We shall have stirring times here. Our troops are to be marched through Richmond immediately, for the defense of Yorktown—the same town surrendered by Lord Cornwallis to Washington. But its fall or its successful defense now will signify nothing.

MARCH 5TH.—Martial law has been proclaimed.

MARCH 6TH.—Some consternation among the citizens—they dis-like martial law.

MARCH 7TH.—Gen. Winder has established a guard with fixed bayonets at the door of the passport office. They let in only a few at a time, and these, when they get their passports, pass out by the rear door, it being impossible for them to return through the crowd.

MARCH 8TH.—Gen. Winder has appointed Capt. Godwin Pro-vost Marshal.

MARCH 9TH.—Gen. Winder has appointed Col. Porter Provost Marshal,—Godwin not being high enough in rank, I suppose.

MARCH 10TH.—One of the friends of the Secretary of War came to me to-day, and proposed to have some new passports printed, with the likeness of Mr. Benjamin engraved on them. He said, I think, the engraving had already been made. I denounced the project as absurd, and said there were some five or ten thou-sand printed passports on hand.

MARCH 11TH.—I have summed up the amounts of patriotic contributions received by the army in Virginia, and registered on my book, and they amount to $1,515,898.*

The people of the respective States contributed as follows:

North Carolina	$325,417
Alabama	317,600
Mississippi	272,670
Georgia	244,885
South Carolina	137,206
Texas	87,800
Louisiana	61,950
Virginia*	48,070
Tennessee	17,000
Florida	2,350
Arkansas	950

MARCH 12TH.—Gen. Winder moved the passport office up to the corner of Ninth and Broad Streets.

The office at the corner of Ninth and Broad Streets was a filthy one; it was inhabited—for they slept there—by his rowdy clerks. And when I stepped to the hydrant for a glass of water, the tumbler repulsed me by the smell of whisky. There was no towel to wipe my hands with, and in the long basement room underneath, were a thousand garments of dead soldiers, taken from the hospitals and the battle-field, and exhaling a most disagreeable, if not deleterious, odor.

MARCH 13TH.—Nevertheless, I am (temporarily) signing my name to the passports, yet issued by the authority of the Secretary of War. They are filled up and issued by three or four of the Provost Marshal's clerks, who are governed mainly by my directions, as neither Col. Porter nor the clerks, nor Gen. Winder himself, have the slightest idea of the geography of the country occupied by the enemy. The clerks are all Marylanders, as well as the detectives, and the latter intend to remain here to my great chagrin.

MARCH 14TH.—The Provost Marshal, Col. Porter, has had new passports printed, to which his own name is to be appended. I am requested to sign it for him, and to instruct the clerks generally.

* Virginia undoubtedly contributed more than any other State, but they were not registered.

MARCH 15TH.—For several days troops have been pouring through the city, marching down the Peninsula. The enemy are making demonstrations against Yorktown.

MARCH 16TH.—I omitted to note in its place the gallant feat of Commodore Buchanan with the iron monster Merrimac in Hampton Roads. He destroyed two of the enemy's best ships of war. My friends, Lieutenants Parker and Minor, partook of the glory, and were severely wounded.

MARCH 17TH.—Col. Porter has resigned his provost marshalship, and is again succeeded by Capt. Godwin, a *Virginian*, and I like him very well, for he is truly Southern in his instincts.

MARCH 18TH.—A Mr. MacCubbin, of Maryland, has been appointed by Gen. Winder the Chief of Police. He is wholly illiterate, like the rest of the policemen under his command.

MARCH 19TH.—Mr. MacCubbin, whom I take to be a sort of Scotch-Irishman, though reared in the mobs of Baltimore, I am informed has given some passports, already signed, to some of his friends. This interference will produce a rupture between Capt. Godwin and Capt. MacCubbin; but as the former is a Virginian, he may have the worst of it in the bear fight.

MARCH 20TH.—There is skirmishing every day on the Peninsula. We have not exceeding 60,000 men there, while the enemy have 158,000. It is fearful odds. And they have a fleet of gun-boats.

MARCH 21ST.—Gen. Winder's detectives are very busy. They have been forging prescriptions to *catch* the poor Richmond apothecaries. When the brandy is thus obtained it is confiscated, and the money withheld. They drink the brandy, and imprison the apothecaries.

MARCH 22D.—Capt. Godwin, the Provost Marshal, was swearing furiously this morning at the policemen about their iniquitous *forgeries*.

MARCH 23D.—Gen. Winder was in this morning listening to something MacCubbin was telling him about the Richmond *Whig*. It appears that, in the course of a leading article, enthusiastic for the cause, the editor remarked, "we have arms and ammunition now." The policemen, one and all, interpreted this as a violation of the order to the press to abstain from speaking of the arrivals of arms, etc. from abroad. Gen. Winder, without looking at the paper, said in a loud voice, "Go and arrest the editor—and close his office!" Two or three of the policemen started off on this errand. But I interposed, and asked them to wait a moment, until I could examine the paper. I found no infraction of the order in the truly patriotic article, and said so to Gen. Winder. "Well," said he, "if he has not violated the order, he must not be arrested." He took the paper, and read for himself; and then, without saying anything more, departed.

When he was gone, I asked MacCubbin what was the phraseology of the order that "had been served on the editors." He drew it from his pocket, saying it had been shown to them, *and not left with them.* It was in the handwriting of Mr. Benjamin, and signed by Gen. Winder. And I learned that all the orders, sumptuary and others, had been similarly written and signed. Mr. Benjamin used the pencil and not the pen in writing these orders, supposing, of course, they would be copied by Gen. W.'s clerks. But they were not copied. The policemen threaten to stop the *Examiner* soon, for that paper has been somewhat offensive to the *aliens* who now have rule here.

MARCH 24TH.—Gen. Walker, of Georgia—the same who had the scene with Col. Bledsoe—has resigned. I am sorry that the Confederate States must lose his services, for he is a brave man, covered with honorable scars. He has displeased the Secretary of War.

MARCH 25TH.—Gen. Bonham, of South Carolina, has also resigned, for being overslaughed. His were the *first* troops that entered Virginia to meet the enemy; and because some of his three months' men were reorganized into fresh regiments, his brigade was dissolved, and his commission canceled.

Price, Beauregard, Walker, Bonham, Toombs, Wise, Floyd, and others of the brightest lights of the South have been somehow successively obscured. And Joseph E. Johnston is a doomed fly, sooner or later, for he said, not long since, that there could be no hope of success as long as Mr. Benjamin was Secretary of War. These words were spoken at a dinner-table, and will reach the ears of the Secretary.

MARCH 26TH.—The apothecaries arrested and imprisoned some days ago have been tried and acquitted by a court-martial. Gen. Winder indorsed on the order for their discharge: "*Not approved, and you may congratulate yourselves upon escaping a merited punishment.*"

MARCH 27TH.—It is said Mr. Benjamin has been dismissed, or resigned.

MARCH 28TH.—Mr. Benjamin has been promoted. He is now Secretary of State.

His successor in the War Department is G. W. Randolph, a lawyer of modest pretensions, who, although he has lived for several years in this city, does not seem to have a dozen acquaintances. But he inherits a name, being descended from Thomas Jefferson, and, I believe, likewise from the Mr. Randolph in Washington's cabinet. Mr. Randolph was a captain at Bethel under Magruder; and subsequently promoted to a colonelcy. Announcing his determination to quit the military service more than a month ago, he entered the field as a competitor for the seat in Congress left vacant by the death of President Tyler. Hon. James Lyons was elected, and Col. Randolph got no votes at all.

MARCH 30TH.—Gen. Lee is to have command of all the armies—but will not be in the field himself. He will reside here. Congress passed an act to create a commanding general; but this was vetoed, for trenching on the executive prerogative—or failed in some way. The proceedings were in secret session.

MARCH 31ST.—Gen. Joseph E. Johnston is to command on the Peninsula. The President took an affectionate leave of him the other day; and Gen. Lee held his hand a long time, and admonished him to take care of his life. There was no necessity for him to endanger it—as had just been done by the brave Sydney Johnston at Shiloh, whose fall is now universally lamented. This Gen Johnston (Joseph E.) I believe has the misfortune to be wounded in most of his battles.

CHAPTER XIII.

Gen. Beauregard succeeds Gen. Sydney Johnston.—Dibble, the traitor.—Enemy at Fredericksburg.—They say we will be subdued by the 15th of June.—Lee rapidly concentrating at Richmond.—Webster, the spy, hung.

April 1st.—Gen. Sydney Johnston having fallen in battle, the command in the West devolved on Gen. Beauregard, whose recent defense at Island No. 10 on the Mississippi, has revived his popularity. But, I repeat, he is a doomed man.

April 2d.—Gen. Wise is here with his report of the Roanoke disaster.

April 3d.—Congress is investigating the Roanoke affair. Mr. Benjamin has been denounced in Congress by Mr. Foote and others as the sole cause of the calamities which have befallen the country.

I wrote a letter to the President, offering to show that I had given no passport to Mr. Dibble, the traitor, and also the evidences, in his own handwriting, that Mr. Benjamin granted it.

April 4th.—The enemy are shelling our camp at Yorktown. I can hear the reports of the guns, of a damp evening. We are sending back defiance with our guns.

The President has not taken any notice of my communication. Mr. Benjamin is too powerful to be affected by such proofs of such small matters.

April 5th.—Newbern, N. C., has fallen into the hands of the enemy! Our men, though opposed by greatly superior numbers, made a brave resistance, and killed and wounded 1000 of the invaders.

The enemy were piloted up the river to Newbern by the same *Mr. Dibble* to whom I refused a passport, but to whom the Secretary of War granted one.

The press everywhere is commenting on the case of Dibble—*but Mordecai still sits at the gate.*

April 6th.—Two spies (Lincoln's detective police) have been

arrested here, tried by court-martial, and condemned to be hung. There is an awful silence among the Baltimore detectives, which bodes no harm to the condemned. They will not be executed, though guilty.

April 7th.—R. G. H. Kean, a young man, and a connection of Mr. Randolph, has been appointed Chief of the Bureau of War in place of Col. Bledsoe, resigned at last. Mr. Kean was, I believe, a lieutenant when Mr. Randolph was colonel, and acted as his adjutant.

April 8th.—Col. Bledsoe has been appointed Assistant Secretary of War by the President. Now he is in his glory, and has forgotten me.

April 9th.—There are several young officers who have sheathed the sword, and propose to draw the pen in the civil service.

To-day I asked of the department a month's respite from labor, and obtained it. But I remained in the city, and watched closely, still hoping I might serve the cause, or at least prevent more injury to it, from the wicked facility hitherto enjoyed by spies to leave the country.

April 10th.—The condemned spies have implicated *Webster*, the letter-carrier, who has had so many passports. He will hang, probably. Gen. Winder himself, and his policemen, wrote home by him. I don't believe him any more guilty than many who used to write by him; and I mean to tell the Judge Advocate so, if they give me an opportunity.

April 11th.—The enemy are at Fredericksburg, and the Yankee papers say it will be all over with us by the 15th of June. I doubt that.

April 12th.—The committee (Congressional) which have been investigating the Roanoke Island disaster have come to the conclusion, unanimously, and the House has voted accordingly, and with unanimity, that the blame and guilt of that great calamity rest solely upon "Gen. Huger and Judah P. Benjamin."

April 13th.—Gen. Wise now resolved to ask for another command, to make another effort in defense of his country. But, when he waited upon the Secretary of War, he ascertained that there was no brigade for him. Returning from thence, some of his officers, who had escaped the trap at Roanoke, crowded round him to learn the issue of his application.

"There is no Secretary of War!" said he.

"What is Randolph?" asked one.

"He is not Secretary of War!" said he; "he is merely a *clerk*, an underling, and cannot hold up his head in his humiliating position. He never will be able to hold up his head, sir."

APRIL 14TH.—There will soon be hard fighting on the Peninsula.

APRIL 15TH.—Gen. Beauregard has written to Gen. Wise, offering him a command in his army, if the government will consent to it. It will not be consented to.

APRIL 16TH.—Troops are being concentrated rapidly in Virginia by Gen. Lee.

APRIL 17TH.—To-day Congress passed an act providing for the termination of martial law within thirty days after the meeting of the next session. This was as far as they could *venture*; for, indeed, a majority seem to be intimidated at the glitter of bayonets in the streets, wielded by the authority of martial law. The press, too, has taken the alarm, and several of the publishers have confessed a fear of having their offices closed, if they dare to speak the sentiments struggling for utterance. It is, indeed, a reign of terror! Every Virginian, and other loyal citizens of the South—members of Congress and all—must now, before obtaining Gen. Winder's permission to leave the city for their homes, bow down before the *aliens* in the Provost Marshal's office, and subscribe to an oath of allegiance, while a file of bayonets are pointed at his back!

APRIL 18TH.—The President is thin and haggard; and it has been whispered on the street that he will immediately be baptized and confirmed. I hope so, because it may place a great gulf between him and the descendant of those who crucified the Saviour. Nevertheless, some of his enemies allege that professions of Christianity have sometimes been the premeditated accompaniments of usurpations. It was so with Cromwell and with Richard III. Who does not remember the scene in Shakspeare, where Richard appears on the balcony, with prayer book in hand and a priest on either side?

APRIL 19TH.—All believe we are near a crisis, involving the possession of the capital.

APRIL 21ST.—A calm before the storm.

April 22d.—Dibble, the traitor, has been captured by our soldiers in North Carolina.

April 23d.—The North Carolinians have refused to give up Dibble to Gen. Winder. And, moreover, the governor has demanded the rendition of a citizen of his State, who was arrested there by one of Gen. Winder's detectives, and brought hither. The governor says, if he be not delivered up, he will institute measures of retaliation, and arrest every alien policeman from Richmond caught within the limits of his jurisdiction.

Is it not shameful that martial law should be playing such fantastic tricks before high heaven, when the enemy's guns are booming within hearing of the capital?

April 24th —Webster has been tried, condemned, and *hung*.

April 25th.—Gen. Wise, through the influence of Gen. Lee, who is a Christian gentleman as well as a consummate general, has been ordered into the field. He will have a brigade, but not with Beauregard. The President has unbounded confidence in Lee's capacity, modest as he is.

Another change! Provost Marshal Godwin, for rebuking the Baltimore chief of police, is to leave us, and to be succeeded by a Marylander, Major Griswold, whose family is now in the enemy's country.

April 26th.—Gen. Lee is doing good service in bringing forward reinforcements from the South against the day of trial—and an awful day awaits us. It is understood that he made fully known to the President his appreciation of the desperate condition of affairs, and demanded *cartē blanche* as a condition of his acceptance of the position of commanding general. The President wisely agreed to the terms.

April 27th.—Gen. Lee is calm—but the work of preparation goes on night and day.

April 28th.—We have rumors of an important cabinet meeting, wherein it was resolved to advise or command Gen. Johnston to evacuate Yorktown and retire toward Richmond! Also that Norfolk is to be given up! I don't believe it; Lee's name is not mentioned.

April 29th.—Major Griswold is here, and so is a new batch of Marylanders.

April 30th.—Troops from the South are coming in and marching down the Peninsula.

CHAPTER XIV.

Disloyalists entrapped.—Norfolk abandoned.—Merrimac blown up.—Army falling back.—Mrs. Davis leaves Richmond.—Preparing to burn the tobacco.—Secretary of War trembles for Richmond.—Richmond to be defended.—The tobacco.—Winking and blinking.—Johnston's great battle.—Wounded himself.—The wounded.—The hospitals.

MAY 1ST.—The ladies shower loaves of bread and slices of ham on the passing troops.

MAY 2D.—An iniquitous-looking prisoner was brought in to-day from Orange C. H., by the name of Robert Stewart. The evidence against him is as follows: He is a Pennsylvanian, though a resident of Virginia for a number of years, and owns a farm in Orange County. Since the series of disasters, and the seeming downward progress of our affairs, Stewart has cooled his ardor for independence. He has slunk from enrollment in the militia, and under the Conscription Act. And since the occupation of Fredericksburg by the enemy he has made use of such equivocal language as to convince his neighbors that his sympathies are wholly with the Northern invader.

A day or two since, near nightfall, three troopers, weary and worn, halted at Stewart's house and craved food and rest for themselves and horses. Stewart, supposing them to be Confederate soldiers, declared he had nothing they wanted, and that he was destitute of every description of refreshments. They said they were sorry for it, as it was a long ride to Fredericksburg.

"Are you *Union* soldiers?" asked Stewart, quickly.

"Yes," said they, "and we are on scouting duty."

"Come in! Come in! I have everything you want!" cried Stewart, and when they entered he embraced them.

A sumptuous repast was soon on the table, but the soldiers refused to eat! Surprised at this, Stewart demanded the reason; the troopers rose, and said they were Confederate soldiers, and it was their duty to arrest a traitor. They brought him hither. Will he, too, escape merited punishment?

MAY 3D —I fear there is something in the rumor that Norfolk and Portsmouth and Yorktown and the Peninsula will be *given* up. The Secretaries of War and Navy are going down to Norfolk.

MAY 4TH.—The Yankees on the Peninsula mean to fight. Well, that is what our brave army pants for.

MAY 5TH.—The prospect of battle produces a joyous smile on every soldier's face to-day.

MAY 6TH, 7TH.—We have not yet reached the lowest round of the ladder. The Secretary is at Norfolk, and the place is to be evacuated. I would resign first.

MAY 8TH.—Norfolk and Portsmouth are evacuated! Our army falling back! The Merrimac is to be, or has been, blown up!

MAY 9TH.—My family, excepting my son Custis, started to-day for Raleigh, N. C., where our youngest daughter is at school. But it is in reality another flight from the enemy. No one, scarcely, supposes that Richmond will be defended. But it must be!

MAY 10TH.—The President's family have departed for Raleigh, and the families of most of the cabinet to their respective homes, or other places of refuge. The President has been baptized (at home) and privately confirmed in St. Paul's Church.

MAY 11TH.—The Baltimore detectives are the lords of the ascendant. They crook a finger, and the best carriages in the street pause, turn round, and are subject to their will. They loll and roll in glory. And they ride on horseback, too—government horses, or horses *pressed* from gentlemen's stables. One word of remonstrance, and the poor victim is sent to Castle Godwin.

MAY 12TH.—I suggested to the Provost Marshal several days ago that there was an act of Congress *requiring* the destruction of tobacco, whenever it might be in danger of falling into the hands of the enemy. He ran to Gen. Winder, and he to some one else, and then a hundred or more negroes, and as many wagons, were "pressed" by the detectives. They are now gathering the weed from all quarters, and piling it in "pressed" warehouses, mixed with "combustibles," ready for the conflagration.

And now the consuls from the different nations are claiming that all bought on foreign account ought to be spared the torch. Mr. Myers, the little old lawyer, has been employed to aid them. He told me to-day that none ought to be burnt, that the Yankees having already the tobacco of Missouri, Kentucky, and Maryland, if we burn ours it will redound to their benefit, as it will enhance the price of that in their hands. That is a Benjamite argument. He hastened away to see the Secretary of State, and returned, saying, in high glee (supposing I concurred with him, of course), Mr. B. agreed with him. I told him, very gravely, that it mattered not who agreed with him; so soon as the enemy came to Richmond all the tobacco would be burned, as the retiring army would attend to it; several high officers were so resolved. He looked astounded, and departed.

MAY 13TH.—This morning I learned that the consuls had carried the day, and were permitted to collect the tobacco *alleged* to be bought on foreign account in separate warehouses, and to place the flags of their respective nations over them. This was saving the property claimed by foreigners whose governments refused to recognize us (these consuls are accredited to the United States), and destroying that belonging to our own citizens. I told the Provost Marshal that the act of Congress included *all* tobacco and cotton, and he was required by *law* to see it all destroyed. He, however, acknowledged only martial law, and was, he said, acting under the instructions of the Secretary of State. What has the Secretary of State to do with *martial law?* Is there really no Secretary of War?

Near the door of the Provost Marshal's office, guarded by bayoneted sentinels, there is a desk presided over by Sergeant Crow, who orders *transportation* on the cars to such soldiers as are permitted to rejoin their regiments. This Crow, a Marylander, keeps a little black-board hung up and notes with chalk all the regiments that go down the Peninsula. To-day, I saw a man whom I suspected to be a Yankee spy, copy with his pencil the list of regiments; and when I demanded his purpose, he seemed confused. This is the kind of information Gen. McClellan can afford to pay for very liberally. I drew the Provost Marshal's attention to this matter, and he ordered a discontinuance of the practice.

MAY 14TH.—Our army has fallen back to within four miles of Richmond. Much anxiety is felt for the fate of the city. Is there no turning point in this long lane of downward progress? Truly it may be said, our affairs at this moment are in a critical condition. I trust in God, and the chivalry and patriotism of the South *in the field.*

The enemy's fleet of gun-boats are ascending James River, and the obstructions are not completed. We have but one or two casemated guns in battery, but we have brave men there.

MAY 15TH.—The enemy's gun-boats, Monitor, Galena, etc. are at Drewry's Bluff, eight miles below the city, shelling our batteries, and our batteries are bravely shelling them. The President rode down to the vicinity this morning, and observed the firing.

The guns are heard distinctly in the city, and yet there is no consternation manifested by the people. If the enemy pass the obstructions, the city will be, it is true, very much at their mercy. They may shell us out of it, and this may occur any hour. South of the city the enemy have no forces, and we can find refuge there. I suppose the government would go to Lynchburg. I shall remain with the army, *and see that the tobacco be burnt, at all hazards, according to law.* I have seen some of our generals, and am convinced that the Baltimore rabble, and those that direct them, will be suppressed, or exterminated, if they attempt to throw impediments in the way of our soldiers in the work of destroying the tobacco, as enjoined by Congress.

Our marksmen will keep up an incessant fire into the port-holes of the gun-boats; and if it be at all practicable, we will board them. So hope is by no means extinct. But it is apprehended, if the enemy get within shelling distance of the city, there will be an attack along our lines by McClellan. We must beat him there, as we could never save our guns, stores, etc. retreating across the river. And we *will* beat him, for we have 80,000 men, and more are coming.

Joyful tidings! the gun-boats have been repulsed! A heavy shot from one of our batteries ranged through the Galena from stem to stern, making frightful slaughter, and disabling the ship; and the whole fleet turned about and steamed down the river! We have not lost a dozen men. We breathe freely; and the government will lose no time in completing the obstructions and strengthening the batteries.

MAY 16TH.—McClellan is intrenching—that is, at least, significant of a respite, and of apprehension of attack.

MAY 17TH.—Gen. Lee has admonished Major Griswold on the too free granting of passports. Will it do any good?

MAY 18TH.—All quiet to-day except the huzzas as fresh troops arrive.

MAY 19TH.—We await the issue before Richmond. It is still believed by many that it is the intention of the government and the generals to evacuate the city. If the enemy were to appear in force on the south side, and another force were to march on us from Fredericksburg, we should be inevitably taken, in the event of the loss of a battle—an event I don't anticipate. Army, government, and all, might, it is true, be involved in a common ruin. Wrote as strong a letter as I could to the President, stating what I have every reason to believe would be the consequences of the abandonment of Richmond. There would be demoralization and even insubordination in the army. Better die here! With the exception of the business portion of the city, the enemy could not destroy a great many houses by bombardment. But if defeated and driven back, our troops would make a heroic defense in the streets, in the walled grave-yards, and from the windows. Better electrify the world by such scenes of heroism, than surrender the capital and endanger the cause. I besought him by every consideration, not to abandon Richmond to the enemy short of the last extremity.

The legislature has also passed resolutions calling upon the C. S. Government to defend Richmond at all hazards, relieving the Confederate authorities, in advance, of all responsibility for any damage sustained.

This will have its effect. It would be pusillanimous to retire now.

But every preparation had been made to abandon it. The archives had been sent to Columbia, S. C., and to Lynchburg. The tracks over the bridges had been covered with plank, to facilitate the passage of artillery. Mr. Randolph had told his page, and cousin, "you must go with my wife into the country, for to-morrow the enemy will be here." Trunks were packed in readiness—for what? Not one would have been taken on the cars! The Secretary of the Treasury had a special locomotive and cars, constantly with steam up, in readiness to fly with the treasure.

Nevertheless, many of the *old* secessionists have resolved not to leave their homes, for there were no other homes for them to fly to. They say they will never take the oath of allegiance to the despised government of the North, but suffer whatever penalties may be imposed on them. There is a sullen, but generally a calm expression of inflexible determination on the countenances of the people, men, women, and children. But there is no consternation; we have learned to contemplate death with composure. It would be at least an effectual escape from dishonor; and Northern domination is dishonor.

MAY 20TH.—The President, in response to the Legislative Committee, announced that Richmond would be defended. A thrill of joy electrifies every heart, a smile of triumph is on every lip. The inhabitants seem to know that their brave defenders in the field will prove invincible; and it is understood that Gen. Lee considers the city susceptible of successful defense. The ladies are in ecstasies.

MAY 21ST.—There are skirmishes every day, and we can hear both the artillery and musketry from the hills on the outskirts of the city, whither some of us repair every afternoon.

But the Provost Marshal's administration is abominable. Mr. Garnett, M. C., told me that in an interview with the President, the latter informed him that he had just received a letter from Gen. Johnston, stating that the enemy not only knew everything going on within our lines, but seemed absolutely to know what we intended doing in the future, as if the most secret counsels of the cabinet were divulged.

Count Mercier, the French Minister residing at Washington, has been here on a mysterious errand. They said it referred to our recognition. He had prolonged interviews with Mr. Benjamin. I think it was concerning tobacco. There are $60,000,000 worth in Richmond, at French prices. For $1,000,000, Mr. Seward might afford to wink very hard; and, after distributing several other millions, there would be a grand total profit both to the owners and the French Emperor. I smile at their golden expectations, for I know they will not be realized. If one man can prevent it, the South shall never be betrayed for a crop of tobacco. This is a holy cause we are embarked in, worthy to die for.

The British Minister, Lord Lyons, has embarked for England, to report to his government that "the rebellion is on its last legs," and must speedily succumb. He is no prophet, or the son of a prophet.

MAY 22D.—There is lightning in the Northwest, and the deep thunder of avenging guns is heard at Washington! Gen. Jackson, sent thither by Gen. Lee, is sweeping everything before him, defeating Shields, Banks, Fremont, and one or two other Yankee major-generals, with his little *corps d'armée!* And his coadjutor, Ewell, is worthy of his companionship. He has swept them out of the valley, scattering their hosts like quails before the fowler! They fly in every direction; and the powers at Washington are trembling for the safety of their own capital. Glorious Jackson! and he gives, as is justly due, the glory to God.

MAY 23D.—Oh, the extortioners! Meats of all kinds are selling at 50 cts. per pound; butter, 75 cts.; coffee, $1.50; tea, $10; boots, $30 per pair; shoes, $18; ladies' shoes, $15; shirts, $6 each. Houses that rented for $500 last year, are $1000 now. Boarding, from $30 to $40 per month. Gen. Winder has issued an order fixing the maximum prices of certain articles of marketing, which has only the effect of keeping a great many things out of market. The farmers have to pay the merchants and Jews their extortionate prices, and complain very justly of the partiality of the general. It does more harm than good.

MAY 24TH.—Every day the two armies are shelling each other, more or less; and every gun can be heard from the Hospital Hill, north of the city, whither many repair to listen.

MAY 25TH.—The enemy send up several balloons every day. Sometimes three can be seen at once. They are stationary, being fastened by ropes to trees; and give us an idea of the extent of his lines. But with glasses they can not only see our camps around the city, but they can view every part of the city itself.

MAY 26TH.—Gen. Lee is still strengthening the army. Every day additional regiments are coming. We are now so strong that no one fears the result when the great battle takes place. McClellan has delayed too long, and he is doomed to defeat. The tobacco savers know it well, and their faces exhibit chagrin and disappointment. Their fortunes will not be made this year, and so their reputations may be saved.

MAY 27TH.—More troops came in last night, and were marched to the camp at once, so that the Yankees will know nothing of it.

MAY 28TH.—Prisoners and deserters from the enemy say the Yankees get the Richmond papers, every day, almost as soon as we do. This is a great advantage they possess; and it demonstrates the fact that the Provost Marshal has interposed no effectual barriers between us and the enemy.

MAY 29TH.—More troops are marching into the city, and Gen. Lee has them sent out in such manner and at such times as to elude the observations of even the spies.

MAY 30TH.—It is said some of the enemy's mounted pickets rode through the city last night! Northern papers manifest much confidence in the near approach of the downfall of Richmond, and the end of the "rebellion." The 15th of June is the utmost limit allowed us for existence. A terrific storm arose yesterday; and as our scouts report the left wing of the enemy on this side of the Chickahominy, Gen. Johnston has determined to attack it to-morrow. Thank God, we are strong enough to make the attack!

MAY 31ST.—Everybody is upon the tip-toe of expectation. It has been announced (in the streets!) that a battle would take place this day, and hundreds of men, women, and children repaired to the hills to listen, and possibly to see, the firing. The great storm day before yesterday, it is supposed, has so swollen the Chickahominy as to prevent McClellan's left wing from retreating, and reinforcements from being sent to its relief. The time is well chosen by Gen. Johnston for the attack, but it was bad policy to let it be known where and when it would be made; for, no doubt, McClellan was advised of our plans an hour or so after they were promulged in the streets. Whose fault is this? Johnston could hardly be responsible for it, because he is very reticent, and appreciates the importance of keeping his purposes concealed from the enemy. Surely none of his subordinates divulged the secret, for none but generals of division knew it. It must have been found out and proclaimed by some one in the *tobacco* interest. It is true, Mr. Randolph told Mr. Jacques a great battle would begin at 8 A.M., to-day; but he would not propagate such news as that!

But the battle did not occur at the time specified. Gen. Huger's division was not at the allotted place of attack at the time fixed upon. His excuse is that there was a stream to cross, and understanding Gen. Longstreet was his senior in command (which is not the fact, however), he permitted his division to have *precedence*. All the divisions were on the ground in time but Huger's, but still no battle. Thousands of impatient spectators are venting their criticisms and anathemas, like an audience at a theater when some accident or disarrangement behind the scenes prevents the curtain from rising.

At last, toward noon, a few guns are heard; but it was not till 4 P.M. that Huger's division came upon the field. Nevertheless, the battle began in earnest before that hour; and we could hear distinctly not only the cannon but the musketry.

The hearts of our soldiers have been inspired with heroic resolution, and their arms nerved with invincible power to overcome the difficulties known to be in the way. Every one is aware that the camp of the enemy, on this side of the Chickahominy, is almost impregnably intrenched; and in front of the works trees have been cut down and the limbs sharpened, so as to interpose every obstacle to our advance.

Ever and anon after rapid firing of cannon, and a tremendous rattle of musketry, a pause would ensue; and we knew what this meant! A battery had been taken at the point of the bayonet, and we cheered accordingly. One after another, we could in this manner perceive the strongholds of the enemy fall into our hands.

Toward sundown it was apparent that the intrenched camp had been taken; and as the deep booming of cannon became more distant, and the rattle of musketry less distinct, we felt certain that the foe was flying, and that our men were pursuing them. But we *knew* that our men would take everything they were ordered to take. *They* care not for wounds and death. This is their only country. But the enemy have a country to run to, and they hope to live, even if defeated here. If they kill all our young men, the old men and women, and even our children, will seize their arms and continue the conflict.

At night. The ambulances are coming in with our wounded. They report that all the enemy's strong defenses were stormed, just as we could perceive from the sounds. They say that our brave men suffered much in advancing against the intrenchments, exposed to the fire of cannon and small arms, without being able to see the foe under their shelter; but when they leaped over the breastworks and turned the enemy's guns on them, our loss was more than compensated. Our men were shot in front; the enemy in the back—and terrible was the slaughter. We got their tents, all standing, and a sumptuous repast that had just been served up when the battle began. Gen. Casey's headquarters were taken, and his *plate* and smoking viands were found on his table. His papers fell into our hands. We got a large amount of stores and refreshments, so much needed by our poor braves! There were boxes of lemons, oranges, brandies and wines, and all the luxuries of distant lands which enter the unrestricted ports of the United States. These things were narrated by the pale and bleeding soldiers, who smiled in triumph at their achievement. Not one in the long procession of ambulances uttered a complaint. Did they really suffer pain from their wounds? This question was asked by thousands, and the reply was, "not much." Women and children and slaves are wending to the hospitals, with baskets of refreshments, lint, and bandages. Every house is offered for a hospital, and every matron and gentle daughter, a tender nurse.

But how fares it with the invader? Unable to recross the swollen Chickahominy, the Yankees were driven into an almost impenetrable swamp, where they must pass the night in water up to their knees. The wounded borne off by them will have no ministrations from their sisters and mothers, and their dead are abandoned on the field. If Huger had come up at the time appointed, the enemy would have been ruined.

CHAPTER XV.

Huger fails again.—A wounded boy.—The killed and wounded.—Lee assumes command.—Lee prepares to attack McClellan.—Beauregard watches the gold.—Our generals scattered.—Hasty letter from Gen. Lee.—Opening of grand battle.—First day, 26th June.—Second, etc.—Lee's consummate skill.—Every day for a week it rages.—Streets crowded with Blue Jackets.—McClellan retires.

JUNE 1ST.—The ambulances are now bringing in the enemy's wounded as well as our own. It is the prompting of humanity. They seem truly grateful for this magnanimity, as they call it; a sentiment hitherto unknown to them.

The battle was renewed to-day, but not seriously. The failure of Gen. Huger to lead his division into action at the time appointed, is alleged as the only reason why the left wing of the enemy was not completely destroyed. But large masses of the enemy did cross the river, on bridges constructed for the purpose, and they had 50,000 men engaged against a much less number on our part; and their batteries played upon us from the north bank of the Chickahominy. The flying foe kept under shelter of this fire—and these guns could not be taken, as the pontoon bridge was defended by heavy artillery.

All day the wounded were borne past our boarding-house in Third Street, to the general hospital; and hundreds, with shattered arms and slight flesh wounds, came in on foot. I saw a boy, not more than fifteen years old (from South Carolina), with his hand in a sling. He showed me his wound. A ball had entered between the fingers of his left hand and lodged near the wrist, where the flesh was much swollen. He said, smiling, "I'm going to the hospital just to have the ball cut out, and will then return to the battle-field. I can fight with my right hand."

The detectives are jubilant to-day. They say one of their number, ——, did heroic feats of arms on the field, killing a Yankee colonel, and a private who came to the rescue. At all events, they brought in a colonel's sword, pistols, and coat, as trophies. This story is to be in the papers to-morrow!

June 2d.—Great indignation is expressed by the generals in the field at the tales told of the heroism of the amateur fighters. They say —— stripped a dead colonel, and was never in reach of the enemy's guns. Moreover, the civilians in arms kept at such a distance from danger that their balls fell among our own men, and wounded some of them! An order has been issued by one of the major-generals, that hereafter any stragglers on the field of battle shall be shot. No civilians are to be permitted to be there at all, unless they go into the ranks.

Gen. Johnston is wounded—badly wounded, but not mortally. It is his misfortune to be wounded in almost every battle he fights. Nevertheless, he has gained a glorious victory. Our loss in killed and wounded will not exceed 5000; while the enemy's killed, wounded, and prisoners will not fall short of 13,000. They lost, besides, many guns, tents, and stores—all wrung from them at the point of the bayonet, and in spite of their formidable abattis. Prisoners taken on the field say: "The Southern soldiers would charge into hell if there was a battery before them—and they would take it from a legion of devils!" The moral effect of this victory must be great. The enemy have been taught that none of the engines of destruction that can be wielded against us, will prevent us from taking their batteries; and so, hereafter, when we charge upon them, they might as well run away from their own guns.

JUNE 3D.—Gen. Lee henceforth assumes command of the army in person. This may be hailed as the harbinger of bright fortune.

JUNE 4TH.—Col. Bledsoe sent word to me to-day by my son that he wished to see me. When I met him he groaned as usual, and said the department would have to open another passport office, as the major-generals in the field refused to permit the relatives of the sick and wounded in the camps to pass with orders from Brig.-Gen. Winder or his Provost Marshal.

JUNE 5TH.—I reopened my office in the department.

JUNE 6TH.—Gen. Winder getting wind of what was going on, had an interview, first with Mr. Benjamin, who instructed him what to say; and then bringing forward the Provost Marshal, they had a rather stormy interview with Mr. Randolph, who, as usual, yielded to their protestations against having *two* passport offices, while martial law existed.

And so Col. Bledsoe came in and told me to "shut up shop." The Secretary had revoked his order.

JUNE 7TH.—But business is in a great measure suspended, and so I have another holiday.

JUNE 8TH.—I learn that Col. Bledsoe has to grant passports to the army, as the pickets have been instructed to let no one pass upon the order of Gen. Winder or his Provost Marshal.

JUNE 9TH.—It is now apparent that matters were miserably managed on the battle-field, until Gen. Lee assumed command in person. Most of the trophies of the victory, and thousands of arms, stores, etc. were pillaged by the promiscuous crowds of aliens and Jews who purchased passports thither from the Provost Marshal's detectives.

JUNE 10TH.—Col. Bledsoe sent for me again. This time he wanted me to take charge of the letter room, and superintend the young gentlemen who briefed the letters. This I did very cheerfully; I opened all the letters, and sent to the Secretary the important ones immediately. These, for want of discrimination, had sometimes been suffered to remain unnoticed two or three days, when they required instant action.

JUNE 11TH, 12TH.—Gen. Smith, the New York street commissioner, had been urged as commander-in-chief.

JUNE 13TH.—Gen. Lee is satisfied with the present posture of affairs—and McClellan has no idea of attacking us now. He don't say what he means to do himself.

JUNE 14TH.—The wounded soldiers bless the ladies, who nurse them unceasingly.

JUNE 15TH.—What a change! No one now dreams of the loss of the capital.

JUNE 17TH.—It is not yet ascertained what amount of ordnance stores we gained from the battle.

JUNE 18TH.—Lee is quietly preparing to attack McClellan. The President, who was on the battle-field, is very cheerful.

JUNE 19TH.—To-day so many applications were made to the Secretary himself for passports to the armies, and beyond the lines of the Confederate States, that, forgetting the revocation of his former order, he sent a note into the Assistant Secretary, saying he thought a passport agent had been appointed to attend to such cases; and he now directed that it be done. Bledsoe came to me immediately, and said: "Jones, you'll have to open a passport office again—I shall sign no more."

JUNE 20TH.—Moved once more into the old office.

JUNE 21ST.—Gen. Beauregard is doubly doomed. A few weeks ago, when the blackness of midnight brooded over our cause, there were some intimations, I know not whether they were well founded, that certain high functionaries were making arrangements for a flight to France; and Gen. Beauregard getting intimation of an order to move certain sums in bullion in the custody of an Assistant Treasurer in his military department, forbid its departure until he could be certain that it was not destined to leave the Confederacy. I have not learned its ultimate destination; but the victory of the Seven Pines intervening, Gen. Beauregard has been relieved of his command, "on sick leave." But I know his army is to be commanded permanently by Gen. Bragg. There are charges against Beauregard. It is said the Yankee army might have been annihilated at Shiloh, if Beauregard had fought a little longer.

June 23d.—And Gen. Johnston, I learn, has had his day. And Magruder is on "sick leave." He is too open in his censures of the late Secretary of War. But Gen. Huger comes off scot-free; he has always had the confidence of Mr. Benjamin, and used to send the flag of truce to Fortress Monroe as often as could be desired.

June 24th.—Gen. Lee's plan works like a charm! Although I have daily orders from Mr. Randolph to send persons beyond our lines, yet the precautions of Lee most effectually prevent any spies from knowing anything about his army. Even the Adjutant-General, S. Cooper, don't know how many regiments are ordered into Virginia, or where they are stationed. Officers returning from furlough, cannot ascertain in the Adjutant-General's office where their regiments are! They are referred to me for passports to Gen. Lee's headquarters. No man with a passport from Gen. Winder, or from his Provost Marshal, can pass the pickets of Gen. Lee's army. This is the harbinger of success, and I predict a career of glory for Lee, and for our country! There are some vague rumors about the approach of Stonewall Jackson's army; but no one knows anything about it, and but few believe it. Recent Northern papers say he is approaching Winchester, and I see they are intrenching in the valley to guard against his terrible blows. This is capital! And our people are beginning to *fear* there will be no more fighting around Richmond until McClellan *digs* his way to it. The moment fighting ceases, our people have fits of gloom and despondency; but when they snuff battle in the breeze, they are animated with confidence. They regard victory as a matter of course; and are only indignant at our long series of recent reverses, when they reflect that our armies have so seldom been led against the embattled hosts of the enemy.

June 25th.—The people of Louisiana are protesting strongly against permitting Gen. Lovell to remain in command in that State, since the fall of New Orleans (which I omitted to note in regular order in these chronicles), and they attribute that disgraceful event, some to his incompetency, and others to treason. These remonstrances come from such influential parties, I think the President must listen to them. Yes, a Massachusetts man (they say Gen. L. came from Boston) was in command of the troops of New Orleans when that great city surrendered without firing a gun. And this is one of the Northern generals who came over to our side *after* the battle of Manassas.

JUNE 26TH.—To-day a letter, hastily written by Gen. Lee to the Secretary of War, stated that his headquarters would be at ——, or *beyond* that point, whence couriers could find him if there should be anything of importance the Secretary might desire to communicate during the day. *This is the day of battle!* Jackson is in the rear of McClellan's right wing! I sent this note to the Secretary at once. I *suppose* Mr. Randolph had been previously advised of Gen. Lee's intention to fight to-day; but I do not *know* it. I know some of the brigadier-generals in the army do not know it; although they have all been ordered to their commands. This is no uncommon order; but it is characteristic of Lee's secretiveness to keep *all* of his officers in profound ignorance of his intentions, except those he means to be engaged. The *enemy* cannot possibly have any intimation of his purpose, because the spies here have no intelligence; and none are permitted to pass the rear pickets in sight of the city without my passport. What a change since the last battle!

To-day, in compliance with an intimation of the President, all in the departments, who felt so disposed, formed a military organization for the defense of the city, and especially of the archives, which had been brought back since the assumption of command by Gen. Lee. Col. Bledsoe denounced the organization as a humbug! Defending the government, or readiness to defend it, in such times as these, is no humbug! In the fluctuations of a great battle, almost in the suburbs of the city, a squadron of the enemy's horse might penetrate even to the office of the Chief Executive, when a few hundred muskets, in the hands of old men and boys, might preserve the papers.

After dinner I repaired, with Custis and a few friends, to my old stand on the hill north of the Jews' Cemetery, and sat down in the shade to listen. Many persons were there as usual—for every day some firing could be heard—who said, in response to my inquiries, that distant guns had been heard in the direction of the Pamunky River.

"That is *Jackson!*" I exclaimed, as the sounds were distinctly discerned by myself; "and he is in their rear, behind their right wing!"

All were incredulous, and some doubted whether he was within a hundred miles of us. But the sounds grew more distinct, and more frequent, and I knew he was advancing. But how long could he advance in that direction without being overwhelmed? Everywhere else along the line a deathlike silence reigned, that even the dropping fire of the pickets, usually so incessant, could be heard.

This suspense continued only a few minutes. Two guns were then heard northeast of us, and in such proximity as to startle some of the anxious listeners. These were followed by three or four more, and then the fire continued with increasing rapidity. This was Gen. A. P. Hill's division in *front* of the enemy's right wing, and Lee's plan of battle was developed. Hill was so near us as to be almost in sight. The drums and fifes of his regiments, as they marched up to the point of attack, could be easily heard; how distinctly, then, sounded his cannon in our ears! And the enemy's guns, pointed in the direction of the city, were as plainly discerned. I think McClellan is taken by surprise.

One gentleman, who had been incredulous on the subject of a battle to-day, held his watch in his hand ten minutes, during which time one hundred and ninety guns were heard. Saying he believed a battle was in progress, he replaced the watch in his pocket, and sat down on the ground to listen.

Another hour, and the reports come with the rapidity of seconds, or 3600 per hour! And now, for the first time, we hear the rattle of small arms. And lo! two guns farther to the right,—from Longstreet's division, I suppose. And they were followed by others. This is Lee's grand plan of battle: Jackson first, then Hill, then Longstreet—time and distance computed with mathematical precision! The enemy's balloons are not up now. They *know* what is going on, without further investigations up in the air. The business is upon earth, where many a Yankee will breathe his last this night! McClellan must be thunderstruck at this unexpected opening of a decisive battle. Our own people, and even our own general officers, except those who were to participate in the attack, were uninformed of Lee's grand purpose, until the booming of Jackson's guns were heard far on our left.

As the shades of evening fall, the fire seems to increase in rapidity, and a gentle breeze rising as the stars come out, billows of smoke are wafted from the battle-field. And now, occasionally, we can distinctly see the bursting of shells in the air, aimed too high by the enemy, and exploding far this side of our line of battle.

Darkness is upon us, save the glimmer of the stars, as the sulphurous clouds sink into the humid valleys. But the flashes of the guns are visible on the horizon, followed by the deep intonations of the mighty engines of destruction, echoing and reverberating from hill to hill, and through the vast valley of the James in the rear.

Hundreds of men, women, and children were attracted to the heights around the city to behold the spectacle. From the Capitol and from the President's mansion, the vivid flashes of artillery could be seen; but no one doubted the result. It is only silence and inaction we dread. The firing ceased at nine o'clock P.M. The President was on the field, but did not interfere with Lee.

JUNE 27TH.—At the first dawn of day, the battle recommenced, farther round to the east. This was enough. The enemy had drawn in his right wing. And courier after courier announced the taking of his batteries by our brave defenders! But the battle rages loud and long, and the troops of Jackson's corps, like the march of Fate, still upon McClellan's right flank and rear. Jackson's horse, and the gallant Stuart, with his irresistible cavalry, have cut the enemy's communications with their base on the Pamunky. It is said they are burning their stores!

What genius! what audacity in Lee! He has absolutely taken the greater portion of his army to the north side of the Chickahominy, leaving McClellan's center and left wing on the south side, with apparently easy access to the city. This is (to the invaders) impenetrable strategy. The enemy believes Lee's main forces are *here*, and will never think of advancing. We have so completely closed the avenues of intelligence that the enemy has not been able to get the slightest intimation of our strength or the dispositions of our forces.

JUNE 28TH.—The President publishes a dispatch from Lee,

announcing a victory! The enemy has been driven from all his intrenchments, losing many batteries.

Yesterday the President's life was saved by Lee. Every day he rides out near the battle-field, in citizen's dress, marking the fluctuations of the conflict, but assuming no direction of affairs in the field. Gen. Lee, however, is ever apprised of his position; and once, when the enemy were about to point one of their most powerful batteries in the direction of a certain farm-house occupied by the President, Lee sent a courier in haste to inform him of it. No sooner had the President escaped than a storm of shot and shell riddled the house.

Some of the people still think that their military President is on the field directing every important movement in person. A gentleman told me to-day, that he met the President yesterday, and the day before, alone, in the lanes and orchards, near the battle-field. He issued no orders; but awaited results like the rest of us, praying fervently for abundant success.

To-day some of our streets are crammed with thousands of blue-jackets—Yankee prisoners. There are many field officers, and among them several generals.

General Reynolds, who surrendered with his brigade, was thus accosted by one of our functionaries, who knew him before the war began:

"General, this is in accordance with McClellan's prediction; you are in Richmond."

"Yes, sir," responded the general, in bitterness; "and d—n me, if it is not precisely in the manner I anticipated."

"Where is McClellan, general?"

"I know not exactly; his movements have been so frequent of late. But I think it probable he too may be here before night!"

"I doubt that," said his fellow-prisoner, Gen. McCall; "beware of your left wing! Who commands there?"

"Gen. Jackson."

"Stonewall Jackson? Is he in this fight? Was it really Jackson making mince-meat of our right? Then your left wing is safe!"

Four or five thousand prisoners have arrived.

June 29th.—The battle still rages. But the scene has shifted farther to the east. The enemy's army is now entirely on *this* side of the Chickahominy. McClellan is doggedly retiring toward the James River.

JUNE 30TH.—Once more all men are execrating Gen. Huger. It is alleged that he *again* failed to obey an order, and kept his division away from the position assigned it, which would have prevented the escape of McClellan. If this be so, who is responsible, after his alleged misconduct at the battle of the Seven Pines?

CHAPTER XVI.

Terrific fighting.—Anxiety to visit the battle-field.—Lee prepares for other battles.—Hope for the Union extinct.—Gen. Lee brings forward conscripts.—Gen. Cobb appointed to arrange exchange of prisoners.—Mr. Ould as agent.—Pope, the braggart, comes upon the stage.—Meets a braggart's fate.—The war transferred to Northern Virginia.

JULY 1ST.—To-day Gen. Magruder led his division into action at Malvern Hill, it is said, contrary to the judgment of other commanders. The enemy's batteries commanded all the approaches in most advantageous position, and fearful was the slaughter. A wounded soldier, fresh from the field to-night, informs me that our loss in killed in this engagement will amount to as many as have fallen in all the others combined.

JULY 2D.—More fighting to-day. The enemy, although their batteries were successfully defended last night at Malvern Hill, abandoned many guns after the charges ceased, and retreated hastily. The grand army of invasion is now some twenty-five miles from the city, and yet the Northern papers claim the victory. They say it was a masterly strategic movement of McClellan, and a premeditated change of base from the Pamunky to the James; and that he will certainly take Richmond in a week and end the rebellion.

JULY 3D.—Our wounded are now coming in fast, under the direction of the Ambulance Committee. I give passports to no one not having legitimate business on the field to pass the pickets of the army. There is no pilfering on this field of battle; no "Plug Ugly" detectives stripping dead colonels, and, Falstaff like, claiming to be made "either Earl or Duke" for killing them.

So great is the demand for vehicles that the brother of a North Carolina major, reported mortally wounded, paid $100 for a hack to bring his brother into the city. He returned with him a few hours after, and, fortunately, found him to be not even dangerously wounded.

I suffer no physicians not belonging to the army to go upon the battle-field without taking amputating instruments with them, and no private vehicle without binding the drivers to bring in two or more of the wounded.

There are fifty hospitals in the city, fast filling with the sick and wounded. I have seen men in my office and walking in the streets, whose arms have been amputated within the last three days. The realization of a great victory seems to give them strength.

JULY 4TH.—Lee does not follow up his blows on the whipped enemy, and some sage critics censure him for it. But he knows that the fatal blow has been dealt this "grand army" of the North. The serpent has been killed, though its tail still exhibits some spasmodic motions. It will die, so far as the Peninsula is concerned, after sunset, or when it thunders.

The commanding general neither sleeps nor slumbers. Already the process of reorganizing Jackson's corps has been commenced for a blow at or near the enemy's capital. Let Lincoln beware the hour of retribution.

The enemy's losses in the seven days' battles around Richmond, in killed, wounded, sick, and desertions, are estimated at 50,000 men, and their losses in cannon, stores, etc., at some $50,000,000. Their own papers say the work is to be begun anew, and subjugation is put off six months, which is equivalent to a loss of $500,000,000 inflicted by Lee's victory.

By their emancipation and confiscation measures, the Yankees have made this a war of extermination, and added new zeal and resolution to our brave defenders. All hope of a reconstruction of the Union is relinquished by the few, comparatively, in the South, who still clung to the delusion. It is well. If the enemy had pursued a different course we should never have had the same unanimity. If they had made war only on men in arms, and spared private property, according to the usages of civilized nations, there would, at least, have been a *neutral* party in the South, and never the same energy and determination to contest the last inch of soil with the cruel invader. Now they will find that 3,000,000 of troops cannot subjugate us, and if subjugated, that a standing army of half a million would be required to keep us in subjection.

JULY 5TH.—Gen. Lee is bringing forward the conscript regiments with rapidity; and so large are his powers that the Secretary of War has but little to do. He is, truly, but a mere clerk. The correspondence is mostly referred to the different bureaus for action, whose experienced heads know what should be done much better than Mr. Randolph could tell them.

JULY 6TH.—Thousands of fathers, brothers, mothers, and sisters of the wounded are arriving in the city to attend their suffering relations, and to recover the remains of those who were slain.

JULY 7TH.—Gen. Huger has been relieved of his command. He retains his rank and pay as major-general "of ordnance."

Gen. Pope, Yankee, has been assigned to the command of the army of invasion in Northern Virginia, and Gen. Halleck has been made commanding general, to reside in Washington. Good! The Yankees are disgracing McClellan, the best general they have.

JULY 8TH.—Glorious Col. Morgan has dashed into Kentucky, whipped everything before him, and got off unharmed. He had but little over a thousand men, and captured that number of prisoners. Kentucky will rise in a few weeks.

JULY 9TH.—Lee has turned the tide, and I shall not be surprised if we have a long career of successes. Bragg, and Kirby Smith, and Loring are in motion at last, and Tennessee and Kentucky, and perhaps Missouri, will rise again in "Rebellion."

JULY 10TH.—I forgot to note in its place a feat of Gen. Stuart and his cavalry, before the recent battles. He made a complete girdle around the enemy, destroying millions of their property, and returned without loss. He was reconnoitering for Jackson, who followed in his track. This made Stuart major-general.

I likewise omitted to note the death of the brave Gen. Ashby, who fell in one of Jackson's brilliant battles in the Valley. But history will do him justice. [My chronicles are designed to assist history, and to supply the smaller incidents and details which the grand historian would be likely to omit.]

JULY 11TH.—Gen. Howell Cobb has been sent down the river under flag of truce to negotiate a cartel with Gen. Dix for the exchange of prisoners. It was decided that the exchange should be conducted on the basis agreed to between the United States and the British Government during the war of 1812, and all men taken hereafter will be released on parole within ten days after their capture. We have some 8000 prisoners in this city, and altogether, I dare say, a larger number than the enemy have of our men.

JULY 12TH.—Mr. Ould has been appointed agent to effect exchanges of paroled men. He is also acting as judge advocate.

JULY 13TH.—We have some of Gen. Pope's proclamations and orders. He is simply a braggart, and will meet a braggart's fate. He announces his purpose to subsist his army in our country, and moreover, he intends to shoot or hang our non-combating citizens that may fall into his hands, in retaliation for the killing of any of his thieving and murdering soldiers by our avenging guerrillas. He says his headquarters will be on his horse, and that he will make no provision for retreat. That he has been accustomed to see the *backs* of his enemies! Well, we shall see how he will face a Stonewall!

JULY 14TH.—Jackson and Ewell and Stuart are after Pope, but I learn they are not allowed to attempt any enterprise for some weeks yet. Fatal error, I fear. For we have advices at the department that Pope has not now exceeding 20,000 men, but that all the rolling stock of the Baltimore and Ohio Railroad is ordered West to bring reinforcements. Besides, the United States Government is calling for 600,000 additional men. Then again, McClellan and Burnside will form a junction with Pope, and we will be outnumbered. But the President and Gen. Lee know best what is to be done. We have lost many of the flower of Southern chivalry in the late conflicts.

JULY 15TH—Gen. Pendleton has given McClellan a scare, and might have hurt him if he had fired lower. He planted a number of batteries (concealed) on the south side of the river, just opposite the enemy's camp. The river was filled with gun-boats and transports. At a signal, all the guns were fired, at short range, too, for some minutes with great rapidity, and then the batteries were withdrawn. I happened to be awake, and could not conjecture what the rumpus meant. But we fired too high in the dark, and did but little execution. Our shells fell beyond the enemy's camp on the opposite side of the river. We lost a few men, by accident, mostly. But hereafter in "each bush they fear an officer."

JULY 16TH.—Gen. Lee is hurrying up reinforcements from the South, old regiments and conscripts, and pays very little attention to McClellan on the Peninsula, knowing no further enterprises will be attempted by the enemy in that quarter for some time to come.

JULY 17TH.—The people are too jubilant, I fear, over our recent successes near the city. A great many *skulkers* from the army are seen daily in the streets, and it is said there are 3000 men here subject to conscript duty, who have not been enrolled. The business of purchasing substitutes is prevailing alarmingly.

JULY 18TH.—To-day several ladies applied in person to the Secretary of War for passports to Norfolk and Baltimore, and he sent me written orders to grant them. They next applied to Gen. Winder to go with the flag of truce, exhibiting their passports. He repudiated them, however, and sent the ladies back to me, saying he wanted something with the Secretary's signature, showing me to be authorized to sign them. I wrote such a note as I supposed he wanted, and the Secretary signed it as follows:

"RICHMOND, July 18th, 1862.

"BRIG.-GEN. J. H. WINDER.

"SIR:—The passports issued by J. B. Jones from this Department to pass the lines of the Confederate armies, and the lines of the Confederate States, are granted by my direction, evidences of which are on file in the Passport Office.

"Respectfully,

"G. W. RANDOLPH,

"*Secretary of War.*"

This, one of the ladies delivered to him. I hope I am now done with Gen. Winder and his "Plug Ugly" dynasty.

JULY 19TH.—This morning early, while congratulating myself on the evidence of some firmness and independence in the new Secretary, I received the following note:

"RICHMOND, July 19th, 1862.

"Mr. J. B. JONES.

"SIR:—I have just been directed by the Secretary of War that he has turned over the whole business of passports to Gen. Winder, and that applications for passports will not be received at this office at all.

"Very respectfully,

"A. G. BLEDSOE,

"*Asst. Sec. War.*"

Of course I ceased operations immediately. So large a concourse of persons now accumulated in the hall, that it was soon necessary to put up a notice that Gen. Winder would grant them passports. But the current set back again. Gen. Winder *refused* to issue passports to the relatives of the sick and wounded in the camps, well knowing the generals, his superiors in rank, would not recognize his authority. He even came into the department, and tore down the notice with his own hands.

JULY 20TH.—I am back again, signing passports to the army. But yesterday, during the *interregnum*, the Beaverdam Depot was burnt by the enemy, information of its defenseless condition having been given by a Jew peddler, who obtained no passport from me.

JULY 21ST.—A Marylander, a lieutenant employed by Gen. Winder to guard the prisoners (the generals and other high Yankee officers), came to me to-day, with a friend who had just arrived from Baltimore, and demanded passports to visit Drewry's Bluff, for the purpose of inspecting the defenses. I refused, fearing he might (I did not like his face) have been corrupted by his prisoners. He said very significantly that he would go in spite of me. This I reported to the Assistant Adjutant-General, and also wrote a note to Gen. Wise, to examine him closely if he came within his lines.

JULY 22D.—To-day Gen. Winder came into my office in a passion with a passport in his hand which I had given, a week before, to Mr. Collier, of Petersburg, on the order of the Assistant Secretary of War—threatening me with vengeance and the terrors of Castle Godwin, his Bastile! if I granted any more passports to Petersburg where he was military commander, that city being likewise under martial law. I simply uttered a defiance, and he departed, boiling over with rage.

JULY 23D.—To-day I received the following note from the Secretary:

"JULY 23D, 1862.

"J. B. JONES, ESQ.

"SIR:—You will not issue passports except to persons going to the camps near Richmond.

"Passports elsewhere will be granted by Brig.-Gen. Winder.

"Respectfully,

"GEO. W. RANDOLPH,

"*Secretary of War.*"

JULY 24TH.—Already the flood-gates of treasonable intelligence flowing North seem to be thrown wide open. The Baltimore papers contain a vast amount of information concerning our condition, movements in progress, and projected enterprises. And to crown all, these rascals publish in the same papers *the passports given them by Gen. Winder.* I doubt not they are sold by the detectives, Winder being ignorant.

JULY 25TH.—More Northern papers received to-day, containing news from the South. Most fortunately, they can know nothing reliable of what is passing within Gen. Lee's lines. The responsibility of keeping his gates closed against spies rests in a great measure on myself, and I endeavor to keep even our own people in profound ignorance of what transpires there.

JULY 26TH.—There is a pause in the depreciation of C. S. securities.

JULY 27TH.—Gen. Lovell, it is said, will be tried by a court-martial. The same has been said of Generals Magruder and Huger. But I doubt it.

JULY 28TH.—The Examining Board of Surgeons, established by the Secretary of War, has been abolished by order of Gen. Lee. It was the only idea of the Secretary yet developed, excepting the "handing over" of the "whole business of passports to Gen. Winder."

JULY 29TH.—Pope's army, greatly reinforced, are committing shocking devastations in Culpepper and Orange Counties. His brutal orders, and his bragging proclamations, have wrought our men to such a pitch of exasperation that, when the day of battle comes, there will be, must be terrible slaughter.

JULY 30TH.—Both Gen. Jackson and Gen. Stuart were in the department to-day. Their commands have preceded them, and must be near Orange C. H. by this time. These war-worn heroes (neither of them over forty years of age) attracted much attention. Everybody wished to see them; and if they had lingered a few minutes longer in the hall, a crowd would have collected, cheering to the echo. This they avoided, transacting their business in the shortest possible space of time, and then escaping observation. They have yet much work to do.

JULY 31ST.—Gen. Breckinridge has beaten the Yankees at Baton Rouge, but without result, as we have no co-operating fleet.

CHAPTER XVII.

Vicksburg shelled.—Lee looks toward Washington.—Much manœuvring in Orange County.—A brigade of the enemy annihilated.—McClellan flies to Washington.—Cretans.—Lee has a mighty army.—Missouri risings.—Pope's coat and papers captured.—Cut up at Manassas.—Clothing captured of the enemy.

AUGUST 1ST.—Vicksburg has triumphantly withstood the shelling of the enemy's fleet of gun-boats. This proves that New Orleans might have been successfully defended, and could have been held to this day by Gen. Lovell. So, West Point is not always the best criterion of one's fitness to command.

AUGUST 2D.—The Adjutant-General, "by order" (I suppose of the President), is annulling, one after another, all Gen. Winder's despotic orders.

AUGUST 3D.—There is a rumor that McClellan is "stealing away" from his new base! and Burnside has gone up the Rappahannock to co-operate with Pope in his "march to Richmond."

AUGUST 4TH.—Lee is making herculean efforts for an "on to Washington," while the enemy think he merely designs a defense of Richmond. Troops are on the move, all the way from Florida to Gordonsville.

AUGUST 5TH.—The enemy have postponed drafting, that compulsory mode of getting men being unpopular, *until after the October elections.* I hope Lee will make the most of his time, and annihilate their drilled and seasoned troops. He can put more *fighting* men in Virginia than the enemy, during the next two months. "Now's the day, and now's the hour!"

AUGUST 6TH.—Jackson is making preparations to fight. I know the symptoms. He has made Pope believe he's afraid of him.

AUGUST 7TH.—Much incomprehensible manœuvring is going on in Orange County.

AUGUST 8TH.—We hear of skirmishing in Orange County, and the enemy seem as familiar with the paths and fords as our own people; hence some surprises, attempted by our cavalry, have failed.

AUGUST 9TH.—Jackson and Ewell are waiting and watching. Pope will expose himself soon.

AUGUST 10TH.—Jackson struck Pope yesterday! It was a terrible blow, for the numbers engaged. Several thousand of the enemy were killed, wounded, and taken prisoners. Among the latter is Gen. Prince, who arrived in this city this morning. He affected to be ignorant of Pope's brutal orders, and of the President's retaliatory order concerning the commissioned officers of Pope's army taken in battle. When Prince was informed that he and the fifty or sixty others taken with him were not to be treated as prisoners of war, but as *felons,* he vented his execrations upon Pope. They were sent into close confinement.

AUGUST 11TH.—Our killed, wounded, and captured did not amount to more than 600. We might have captured a whole brigade at one time during the battle, but *did not.* They charged our batteries, not perceiving a brigade of our own lying concealed just in the rear of the guns: so, when they advanced, shouting, to within *thirty yards* of our troops, they rose and "let them have it." Nine-tenths of the enemy fell, and the rest were soon dispatched, before they could get away. One of their dying officers said they would have surrendered to us, if we had demanded it. He was reminded of Pope's beastly orders, and died with a horrible groan.

AUGUST 12TH.—Pope claims a victory! So did McClellan. But truth will rise, in spite of everything. I will not quote Bryant literally, because he is an enemy in this war, and falsifies his own precepts.

AUGUST 13TH.—McClellan is gone, bag and baggage, abandoning his "*base;*" to attain which, he said he had instituted his magnificent strategic movements, resulting in an unmolested retreat from the Peninsula and flight to Washington, for the defense of his own capital. So the truth they crushed to earth on the Chickahominy has risen again, and the Yankees, like the Cretans, are to be known henceforth as a nation of liars.

AUGUST 14TH.—Lee has gone up the country to command in person. Now let Lincoln beware, for there *is* danger. A mighty army, such as Napoleon himself would have been proud to command, is approaching his capital. This is the triumph Lee has been providing for, while the nations of the earth are hesitating whether or not to recognize our independence.

AUGUST 15TH.—Moved my office to an upper story of the Bank of Virginia, where the army intelligence office is located—an office that keeps a list of the sick and wounded.

AUGUST 16TH.—We have intelligence from the West of a simultaneous advance of several of our columns. This is the work of Lee. May God grant that our blows be speedy and effectual in hurling back the invader from our soil!

AUGUST 17TH.—We have also news from Missouri of indications of an uprising which will certainly clear the State of the few Federal troops remaining there. The *draft* will accelerate the movement. And then if we get Kentucky, as I think we must, we shall add a hundred thousand to our army!

AUGUST 18TH.—From Texas, West Louisiana, and Arkansas, we shall soon have tidings. The clans are gathering, and 20,000 more, half mounted on hardy horses, will soon be marching for the *prairie* country of the enemy. Glorious Lee! and glorious Jackson! They are destined to roll the dark clouds away from the horizon.

AUGUST 19TH.—Day and *night* our troops are marching; they are now *beyond* the right wing of Pope, and will soon be accumulated there in such numbers as to defy the combined forces of Pope, Burnside, and McClellan!

AUGUST 20TH.—We have now a solution of the secret of Pope's familiarity with the country. *His guide and pilot is the identical Robt. Stewart who was sent here to the Provost Marshal—a prisoner.* How did he get out? They say money did it.

AUGUST 21ST.—Some apprehensions are felt by a few for the safety of this city, as it is supposed that *all* the troops have been withdrawn. This is not so, however. From ten to fifteen *thousand* men could be concentrated here in twenty-four hours. Richmond is not in half the danger that Washington is.

AUGUST 22D.—Saw Vice-President Stephens to-day, as cordial and enthusiastic as ever.

AUGUST 23D.—Members of Congress are coming to my office every day, getting passports for their constituents. Those I have seen (Senator Brown, of Mississippi, among the rest) express a purpose not to renew the act, to expire on the 18th September, authorizing martial law.

AUGUST 24TH.—In both Houses of Congress they are thundering away at Gen. Winder's Provost Marshal and his Plug Ugly alien policemen. Senator Brown has been very bitter against them.

AUGUST 25TH.—Mr. Russell has reported a bill which would give us martial law in such a modified form as to extract its venom.

AUGUST 26TH.—Mr. Russell's bill will not pass. The machinery of legislation works too slowly.

Fredericksburg has been evacuated by the enemy! It is said the Jews rushed in and bought boots for $7.00, which they now demand $25.00 for, and so with various other articles of merchandise. They are now investing money in real estate for the first time, which is evidence that they have no faith in the ultimate redemption of Confederate money.

AUGUST 27TH.—Huzza for Gen. Stuart! He has made another *circumvention* of the enemy, getting completely in Pope's rear, and destroying many millions worth of stores, etc.

AUGUST 28TH.—Pope's coat was captured, and all his papers. The braggart is near his end.

AUGUST 29TH.—Bloody fighting is going on at Manassas. All the news is good for us. It appears that Pope, in his consummate egotism, refused to believe that he had been outwitted, and "pitched into" our corps and divisions, believing them to be merely brigades and regiments. He has been terribly cut up.

August 30th.—Banks, by the order of Pope, has burnt 400 Yankee cars loaded with quartermaster's and commissary stores. But our soldiers have fared sumptuously on the enemy's provisions, and captured clothing enough for half the army.

August 31st.—Fighting every day at Manassas.

CHAPTER XVIII.

Lee announces a victory.—Crosses the Potomac.—Battle of Sharpsburg.—McClellan pauses at the Potomac.—Lee moves mysteriously.—The campaign a doubtful one in its material results.—Horrible scene near Washington.—Conscription enlarged.—Heavy loss at Sharpsburg.—10,000 in the hospitals here.

September 1st.—Official dispatches from Lee, announcing a "signal victory," by the blessing of God, "over the combined forces of the enemy." That is glory enough for a week. When *Lee* says "signal victory," we know exactly what it means, and we breathe freely. *Our* generals *never* modify their reports of victories. They see and know the extent of what has been done before they speak of it, and they never mislead by exaggerated accounts of successes.

September 2d.—Winchester is evacuated! The enemy fled, and left enough ordnance stores for a campaign! It was one of their principal depots.

September 3d.—We lament the fall of *Ewell*—not killed, but his leg has been amputated. The enemy themselves report the loss, in killed and wounded, of *eight generals!* And Lee says, up to the time of writing, he had paroled 7000 prisoners, taken 10,000 stand of small arms, 50 odd cannon, and immense stores!

September 4th.—The enemy's loss in the series of battles, in killed, wounded, and prisoners, is estimated at 30,000. Where is the braggart Pope now? Disgraced eternally, deprived of his command by his own government, and sent to Minnesota to fight the Indians! Savage in his nature, he is only fit to fight with savages!

SEPTEMBER 5TH—Our army knows no rest. But I fear this incessant marching and fighting may prove too much for many of the tender boys.

SEPTEMBER 6TH.—We have authentic accounts of our army crossing the Potomac without opposition.

SEPTEMBER 7TH.—We see by the Northern papers that Pope claimed a great victory over Lee and Jackson! It was too much even for the lying editors themselves! The Federal army being hurled back on the Potomac, and then compelled to cross it, it was too transparently ridiculous for the press to contend for the victory. And now they confess to a series of defeats from the 26th June to the culminating calamity of the 30th August. They acknowledge they have been beaten—badly beaten—*but they will not admit that our army has crossed into Maryland.* Well, Lee's dispatch to the President is dated "Headquarters, Frederick City." We believe him.

SEPTEMBER 8TH.—But the Marylanders have not risen *yet.* Some of our divisions have touched the soil of *Pennsylvania.* And I believe the whole Yankee host would leave Washington, escaping by the Potomac, if it were not for the traitors here, who go to Norfolk and Baltimore by flag of truce, and inform the Lincoln Government (for pay) that we have no troops here—none between this and Manassas, none all the way to Lee, while thousands in the army are prostrated with physical exhaustion.

SEPTEMBER 9TH.—Lord, what a scare they are having in the North! They are calling everybody to arms for the defense of *Philadelphia,* and they are removing specie, arms, etc., from Harrisburg and all the intervening towns. This is the chalice so long held by them to our lips.

SEPTEMBER 10TH.—On the very day that Lee gained the signal victory at Manassas, Kirby Smith gained one at Richmond, Kentucky, capturing thousands of prisoners. This is not chance—it is God, to whom all the glory is due.

SEPTEMBER 11TH—And Cincinnati is trembling to its center. That abolition city, half foreign and half American, is listening for the thunder of our avenging guns.

SEPTEMBER 12TH.—The ranks of the enemy are broken everywhere in the West. Buell is flying to Nashville as a city of refuge, but we have invincible columns interposed between him and his country.

SEPTEMBER 13TH.—Buell has impressed 10,000 slaves, and is fortifying Nashville.

SEPTEMBER 14TH.—Our army has entered the City of Lexington, and the population hail our brave soldiers as deliverers. Three regiments were organized there in twenty-four hours, and thirty thousand recruits, it is thought, will flock to our standard in Kentucky.

SEPTEMBER 15TH.—Our flag floats over the Capitol at Frankfort! And Gen. Marshall, lately the exile and fugitive, is encamped with his men on his own farm, near Paris.

SEPTEMBER 16TH.—Intelligence from Missouri states that the Union militia have rallied on the side of the South.

SEPTEMBER 17TH.—Everything seems to indicate the "breaking up" of the armies of our enemies, as if our prayers had been answered, and the hosts of Lincoln were really to be "brought to confusion."

SEPTEMBER 18th.—To-day, in response to the President's proclamation, we give thanks to Almighty God for the victories HE has blessed us with.

SEPTEMBER 19TH.—And God has blessed us even more abundantly than we supposed. The rumor that our invincible Stonewall Jackson had been sent by Lee to Harper's Ferry, and had taken it, is TRUE. Nearly 12,000 men surrendered there on the 15th inst., after the loss of two or three hundred on their side, and only *three* killed and a few wounded on ours. We got 90 guns, 15,000 stand of small arms, 18,000 fine horses, 200 wagons, and stores of various kinds, worth millions.

SEPTEMBER 20TH.—While Jackson was doing his work, McClellan, who has been restored to command, marched at the head of 100,000 men to the rescue of Harper's Ferry, but D. P. Hill, with his single division, kept him at bay for many hours, until Longstreet came to his assistance, and night fell upon the scene.

But Lee soon concentrated his weary columns at Sharpsburg, near Shepherdstown, and on the 17th inst. gave battle. We got the first news of this battle from a Northern paper—the *Philadelphia Inquirer*—which claimed a great victory, having killed and taken 40,000 of our men, made Jackson prisoner, and wounded Longstreet! But the truth is, we lost 5000 and the enemy 20,000. At the next dawn Lee opened fire again—but, lo! the enemy had fled!

SEPTEMBER 21ST.—We have one day of gloom. It is said that our army has retreated back into Virginia.

SEPTEMBER 22D.—There are rumors that only Jackson's corps recrossed the Potomac to look after a column of the enemy sent to recapture Harper's Ferry and take Winchester, our grand depot.

SEPTEMBER 23D.—Jackson, the ubiquitous and invincible, fell upon Burnside's division and annihilated it. This intelligence has been received by the President.

We have, also, news from Kentucky. It comes this time in the *New York Herald*, and is true, as far as it goes. A portion of Buell's army, escaping from Nashville, marched to Mumfordsville, where Bragg cut them to pieces, taking 5000 prisoners! It cannot be possible that this is more than half the truth.

The newsboys are selling extras in the streets containing these glorious accounts.

SEPTEMBER 24TH.—The papers this morning are still in doubt whether Lee has returned to the Virginia side of the Potomac, or remains in Maryland. My theory is that he is *perdue* for the present, hoping all the enemy's forces will enter Virginia, from Washington—when he will pounce upon that city and cut off their retreat.

The Northern papers contain intimations of the existence of a conspiracy to *dethrone* Lincoln, and put a military Dictator at the head of the government. Gen. Fremont is named as the man. It is alleged that this movement is to be made by the Abolitionists, as if Lincoln were not sufficiently radical for them!

A call has been made by Congress for explanations of the arrest of a citizen of Virginia, by Gen. Winder, for procuring a substitute for a relative. Gen. W., supposing his powers ample, under martial law, had forbidden agents to procure substitutes. This was in contravention of an act of Congress, legalizing substitutes. If Winder be sustained, it is said we shall have inaugurated a military despotism.

I have just seen persons from the Eastern Shore of Virginia.

They say my farm there has not been disturbed* by the enemy. I think it probable they knew nothing about its ownership, or it would have been devastated. My agent sent me a little money, part of the rent of year before last. My tenant is getting rich. After peace I shall reside there myself. How I long for the independent life of a farmer!

Wood is selling at $16 per cord, and coal at $9 per load. How can we live here, unless our salaries are increased? The matter is under consideration by Congress, and we *hope* for favorable action.

Col. Bledsoe has resigned and gone back to his school at Charlottesville.

SEPTEMBER 25TH.—Blankets, that used to sell for $6, are now $25 per pair; and sheets are selling for $15 per pair, which might have been had a year ago for $4. Common 4-4 bleached cotton shirting is selling at $1 a yard.

Gen. Lee's locality and operations, since the battle of Sharpsburg or Shepherdstown, are still enveloped in mystery.

About one hundred of the commissioned officers of Pope's army, taken prisoners by Jackson, and confined as felons in our prisons, in conformity to the President's retaliatory order, were yesterday released on parole, in consequence of satisfactory communications from the United States Government, disavowing Pope's orders, I presume, and stating officially the fact that Pope himself has been relieved from command.

We have taken, and paroled, within the last twelve or fifteen weeks, no less than *forty odd thousand prisoners!* The United States must *owe* us some thirty thousand men. This does not look like progress in the work of subjugation.

Horrible! I have seen men just from Manassas, and the battle-field of the 30th August, where, they assure me, hundreds of dead Yankees still lie unburied! They are swollen "as large as cows," say they, "and are as black as crows." No one can now undertake to bury them. When the wind blows from that direction, it is said the scent of carrion is distinctly perceptible at the *White*

---

* It is held by the government *now*, January, 1866, and my family are homeless and destitute. *Onancock, Accomac County, Va.*—J. B. J.

House in Washington. It is said the enemy are evacuating Alexandria. I do not believe this.

A gentleman (Georgian) to whom I gave a passport to visit the army, taking two substitutes, over forty-five years of age, in place of two sick young men in the hospitals, informs me that he got upon the ground just before the great battle at Sharpsburg commenced. The substitutes were mustered in, and in less than an hour after their arrival, one of them was shot through the hat and hair, but his head was untouched. He says they fought as well as veterans.

SEPTEMBER 26TH.—The press here have no knowledge of the present locality of Gen. Lee and his army. But a letter was received from Gen. L. at the department yesterday, dated on this side of the Potomac, about eighteen miles above Harper's Ferry.

It is stated that several hundred prisoners, taken at Sharpsburg, are paroled prisoners captured at Harper's Ferry. If this be so (and it is said they will be here to-night), I think it probable an example will be made of them. This unpleasant duty may not be avoided by our government.

After losing in killed and wounded, in the battle of Sharpsburg, ten generals, and perhaps twenty thousand men, we hear no more of the advance of the enemy; and Lee seems to be lying *perdue*, giving them an opportunity to ruminate on the difficulties and dangers of "subjugation."

I pray we may soon conquer a peace with the North; but then I fear we shall have trouble among ourselves. Certainly there is danger, after the war, that Virginia, and, perhaps, a sufficient number of the States to form a new constitution, will meet in convention and form a new government.

Gen. Stark, of Mississippi, who fell at Sharpsburg, was an acquaintance of mine. His daughters were educated with mine at St. Mary's Hall, Burlington, N. J.—and were, indeed, under my care. Orphans now!

SEPTEMBER 27TH.—The papers this morning contain accounts of the landing of Yankees at White House, York River; and of reinforcements at Williamsburg and Suffolk. They might attempt to take Richmond, while Lee's army is away; for they know we have no large body of troops here.

A battery passed through the city this morning early, at *double-quick*, going eastward.

Yesterday Congress passed an act, supplemental and amendatory to the Conscription Act of last April, authorizing the President to call into the military service all residents between the ages of thirty-five and forty-five. The first act included only those between the ages of eighteen and thirty-five.

By the 1st of January there will be $300,000,000 Treasury notes in circulation. It is proposed in Congress to make a forced loan of one-fifth of the incomes of the people.

It is said Lincoln has issued a proclamation declaring the slaves of Rebels free, on and after the 1st of January, 1863. This will only intensify the war, and add largely to our numbers in the field.

A letter was received from General Lee to-day, dated at Martinsburg, giving a sad account of the army. It seems that without some additional power given the President by Congress to enforce discipline, he fears the army will melt away. He suggests that incompetent officers be reduced to the ranks, and that more stringent regulations be adopted. He is in no condition to advance now, since so many thousands of his men are permitted to wander away. We shall be afflicted with fresh invasions—and that, if nothing else, may cause the stragglers to return.

The substance of Lee's letter has been communicated to Congress, and that body, I understand, has postponed the day of adjournment until the 6th October.

In future times, I wonder if it will be said that we had great men in this Congress? Whatever may be *said*, the truth is, there are not a dozen with any pretensions to statesmanship.

SEPTEMBER 29TH.—We have Lincoln's proclamation, freeing all the slaves from and after the 1st January next. And another, declaring martial law throughout the United States! Let the Yankees ruminate on that! Now for a *fresh* gathering of our clans for another harvest of blood.

On Saturday the following resolutions were reported by Mr. Semmes, from the Committee of the Judiciary, in the Senate:

"1st. That no officer of the Confederate Government is by law empowered to vest Provost Marshals with any authority whatever over citizens of the Confederate States not belonging to the land and naval forces thereof, or with general police powers and duties for the preservation of the peace and good order of any city, town, or municipal district in any State of this Confederacy, and any such exercise of authority is illegal and void.

"2d. That no officer of the Confederate Government has constitutional or other lawful authority to limit or restrict, or in any manner to control, the exercise of the jurisdiction of the civil judicial tribunals of the States of this Confederacy, vested in them by the Constitution and laws of the States respectively; and all orders of any such officer tending to restrict or control or interfere with the full and normal exercise of the jurisdiction of such civil judicial tribunals are illegal and void."

We shall see what further action will follow. This is in marked contrast to the despotic rule in the Yankee nation. Nevertheless, the Provost Marshal here keeps his establishment in full blast. He was appointed by Gen. Winder, of Maryland, who has been temporarily subordinated by Major-Gen. Smith, of New York.

Since Gen. Smith has been in command, the enemy has made raids to Leesburg, Manassas, and even Warrenton, capturing and paroling our sick and wounded men. Who is responsible?

Accounts from Nashville state that our cavalry is beleaguering that city, and that both the United States forces there, and the inhabitants of the town, are reduced nearly to starvation.

Buell, it is said, has reached Louisville. We hope to hear soon of active operations in Kentucky. Bragg, and Smith, and Price, and Marshall are there with abundant forces to be striking heavy blows.

Beauregard is assigned to the defense of South Carolina and Georgia.

Harper's Ferry is again occupied by the enemy—but we have removed everything captured there. The Northern papers now admit that the sanguinary battle of Sharpsburg was without result.

I sent my wife money to-day, and urged her to return to Richmond as soon as possible, as the enemy may cut the communications—being within forty miles of the railroad. How I should like to think they were cut to pieces! Then they would let us alone.

Hitherto 100,000 sick and wounded patients have been admitted into the army hospitals of this city. Of these, about 10,000 have been furloughed, 3000 discharged from the service, and only 7600 have died. At present there are 10,000 in the hospitals. There is not so much sickness this year as there was last, nor is it near so fatal.

Many of the Northern papers seem to dissent from the policy of Lincoln's proclamation, and *hope* that evil consequences may not grow out of it. But how can it be possible for the people of the North to submit to martial law? The government which directs and enforces so obnoxious a tyranny cannot be sure of its stability. And when the next army of invasion marches southward, it will be likely to have enemies in its rear as well as in its front. The *Tribune* exclaims "God bless Abraham Lincoln." Others, even in the North, will pray for "God to —— him!"

SEPTEMBER 30TH.—Lincoln's proclamation was the subject of discussion in the Senate yesterday. Some of the gravest of our senators favor the raising of the *black flag*, asking and giving no quarter hereafter.

The yellow fever is raging at Wilmington, North Carolina.

The President, in response to a resolution of inquiry concerning Hyde, the agent who procured a substitute and was arrested for it, sent Congress a letter from the Secretary of War, stating that the action of Gen. Winder had not been approved, and that Mr. Hyde had been discharged. The Secretary closes his letter with a *sarcasm*, which, I think, is not his own composition. He asks, as martial law is still existing, though the writ of *habeas corpus* is not suspended, for instructions as to the power of the military commander, Winder, to *suppress tippling shops!* Several members declared that martial law existed in this city without any constitutional warrant. There is much bad feeling between many members and the Executive.

No fighting has occurred on the Peninsula, and I believe Gen. Wise has returned with his forces to Chaffin's Bluff.

CHAPTER XIX.

McClellan has crossed the Potomac.—Another battle anticipated.—I am assured here that Lee had but 40,000 men engaged at Sharpsburg.—He has more now, as he is defending Virginia.—Radicals of the North want McClellan removed.—Our President has never taken the field.—Lee makes demonstrations against McClellan.—A Jew store robbed last night.—We have 40,000 prisoners excess over the enemy.—My family arrived from Raleigh.—My wife's substitute for coffee.—Foul passports.—My friend Brooks dines and wines with members of Congress.—The Herald and Tribune tempt us to return to the Union —Lee writes, no immediate advance of McClellan.—Still a rumor of Bragg's victory in Kentucky.—Enemy getting large reinforcements.—Diabolical order of Governor Baylor.—Secretary's estimate of conscripts and all others, 500,000.—Bragg retreating from Kentucky.—Bickering between Bragg and Beauregard.—Lee wants Confederate notes made a legal tender.—There will be no second Washington.

OCTOBER 1ST.—They are still striking at martial law in the Senate, as administered by Gen. Winder. A communication from the Secretary of War admits that Gen. W. was authorized to suppress substitute agencies—"but this did not justify impressment and confiscation." It appears that Gen Winder ordered the agents to be impressed into the service, and the money paid for substitutes to be confiscated! Notwithstanding his blundering ignorance is disavowed, he is still retained in command.

The enemy are at Warrenton; and McClellan's army has crossed the Upper Potomac. Another battle is imminent—and fearful will be the slaughter this time. Lee had but little if any more than 40,000 in the battle of Sharpsburg; the Northern papers said McClellan had 200,000! a fearful odds. But Lee now has 70,000—and, besides, he will be defending Virginia. McClellan, with his immense army, *must* advance, or else relinquish command. The Abolitionists of the North have never liked him, and they wield the power at present. A defeat of Lee near Winchester would produce consternation here.

There are, as usual, thousands of able-bodied men still in our streets. It is probable every man, able to march, will be required on the field of battle. If we can get out *all*, we shall certainly gain the day, and establish our independence.

How shall we subsist this winter? There is not a supply of wood or coal in the city—and it is said there are not adequate means of transporting it hither. Flour at $16 per barrel, and bacon at 75 cts. per pound, threaten a famine. And yet there are no beggars in the streets. We must get a million of men in arms and drive the invader from our soil. We are capable of it, and we must do it. Better die in battle than die of starvation produced by the enemy.

The newspapers are printed on half sheets—and I think the publishers make money; the extras (published almost every day) are sold to the newsboys for ten cents, and often sold by them for twenty-five cents. These are mere slips of paper, seldom containing more than a column—which is reproduced in the next issue. The *matter* of the extras is mostly made up from the Northern papers, brought hither by persons running the blockade. The supply is pretty regular, and dates are rarely more than three or four days behind the time of reception. We often get the first accounts of battles at a distance in this way, as our generals and our government are famed for a prudential reticence. When the Northern papers simply say they have gained a victory, we rejoice, knowing their Cretan habits. The other day they announced, for European credulity, the capture and killing of 40,000 of our men: this staggered us; but it turned out that they did capture 700 of our stragglers and 2000 wounded men in field hospitals. *Now* they are under the necessity of admitting the truth. Truth, like honesty, is always the best policy.

OCTOBER 2D.—News from the North indicate that in Europe all expectation of a restoration of the Union is at an end; and the probability is that we shall soon be recognized, to be followed, possibly, by intervention. Nevertheless, we must rely upon our own strong arms, and the favor of God. It is said, however, an iron steamer is being openly constructed in the Mersey (Liverpool), for the avowed purpose of opening the blockade of Charleston harbor.

Yesterday in both Houses of Congress resolutions were introduced for the purpose of retaliating upon the North the barbarities contemplated in Lincoln's Emancipation Proclamation.

The Abolitionists of the North want McClellan removed—I hope they may have their will. The reason assigned by his friends for his not advancing farther into Virginia, is that he has not troops enough, and the Secretary of War has them not to send him. I hope this may be so. Still, I think he must fight soon if he remains near Martinsburg.

The yellow fever is worse at Wilmington. I trust it will not make its appearance here.

A resolution was adopted yesterday in the Senate, to the effect that martial law does not apply to civilians. But it *has* been applied to them here, and both Gen. Winder and his Provost Marshal threatened to apply it to me.

Among the few measures that may be attributed to the present Secretary of War, is the introduction of the telegraph wires into his office. It may possibly be the idea of another; but it is not exactly original; and it has not been productive of good. It has now been in operation several weeks, all the way to Warrenton; and yet a few days ago the enemy's cavalry found that section of country undefended, and took Warrenton itself, capturing in that vicinity some 2000 wounded Confederates, in spite of the Secretary's expensive vigilance. Could a Yankee have been the inventor of the Secretary's plaything? One amused himself telegraphing the Secretary from Warrenton, that all was quiet there; *and that the Yankees had not made their appearance in that neighborhood, as had been rumored!* If we had imbeciles in the field, our subjugation would be only pastime for the enemy. It is well, perhaps, that Gen. Lee has razeed the department down to a second-class bureau, of which the President himself is the chief.

I see by a correspondence of the British diplomatic agents, that their government have decided no reclamation can be made on us for burning cotton and tobacco belonging to British subjects, where there is danger that they may fall into the hands of the enemy. Thus the British government do not even claim to have their subjects in the South favored above the Southern people. But Mr. Benjamin is more liberal, and he directed the Provost Marshal to save the tobacco bought on foreign account. So far, however, *the grand speculation has failed.*

OCTOBER 3D.—Gen. Wise was countermanded in his march against Williamsburg, by Major-Gen. Gustavus W. Smith. He had 2700 men, the enemy 1500, and he would have captured and slain them all. Gen. Wise was the trusted and revered Governor of Virginia, while Smith was the Street Commissioner in New York.

A strong letter from Vice-President Stephens is published to-day, in which it is successfully maintained that no power exists, derived either from the Constitution or acts of Congress, for the declaration of martial law. He says all punishments inflicted by military governors on civilians are clearly illegal.

There is a rumor that we have Louisville, but it does not seem to be authentic. We have nothing from Lee, and know not exactly where McClellan is.

Many people thought the President himself would take the field. I doubt not he would have done so if the Provisional Government had continued in existence until independence was achieved.

OCTOBER 4TH.—A splendid aurora borealis last night.

Yesterday, most of the delegation in Congress from Kentucky and Tennessee petitioned the President to order Gen. Breckinridge, at Knoxville, to march to the relief of Nashville, and expel the enemy, without waiting for orders from Gen. Bragg, now in Kentucky. The President considers this an extraordinary request, and will not, I suppose, grant it.

It is said Gen. Lee is advancing against Gen. McClellan at Martinsburg. If Lee attacks him, and beats him, he will probably be ruined, for the Potomac will be in his rear.

The enemy's paper, printed at Nashville, thinks Bragg has taken Louisville. I hope so. I think we shall get Nashville soon.

Gen. Butler, the Yankee commander in New Orleans, has issued an order to all the inhabitants of that city, sympathizing with the Southern Confederacy, to present themselves immediately, and take the oath of allegiance, when they will be recommended for *pardon*. If they do not comply with the order, they will be arrested by his police, cast into prison, and their property confiscated. These are the orders which rally our men and make them fight like heroes. How many Yankees will bleed and die in consequence of this order? And Lincoln's Emancipation Proclamation will seal the doom of one hundred thousand of his own people!

A letter from Gen. Lee, dated October 1st, says that McClellan has not crossed the Potomac. Some of his scouts have been at Martinsburg, or in its vicinity. It is not to be supposed that Lee can be *amused* by McClellan, while a force of any magnitude is sent against Richmond. Some fear this, but I don't.

OCTOBER 6TH, MONDAY.—A Jew store, in Main Street, was robbed of $8000 worth of goods on Saturday night. They were carted away. This is significant. The prejudice is very strong against the extortionists, and I apprehend there will be many scenes of violence this winter. And our own people, who ask four prices for wood and coal, may contribute to produce a new Reign of Terror. The supplies necessary for existence should not be withheld from a suffering people. It is dangerous.

There is great diversity of opinion yet as to the locality of McClellan's army and Lee's intentions.

A dispatch from Gen. Van Dorn, in West Tennessee, indicates that we are *gaining* a victory over Rosecrans. The battle was in *progress*, not completed.

OCTOBER 7TH.—Nothing further has been heard from Corinth. A great battle is looked for in Kentucky. All is quiet in Northern Virginia.

Some 2500 Confederate prisoners arrived from the North last evening. They are on parole, and will doubtless be exchanged soon, as we have taken at least 40,000 more of the enemy's men than they have captured of ours.

Yesterday, Congress, which has prolonged the session until the 13th instant, passed a bill increasing the pay of soldiers four dollars per month. I hope they will increase *our* pay before they adjourn. Congress also, yesterday, voted down the proposition of a *forced loan* of one-fifth of all incomes. But the Committee of Ways and Means are instrutcted to bring forward another bill.

This evening Custis and I expect the arrival of my family from Raleigh, N. C. We have procured for them one pound of sugar, 80 cents; one quart of milk, 25 cents; one pound of sausage-meat, 37½ cents; four loaves of bread, as large as my fist, 20 cents each; and we have a little coffee, which is selling at $2.50 per pound. In the morning, some one must go to market, else there will be short-commons. Washing is $2.50 per dozen pieces. Common soap is worth 75 cents per pound.

OCTOBER 8TH.—At last we have definite accounts of the battle of Corinth, on Friday, Saturday, and Sunday last. We have been defeated, and fearful has been the slaughter on both sides. The enemy had overwhelming numbers. We have no particulars, further than that our army retreated This is bad for Van Dorn and Price.

My family arrived last night, well, and pleased with the cottage, which they call Robin's Nest. But we were saddened by the loss of a trunk—the most valuable one—containing some heavy spoons, forks, and other plate, saved from the wreck at Burlington; my wife's velvet cloak, satin dress (bought in Paris), my daughter's gold watch, and many other things of value. Twelve trunks, the right number, were delivered; but one did not belong to us.

OCTOBER 9TH.—Early this morning I was at the depot. The superintendent suggested that I should send some one to Weldon in search of the trunk. He proffered to pass him free. This was kind; but I desired first to look among the baggage at the depot, and the baggage-master was called in. Only two were unclaimed last night; but he said a gentleman had been there early in the morning looking for his trunk, who stated that by some mistake he had got the *wrong* one last night. He said he stopped at the Exchange, and I repaired thither without delay, where I found my trunk, to the mutual joy of the traveler and myself. It was sent to the cottage, and the stranger's taken to the hotel. Had it not been for my lucky discovery, we should have had no spoons, forks, etc.

My wife has obviated one of the difficulties of the blockade, by a substitute for coffee, which I like very well. It is simply *corn meal, toasted like coffee*, and served in the same manner. It costs five or six cents per pound—coffee, $2.50.

I heard a foolish North Carolinian abusing the administration to-day. He said, among other things, that the President himself, and his family, had Northern proclivities. That the President's family, when they fled from Richmond, in May, took refuge at St. Mary's Hall, Raleigh, the establishment of the Rev. Dr. Smedes, a Northern man of open and avowed partiality for the Union; and that the Rev. Dr. Mason of the same place, with whom they were in intimate association, was a Northern man, and an open Unionist. That the President's aid, and late Assistant Secretary of State, was an Englishman, imported from the North; Gen. Cooper, the highest in rank of any military officer, was a Northern man; Col. Gorgas, Chief of Ordnance, was also a Northern man; Gen. Lovell, who was in the defeat at Corinth, and who had surrendered New Orleans, was from Pennsylvania; Gen. Smith, in command of Virginia and North Carolina, from New York; and Gen. Winder, commanding this metropolis, a Marylander, and his detectives strangers and aliens, who sold passports to Lincoln's spies for $100 each. He was furious, and swore all the distresses of the people were owing to a Nero-like despotism, originating in the brain of Benjamin, the Jew, whose wife lived in Paris.

The Senate, yesterday, passed the following resolutions, almost unanimously:

1*st. Resolved by the Congress of the Confederate States of America,* That no officer of the Confederate Government is *by law* empowered to vest Provost Marshals with any authority whatever over citizens of the Confederate States not belonging to the land or naval forces thereof or with general police powers and duties for the preservation of the peace and good order of any city, town, or municipal district in any State of this Confederacy, and any such exercise of authority *is illegal and void.*

2*d. Resolved,* That no officer of the Confederate Government has constitutional or other lawful authority to limit or restrict, or in any manner to control the exercise of the jurisdiction of the civil judicial tribunals of the States of this Confederacy, vested in them by the constitutions and laws of the States respectively, and all orders of any such officer, tending to restrict or control or interfere with the full and normal exercise of the jurisdiction of such civil judicial tribunals *are illegal and void.*

3*d. Resolved,* That the military law of the Confederate States is, by the courts and the enactments of Congress, limited to the land and naval forces and the militia when in actual service, and to such other persons as are within the lines of any army, navy, corps, division or brigade of the army of the Confederate States.

Yesterday, the *Dispatch* contained an article, copied from the *Philadelphia Inquirer,* stating that a certain person who had been in prison here, arrested by order of Gen. Winder, for disloyalty, and for attempting to convey information to the enemy, had succeeded in obtaining his release; and, for a *bribe* of $100, a passport to leave the Confederacy had been procured from Gen. Winder's alien detectives. The passport is printed in the Philadelphia paper, and the bearer, the narrative says, has entered the United States service.

This must have been brought to the attention of the President; for a lady, seeking a passport to go to her son, sick and in prison in the North, told me that when she applied to Gen. Winder today, he said *the President had ordered him to issue no more passports*. And subsequently several parties, government agents and others, came to me with orders from the Secretary (which I retain on file), to issue passports for them. I hope this may be the end of Winder's reign.

A letter from Gen. Lee states that, in view of certain movements, he had, without waiting for instructions, delivered the sword, horse, etc. of Gen. Kearney, lately killed, to his wife, who had made application for them. The *movements* referred to we shall know more about in a few days.

Gen. Van Dorn dispatches the department that his army is safe; that he took thirteen guns and 700 prisoners. So it was not so disastrous a defeat. But the idea of charging five times his number!

OCTOBER 10TH.—Mr. Brooks called this morning to get me to draft a passport bill, which he said he would get Congress to pass. I doubt it. I wrote the bill, however. He says fifteen or twenty members of Congress visit his house daily. They dine with him, and drink his old whisky. Mr. B. has a superb mansion on Clay Street, which he bought at a sacrifice. He made his money at trade. In one of the rooms Aaron Burr once dined with Chief Justice Marshall, and Marshall was assailed for it afterward by Mr. Jefferson. It was during Burr's trial, and Marshall was his judge. Mr. Wickham, who was Burr's counsel, then occupied the house, and gave a dinner party. Marshall did not know Burr was to be one of the guests. I got these facts from Mr. Foote, whom I met there the other evening.

A letter from Gen. Bragg to the President, indicates but too clearly that the people of Kentucky hesitate to risk the loss of property by joining us. Only one brigade has been recruited so far. The general says 50,000 more men are requisite. Can he have them? None!

OCTOBER 11TH.—There are rumors of Abolition gun-boats in the York and James Rivers. A battery of long range guns was sent down yesterday.

It is said that an army of raw Abolitionists, under Sigel, has marched from Alexandria toward Culpepper County. If this be so, we shall soon have more fighting, and more running, I hope. Lee keeps his own counsel—*wisely*.

OCTOBER 13TH.—Northern papers, received last night, speak of a battle at Perryville, Kentucky, on the 9th instant, in which the Abolitionists lost, by their own confession, 2000 killed and wounded, which means 10,000. They say Bragg's forces held a *portion* of the field after the battle. If this prove not a glorious victory for our arms, I don't know how to read Abolition journals.

I see that our Congress, late on Saturday night (they adjourn to-day), passed an act increasing the salaries of officers and employees in the departments residing at Richmond. This will make the joint compensation of my son and myself $3000; this is not equal to $2000 a year ago. But Congress failed to make the necessary appropriation. The Secretary might use the contingent fund.

Another act authorizes the President to appoint twenty additional brigadier-generals, and a number of lieutenant-generals.

The *New York Herald*, and even the *Tribune*, are *tempting* us to return to the Union, by promises of *protecting slavery*, and an offer of a convention to alter the Constitution, giving us such guarantees of safety as we may demand. *This is significant.* We understand the sign.

Letters from Gen. Lee do not indicate an immediate purpose to retire from the Potomac; on the contrary, he has ordered Gen. Loring, if practicable, to menace Wheeling and Pennsylvania, and form a junction with him *via* the Monongahela and Upper Potomac. But Loring does not deem it safe to move all his forces (not more than 6000) by that route; he will, however, probably send his cavalry into Pennsylvania.

And Gen. Lee does not want any more raw conscripts. They get sick immediately, and prove a burden instead of a benefit. He desires them to be kept in camps of instruction, until better *seasoned* (a term invented by Gen. Wise) for the field.

Senator Brown, of Mississippi, opposed the bill increasing our salaries, on the ground that letters from himself, indorsed by the President, applying for clerkships for his friends, *remained unanswered.* He did not seem to know that this was exclusively the fault of the head clerk, Mr. Randolph, who has the title of Secretary of War.

And the *Examiner* denounces the bill, because it seems to sanction a depreciation of our currency! What statesmanship! What logic!

OCTOBER 14TH.—Congress adjourned yesterday at five o'clock P.M. I have heard nothing of Mr. Brooks and the Passport Bill I drafted. The truth is that, with few exceptions, the members of this Congress are very weak, and very subservient to the heads of departments.

Congress has given him (the President) power to suspend the writ of *habeas corpus* anywhere, until thirty days after the reassembling of Congress—and they have failed to pass the joint resolution declaring no power exists under the Constitution to institute martial law. They voted it separately, but *flinched* when put to the test to act conjointly; and martial law still exists in this city.

We have Northern accounts of a dash into Pennsylvania by Gen. Stuart and 1500 of his cavalry. He went as far as Chambersburg, which surrendered; and he was gathering horses, etc., for the use of the army, paying for them in Confederate notes. They say he did not disturb any other description of private property without paying for it. I hope he is safely back again by this time. The Northern papers claim a victory in Kentucky—but I shall wait until we hear from Bragg.

Gen. Magruder has been assigned to duty in Texas. What Gen. Johnston is to do, does not yet appear. A great many new assistant adjutants and inspector-generals are to be appointed for the generals, lieutenant-generals, majors, and brigadier-generals, having rank and pay of colonels, majors, captains, and lieutenants of cavalry. Like the Russian, perhaps, we shall have a purely military government; and it may be as good as any other.

Gold, in the North, is selling at 28 per cent. premium; and Exchange on England at $1.40. This is an indication that the Abolitionists are bringing distress upon their own country.

The financial bill did not pass—so there is to be no forced loan. Neither did a bill, making Confederate notes a legal tender—so there will be a still greater depreciation.

Gen. Hardee is a lieutenant-general.

OCTOBER 15TH.—A young man showed me a passport to-day to return to Washington. It appears that Secretary Randolph has adopted another plan, which must be a rare stroke of genius. The printed passport is "by order of the Secretary of War," and is signed by "J. H. Winder, Brig.-Gen." But this is not all: on the back it is "*approved*—by order of Major-Gen. Gustavus W. Smith," and signed by one of Smith's "adjutants." So the command of the Secretary of War is approved by the New Yorker, Smith, after being first manipulated by Winder. It is an improvement, at all events, on the late mode of sending out spies—they cannot get passports for bribes now, without Smith's adjutant knowing something about it. Heretofore the "Plug Uglies" might take the bribe, and by their influence with Gen. Winder, obtain his signature to a blank passport.

The following was received yesterday:

"WINCHESTER, VA., Oct. 14, 1862.

"HON. G. W. RANDOLPH.

"The cavalry expedition to Pennsylvania has returned safe. They passed through Mercersburg, Chambersburg, Emmetsburg, Liberty, New Market, Syattstown, and Burnesville. The expedition crossed the Potomac above Williamsport, and recrossed at White's Ford, making the entire circuit, cutting the enemy's communications, destroying arms, etc., and obtaining many recruits.

"R. E. LEE, General."

Thus, Gen. Stuart has made another circle round the enemy's army; and hitherto, every time he has done so, a grand battle followed. Let McClellan beware!

A letter, just received from Gen. Lee, says there is no apprehension of an immediate advance of McClellan's army. This he has ascertained from his scouts sent out to obtain information. He says the enemy is in no condition to advance. Will they go into winter quarters? Or will Lee beat them up in their quarters?

But the government has desired Lee to fall back from the Potomac; and Lee, knowing best what he should do at present, declines the *honor*. He says he is now subsisting his army on what, if he retreated, would subsist the enemy, as he has but limited means of transportation. He says, moreover, that our cavalry about Culpepper and Manassas (belonging to the command of Gen. Gustavus W. Smith), should be more *active* and *daring* in dashing at the enemy; and then, a few weeks hence, McClellan would go into winter quarters. That would insure the safety of Richmond until spring.

There is a rumor, generally credited, that Bragg has led the enemy, in Kentucky, into an ambuscade, and slaughtered 25,000. A traveler from the West reports having read an account to this effect in the Louisville *Journal*. If the *Journal* really says so—that number won't cover the loss. The Abolitionist journals are incorrigible liars. And, indeed, so are many of those who bring us news from the West.

OCTOBER 16TH.—There is no confirmation of the reported victory in Kentucky.

An Englishman, who has been permitted to go North, publishes there a minute and pretty accurate description of our river defenses.

I have written a leading article for the *Whig* to-morrow, on "Martial Law and Passports." My plan is to organize committees in all the border counties to examine the passports of strangers seeking egress from the country; and to permit loyal citizens, not desiring to pass our borders, or the lines of the armies, to travel without passports. An officer and a squad of soldiers at the depots can decide what soldiers are entitled to pass on the roads.

OCTOBER 17TH.—The article in the *Whig* is backed by one of a similar character in the *Examiner*. We shall see what effect they will have on the policy adopted by the Secretary of War.

Although still unofficial, we have confirmatory accounts of Bragg's victory in Kentucky. The enemy lost, they say, 25,000 men. Western accounts are generally exaggerated.

The President has appointed the following lieutenant-generals: Jackson, Longstreet, (Bishop) Polk, Hardee, Pemberton, Holmes, and Smith (Kirby).

The raid of Stuart into Pennsylvania was a most brilliant affair. He captured and destroyed much public property—respecting that of individuals. The Abolitionists are much mortified, and were greatly frightened. The plan of this expedition was received at the department to-day—just as conceived and prepared by Lee, and it was executed by Stuart in a masterly manner.

Advices from Winchester inform the government that McClellan is receiving large reinforcements. He may be determined to cross the Potomac and offer battle—as nothing less will satisfy the rabid Abolitionists. Gen. Lee is tearing up the rails on the road from Harper's Ferry.

Our improvident soldiers lose a great many muskets. We should not have arms enough on the Potomac, were it not for those captured at Harper's Ferry. An order will be issued, making every man responsible for the safe-keeping of his gun.

OCTOBER 18TH.—Major-Gen. Jones telegraphs from Knoxville, Tenn., that a wounded officer arrived from Kentucky, reports a victory for Bragg, and that he has taken over 10,000 prisoners. We shall soon have positive news.

A letter from Admiral Buchanan states that he has inspected the defenses of Mobile, and finds them satisfactory.

I traversed the markets this morning, and was gratified to find the greatest profusion of all kinds of meats, vegetables, fruits, poultry, butter, eggs, etc. But the prices are enormously high. If the army be kept away, it seems the supply must soon be greater than the demand. Potatoes at $5 per bushel, and a large crop! Half-grown chickens at $1 each! Butter at $1.25 per pound! And other things in the same proportion.

Here is a most startling matter. Gov. Baylor, appointed Governor of Arizona, sent an order some time since to a military commander to assemble the Apaches, under pretense of a treaty—*and when they came, to kill every man of them, and sell their children to pay for the whisky.* This order was sent to the Secretary, who referred it to Gen. Sibley, of that Territory, to ascertain if it were genuine. To-day it came back from Gen. S. indorsed *a true bill*. Now it will go to the President—and we shall see what will follow. He cannot sanction such a perfidious crime. I predict he will make Capt. Josselyn, his former private Secretary, and the present Secretary of the Territory, Governor in place of Baylor.

OCTOBER 20TH.—The news from Kentucky is very vague. It seems there has been a battle, which resulted favorably for us, so far as the casualties are concerned. But then Bragg has fallen back forty miles, and is probably retiring toward Cumberland Gap, that he may not be taken in the rear by the enemy's forces lately at Corinth.

The President intends suspending the Conscription Act in Western Virginia, for the purpose, no doubt, of organizing an army of Partisan Rangers in that direction.

It seems, from recent Northern papers received in this city, that the elections in Pennsylvania, Ohio, and Indiana have gone against the Abolitionists. What then? If the war should be waged by the Democrats for the restoration of the Union, and waged according to the rules of civilized nations, respecting non-combatants, and exempting private property from pillage, it would be a still more formidable war than that now waged against us.

I have just received the following note from the Secretary:

"OCTOBER 17th, 1862.

"MR. J. B. JONES will hereafter refer all applicants for passports to Gen. Smith's Adjutant-General, and grant none from the department.

"GEORGE W. RANDOLPH,
"*Sec. of War.*"

Neither the acting Assistant Secretary, nor Mr. Kean, with his whole alphabet of initials, could be certain whether the order referred merely to applicants to go out of the Confederacy, or all applicants of whatever kind. If the latter, I am *functus officio*, so far as passports are concerned. But Capt. Kean says there is plenty of work for me to do; and I presume I will not be entirely out of employment.

I took a good look at Mr. Randolph to-day. He is thin, frail. His face is pale, and will soon be a mass of wrinkles, although he is not over forty. His eyes are extremely small, blue, and glisten very much.

OCTOBER 21ST.—Still nothing definite from Kentucky, more than the retreat of Bragg. Gen. Loring is here—he would not act upon the suggestions of Lee, and so he is recalled.

The government is uneasy about Richmond. They want a portion of Lee's army sent hither. But Lee responds, that although he is not advised of the condition of things on the south side of James River, yet, if he detaches a portion of his army, he may be too weak to encounter McClellan, if he should advance.

I saw the Secretary again this morning; he wished me to turn over all the passport business to the military. I said I was glad to be rid of that business, and would never touch it again.

OCTOBER 22D.—Back at the department at work, but not much to do yet. The mails are not heavy.

We have Bragg's report of the battle of Perryville. He beat the enemy from his positions, driving him back two miles, when night set in. But finding overwhelming masses accumulating around him, he withdrew in good order to Bryattsville. Thus Kentucky is given up for the present!

McClellan has retired back into Maryland, hoping, I suppose, Lee will follow and fall into his ambuscade.

The President will call out, under the Conscription Act, all between the ages of eighteen and forty. This will furnish, according to the Secretary's estimate, 500,000, after deducting the exempts. A great mistake.

A letter from Gen. Lee indicates that he is in favor of making Treasury notes a legal tender. It was so with Washington concerning Continental money—but Congress pays no attention to the subject. Why does not the President recommend it? It would then pass—for, at present, he is master.

The paper from the Provost Marshal, referred by the latter to the President, came back to-day. The Secretary, in referring it, seems to incline to the opinion that the writ of *habeas corpus* not being suspended, there was no remedy for the many evils the Provost Marshal portrayed. The President, however, did not wholly coincide in that opinion. He says: "The introduction and sale of liquors must be prevented. Call upon the city authorities to withhold licenses, and to abate the evil in the courts, *or else an order will be issued, such as the necessity requires.*"

Judge Campbell, late of the United States Supreme Court, has been appointed Assistant Secretary of War.

OCTOBER 23D.—The Gov. of Florida calls for aid, or he thinks his State will fall.

Albert Pike, writing from Texas, says if the Indian Territory be not attended to "*instantly,*" it will be lost.

Per contra, we have a rumor that Lee is recrossing the Potomac into Maryland.

OCTOBER 24TH.—Bragg is in full retreat, leaving Kentucky, and racing for Chattanooga—the point of interest now. But Beauregard, from whom was taken the command of the Western army, day before yesterday repulsed with slaughter a large detachment of the Yankees that had penetrated to the Charleston and Savannah Railroad. Thus, in spite of the fantastic tricks of small men here, the *popular* general is destined to rise again.

OCTOBER 25TH.—Many severe things are alleged against the President for depriving Beauregard of the command of the Western army. It is alleged that Bragg reported that the enemy would have been annihilated at Shiloh, if Beauregard had fought an hour longer. Now, it appears, that Bragg would have annihilated the enemy at Perryville, if he had fought an hour longer! And just at the moment of his flying out of Kentucky, news comes of Beauregard's victory over the enemy in the South. Nor is this all. The enemy some time since intercepted a letter from Beauregard to Bragg (a copy of which was safely sent to the government here), detailing his plan of the campaign in the West, if he had not been unjustly deprived of the command. But Bragg chose to make a plan of his own, or was directed to disregard Beauregard's advice. No one doubts that Beauregard's plan would have been successful, and would have given us Cincinnati and Louisville; but that of Bragg, as the one sent him by the government, has resulted in the loss of Kentucky, and, perhaps, Tennessee!

Brig.-Gen. Edward Johnson is recommended by Gen. Lee for promotion to major-general, and to be placed in command of the army in Western Virginia.

OCTOBER 27TH.—From information (pretty direct from Washington), I believe it is the purpose of the enemy to make the most strenuous efforts to capture Richmond and Wilmington this fall and winter. It has been communicated to the President that if it takes their last man, and all their means, these cities must fall. Gen. Smith is getting negroes to work on the defenses, and the subsistence officers are ordered to accumulate a vast amount of provisions here.

Letters from Beauregard show that the Commissary-General, because *he* thinks Charleston cannot be defended, opposes the provisioning the forts as the general would have it done! The general demands of the government to know whether he is to be overruled, and if so, he must not be held responsible for the consequences. We shall see some of these days which side the President will espouse. Beauregard is *too popular*, I fear, to meet with favor here. But it is life or death to the Confederacy, and danger lurks in the path of public men who endanger the liberties of the people.

OCTOBER 28TH.—Gen. Bragg is here, but will not probably be deprived of his command. He was opposed by vastly superior numbers, and succeeded in getting away with the largest amount of provisions, clothing, etc., ever obtained by an army. He brought out 15,000 horses and mules, 8000 beeves, 50,000 barrels of pork, a great number of hogs, 1,000,000 yards of Kentucky cloth, etc. The army is now at Knoxville, Tennessee, in good condition. But before leaving Kentucky, Morgan made still another capture of Lexington, taking a whole cavalry regiment prisoners, destroying several wagon trains, etc. It is said Bragg's train of wagons was forty miles long! A Western *tale*, I fear.

Letters from Lee urge the immediate completion of the railroad from Danville to Greenville, North Carolina, as of *vital importance.* He thinks the enemy will cut the road between this and Weldon. He wants Confederate notes made a legal tender; and the President says that, as the courts cannot enforce payment in anything else, they are substantially a legal tender already. And he suggests the withholding of pay from officers during their absence from their regiments. A good idea.

Everything indicates that Richmond will be assailed this fall, and that operations in the field are not to be suspended in the winter.

Polk, Bragg, Cheatham, etc. are urging the President to make Col. Preston Smith a brigadier-general. Unfortunately, Bragg's letter mentioned the fact that Beauregard had given Smith command of a brigade at Shiloh; and this attracting the eye of the President, he made a sharp note of it with his pencil. "What authority had he for this?" he asked; and Col. Smith will not be appointed.

OCTOBER 29TH.—There was a rumor yesterday that the enemy were marching on Weldon; but we have no confirmation of it to-day.

Loring, after all, did not send his cavalry into Pennsylvania, I presume, since nothing has been heard of it.

The *Charleston Mercury* has some strictures on the President for not having Breckinridge in Kentucky, and Price in Missouri, this fall. They would doubtless have done good service to the cause. The President is much absorbed in the matter of appointments.

Gen. Wise was again ordered down the Peninsula last Saturday; and again ordered back when he got under way. They will not let him fight.

OCTOBER 30TH.—The Commissary-General is in hot water on account of some of his contracts, and a board of inquiry is to sit on him.

The President has delayed the appointment of Gen. E. Johnson, and Gen. Echols writes that several hundred of his men have deserted; that the enemy, 10,000 or 15,000 strong, is pressing him, and he must fall back, losing Charleston, Virginia, the salt works, and possibly the railroad. He has less than 4000 men!

But we have good news from England—if it be true. The New York *Express* says Lord Lyons is instructed by England, and perhaps on the part of France and other powers, to demand of the United States an armistice; and in the event of its not being acceded to, the governments will recognize our independence. One of the President's personal attendants told me this news was regarded as authentic by our government. I don't regard it so.

Yesterday the whole batch of "Plug Ugly" policemen, in the Provost Marshal's "department," were summarily dismissed by Gen. Winder, for "malfeasance, corruption, bribery, and incompetence." These are the branches: the roots should be plucked up, and Gen. Winder and his Provost Marshal ought to resign. I believe the President ordered the removal.

OCTOBER 31ST.—If it be not a Yankee electioneering trick to operate at the election in New York, on the fourth of November, the Northern correspondence with Europe looks very much like speedy intervention in our behalf.

Winder has really dismissed all his detectives excepting Cashmeyer, about the worst of them.

If we gain our independence by the valor of our people, or assisted by European intervention, I wonder whether President Davis will be regarded by the world as a second Washington? What will his own country say of him? I know not, of course; but I know what quite a number here say of him now. They say he is a small specimen of a statesman, and no military chieftain at all. And worse still, that he is a capricious tyrant, for lifting up Yankees and keeping down great Southern men. Wise, Floyd, etc. are kept in obscurity; while Pemberton, who commanded the Massachusetts troops, under Lincoln, in April, 1861, is made a lieutenant-general; G. W. Smith and Lovell, who were office-holders in New York, when the battle of Manassas was fought, are made major-generals, and the former put in command over Wise in Virginia, and all the generals in North Carolina. Ripley, another Northern general, was sent to South Carolina, and Winder, from Maryland, has been allowed to play the despot in Richmond and Petersburg. Washington was maligned.

CHAPTER XX.

General Lee in Richmond: beard white.—First proposition to trade cotton to the enemy.—Secretary in favor of it.—All the letters come through my hands again.—Lee falling back.—5000 negroes at work on the fortifications.—Active operations looked for.—Beauregard advises non-combatants to leave the city.—Semmes's operations.—Making a nation.—Salt works lost in Virginia.—Barefooted soldiers.—Intrigues of Butler in New Orleans.—Northern army advancing everywhere.—Breach between the President and Secretary of War.—President's servant arrested for robbing the Treasury.—Gen. J. E. Johnston in town.—Secretary has resigned.—Hon. J. A. Seddon appointed Secretary of War.—The enemy marching on Fredericksburg.—Lee writes that he will be ready for them.—Kentuckians will not be hog drivers.—Women and children flying from the vicinity of Fredericksburg.—Fears for Wilmington.—No beggars.—Quiet on the Rappahannock.—M. Paul, French Consul, saved the French tobacco.—Gen. Johnston goes West.—President gives Gov. Pettit full authority to trade cotton to France.

NOVEMBER 1ST.—Gen. Winder's late policemen have fled the city. Their monstrous crimes are the theme of universal execration. But I reported them many months ago, and Gen. Winder was cognizant of their forgeries, correspondence with the enemy, etc. The Secretary of War, and the President himself, were informed of them, but it was thought to be a "small matter."

Gen. Lee made his appearance at the department to-day, and was hardly recognizable, for his beard, now quite white, has been suffered to grow all over his face. But he is quite robust from his exercises in the field. His appearance here, coupled with the belief that we are to have the armistice, or recognition and intervention, is interpreted by many as an end of the war. But I apprehend it is a symptom of the falling back of our army.

I have been startled to-day by certain papers that came under my observation. The first was written by J. Foulkes, to L. B. Northrop, Commissary-General, proposing to aid the government in procuring meat and bread for the army *from ports in the enemy's possession. They were to be paid for in cotton.* The next was a letter from the Commissary-General to G. W. Randolph, Secretary of War, urging the acceptance of the proposition, and saying without it, it would be impossible to subsist the army. He says the cotton proposed to be used, in the Southwest will either be burned or fall into the hands of the enemy; and that more than two-thirds is never destroyed when the enemy approaches. But to effect his object, it will be necessary for the Secretary to sanction it, and to give orders for the cotton to pass the lines of the army. The next was from the Secretary to the President, dated October thirtieth, which not only sanctioned Colonel Northrop's scheme, but went further, and embraced shoes and blankets for the Quartermaster-General. This letter inclosed both Foulkes's and Northrop's. They were all sent back to-day by the President, with his remarks. He hesitates, and does not concur. But says the Secretary will readily see the propriety of *postponing* such a resort until January—and he hopes it may not be necessary then to depart from the settled policy of the government—to forbear trading cotton to the Yankees, etc. etc.

Mr. Benjamin, Secretary of State, has given Mr. Dunnock permission to sell cotton to the Yankees and the rest of the world on the Atlantic and Gulf coast. Can it be that the President knows nothing of this? It is obvious that the cotton sold by Mr. Dunnock (who was always licensed by Mr. Benjamin to trade with people in the enemy's country beyond the Potomac) will be very *comfortable* to the enemy. And it may aid Mr. Dunnock and others in accumulating a fortune. The Constitution defines *treason* to be giving aid and comfort to the enemy. I never supposed Mr. Randolph would suggest, nay *urge,* opening an illicit trade with "Butler, the Beast." This is the first really dark period of our struggle for independence.

We have acres enough, and laborers enough, to subsist 30,000,000 of people; and yet we have the spectacle of high functionaries, under Mr. Davis, urging the necessity of bartering cotton to the enemy for stores essential to the maintenance of the army! I cannot believe it is a necessity, but a destitution of that virtue necessary to achieve independence. If they had any knowledge of these things in Europe, they would cease their commendations of President Davis.

Mr. Randolph says, in his letter to the President, that trading with ports in possession of the enemy is forbidden to citizens, and not to the government! The archives of the department show that this is not the first instance of the kind entertained by the Secretary. He has granted a license to *citizens* in Mobile to trade cotton in New Orleans for certain supplies in exchange, in exact compliance with Gen. Butler's proclamation. Did Pitt ever practice such things during his contest with Napoleon? Did the Continental Government ever resort to such equivocal expedients? A member of Washington's cabinet (and he, too, was a Randolph) once violated the "settled policy of the government," but he was instantly deprived of the seals of office. He acted under the advice of Jefferson, who sought to destroy Washington; and the present Secretary Randolph is a grandson of Jefferson. Washington, the inflexible patriot, frowned indignantly upon every departure from the path of rectitude.

I can do nothing more than record these things, and WATCH!

NOVEMBER 2D, SUNDAY.—I watch the daily orders of Adjutant and Inspector-Gen. Cooper. These, when "by command of the Secretary of War," are intelligible to any one, but not many are by his command. When simply "by order," they are promulgated by order of the President, without even consulting the Secretary; and they often annul the Secretary's orders. They are *edicts*, and sometimes thought very arbitrary ones. One of these orders says liquor shall not be introduced into the city; and a poor fellow, the other day, was sentenced to the ball-and-chain for trying to bring hither his whisky from Petersburg. On the same day Gov. Brown, of Georgia, seized liquor in his State, in transitu over the railroad, belonging to the government!

Since the turning over of the passports to Generals Smith and Winder, I have resumed the position where all the letters to the department come through my hands. I read them, make brief statements of their contents, and send them to the Secretary. Thus all sent by the President to the department go through my hands, being epitomized in the same manner.

The new Assistant Secretary, Judge Campbell, has been ordering the Adjutant-General too peremptorily; and so Gen. Cooper has issued an order making Lieut.-Col. Deas an Acting Assistant Secretary of War, thus creating an office in defiance of Congress.

NOVEMBER 3D.—The right wing of Lee's army has fallen back

as far as Culpepper County, and the enemy advances. Active movements are speedily looked for; many suppose a desperate attempt to take Richmond.

Our government has decided that *no one* shall be permitted to go North for thirty days.

A requisition for heavy guns to defend Cumberland Gap, elicited from the Inspector of Ordnance a statement of the fact that we are "short" of guns for the defense of Richmond.

There was a rumor yesterday that the enemy was marching in force on Petersburg. This, at all events, was premature.

A letter from Hon. C. C. Clay, Senator, says there is much defection in North Alabama, and that many people are withdrawing themselves to avoid conscription.

Just at this time, if it were not for Lincoln's proclamation, if the war were conducted according to the rules of civilized nations, I verily believe a very formidable party in favor of RECONSTRUCTION might spring up in the South. With a united South, two million of Abolitionists could not subjugate us.

NOVEMBER 4TH.—An exposé of funds in the hands of disbursing agents shows there are nearly seventy millions of dollars not accounted for!

The members of the legislature are fearful of an attack on the Southern Railroad, and asks that Gen. Mahone be sent to Petersburg.

The government is impressing flour at $12 per barrel, when it is selling at $24; and as the railroads are not allowed to transport any for private use, *it may be hoped we shall have our bread cheaper some of these days.* But will the government make itself popular with the people?

The *Examiner* says a clerk in the War Department is making money in the substitute business. If this be true, it is rank corruption! But, then, what is the cotton business?

The Chief of Ordnance Bureau, Col. J. Gorgas (Northern by birth), recommends the Secretary of War to remove the lighter guns, some sixty in number, from the lower tiers of Forts Sumter, Moultrie, and Morgan, for the defense of the rivers likely to be ascended by the enemy's gun-boats.

I saw, to-day, the President's order to revoke the authority heretofore given Gov. Baylor to raise a brigade, and in regard to his conduct as governor (ordering the massacre of the Indians after collecting them under pretense of forming a treaty of peace). The President suggests that nothing be done until the Governor *be heard in his own defense.* It was diabolical! If it had been consummated, it would have affixed the stigma of infamy to the government in all future time, and might have doomed us to merited subjugation.

NOVEMBER 5TH —Major Ruffin, in the Commissary Department, says the army must go on half rations after the 1st of January next.

It is alleged that certain favorites of the government have a monopoly of transportation over the railroads, for purposes of speculation and extortion!

NOVEMBER 6TH.—I believe the commissaries and quartermasters are cheating the government. The Quartermaster-General sent in a paper, to-day, saying he did not need the contributions of clothes tendered by the people of Petersburg, but still would pay for them. They were offered for nothing.

The Commissary-General to-day says there is not wheat enough in Virginia (when a good crop was raised) for Gen. Lee's army, and unless he has millions in money and cotton, the army must disband for want of food. I don't believe it.

There are 5000 negroes working on the fortifications near the city, and 2500 are to work on the Piedmont Railroad.

We are all hoping that New York and other States declared against the Republicans, at the elections in the United States, on Tuesday last. Such a communication would be regarded as the harbinger of peace. We are all weary of the war, but *must* and *will* fight on, for no other alternative remains. Everything, however, indicates that we are upon the eve of most interesting events. This is the time for England or France to come to the rescue, and enjoy a commercial monopoly for many years. I think the Secretary of War has abandoned the idea of trading cotton to the enemy. It might cost him his head.

NOVEMBER 7TH.—Yesterday I received from the agent of the City Councils fourteen pounds of salt, having seven persons in my family, including the servant. One pound to each member, per month, is allowed at 5 cts. per pound. The extortionists sell it at 70 cts. per pound. One of *them* was drawing for his family. He confessed it; but said he paid 50 cts. for the salt he sold at 70 cts. Profit $10 per bushel! I sent an article to-day to the *Enquirer*, suggesting that fuel, bread, meat, etc. be furnished in the same manner. We shall soon be in a state of siege.

Last night there was a heavy fall of *snow*.

The authorities of Charleston, with the concurrence of Beauregard, advise all the non-combating population to leave the city, and remove their personal property. The city will be defended to the last extremity.

What a change in the Executive Department! Before the election, the President was accessible to all; and even a member of Congress had no preference over the common citizen. But now there are *six* aids, cavalry colonels in rank and pay, and one of them an Englishman, who see the people, and permit only certain ones to have access to the President. This looks like the beginning of an imperial court. But what may not its ending be?

I see that Mr. Hurlbut, incarcerated once as a spy, or as a writer for an Abolition paper in New York, and a Northern man himself, after being protected by Mr. Browne (the English A.D.C. of the President) and released by Mr. Benjamin from prison, has escaped to the North, and is out in a long article in the *Times!* He says he got a passport from Gen. Winder's Provost Marshal. Mr. James Lyons thought he had made H. a Southern man; what does he think now?

The "290" or Alabama, the ship bought in Europe, and commanded by Capt. Semmes, C. S. N., is playing havoc with the commerce of the United States. If we had a dozen of them, our foes would suffer incalculably, for they have an immense amount of shipping. I see Semmes had captured the Tonawanda, that used to lie at the foot of Walnut Street, Philadelphia; but he released her, first putting the master under bond to pay President Davis $80,000 after the war. I hope he will pay it, for I think the President will want the money.

NOVEMBER 8TH.—The European statesmen, declining intervention in our behalf, have, nevertheless, complimented our President by saying he has, at all events, "made a nation." He is pleased with this, I understand. But it is one of the errors which the wise men over the water are ever liable to fall into. The "nation" was made before the President existed: indeed, the nation made the President.

We have rumors of fighting near the mouth of the Shenandoah, and that our arms were successful. It is time both armies were in winter quarters. Snow still lies on the ground here.

We have tidings from the North of the triumph of the Democrats in New York, New Jersey, etc. etc. This news produces great rejoicing, for it is hailed as the downfall of Republican despotism. Some think it will be followed by a speedy peace, or else that the European powers will recognize us without further delay. I should not be surprised if Seward were now to attempt to get the start of England and France, and cause our recognition by the United States. I am sure the Abolitionists cannot now get their million men. The drafting must be a failure.

The Governor of Mississippi (Pettus) informs the President that a Frenchman, perhaps a Jew, proposes to trade salt for cotton—ten sacks of the first for one of the latter. The Governor says he don't *know* that he has received the consent of "Butler, the Beast" (but he knows the trade is impossible without it), but that is no business of his. He urges the traffic. And the President has consented to it, and given him power to conduct the exchange in spite of the military authorities. The President says, however, that twenty sacks of salt ought to be given for one of cotton. Salt is worth in New Orleans about one dollar a sack, cotton $160 per bale. The President informed the Secretary of what had been *done,* and sends him a copy of his dispatch to Gov. Pettus. He don't even ask Mr. Randolph's *opinion.*

November 9th.—It is too true that Charleston, Va., and the great Kanawha salt works have been abandoned by Gen. Echols for the want of an adequate force to hold them. If the President had only taken Gen. Lee's advice a month ago, and ordered a few thousand more men there, under the command of Gen. Ed. Johnson, we should have kept possession of the works. The President may seem to be a good nation-maker in the eyes of distant statesmen, but he does not seem to be a good salt-maker for the nation. The works he has just relinquished to the enemy manufacture 7000 bushels of salt per day—two million and a half a year—an ample supply for the entire population of the Confederacy, and an object adequate to the maintenance of an army of 50,000 in that valley. Besides, the troops necessary for its occupation will soon be in winter quarters, and quite as expensive to the government as if in the valley. A Cæsar, a Napoleon, a Pitt, and a Washington, all great nation-makers, would have deemed this work worthy their attention.

Only three days ago the President wrote to the Secretary that the idea of trading cotton to the enemy must be postponed until the first of January, and perhaps indefinitely, but now he informs Mr. Randolph that he has sent the requisite authority to his friend, Gov. Pettus, to launch out in that trade.

No, the people have made the nation. It is a people's war, and it is the momentum of a united, patriotic people, which carries everything with it. Our brave men win victories under adverse circumstances, and often under incompetent officers, and the people feed and clothe the armies in spite of the shortcomings of dishonest commissaries and quartermasters. They are now sending ten thousand pairs of shoes to Lee's army in opposition to the will of the Jew Myers, Quartermaster-General, who says everything must be contracted and paid for by his agents, according to red-tape rule and regulation.

The weather continues cold, 38°, and snow still lies on the ground. This *must* produce a cessation of hostilities, and afford Lincoln's drafted recruits opportunity for meditation.

If it be true that the Democrats have carried the day in the North, I think the war is approaching a termination.

NOVEMBER 10TH.—A day or two ago some soldiers marched through the city without shoes, *in the snow.* A committee of citizens to-day obtained an order from the War Department, for the impressment of all the boots, shoes, blankets, and overcoats in the shops. What a commotion among the Jews!

It is *certain* that the enemy are advancing upon Culpepper, on the way to Richmond, in great force. This we have in letters from Gen. Lee, dated 7th inst., near Culpepper C. H. He says the enemy's cavalry is very numerous, while our horses have the "sore tongue," and tender hoofs. Lee has ordered the stores, etc. from Gordonsville to Lynchburg. He says Jackson may possibly march through one of the gaps and fall upon the enemy's flank, and intimates that an opportunity may be offered to strike the invaders "a blow."

Yesterday, Sunday, a cavalry company dashed into Fredericksburg, and after robbing the stores, and reporting that the Democrats had swept the North, that England and France had recognized us, etc., they dashed out again.

The President sent to the department to-day, *without comment*, a defense by Col. Baylor of his atrocious order for the massacre of the Indians. It was in a Texas paper. Baylor acknowledges its genuineness, and says the Apaches murdered our people invited to make a treaty with them, and he says it is his intention to retaliate by extermination of them.

Another proposition was received by the government to-day from a French firm of *New Orleans* merchants, to furnish us salt, meat, shoes, blankets, etc., in unlimited quantities, *and guarantee their delivery*, if we will allow them, with the proceeds of salt, the privilege of buying cotton on the Mississippi River, and they will, moreover, freight French ships above New Orleans, and guarantee that not a bale shall be landed in any U. S. port. Is it not *certain* that "Butler, the Beast," is a party to the speculation? This is a strong temptation, and we shall see what response our government will make to this proposition to violate an act of Congress.

NOVEMBER 11TH.—More projects from the Southwest. Mr. Jno. A. S. has *just* arrived from *New Orleans*, where, he states in his communication to the government, he had interviews and correspondence with the U. S. authorities, Butler, etc., and they had given him positive assurances that he will be permitted to take any supplies to the planters (excepting arms and ammunition) in exchange for cotton, which may be shipped to any part of the world. S. says that Butler will let us have *anything* for a bribe. No doubt! And Mr. L., President of the L. Bank, writes that he will afford facilities to Mr. S. It remains to be seen what our government will do in these matters. They smack of treason.

It is said heavy firing was heard yesterday in the direction of Culpepper C. H., and it is supposed a battle is in progress to-day. No danger of it.

NOVEMBER 12TH.—The heavy firing heard did no execution. Letters from Gen. Lee indicate no battle, unless the enemy should make an egregious blunder. He says he has *not half men enough* to resist McClellan's advance with his mighty army, and prefers manœuvring to risking his army. He says three-fourths of our cavalry horses are sick with sore-tongue, and their hoofs are falling off, and the soldiers are not fed and clad as they should be. He urges the sending of supplies to Gordonsville.

And we have news of a simultaneous advance of Northern armies everywhere; and everywhere we have the same story of deficiency of men and provisions. North and south, east and west of us, the enemy is reported advancing.

Soon we shall have every one blaming the Secretary of War for the deficiency of men, and of quartermaster and commissary stores.

The Commissary-General, backed by the Secretary of War, made another effort to-day to obtain the President's permission to trade cotton with "Butler, the Beast." But the President and Gov. Pettus will manage that *little* matter without their assistance.

Major Ruffin's (Commissary's Bureau) statement of the alarming prospects ahead, unless provisions be obtained outside of the Confederacy (for cotton), was induced by reports from New Orleans. A man was in the office to-day exhibiting Butler's passport, and making assurances that all the Yankee generals are for sale—for cotton. Butler will make a fortune—and so will some of our great men. Butler says the reason he don't send troops into the interior is that he is afraid we will burn the cotton.

It is reported that a fleet of the enemy's gun-boats are in the James River.

NOVEMBER 13TH.—The President has rebuked the Secretary of War in round terms for ordering Gen. Holmes to assume the command on *this* side the Mississippi. Perhaps Mr. Randolph has resolved to be really Secretary. This is the first thing I have ever known him to do without previously obtaining the President's sanction—and it must be confessed, it was a matter of some gravity and importance. Of course it will be countermanded. I have not been in the Secretary's office yet, to see if there is an envelope on his table directed to the President marked "*Immediate*." But he has not been to see the President—and that may be significant, as this is the usual day.

A gentleman, arrived to-day from Maryland, reports that Gen. McClellan has been removed, and the command given to Burnside! He says, moreover, that this change has given umbrage to the army. This may be our deliverance; for if McClellan had been let alone two weeks longer (provided he ascertained our present condition), he might have captured Richmond, which would be holding all Eastern and much of Central Virginia. This blunder seems providential.

We learn, also, that the Democracy have carried Illinois, Mr. Lincoln's own State, by a very large majority. This is hailed with gladness by our people; and if there should be a "rebellion in the North," as the *Tribune* predicts, this intervention of the Democrats will be regarded altogether in our favor. Let them put down the radical Abolitionists, and then, no doubt, they will recover some of our trade. It will mortify the Republicans, hereafter, when the smoke clears away, to learn that Gen. Butler was trading supplies for our army during this November, 1862—and it will surprise our secessionists to learn that our government is trading him cotton!

NOVEMBER 14TH.—An order has gone forth to-day from the Secretary of War, that no more flour or wheat shall leave the States. This order was given some time ago—then relaxed, and now reissued. How soon will he revoke it again?

Never before did such little men rule such a great people. Our rulers are like children or drunken men riding docile horses, that absolutely keep the riders from falling off by swaying to the right and left, and preserving an equilibrium. There is no rule for anything, and no stability in any policy.

To-day more propositions from Frenchmen (in New Orleans) have been received. Butler is preparing to do a great business—and no objection to the illicit traffic is filed by the Secretaries of State or Treasury.

Yesterday one of the President's servants was arrested for stealing Treasury notes. The Treasury Department is just under the Executive Department; and this negro (slave) has been used by the President to take important papers to the departments. The amount abstracted was $5000—unsigned—but some one, perhaps the negro, for he is educated, forged the Register's and Treasurer's names.

I saw Gen. J. E. Johnston standing idle in the street to-day.

NOVEMBER 15TH.—"Now, by St. George, the work goes bravely on!" Another letter on my desk from the President to the Secretary. Well, being in an official envelope, it was my duty to open it, note its contents, and send it to the Secretary. The Secretary has been responding to the short espistle he received yesterday. It appears he could not clearly understand its purport. But the President has used such plain language in this, that it must be impossible to misunderstand him. He says that the transferring of generals commanding important military districts, without conference with him and his concurrence; and of high disbursing officers; and, above all, the making of appointments without his knowledge and consent, are prerogatives that do not pertain to the Secretary of War in the first instance; and can only be exercised by him under the direction of the Chief Executive. In regard to *appointments*, especially, the President has no constitutional authority nor any disposition to transfer the power. He discussed their relative duties,—for the benefit of all future Secretaries, I suppose.

But it looks like a rupture. It seems, then, after acting some eight months merely in the humble capacity of clerk, Mr. Randolph has all at once essayed to act the PRESIDENT.

The Secretary of War did not go to the President's closet today. This is the third day he has absented himself. Such incidents as these preceded the resignation of Mr. Walker. It is a critical time, and the Secretary of War ought to confer freely with the President.

NOVEMBER 16TH, SUNDAY.—Yesterday the Secretary of War resigned his office, and his resignation was promptly accepted by the President.

NOVEMBER 17TH.—A profound sensation has been produced in the outside world by the resignation of Mr. Randolph; and most of the people and the press seem inclined to denounce the President, for they know not what. In this matter the President is not to blame; but the Secretary has acted either a very foolish or a very desperate part. It appears that he wrote a note in reply to the last letter of the President, stating that as no discretion was allowed him in such matters as were referred to by the President, he begged respectfully to tender his resignation. The President responded, briefly, that inasmuch as the Secretary declined acting any longer as one of his constitutional advisers, and also declined a personal conference, no alternative remained but to accept his resignation.

Randolph's friends would make it appear that he resigned in consequence of being restricted in his action; but he knows very well that the latitude allowed him became less and less circumscribed; and that, hitherto, he was well content to operate within the prescribed limits. Therefore, if it was not a silly caprice, it was a deliberate purpose, to escape a cloud of odium he knew must sooner or later burst around him.

A letter from Gen. Magruder, dated 10th inst., at Jackson, Mississippi, intimates that we shall lose Holly Springs. He has also been in Mobile, and doubts whether that city can be successfully defended by Gen. Forney, whose liver is diseased, and memory impaired. He recommends that Brig.-Gen. Whiting be promoted, and assigned to the command in place of Forney, relieved.

A letter from Gen. Whiting, near Wilmington, dated 13th. inst., expresses serious apprehensions whether that place can be held against a determined attack, unless a supporting force of 10,000 men be sent there immediately. It is in the command of Major-Gen. G. A. Smith.

More propositions to ship cotton in exchange for the supplies needed by the country. The President has no objection to accepting them all, provided the cotton don't go to any of the enemy's ports. How *can* it be possible to avoid this liability, if the cotton be shipped from the Mississippi River?

NOVEMBER 18TH.—Well, the President is a bold man! He has put in Randolph's place, temporarily at least, Major-Gen. Gustavus W. Smith—who was Street Commissioner in the City of New York, on the day that Capt. G. W. Randolph was fighting the New Yorkers at Bethel!

Gen. Wise is out in a card, stating that in response to a requisition for shoes for his suffering troops, Quartermaster-Gen. A. C. Myers said, "Let them suffer."

The enemy attacked Fredericksburg yesterday, and there was some skirmishing, the result of which we have not heard. It is rumored they are fighting there to-day. We have but few regiments between here and Fredericksburg.

NOVEMBER 19TH.—Hon. James A. Seddon (Va.) has been appointed Secretary of War. He is an able man (purely a civilian), and was member of our Revolutionary Convention, at Metropolitân Hall, 16th April, 1861. But some thought him then rather inclined to restrain than to urge decisive action. He is an orator, rich, and frail in health. He will not remain long in office if he attempts to perform all the duties.

Two letters were received from Gen. Lee to-day. Both came unsealed and open, an omission of his adjutant-general, Mason. The first inclines to the belief that Burnside intends to embark his army for the south side of James River, to operate probably in Eastern North Carolina.

The second, dated 17th inst. 6½ P.M., says the scouts report large masses advancing on Fredericksburg, and it may be Burnside's purpose to make that town his base of operations. (Perhaps for a pleasant excursion to Richmond.) Three brigades of the enemy had certainly marched to Fredericksburg. A division of Longstreet's corps were marched thither yesterday, 18th, at early dawn. Lee says if the reports of the scouts be confirmed, the entire corps will follow immediately. And he adds: "Before the enemy's trains can leave Fredericksburg (for Richmond) this whole army will be in position." These letters were sent immediately to the President.

A letter from Gen. Holmes calls for an immediate supply of funds ($24,000,000) for the trans-Mississippi Department. A letter from Gen. Pike says if Gen. Hindman (Ark.) is to control there, the Indian Country will be lost.

We shall soon have a solution of Burnside's intentions. Lee is in spirits. He knows Burnside can be easily beaten with greatly inferior numbers.

We hear of sanguinary acts in Missouri—ten men (civilians) being shot in retaliation for one killed by our rangers. These acts exasperate our people, and will stimulate them to a heroic defense.

The cars this afternoon from the vicinity of Fredericksburg were crowded with negroes, having bundles of clothing, etc., their owners sending them hither to escape the enemy. A frightened Jew, who came in the train, said there was an army of 100,000 near Fredericksburg, and we should hear more in a few days. I doubt it not.

Salt sold yesterday at auction for $1.10 per pound. Boots are now bringing $50 per pair; candles (tallow) 75 cts. per pound; butter $2.00 per pound. Clothing is almost unattainable. We are all looking shabby enough.

Mr. K., the young Chief of the Bureau, who came in with Mr. Randolph, declines the honor of going out with him, to the great chagrin of several anxious applicants. It is an office "for life."

I shall despair of success unless the President puts a stop to Gen. Winder's passport operations, for, if the enemy be kept advised of our destitute condition, there will be no relaxation of efforts to subjugate us. And Europe, too, will refuse to recognize us. I believe there are traitors in high places here who encourage the belief in the North and in Europe that we must soon succumb. And some few of our influential great men might be disposed to favor reconstruction of the Union on the basis of the Democratic party which has just carried the elections in the North.

Everything depends upon the result of approaching military operations. If the enemy be defeated, and the Democrats of the North should call for a National Convention—but why anticipate?

NOVEMBER 20TH.—A letter from Brig. H. Marshall, Abingdon, Ky., in reply to one from the Secretary, says his Kentuckians are not willing to be made Confederate *hog-drivers*, but they will protect the commissary's men in collecting and removing the hogs. Gen. M. criticises Gen. Bragg's campaign very severely. He says the people of Kentucky looked upon their fleeting presence as a *horse-show*, or military pageantry, and not as indicating the stern reality of war. Hence they did not rise in arms, and hence their diffidence in following the fortunes of the new Confederacy. Gen. M. asks if it is the purpose of the government to *abandon* Kentucky, and if so, is he not *functus officio*, being a Kentucky general, commanding Kentucky troops?

Col. Myers has placed on file in the department a denial of having said to Gen. Wise's quartermaster, "Let them suffer."

Several ladies, near relatives of Judge Campbell, Assistant Secretary of War, came over yesterday under flag of truce. They lived, I believe, in Alexandria.

Another requisition has been made by the engineer for 5000 negroes to work on the fortifications of Richmond.

No letters were received from Gen. Lee to-day, and he may be busy in the field. Accounts say the enemy is planting batteries on the heights opposite Fredericksburg.

It has been raining occasionally the last day or two. I hope the ground is *soft*, and the mud deep; if so, Burnside cannot move on Richmond, and we shall have time to prepare for "contingencies."

Yesterday salt sold at auction for $1.30 per pound. We are getting into a pretty extreme condition.

NOVEMBER 21ST.—It rained all night, which may extinguish Burnside's ardent fire. He cannot drag his wagons and artillery through the melting snow, and when it dries we may look for another rain.

The new Secretary is not yet in his seat. It is generally supposed he will accept.

President Davis hesitates to retaliate life for life in regard to the Missouri military executions.

Common shirting cotton, and Yankee calico, that used to sell at 12½ cts. per yard, is now $1.75! What a temptation for the Northern manufacturers! What a *rush* of trade there would be if peace should occur suddenly! And what a party there would be in the South for peace (and unity with Northern Democrats) if the war were waged somewhat differently. The excesses of the Republicans *compel* our people to be almost a unit. This is all the better for us. Still, we are in quite a bad way now, God knows!

The passengers by the cars from Fredericksburg this morning report that Gen. Patrick (Federal) came over under a flag of truce, demanding the surrender of the town, which was refused by Gen. Lee, in compliance with the unanimous sentiments of the people. Gen. Patrick, it is stated, said if it were not surrendered by 9 A.M. to-day, it would be shelled.

Mr. Dargan, M. C., writes to the President from Mobile that the inhabitants of that city are in an awful condition. Meal is selling for $3.50 per bushel, and wood at $15 per cord, and that the people are afraid to bring supplies, apprehending that the government agents will seize them. The President (thanks to him!) has ordered that interference with domestic trade must not be permitted.

Mr. Seddon has taken his seat. He has, at least, a manly appearance—his predecessor was said to look like a m——y.

The President has ordered our generals in Missouri, if the Yankee accounts of the executions of our people be true, to execute the next ten Federal officers taken in that State.

The *Enquirer*, to-day, publishes Col. Baylor's order to execute the Indians in Arizona, coupled with Mr. Randolph's condemnation of the act. Who furnished this for publication?

It is rumored that Fredericksburg is in flames, shelled by the enemy. We will know how true this is before night.

NOVEMBER 23D.—The cars which came in from the North last night brought a great many women, children, and negroes from Fredericksburg and its vicinity. The benevolent and patriotic citizens here had, I believe, made some provision for their accommodation. But the enemy had not yet shelled the town.

There is a rumor that Jackson was to appear somewhere in the rear of the enemy, and that the Federal stores which could not be moved with the army had been burnt at Manassas.

Yesterday the President remitted the sentence of a poor lad, sentenced to ball-and-chain for six months, for cowardice, etc. He had endured the penalty three months. I like this act, for the boy had enlisted without the consent of his parents, and was only sixteen years of age.

J. R. Anderson & Co. (having drawn $500,000 recently on the contract) have failed to furnish armor for the gun-boats—the excuse being that iron could not be had for their rolling-mills. The President has ordered the Secretaries of the Navy and War to consult on the propriety of taking railroad iron, on certain tracks, for that purpose.

NOVEMBER 24TH.—Fredericksburg not shelled yet; but the women and children are flying hither. The enemy fired on a train of women and children yesterday, supposing the cars (baggage) were conveying military stores. The Northern press says Burnside is determined to force his way, directly from the Rappahannock to Richmond, by virtue of superior numbers. The thing Lee desires him to attempt.

The enemy are landing troops at Newport News, and we shall soon hear of gun-boats and transports in the James River. But no one is dismayed. We have supped on horrors so long, that danger now is an accustomed condiment. Blood will flow in torrents, and God will award the victory.

Another letter from Gen. Whiting says there is every reason to suppose that Wilmington will be attacked immediately, and if re-inforcements (10,000) be not sent him, the place cannot be defended against a land assault. Nor is this all: for if the city falls, with the present force only to defend it, none of our men can escape. There is no repose for us!

NOVEMBER 25TH.—Fredericksburg is not shelled yet; and, moreover, the enemy have apologized for the firing at the train containing women and children. Affairs remain in *statu quo*—the mayor and military authorities agreeing that the town shall furnish neither aid nor comfort to the Confederate army, and the Federals agreeing not to shell it—for the present.

Gen. Corcoran, last year a prisoner in this city, has landed his Irish brigade at Newport News. It is probable we shall be assailed from several directions simultaneously.

No beggars can be found in the streets of this city. No cry of distress is heard, although it prevails extensively. High officers of the government have no fuel in their houses, and give nearly $20 per cord for wood for cooking purposes. And yet there are millions of tons of coal almost *under* the very city!

NOVEMBER 26TH.—No fighting on the Rappahannock yet, that I hear of; and it is said the enemy are moving farther down the river. Can they mean to cross? Nothing more is heard of Gen. Corcoran, with his Irish bogtrotters, on the Peninsula.

The government has realized 50,000 pounds of leather from two counties in Eastern North Carolina, in danger of falling into the hands of the enemy. This convinces me that there is abundance of leather in the South, if it were properly distributed. It is held, like everything else, by speculators, for extortioners' profits. The government might remedy the evils, and remove the distresses of the people; but instead of doing so, the bureaus aggravate them by capricious seizures, and tyrannical restrictions on transportation. Letters are coming in from every quarter complaining of the despotic acts of government agents.

Mr. J. Foulkes writes another letter to the department on his cotton scheme. He says it must be embraced now or never, as the enemy will soon make such dispositions as would prevent his getting supplies *through their lines.* The Commissary-General approves, and the late Secretary approved; but what will the new one do? The President is non-committal.

What a blunder France and England made in hesitating to espouse our cause! They might have had any commercial advantages.

NOVEMBER 27TH.—Some of the late Secretary's friends are hinting that affairs will go amiss now, as if he would have prevented any disaster! Who gave up Norfolk? That was a calamitous blunder! Letters from North Carolina are distressing enough. They say, but for the influence of Gov. Vance, the *legislature* would favor reconstruction!

Gen. Marshall writes lugubriously. He says his men are all barefoot.

Gen. Magruder writes that Pemberton has only 20,000 men, and should have 50,000 more at once—else the Mississippi Valley will be lost, and the cause ruined. He thinks there should be a concentration of troops there immediately, no matter how much other places might suffer; the enemy beaten, and the Mississippi secured at all hazards. If not, Mobile is lost, and perhaps Montgomery, as well as Vicksburg, Holly Springs, etc.

One of our paroled men from Washington writes the President that, on the 6th instant, Burnside had but seventy regiments; and the President seemed to credit it! The idea of Burnside advancing with seventy regiments is absurd. But how many absurd ideas have been entertained by the government, and have influenced it! *Nous verrons.*

NOVEMBER 28TH.—All is quiet on the Rappahannock; the enemy reported to be extending his line up the river some twenty miles, intending to find a passage. He *might* have come over last week but for a *ruse* of Gen. Lee, who appeared near Fredericksburg twenty-four hours in advance of the army. His presence deceived Burnside, who took it for granted that our general was at the head of his army!

M. Paul carried the day yesterday, in the Confederate Court, in the matter of $2,000,000 worth of tobacco, which, under pretense of its belonging to French citizens (though bought by Belmont, of New York, an alien enemy), is rescued from sequestration. In other words, the recognition of M. Paul as Consul, and the validity of his demands, deprives the Confederate Government of two millions; and really acknowledges the *exequatur* of the United

States, as M. Paul is not Consul to the Confederate States but to the United States. This looks like submission; and a great fee has been realized by somebody. If the enemy were to take Richmond, this tobacco would be destroyed by the *military.*

Gen. Joseph E. Johnston is assigned to the command of the army of the West.

To-day we have a dispatch from Gov. Pettus, saying authority to pass cotton through the lines of the army, and for salt to have ingress, must be given immediately. The President directs the Secretary to transmit orders to the generals to that effect. He says the cotton is to go to France without touching any port in the possession of the enemy.

NOVEMBER 29TH.—The Quartermaster-General publishes a notice that *he* will receive and distribute contributions of clothing, etc. to the army, and even *pay* for the shirts $1 each! Shirts are selling at $12. The people will not trust him to convey the clothing to their sons and brothers, and so the army must suffer on. But he is getting in bad odor. A gentleman in Alabama writes that his agents are speculating in food: the President tells the Secretary to demand explanations, and the Secretary does so. Col. Myers fails, I think, to make the exhibit required, and it may be the worse for him.

I see by the papers that another of Gen. Winder's police has escaped to Washington City, and is now acting as a *Federal* detective. And yet many similar traitors are retained in service here!

The Governor of North Carolina writes the President that his State intends to organize an army of 10,000 men for its own defense, besides her sixty regiments in the Confederate States service; and asks if the Confederate States Government can furnish any arms, etc. The President sends this to the Secretary of War, for his *advice.* He wants to know Mr. Seddon's views on the subject—a delicate and embarrassing predicament for the new Secretary, truly! He must know that the President frowns on all military organizations not under his own control, and that he counteracted all Gen. Floyd's efforts to raise a division under State authority. Beware, Mr. Seddon! The President is a little particular concerning his prerogatives; and by the advice you now give, you stand or fall. What is North Carolina to the Empire? You tread on dangerous ground. Forget your old State-Rights doctrine, or off goes your head.

NOVEMBER 30TH.—It is said there is more concern manifested in the government here on the indications that the States mean to organize armies of non-conscripts for their own defense, than for any demonstration of the enemy. The election of Graham Confederate States Senator in North Carolina, and of H. V. Johnson in Georgia, causes some uneasiness. These men were not original secessionists, and have been the objects of aversion, if not of proscription, by the men who secured position in the Confederate States Government. Nevertheless, they are able men, and as true to Southern independence as any. But they are opposed to despotic usurpation—and their election seems like a rebuke and condemnation of military usurpation.

From all sections of the Confederacy complaints are coming in that the military agents of the bureaus are oppressing the people; and the belief is expressed by many, that a sentiment is prevailing inimical to the government itself.

CHAPTER XXI.

The great crisis at hand.—The rage for speculation raises its head.—Great battle of Fredericksburg.—The States called on for supplies.—Randolph resigns as Brigadier-General.—South Carolina honor.—Loss at Fredericksburg.—Great contracts.—Lee's ammunition bad.—Small-pox here.

DECEMBER 1ST, MONDAY.—There is a rumor to-day that we are upon the eve of a great battle on the Rappahannock. I doubt it not.

I am sorry to see that Col. McRae, a gallant officer, has resigned his commission, charging the President with partiality in appointing junior officers, and even his subordinates, brigadiers over his head. Nevertheless, he tenders his services to the Governor of his State, and will be made a general. But where will this end? I fear in an issue between the State and Confederate authorities.

The news from Europe is not encouraging. France is willing

to interfere, and Russia is ready to participate in friendly mediation to stay the effusion of blood—but England seems afraid of giving offense to the United States. They refer to the then approaching elections in the North, and lay some stress on the anticipated change in public opinion. Popular opinion! What is it worth in the eyes of European powers? If it be of any value, and if the voice of the people should be allowed to determine such contests, why not leave it to a vote of the Southern people to decide under which government they will live? But why make such an appeal to monarchies, while the Republican or Democratic government of the North refuses to permit 8,000,000 of people to have the government they unanimously prefer? Can it be possible that the United States are ignorant of popular sentiment here? I fear so; I fear a few traitors in our midst contrive to deceive even the Government at Washington. Else why a prolongation of the war? They ought to know that, under almost any conceivable adverse circumstances, we can maintain the war twenty years. And if our lines should be everywhere broken, and our country overrun—it would require a half million soldiers to *hold us down*, and this would cost the United States $500,000,000 per annum.

God speed the day of peace! Our patriotism is mainly in the army and among the ladies of the South. The avarice and cupidity of the men at home, could only be excelled by ravenous wolves; and most of our sufferings are fully deserved. Where a people will not have mercy on one another, how can they expect mercy? They depreciate the Confederate notes by charging from $20 to $40 per bbl. for flour; $3.50 per bushel for meal; $2 per lb. for butter; $20 per cord for wood, etc. When we shall have peace, let the extortionists be remembered! let an indelible stigma be branded upon them.

A portion of the people look like vagabonds. We see men and women and children in the streets in dingy and dilapidated clothes; and some seem gaunt and pale with hunger—the speculators, and thieving quartermasters and commissaries only, looking sleek and comfortable. If this state of things continue a year or so longer, they will have their reward. There will be governmental bankruptcy, and all their gains will turn to dust and ashes, dust and ashes!

And I learn they are without shirts in the North—cotton being unattainable. A universal madness rules the hour! Why not throw aside the instruments of death, and exchange commodities with each other? Subjugation is an impossibility. Then why not strive for the possible and the good in the paths of peace? The Quakers are the wisest people, after all. I shall turn Quaker after this war, in one sense, and strive to convince the world that war is the worst remedy for evils ever invented—and MAN the most dangerous animal ever created.

DECEMBER 2D.—There was skirmishing this morning on the line of the Rappahannock. The Chief of Ordnance is ordering arms and ammunition to Gen. Pemberton, in Mississippi. This indicates a battle in the Southwest.

A writer in the London *Times*, who is from Nashville, Tenn., says the South is willing to go into Convention with the North, and be bound by its decisions. I doubt that.

But the *Enquirer* to-day contains a communication from T. E. Chambliss, not the Virginia member of Congress, proposing the election of Commissioners from North and South, to put an end to the war. What can this mean but reconstruction on the old Democratic basis? It will not meet with favor, unless we meet great reverses this winter. Still, but few have faith in foreign intervention, to terminate the war; and there is a growing party both in the North and the South opposed to its indefinite prolongation. If we beat Burnside, *I* think it will be the last battle of magnitude. If he beats us, no one can see the end of the struggle. But from every State complaints are made against the military agents of the Confederate Government, for their high-handed oppressions. We may split up into separate States, and then continue the war—but it will be a sad day for us! The President ought to change his cabinet immediately, and then change his policy. He should cultivate the friendship and support of the people, and be strong in their affections, if he would rule with a strong hand. If he offends and exasperates them, they will break his power to pieces. And he should not attempt to destroy, nor permit others to destroy, the popular leaders. That way lies his own destruction.

DECEMBER 3D.—One of the President's Aids, Mr. Johnston, has asked the Secretary's permission for Mrs. E. B. Hoge, Mrs. M.

Anderson, Miss Judith Venable, and Mrs. R. J. Breckinridge, with children and servants, to leave Richmond by flag of truce, and proceed to their homes in Kentucky. Of course it will be granted—the President sanctions it, but does not commit himself by ordering it.

There was no fighting on the Rappahannock yesterday, and no rumors to-day.

Letters were received from Gen. Lee to-day. He says several thousand of his men are barefoot! He suggests that shoes be *taken* from the extortioners at a *fair price*. That is right. He also recommends a rule of the department putting cavalry on foot when they cannot furnish good horses, and mounting infantry that can and will procure them. This would cause better care to be taken of horses. Gen. Lee also writes for more arms—which may indicate a battle. But the weather is getting bad again, and the roads will not admit of marching.

Mr. Gastrell, M. C., writes to the Secretary of War for permission for Messrs. Frank and Gernot, a Jew firm of Augusta, Ga., to bring through the lines a stock of goods they have just purchased of the Yankees in Memphis. Being a member of Congress, I think his request will be granted. And if all such applications be granted, I think money-making will soon *absorb* the war, and bring down the prices of goods.

We are a confident people. There are no symptoms of trepidation, although a hostile army of 150,000 men is now within two day's march of our capital. A few of guilty consciences, the extortioners, may feel alarm—but not the women and children. They reflect that over one hundred thousand of the enemy were within four miles of the city last spring and summer—and were repulsed.

The negroes are the best-clad people in the South. They have their Sunday clothing, and the half-worn garments of their masters and mistresses; and having worn these but once a week, they have a decidedly fresher aspect than the dresses of their owners. They are well fed, too, at any cost, and present a happy appearance. And they are happy. It is a great mistake of the Abolitionists, in supposing the slaves hail their coming with delight; on the contrary, nearly all the negroes regard their approach with horror.

It might be well for the South if 500,000 of the slaves were suddenly emancipated. The loss would not be felt—and the North would soon be conscious of having gained nothing! My friend, Dr. Powell, near the city, abandoned his farm last summer, when it was partly in possession of the enemy, leaving fifty negroes on it—which he could have sold for $50,000. They promised not to leave him, and they kept their word. Judge Donnell, in North Carolina, has left his plantation with several hundred thousand dollars worth on it—rather risking their loss than to sell them.

DECEMBER 4TH.—All is quiet (before the storm) on the Rappahannock, Gen. Jackson's corps being some twenty miles lower down the river than Longstreet's. It is said Burnside has been removed already and Hooker given the command.

Gen. S. Cooper takes sides with Col. Myers against Gen. Wise. Gen. W.'s letter of complaint of the words, "Let them suffer," was referred to Gen. C., who insisted upon sending the letter to the Quartermaster-General before either the Secretary or the President saw it,—and it was done. Why do the Northern men *here* hate Wise?

Gen. Lee dispatches to-day that there is a very large amount of corn in the Rappahannock Valley, which can be procured, if wagons be sent from Richmond. What does this mean? That the enemy will come over and get it if we do not take it away?

A letter from the President of the Graniteville Cotton Mills, complains that only 75 per ct. profit is allowed by Act of Congress, whose operatives are exempted from military duty, if the law be interpreted to include sales to individuals as well as to the government, and suggesting certain modifications. He says he makes 14,000 yards per day, which is some 4,000,000 per annum. It costs him 20 cts. per yard to manufacture cotton cloth, including, of course, the cotton, and 75 per ct. will yield, I believe, $500,000 profits, which would be equivalent to 32 cts. per yard. But the market price, he says, is 68 cts. per yard, or some $2,000,000 profits! This war is a great encourager of domestic manufacturers, truly!

The Governor sends out a proclamation to-day, saying the President has called on him and other governors for assistance, in returning absent officers and men to their camps; in procuring supplies of food and clothing for the army; in drafting slaves to work on fortifications; and, finally, to put down the extortioners. The Governor invokes the people to respond promptly and fully. But how does this speak for the government, or rather the efficiency of the men who by "many indirect ways" came into power? Alas! it is a sad commentary.

The President sent a hundred papers to the department to-day, which he has been diligently poring over, as his pencil marks bear ample evidence. They were nearly all applications for office, and *this* business constitutes much of his labor.

DECEMBER 5TH.—Yesterday there was some little skirmishing below Fredericksburg. But it rained last night, and still rains. Lee has only 30,000 or 40,000 effective men.

We have the Federal President's Message to-day. It is moderate in tone, and is surprising for its argument on a *new proposition* that Congress pass resolutions proposing amendments to the Constitution, allowing compensation for all slaves emancipated between this and the year 1900! He argues that slaves are property, and that the South is no more responsible for the existence of slavery than the North! The very argument I have been using for twenty years. He thinks if his proposition be adopted that "several of the border States will embrace its terms, and that the Union will be reconstructed." He says the money expended in this way will not amount to so much as the cost of a war of subjugation. He is getting sick of the war, and therein I see the "beginning of the end" of it. It is a good sign for us, perhaps. I should not be surprised if his proposition had advocates in the South.

Lt.-Col. T. C. Johnson sent in a communication to-day. He alludes to an interview with the Secretary, in which the latter informed him that the government intended to exchange cotton for supplies for the army, and Lt.-Col. J. suggests that it be extended to embrace all kinds of merchandise for the people, and informs him that New York merchants are willing to send merchandise to our ports if we will permit their ships to return laden with cotton, at 50 cts. per pound, and pledging themselves to furnish goods at 50 per cent. advance on cost. He advocates a trade of this nature to the extent of $100,000,000, our government (and not individuals) to sell the cotton. The goods to be sold by the government to the merchants here. I know not what answer the Secretary will make. But I know our people are greedy for the merchandise.

The enemy have shelled Port Royal, below Fredericksburg, in retaliation for some damage done their gun-boats in the river by one of our land batteries. And we have news of the evacuation of Winchester by the enemy. The Northern papers say Burnside (who is not yet removed) will beat Lee on the Rappahannock, and that their army on the James River will occupy Richmond. When Lee is beaten, perhaps Richmond will fall.

A large number of our troops, recruited in Kentucky, have returned to their homes. It is said, however, that they will fight the enemy there as guerrillas.

The President has appointed his nephew, J. R. Davis, a brigadier-general. I suppose no president could escape denunciation, nevertheless, it is to be regretted that men of mind, men who wrought up the Southern people, with their pens, to the point of striking for national independence, are hurled into the background by the men who arranged the programme of our government. De Bow was offered a lower clerkship by Mr. Secretary Memminger, which he spurned; Fitzhugh accepted the lower class clerkship Mr. M. offered him after a prolonged hesitation; and others, who did more to produce the revolution than any one of the high functionaries now enjoying its emoluments, are to be found in the lowest subordinate positions; while Tom, Dick, and Harry, never heard of before, young, and capable of performing military service, rich, and able to live without office, are heads of bureaus, chief clerks of departments, and staff-officers flourishing their stars! Even this is known in the North, and they exult over it as a just retribution on those who were chiefly instrumental in fomenting revolution. But they forget that it was ever thus, and that our true patriots and bold thinkers who furnish our lesser men, in greater positions, with ideas, are still true and steadfast in the cause they have advocated so long.

DECEMBER 7TH.—Last night was bitter cold, and this morning there was ice on my wash-stand, within five feet of the fire. Is this the "sunny South" the North is fighting to possess? How much suffering must be in the armies now encamped in Virginia! I suppose there are not less than 250,000 men in arms on the plains of Virginia, and many of them who survive the war will have cause to remember last night. Some must have perished, and thousands, no doubt, had frozen limbs. It is terrible, and few are aware that the greatest destruction of life, in such a war as this, is not produced by wounds received in battle, but by disease, contracted from exposure, etc., in inclement seasons. But the deadly bullet claims its victims. A friend just returned from the battle-field of June, near the city, whither he repaired to recover the remains of a relative, says the scene is still one of horror. So great was the slaughter (27th June) that we were unable to bury our own dead for several days, for the battle raged a whole week, and when the work was completed, the weather having been extremely hot, it was too late to inter the enemy effectually, so the earth was merely thrown over them, forming mounds, which the rains and the wind have since leveled. And now the ground is thickly strewn with the bleaching bones of the invaders. The flesh is gone, but their garments remain. He says he passed through a wood, not a tree of which escaped the missiles of the contending hosts. Most of the trees left standing are dead, being often perforated by scores of Minié-balls, but thousands were prostrated by cannon-balls and shells. It will long remain a scene of desolation, a monument of the folly and wickedness of man.

And what are we fighting for? What does the Northern Government propose to accomplish by the invasion? Is it supposed that six or eight million of free people can be exterminated? How many butchers would be required to accomplish the beneficent feat? More, many more, than can be sent hither. The Southern people, in such a cause, would fight to the last, and when the men all fell, the women and children would snatch their arms and slay the oppressors. Without complete annihilation, it is the merest nonsense to suppose our property can be confiscated.

But if a forced reconstruction of the Union were consummated, does the North suppose any advantage would result to that section? In the Union we could not be compelled to trade with them again. Nor would intercourse of any kind be re-established. Their ships would be destroyed, and their people could never come among us but at the risk of ill treatment. They could not maintain a standing army of half a million, and they could not disarm us in such an extensive territory.

The best plan, the only plan, to redeem the past and enjoy blessings in the future, is to cease this bootless warfare and be the first to recognize our independence. We are exasperated with

Europe, and like the old colonel in Bulwer's play, we can like a brave foe after fighting him. Let the North do this, and we will trade with its people, I have no doubt, and a mutual respect will grow up in time, resulting, probably, in combinations against European powers in their enterprises against governments on this continent.

DECEMBER 8TH.—A letter from Gen. Lee, received to-day, states that, in the recent campaigns, he has experienced the effects of having inferior artillery and fixed ammunition. But this discrepancy is rapidly disappearing, from captures of the enemy's batteries, etc. He recommends that our 12-pounder howitzers and 6-pounder smooth bores be recast into 12-pounder Napoleons, 10-pounder Parrott guns, and 3-inch rifle cannon. He wants four 12-pounder Napoleons sent him immediately, for a *special purpose. His next battle will be principally with artillery.*

Gov. Vance sends a letter, referring to an order of the government that all cotton not removed west of the Weldon and Williamsburg Railroad, by the 16th instant, is to be destroyed. He says his State is purchasing 15,000 to 20,000 bales, to establish a credit in Europe, and asks that the Confederate Government authorities will respect the cotton designed for this purpose. He says he will destroy it himself, when the enemy approaches. He says, moreover, that the order will have an unhappy effect; that many of the people have already lost their slaves, grain, etc. from the inroads of the enemy, and have nothing to live on but their cotton. If it remains where it is, how can they subsist on it without selling it to the enemy? And that would be treason, pretty nearly. But why does the government issue such an order in North Carolina, when the government itself is selling, not destroying, the cotton of Mississippi?

The President of the Central Railroad says that Messrs. Haxhall, Crenshaw & Co., who have the gigantic contract with the government to furnish flour, and who have a preference of transportation by the contract, are blocking up their depots, and fail to remove the grain. They keep whole trains waiting for days to be unladen; and thus hundreds of thousands of bushels, intended for other mills and the people are delayed, and the price kept up to the detriment of the community. Thus it is that the government contractors are aiding and abetting the extortioners. And for this reason large amounts of grain may fall into the hands of the enemy.

DECEMBER 9TH.—W——l, another of Provost Marshal Griswold's policemen, has arrived in Washington. I never doubted he was secretly in the Yankee service here, where many of his fellows still remain, betraying the hand that feeds them. Gen. Winder and the late Secretaries of War must be responsible for all the injury they may inflict upon the country.

Yesterday, the President received a letter from a gentleman well known to him, asserting that if Mississippi and Alabama be overrun by the enemy, a large proportion of the people of those States will certainly submit to the Government of the United States. The President sent this letter to the Secretary of War "for his information."

A letter from W. P. Harris, Jackson, Mississippi, urges the government to abandon the cities and eastern seaboard, and concentrate all the forces in the West, for the defense of the Mississippi Valley and River, else the latter must be lost, which will be fatal to the cause, etc.

Hon. J. H. Reagan has written a savage letter to the Secretary of War, withdrawing certain papers relating to an application for the discharge from service of his brother-in-law, on account of feeble health. He says he will not await the motions (uncertain) of the circumlocution office, and is unwilling to produce evidence of his statements of the disability of his relative. Mr. Seddon will doubtless make a spirited response to this imputation on his office.

We have a rumor that Morgan has made another brilliant raid into Kentucky, capturing 1800 of the enemy.

The small-pox is spreading in this city to an alarming extent. This is the feast to which Burnside is invited. They are vaccinating the clerks in the departments.

Gen. Floyd writes the government that, as the enemy cannot advance from the West before spring, Echol's and Marshall's forces (10,000) might be used on the seaboard. I wish they were here.

The United States forces in the field, by their own estimates, amount to 800,000. We have not exceeding 250,000; but they are not aware of that.

DECEMBER 10TH.—Not a word from the Rappahannock. But there soon will be.

Official dispatches from Gen. Bragg confirm the achievement of Col. Morgan, *acting* as brigadier-general. There was a fight, several hundred being killed and wounded on both sides; but Morgan's victory was complete, his captures amounting to 1800 men, a battery, wagon train, etc.

We have also a dispatch that *Major-Gen. Lovell*, the Yankee, had a battle with the enemy, killing, wounding, and capturing 34!

A characteristic letter was received to-day from Mr. Sanford, Alabama, recommending Col. Dowdell for a brigadiership. I hope he may get it, as he is a gallant *Southerner*. Mr. S. has some hard hits at the government; calling it a government of chief clerks and subordinate clerks. He hopes Mr. Seddon will not be merely a clerk.

Gen. Jos. E. Johnston has written from the West a gloomy letter to Mr. Wigfall, Texan Senator. He says he is ordered to reinforce Lieut.-Gen. Pemberton (another Northern general) from Bragg's army. Pemberton is retreating on Grenada, Mississippi, followed by 40,000 of the enemy. How is he, Gen. J., to get from Tennessee to Grenada with reinforcements, preceded by one army of the enemy, and followed by another?

Mr. Wigfall recommends the Secretary (as if *he* could do it!) to concentrate all the armies of the West, and beat the enemy out of the Mississippi Valley. Gen. Johnston says Lieut.-Gen. Holmes *has* been ordered to reinforce Pemberton. Why, this is the very thing Mr. Randolph did, and lost his *clerkship* for it! The President must have changed his mind.

Gen. Randolph sent in his resignation as brigadier-general to-day. The younger brigadiers, Davis (the President's nephew) and Pryor, have been recently assigned to brigades, and this may have operated on Randolph as an emetic.

There are two war steamers at Charleston from abroad; one a Frenchman, the other an Englishman. Gen. Beauregard entertained the officers of the first the other day.

Gen. Banks has sailed down the coast on an expedition, the nature of which, no doubt, will be developed soon.

DECEMBER 11TH.—Gen. Lee dispatched this morning early that the enemy were constructing three pontoon bridges, and that firing had commenced on both sides. At nine o'clock A.M. the firing increased, and Gen. Lee dispatched for ammunition, looking to the contingency of a prolonged battle.

At three P.M., Gen. Lee says, the enemy had been repulsed in two of their attempts to throw bridges over the river; but the third attempt *would probably succeed*, as it was under cover of batteries which commanded the river, and where his sharpshooters could not reach the workmen. But, he says, *his batteries command the plain* where the enemy must debouch. We may speedily hear of a most sanguinary conflict.

Burnside must have greatly superior numbers, or else he is a great fool to precipitate his men into a plain, where every Southern soldier is prepared to die, in the event of failure to conquer! There is no trepidation here; on the contrary, a settled calm on the faces of the people, which might be mistaken for indifference. They are confident of the success of Lee, and really seem apprehensive that Burnside will not come over and fight him in a decisive battle. We shall soon see, now, of what stuff Burnside and his army are made. I feel some anxiety; because the destruction of our little army on the Rappahannock might be the fall of Richmond.

It is rumored that the President started two days ago for the West—Tennessee and Mississippi. No papers have been sent in by him since Tuesday, and it may be true. If so, he means to return speedily. I think we shall soon have news from the lower James River.

A letter from the Governor of Alabama calls urgently for heavy guns, and a reserve force, for the defense of Mobile.

Major Hause, the government's agent in Europe, has purchased, up to this time, 157,000 stand of arms, besides many cannon, much ammunition, quartermaster's stores, etc. A portion was lost in transitu, however, but not a large amount. Besides the large sums he has expended, he has obtained credit to the extent of $6,000,000!

They are calling for a guard at Petersburg against incendiaries. A factory was burned the other night. This is bad.

Scully and Lewis, condemned to die as spies, have been pardoned by the President, and are to be sent North.

Another dispatch from Gen. Lee, dated 3½ P.M., says the enemy has nearly completed his bridge, and will probably commence crossing this evening or in the morning. The bulletin boards in the city purport to give intelligence of the passage having been effected in part; but I do not see how the editors could have obtained their information.

At 6 P.M., passengers by the Fredericksburg train (which left at 1 P.M.) report the shelling of the town, and a great battle in progress on this side of the river. I doubt both; and I saw but one excited man (a Jew) who said he was in Fredericksburg when the shelling began. I do not believe it. The cars were not within four miles of the town, and perhaps merely *conjectured* the cannonading they heard to be directed at the town. There were no ladies or children in the cars. But doubtless the enemy *will* cross the river, and there will be a battle, which must result in a great mortality.

DECEMBER 12TH.—The enemy have possession of Fredericksburg, and succeeded in crossing a large portion of their force three miles below, on their pontoon bridge. Up to 3 P.M. to-day, we have no other intelligence but that "they are fighting." We shall know more, probably, before night.

The President has passed through East Tennessee on his way to Mississippi.

Lieut.-Col. Nat Tyler, publisher of the *Enquirer*, the organ of the government, was in my office this morning, denouncing Mr. Memminger, Secretary of the Treasury. He says Mr. M.'s head is as worthless as a pin's-head. He also denounced the rules of admission to our Secretary, adopted by Mr. R. G. H. Kean, Chief of the Bureau, and asked for a copy of them, that he might denounce them in his paper. It appears that Mr. Jacques is to say *who* can see the Secretary; and to do this, he must catechize each applicant as to the nature of his business. This is deemed insulting by some of the hot bloods, and will make friend Mr. J.'s position rather a disagreeable and derogatory one.

DECEMBER 13TH.—After all, Fredericksburg was severely shelled—whether designedly or incidentally in the fight, does not yet appear.

Our army has fallen back a little—for a purpose. Lee knows every inch of the ground.

Again we have rumors of a hostile fleet being in the river; and

Major-Gen. G. W. Smith has gone to Petersburg to see after the means of defense, if an attack should be made in that quarter. Some little gloom and despondency are manifested, for the first time, in this community.

Major-Gen. S. Jones writes that although the Federal Gen. Cox has left the valley of the Kanawha, 5000 of his men remain; and he deems it inexpedient, in response to Gen. Lee's suggestion, to detach any portion of his troops for operations elsewhere. He says Jenkins's cavalry is in a bad condition.

Here is an instance of South Carolina honor. During the battle of Williamsburg, last spring, W. R. Erwin, a private in Col. Jenkins's Palmetto sharpshooters, was detailed to take care of the wounded, and was himself taken prisoner. The enemy supposing him to be a surgeon, he was paroled. He now returns to the service; and although the mistake could never be detected, he insists on our government exchanging a private of the enemy's for himself. With the assurance that this will be done, he goes again to battle.

Yesterday flour and tobacco had a fall at auction. Some suppose the bidders had in view the contingency of the capture of the city by the enemy.

In the market-house this morning, I heard a man speaking loudly, denounce a farmer for asking about $6 a bushel for his potatoes, and hoping that the Yankees would take them from him for nothing!

DECEMBER 14TH, SUNDAY.—Yesterday was a bloody day. Gen. Lee telegraphs that the enemy attacked him at 9 A.M., and as the fog lifted, the fire ran along the whole line, and the conflict raged until darkness (6 P.M.) put an end to the battle. The enemy was repulsed at all points, he continued, thanks be to God! But we have to mourn, as usual, a heavy loss. Lee expects another blow at Burnside to-day.

It is understood that Gens. Hood, Texas, was wounded; T. R. R. Cobb, Georgia, and a brigadier from South Carolina were killed. A dispatch says that where our generals fell, the colonels could no longer restrain their regiments; and the men ran into the ranks of the enemy, and, animated with a spirit of desperation, slaughtered the foe in great numbers with their bayonets, pistols, and knives.

Preparations are being made here for the reception of the wounded. The request was to provide for a large number.

Last night, at nine o'clock, a number of regiments which had been encamped among the fortifications northwest of the city, were marched down to Drewry's Bluff. It is probable Gen. Smith has heard of the enemy's approach from that quarter. I hope he may prove the right man in the right place.

It is rumored that we were repulsed yesterday, this side of Suffolk.

At this critical moment the President is away.

A dispatch from Gen. Lee says Gen. Wade Hampton dashed *into Dumfries*, the other side of the Rappahannock, and in the *rear of the enemy*, capturing some wagons, and taking a few men. This seems most extraordinary. If he be not taken himself, the diversion must have a good effect; but if he be taken, it will be considered a wild and desperate sally, boding no good to the cause. But Lee knows what he is about.

From the dispositions of our troops (few in number) in the vicinity of Richmond, at this moment, it seems to me that Gen. Smith is putting the city to great hazard. There are not a thousand men to guard the approach from the head of York River; and if a dozen of the enemy's swift transports were to dash up that river, the city could be surprised by 5000 men!

Ten o'clock A.M. No dispatches from Lee have come over the wires to-day. He may have interdicted others. We got no intelligence whatever. From this I infer the battle was resumed at early dawn, and the general deems it best to have no announcements but *results*. If this be so, it is a day big with events—and upon its issue may depend the fate of governments. And yet our people exhibited no trepidation. The foreign portion of the population may be seen grouped on the pavements indulging in speculation, and occasionally giving vent to loud laughter, when a Jew is asked what will be the price of his shoes, etc. to-morrow. They care not which side gains the day, so they gain the profits.

But our women and children are going to church as usual, to pray for the success of the cause, and not doubting but that our army will triumph as usual on the field of combat. It is a bright and lovely Sabbath morning, and as warm as May.

DECEMBER 15TH.—Yesterday evening several trains laden with

wounded arrived in the city. The remains of Brig.-Gen. T. R. R. Cobb, of Georgia, were brought down. Brig.-Gen. Gregg, of South Carolina, is said to be mortally wounded. It is now believed that Major-Gen. Hood, of Texas, did not fall. The number of our killed and wounded is estimated, by a surgeon who came with the wounded, to be not over a thousand.

To-day, stragglers from the battle-field say that our loss in killed and wounded is 3000. It is all conjecture.

There was heavy skirmishing all day yesterday, and until to-day at noon, when the telegraph operator reports that the firing had ceased. We know not (yet) what this means. We are still sending artillery ammunition to Gen. Lee.

Gen. Evans dispatches from Kinston, N. C., that on the 14th, yesterday, he repulsed the enemy, 15,000 strong, and drove them back to their boats in Neuse River. A portion of Gen. R. A. Pryor's command, in Isle of Wight County, was engaged with the enemy's advance the same day. They have also landed at Gloucester Point. This is pronounced a simultaneous attack on our harbors and cities in Virginia and North Carolina. Perhaps we shall have more before night. Our people seem prepared for any event.

Another long train of negroes have just passed through the city, singing, to work on the fortifications.

DECEMBER 16TH.—To-day the city is exalted to the skies! Gen. Lee telegraphed that the enemy had disappeared from his front, *probably meditating a design to cross at some other place.* Such were his words, which approach nearer to a practical joke, and an inkling of exultation, than anything I have seen from his pen. He has saved the capital. Before the enemy could approach Richmond from "some other place," Lee would be between him and the city, and if he could beat him on the Rappahannock he can beat him anywhere.

Doubtless Burnside has abandoned his heavy stores, siege guns, etc., and at this moment our army must occupy the town. Lee *allowed* the invaders to cross the river, and, in exact accordance with his promise, made a month ago, before they could advance from Fredericksburg, his "whole army *was* in position." They could not debouch without passing through our crescent line, the extreme ends of which touched the river above and below them.

They attempted this on Saturday, and met with a bloody defeat, and until last night, when they retraced their steps, were confined to an exceedingly narrow and uncomfortable strip of land along the south bank of the river.

Our loss in the battle will not exceed, perhaps, 2000 men, not more than 500 being slain. It is estimated that the enemy's loss is over 10,000, and it may greatly exceed that number, as our positions were strong and our batteries numerous. The enemy fought well, charging repeatedly over the plain swept completely by our guns, and leaving the earth strewn with their dead. We have many prisoners, but I have heard no estimate of the number.

The enemy have taken Kinston, N. C., having overwhelming numbers, and a letter from Gen. Bragg, dated at Raleigh, yesterday, says it is probable Goldsborough will fall into their hands. This will cut our railroad communication with Wilmington, which may likewise fall—but not without its price in blood.

Why not let the war cease now? It is worse than criminal to prolong it, when it is apparent that subjugation is an impossibility.

There were no stragglers from Lee's army, and never were men in better spirits and condition. They are well clad and fed, and exceedingly anxious for Burnside to resume his "On to Richmond" after the *skirmish* of Saturday. They call it but a skirmish, for not a brigade was blown, not a regiment fatigued.

Although men shake hands over this result, they all say they never looked for any other termination of Burnside. The ladies say he is now charred all over. Well, he *may* come again by some other route, but I have doubts. The rigors of winter are sufficient punishment for his troops. It is said Burnside intended to resume the battle on Sunday morning, but his generals reported that their men could not be relied upon to approach our batteries again. I shall look with interest for the next Northern papers.

DECEMBER 17TH.—A dispatch from Gen. G. W. Smith, last night, says we have repulsed the enemy from Kinston, N. C., but a dispatch this morning says a cavalry force has cut the railroad near Goldsborough, broken down the wires, and burnt the bridge. We had no letters from beyond that point this morning.

Last night large quantities of ammunition and some more regiments were sent to North Carolina. This is done because Richmond is relieved by the defeat and retreat of Burnside. But suppose it should *not* be relieved, and a force should be sent suddenly up the James and York Rivers?

We have not a word from Fredericksburg, and it is probable Burnside's batteries still command the town. Lee is content and has no idea of crossing the river.

There are two notable rumors in the streets: first, that we have gained a great battle in Tennessee; and, second, that the government at Washington has arrested John Van Buren and many other Democratic leaders in the North, which has resulted in a riot, wherein 1000 have fallen, making the gutters in New York run with blood!

Gen. Lee's official report says our loss in the battle of the 13th in killed and wounded did not exceed 1200, whereas our *papers* said 2050 wounded have already been brought to this city.

Well, our government must have spies at Washington as an offset to Federal spies here among Gen. Winder's policemen; for we knew *exactly* when the enemy would begin operations in North Carolina, and ordered the cotton east of the Weldon Railroad to be burnt on the 16th inst., yesterday, and yesterday the road was cut by the enemy. I have not heard of the cotton being burnt—*and I don't believe it was destroyed.* Nor do I believe Gen. Smith knew that Burnside would be defeated in time to send troops from here to North Carolina.

Elwood Fisher died recently in Georgia, and his pen, so highly prized by the South for its able vindication of her rights, was forgotten by the politicians who have power in the Confederate Government. All Mr. Memminger would offer him was a lowest class clerkship. He died of a broken heart. He was more deserving, but less fortunate, than Mr. M.

It was Mr. *Memminger*, it seems, who refused to contribute anything to supply the soldiers with shoes, and the press is indignant. They say he is not only not a native South Carolinian, but Hessian born.

DECEMBER 18TH.—We have more accounts of the battle of Fredericksburg now in our possession. Our loss in killed and wounded will probably be more than the estimate in the official report, while Federal prisoners report theirs at 20,000. This may be over the mark, but the *Examiner's* correspondent at Fredericksburg puts down their loss at 19,000. The Northern papers of the 14th inst. (while they supposed the battle still undecided) express the hope that Burnside will fight his last man and fire his last cartridge on that field, rather than not succeed in destroying Lee's army! Lee's army, after our victory, is mostly uninjured. The loss it sustained was not a "flea-bite."

The enemy, in their ignominous flight on Saturday night, left their dead propped up as sentinels and pickets, besides 3000 on the plain.

Accounts from North Carolina indicate the repulse of the enemy, though they have burnt some of the railroad bridges. We shall hear more anon. Reinforcements are flying to the scene of action.

DECEMBER 19TH.—Gen. Burnside acknowledges a loss of upwards of 5000, which is good evidence here that his loss was not less than 15,000. The Washington papers congratulate themselves on the *escape* of their army, and say it might have been easily captured by Lee. They propose, now, going into winter quarters.

We have nothing further from North Carolina or Mississippi. Gen. Banks's expedition had passed Hilton Head.

A Mr. Bunch, British Consul, has written an impudent letter to the department, alleging that an Irishman, unnaturalized, is forcibly detained in one of our camps. He says his letters have not been answered, which was great discourtesy, and he means to inform Lord John Russell of it. This letter *was* replied to in rather scathing terms, as the Irishman had enlisted and then deserted. Besides, we are out of humor with England now, and court a French alliance.

The President was at Chattanooga on the 15th instant; and writes the Secretary that he has made some eight appointments of brigadiers, and promotions to major-generals. Major-Gen. Buckner is assigned to command at Mobile.

We are straightened for envelopes, and have taken to turning those we receive. This is economy; something new in the South. My family dines four or five times a week on *liver* and rice. We cannot afford anything better; others do not live so well.

Custis and I were vaccinated to-day, with the rest of the officers of the department.

The Northern papers now want the Federal army to go into winter quarters. This was, confessedly, to be the final effort to take Richmond. It failed. Many of the people regard the disaster of Burnside as the harbinger of peace.

An officer from the field informs me that all our generals were sadly disappointed, when it was discovered that Burnside had fled. They wanted one more blow at him, and he would have been completely destroyed.

DECEMBER 20TH.—Last accounts from Fredericksburg state that the enemy are retiring toward the Potomac and Washington. We have got some of their pontoon bridges, and other things left behind. It is now very cold, with a fair prospect of the Potomac freezing over. Let them beware!

But we were in a bad way: our army, instead of numbering 200,000 as the Federal journals report, did not exceed 50,000 men; and not half that number went into action. The Secretary of War had ordered several regiments from Gen. S. Jones, in Western Virginia; now sent to North Carolina.

There is no mail yet from beyond Goldsborough, and the news from North Carolina seems vague and unsatisfactory. They say we beat the enemy at Kinston; yet they have destroyed a portion of the railroad between Goldsborough and Wilmington. They say the Federals are retreating on Newbern; yet we know they made 500 of our men prisoners after they crossed the Neuse. It is reported that our loss is small, and the enemy's large; and that our 3000 men fought successfully their 18,000. However, we have sent some 15,000 reinforcements.

It is reported that the Federals are evacuating Nashville; but reports from the West are not always reliable.

A communication has been received by Secretary Seddon from S. B. M., of Vicksburg, proposing to purchase shoes, blankets, etc. in the United States, and sell them to the government for cotton or for Confederate notes. This was referred to the Quartermaster-General, who favors it. Now what will Mr. Secretary do? Better wait till the President returns!

The late Secretary of War, Mr. Randolph, has formed a partnership with Mr. G. A. Myers. To-day a paper was sent in by them to the new Secretary, containing the names of ten clients, all Jews and extortioners, who, it appears, at the beginning of the war, and before Virginia had fully seceded, joined several Virginia companies of artillery, but did not drill with them. They hired substitutes for a small sum, all, as the memorial sets forth, being foreigners of the class subsequently exempted by act of Congress. And these counselors demand the exemption of the Jew extortioners on the ground that they once furnished substitutes, now out of the service! And it is probable they will carry their point, and gain large fees. Substitutes now are worth $2000—then, $100.

A dispatch from Charleston to-day says: "Iron steamer Columbia, formerly the Giraffe, of Liverpool, with cargo of shoes, blankets, Whitworth guns, and ammunition, arrived yesterday." I suppose cargoes of this nature have been arriving once a week ever since the war broke out. This cargo, and the ship, belong to the government.

9 O'CLOCK P.M.—After a very cold day, it has become intensely frigid. I have two fires in our little Robin's Nest (frame) on the same floor, and yet ice forms rapidly in both rooms, and we have been compelled to empty the pitchers! This night I doubt not the Potomac will be closed to Burnside and his transports! During the first Revolution, the Chesapeake was frozen over. If we have a winter like that, we shall certainly have an armistice in Virginia without the intervention of any other than the Great Power above. But we shall suffer for the want of fuel: wood is $18 per cord, and coal $14 per cart load.

Gen. Bonham, who somehow incurred the dislike of the authorities here, and was dropped out of the list of brigadiers, has been made Governor of South Carolina.

And Gen. Wise, who is possessed of perhaps the greatest mind in the Confederacy, is still fettered. They will not let him fight a battle, because he is "ambitious!" When Norfolk was (wickedly) given up, his home and all his possessions fell into the hands of the enemy. He is now without a shelter for his head, bivouacing with his devoted brigade at Chaffin's farm, below the city. He is the senior brigadier in the army, and will never be a major-general.

DECEMBER 21ST, SUNDAY.—Nothing, yet, has been done by the immense Federal fleet of iron-clad gun-boats which were to devastate our coast this winter. But the winter is not over yet, and I apprehend something will be attempted. However, we shall make a heroic defense of every point assailed.

I omitted to state, in connection with the partnership formed between Mr. Myers and Mr. Randolph, that the former had already succeeded, when the latter was Secretary of War, in getting the substitutes of the Jew extortioners out of the army, on the ground that they were not domiciled in this country; and now both are intent on procuring the exemption of the principals. This may be good practice, but it is not good service. Every man protected and enriched by the government, owes service to the country in its hour of peril.

I am glad to hear that W. H. B. Custis, of the Eastern Shore of Virginia, takes no part in the war. This is the proper course for him under the circumstances. It is said he declined a high position tendered by the Federal Government. No doubt he has been much misrepresented: his principles are founded on the Constitution, which is violated daily at Washington, and therefore he can have no sympathy with that government.

DECEMBER 22D.—We shall never arrive at the correct amount of casualties at the battle of Fredericksburg. The *Enquirer* to-day indicates that our loss in killed, wounded, and missing (prisoners), amounted to nearly 4000. On the other hand, some of the Federal journals hint that their loss was 25,000. Gen. Armstrong (Confederate), it is said, counted 3500 of their dead on the field; and this was after many were buried. There are five wounded to one killed. But where Burnside is now, or what he will attempt next, no doubt Lee knows; but the rest of our people are profoundly ignorant in relation thereto. The New York *Herald* says: "The finest and best appointed army the world ever saw, has been beaten by a batch of Southern ragamuffins!" And it advises that the shattered remains of the army be put into winter quarters.

The weather has greatly moderated. I hope, now, it will continue moderate!

Mr. Crenshaw, who has the gigantic flour contract with the War Department, effected with Mr. Randolph, has just (in the President's absence) made another contract with Mr. Seddon. The department becomes a partner with him, and another party in England, in a huge commercial transaction, the object of which is to run goods in, and cotton out. We shall have our Girards, as well as the United States. Mr. Crenshaw proceeds to England immediately, bearing letters of credit to Mr. Mason, our Minister, etc.

An immense sum is to be sent West to pay for stores, etc., and Mr. Benjamin recommends the financial agent to the department. The illicit trade with the United States has depleted the country of gold, and placed us at the feet of the Jew extortioners. It still goes on. Mr. Seddon has granted passports to two agents of a Mr. Baumgartien—and how many others I know not. These Jews have the adroitness to carry their points. They have injured the cause more than the armies of Lincoln. Well, if we gain our independence, instead of being the vassals of the Yankees, we shall find all our wealth in the hands of the Jews.

The accounts from North Carolina are still conflicting. It is said the enemy have retired to Newbern; but still we have no letters beyond Goldsborough. From Raleigh we learn that the legislature have postponed the army bill until the 20th of January.

December 23d.—The battle of Fredericksburg is still the topic, or the wonder, and it transpired more than nine days ago. It will have its page in history, and be read by school-boys a thousand years hence. The New York *Times* exclaims, "God help us—for man cannot." This is another war sheet. The *Tribune* is bewildered, and knows not what to say. The *Herald* says "everything by turns, and nothing long." Its sympathies are ever with the winning party. But it is positively asserted that both Seward and his son have resigned, to be followed by the rest of the cabinet. That example might be followed here without detriment to our cause. And it is said Burnside has resigned. I doubt that—but no doubt he will be removed. It is said Fremont has been appointed his successor. That would be good news. I think Halleck will be removed, and McClellan will be recalled. No matter.

It is said our President will command in Mississippi himself—the army having no confidence in Pemberton, because he is a Yankee.

We have a letter to-day from Gen. Pike (another Yankee), saying the Indian country is lost—lost, because Gens. Holmes and Hindman—Southern men—won't let him have his own way!

The news from North Carolina is still cloudy. Gen. G. W. Smith is there (another Northern man).

19*

Gen. Elzey has been appointed to command this department during Gen. L.'s absence. Gen. E. is a Marylander. In the President's absence, it is said this appointment was made by Gen. S. Cooper (another Yankee) to insult Virginia by preventing the capital from being in the hands of a Virginian. The Richmond papers occasionally allude to the fact that the general highest in rank in the Confederacy is a Yankee—Gen. S. Cooper.

Gen. Lee says his ammunition is bad in quality, and that his new guns burst in the late battle—all under charge of the chief of the Bureau of Ordnance—another Yankee. Gen. D. H. Hill writes a scathing letter to the department in response to a rebuke from the new Secretary, occasioned by some complaints of Major Palfrey in Gen. Cooper's (A. and I. General) office. I do not know where Major P. came from; but the fact that he was not in the field, gave the general occasion to rasp him severely. It must have been caused by an order transferring, furloughing, or discharging some soldier in Gen. H.'s division—and his patience vanished at the idea of having his men taken out of the ranks without consulting him, by carpet knights and civilian lawyers. He says 8000 are now absent from his command—and that Gen. Johnston's army, last spring, was reduced from the same cause to 40,000 men, where he had to oppose 138,000 of the "rascally Yankees." He concludes, however, by saying it is the duty of subordinate generals in the field to submit in all humility to the behests of their superiors comfortably quartered in Richmond. But if justice were done, and the opinions of the generals in the field were regarded in the matter of discharges, etc., the lawyers, who have grown fat on fees by thinning our ranks, would be compelled to resort to some more laudable means of making a living.

A letter from Gov. Shorter, of Alabama, introduces Judge Rice, agent for P. S. Gerald and J. R. Powell, who propose to bring goods into the Confederate States through Mexico, to be paid for in cotton, etc. This was referred by the Secretary to the Quartermaster-General—who protests against it on the ground that it might interfere with *his agents already engaged in the business.*

The President publishes a retaliatory proclamation to-day against Gen. Butler, for hanging Mr. Mumford, of New Orleans, who took down the United States flag before the city had surrendered. He declares Butler to be out of the pale of civilization; and orders any commander who may capture him, to hang him as an outlaw. And all commissioned officers serving under Butler, and in arms with negroes, to be reserved for execution.

There is a rumor that an agent of the Federal Government has arrived in the city, to propose an armistice. No armistice, unless on the basis of *uti possidetis ante bellum!*

Bethel, Leesburg, and Fredericksburg are victories memorable for our great success when fighting in advantageous positions. They teach a lesson to generals; and it will be apparent that no necessity exists for so great an expenditure of life in the prosecution of this war. The disparity of numbers should be considered by our generals. I fear the flower of our chivalry mostly perished in storming batteries. It is true a *prestige* was gained.

DECEMBER 24TH.—The *Louisville Journal* says the defeat of Burnside is "sickening," and that this sad condition of affairs cannot be borne long.

It is said that Confederate bonds are bringing quite as much in New York as in Richmond; and that the bonds of Southern men are freely discounted in the North. These, if true, are *indications* of approaching peace. Cotton at 50 cents per pound, and our capacity to produce five million bales per annum, must dazzle the calculating Yankees. A single crop worth $1,000,000,000! What interest or department of industry in the United States can promise such results?

Letters were received to-day from Nassau, dated 12th December. Mr. L. Heyliger, our agent, reports a number of steamers sailing, and about to sail, with large amounts of stores and goods of all kinds, besides *plates for our navy.* A Mr. Wiggs has several steamers engaged in this business. Our government own some, and private individuals (foreign speculators) are largely engaged in the trade. Most of these steamers run sixteen miles an hour.

A Mr. Hart, agent for S. Isaac Campbell & Co., London, proposes to clothe and equip 100,000 men for us, and to receive certificates for specific amounts of cotton. This same house has, on this, it is said, advanced as much as $2,000,000 on our account. This looks cheering. We have credit abroad. But they are JEWS.

Mr. Heyliger says he has seen letters from the United States, conveying information that Charleston is to be attacked about the holidays—the ensuing week—by four iron-clad gun-boats. Well, I believe *we* have three there; so let them come!

Every day we have propositions to supply the army and the country with goods, for cotton; and they succeed in delivering stores, etc., in spite of the vigilance of the Federal blockading squadrons. There is a prospect that we shall have abundance of everything some of these days. But there is some wrangling. The Quartermaster-General complains to-day that Lieut.-Gen. Pemberton has interfered with his agents, trading cotton for stores. Myers is a Jew, and Pemberton a Yankee—so let them fight it out.

DECEMBER 25TH, CHRISTMAS DAY.—Northern papers show that there is much distraction in the North; that both Seward and Chase, who had resigned their positions, were with difficulty persuaded to resume them. This news, coupled with the recent victory, and some reported successes in the West (Van Dorn's capture of Holly Springs), produces some effect on the spirits of the people here; and we have a merrier Christmas than the last one.

It is said the Federal Congress is about to provide for the organization of 100 regiments of negroes. This does not occasion anxiety here. The slaves, once armed, would cut their way back to their masters. The only possible way to restore the Union—if indeed it be possible—is to withdraw all the Federal troops, and maintain an *effective* blockade. There might possibly ensue dissensions among our politicians and States, detrimental to any required unity of purpose. But the Yankees, with all their smartness, cannot perceive this. They can never appal us with horrors, for we have fed upon nothing else for so long a period, that we have become accustomed to them. And they have not men enough to subjugate us and hold us in subjugation. Two millions would not suffice!

The boys are firing Chinese crackers everywhere, and no little gunpowder is consumed in commemoration of the day.

But turkeys are selling at $11 each! Shoes for $25 per pair. Salt, however, has fallen from $1.50 to 33 cents per pound. Fresh meats sell at from 35 to 50 cents per pound.

A silver (lever) watch, which had been lying in my trunk for two years, and which cost me $25, sold at auction yesterday for $75. This sufficed for fuel for a month, and a Christmas dinner. At the end of another month, my poor family must be scattered again, as this house will be occupied by its owner. I have advertised for boarding in the country, but get no response. It would require $300 per month to board my family here, and that is more than my income. What shall we do? Trust in God!

December 26th.—We have no news to-day—not even a rumor. We are ready for anything that may come. No doubt the assailants of Mobile, Wilmington, or Charleston, will meet with determined resistance.

The President will be in Richmond about the first day of January. I saw a man who traveled with him in Alabama.

Vicksburg, I understand, cannot be taken by water. And Grant, the Federal general, is said to be retreating out of Mississippi.

December 27th.—The successes in the West have been confirmed. Morgan captured 2000 and Van Dorn 1500 prisoners at Holly Springs. They likewise destroyed a large amount of stores.

We have intelligence of a great armament, under Gen. Sherman, sailing from Memphis against Vicksburg. At the last accounts the President was at Vicksburg; and he may be witness of this decisive struggle for the possession of the Mississippi River, the result of which involves immense interests. We await with much anxiety the issue of the naval operations during the ensuing month. We are content with the land achievements of this year; and if we should be equally successful in resisting the enemy's fleets, we shall deem ourselves fortunate indeed.

The agents of the Commissary and Quartermaster-General make grievous complaints against Lieut.-Gen. Pemberton, at Grenada, Mississippi; they say he interferes with their arrangements to procure supplies—for cotton; and it is intimated that he has some little arrangements of his own of that nature. This illicit trade is very demoralizing in its nature.

Oh, that peace would return! But with Independence!

December 28th.—We have no news to-day from the West. If the great battle has been fought at Vicksburg, we ought to know it to-day or to-morrow; and if the enemy be beaten, it should be decisive of the war. It would be worse than madness to continue the contest for the Union.

Several fine brass batteries were brought down from Fredericksburg last night, an indication that the campaign is over for the winter in that direction.

If we should have disasters in the West, and on the Southern seaboard, the next session of Congress, to begin a fortnight hence, will be a stormy one.

DECEMBER 29TH.—We have a dispatch from Vicksburg at last. The enemy, 25,000 strong, were repulsed three times yesterday, and finally driven back seven miles, to their gun-boats. It was no battle, for our loss was only 30, and that of the enemy 400. It will be fought to-day, probably.

It is said an attempt will be made this week on Weldon, as well as Charleston.

Our Morgan has been in Kentucky again, and captured 1200 men. Glorious Morgan!

The accounts from the United States are rather cheering. The *Herald* proposes a convention of all the "loyal States," that reconstruction may be tried in that way. A dispatch from Tennessee says, even the New York *Tribune* expresses the opinion that our independence must be recognized. The Philadelphia *Press* proposes another route to Richmond *via* the rivers, and thinks Richmond may be taken yet, and the rebellion crushed.

The surgeon in charge of the Howard Hospital reports that the small-pox is greatly on the increase, and terminating fatally in almost every case. He says men die of it without eruptions on the surface, the disease striking inward. It is proposed to *drive* away the strangers (thousands in number), if they will not leave voluntarily. There are too many people here for the houses, and the danger of malignant diseases very great.

My vaccination was not a success; very little inflammation and a small scab being the only evidences. But I have a cough, and much lassitude.

DECEMBER 30TH.—We have another crisis. Dispatches from Murfreesborough state the hostile armies are facing each other, and not a mile apart; the skirmishing increases, and a decisive battle may occur at any moment.

From Vicksburg we have no further intelligence; but from the

Rappahannock we learn that both artillery and infantry were distinctly heard yesterday in the direction of Dumfries. Is Stuart there?

DECEMBER 31ST.—There were more skirmishes near Vicksburg yesterday; and although several of the Louisiana regiments are said to have immortalized themselves (having lost only two or three men each), I suppose nothing decisive was accomplished. I have not implicit faith in Western dispatches; they are too often exaggerations. And we have nothing further from Murfreesborough.

But there is reliable intelligence from Albemarle Sound, where a large fleet of the enemy's transports appeared yesterday. We must look now for naval operations. Perhaps Weldon is aimed at.

Gen. Wise writes a remarkable letter to the department. His son, just seventeen years old, a lieutenant in 10th Virginia Cavalry, was detailed as ordnance officer of the general's brigade, when that regiment was taken from his father. Now Gen. Cooper, the Northern head of the Southern army, orders him to the 10th Cavalry. The general desires his son to remain with him, or that the lieutenant may be permitted to resign. He says he asks no favors of the administration, and has never received any. His best blood (Capt. O. J. W.) has been given to the country, and his home and property lost by the surrender of Norfolk, etc.

To-day, Gen. Winder's account for disbursement of "secret service" money was sent in. Among the persons who were the recipients of this money, I noticed *Dr. Rossvally*, a notorious spy, and S——w, one of his policemen, who, with W——ll, very recently fled to the enemy, and is now in the service of the United States, at Washington!

Gen. Lee has given the command in Northwestern Virginia to Gen. W. E. Jones; and he asks the Secretary to hold a major he has captured as a hostage for the good conduct of the Federal Gen. Milroy, who is imitating Gen. Pope in his cruelties to civilians.

CHAPTER XXII.

Lee in winter quarters.—Bragg's victory in the Southwest.—The President at Mobile.—Enemy withdraw from Vicksburg.—Bragg retreats as usual. —Bureau of Conscription.—High rents.—Flour contracts in Congress.— Efforts to escape conscription.—Ships coming in freely.—Sneers at negro troops.—Hopes of French intervention.—Gen. Rains blows himself up.— Davis would be the last to give up.—Gov. Vance protests against Col. August's appointment as commandant of conscripts.—Financial difficulties in the United States.

JANUARY 1ST, 1863.—This first day of the year dawned in gloom, but the sun, like the sun of Austerlitz, soon beamed forth in great splendor upon a people radiant with smiles and exalted to the empyrean.

A letter from Gen. H. Marshall informed the government that Gen. Floyd had seized slaves in Kentucky and refused to restore them to their owners, and that if the government did not promptly redress the wrong, the Kentuckians would at once "take the law into their own hands."

We had a rumor (not yet contradicted) that the enemy, or traitors, had burned the railroad bridge between Bristol and Knoxville, cutting our communication with the West.

Then it was said (and it was true) that Gen. Lee had sent his artillery back some 30 miles this side of the Rappahannock, preparatory to going into winter quarters. But this was no occasion for gloom. Lee always knows what is best to be done.

Next there was a rumor (not yet confirmed, but credited) that Stuart had made another of his wonderful reconnoissances, capturing prisoners and destroying much of the enemy's stores beyond the Rappahannock.

Then came a dispatch from Bragg which put us almost "beside" ourselves with joy, and caused even enemies to pause and shake hands in the street. Yesterday he attacked Rosecrans's army near Murfreesborough, and gained a great victory. He says he drove him from all his positions, except on the extreme left, and after ten hours' fighting, occupied the whole of the field except (those exceptions!) the point named. We had, as trophies, thirty-one guns, two generals, 4000 prisoners, and 200 wagons. This is a *Western* dispatch, it is true, but it has Bragg's name to it, and he does not willingly exaggerate. Although I, for one, shall await the next dispatches with anxiety, there can be no question about the victory on the last day of the bloody year 1862. Bragg says the loss was heavy on both sides.

I noticed that one of the brass pieces sent down by Lee to go to North Carolina had been struck by a ball just over the muzzle, and left a glancing mark toward the touch-hole. That ball, probably, killed one of our gunners.

JANUARY 2D.—A dispatch from Gov. Harris gives some additional particulars of the battle near Murfreesborough, Tenn. He says the enemy was driven back six miles, losing four generals killed and three captured, and that we destroyed $2,000,000 commissary and other stores. But still we have no account of what was done yesterday on the "extreme left."

Gen. Stuart has been near Alexandria, and his prisoners are coming in by every train. He captured and destroyed many stores, and, up to the last intelligence, without loss on his side. He is believed, now, *to be in Maryland*, having crossed the Potomac near Leesburg.

The mayor of our city, Jos. Mayo, meeting two friends last night, whom he recognized but who did not recognize him, playfully seized one of them, a judge, and, garroter fashion, demanded his money or his life. The judge's friend fell upon the mayor with a stick and beat him dreadfully before the joke was discovered.

The President was at Mobile on the 30th December, having visited both Murfreesborough and Vicksburg, but not witnessing either of the battles.

We are in great exaltation again! Dispatches from Gen. Bragg, received last night, relieve us with the information that the stronghold of the enemy, which he failed to carry on the day of battle, was abandoned the next day; that Forrest and Morgan were operating successfully far in the rear of the invader, and that Gen. Wheeler had made a circuit of the hostile army after the battle, burning several hundred of their wagons, capturing an ordnance train, and making more prisoners. Bragg says the enemy's telegraphic and railroad communications with his rear have been demolished, and that he will follow up the defeated foe. I think we will get Nashville now.

JANUARY 3D.—To-day we have a dispatch from Vicksburg stating that the enemy had re-embarked, leaving their intrenching instruments, etc., apparently abandoning the purpose of assaulting the city. This is certainly good news.

Gen. Stuart did not cross the Potomac, as reported in the Northern press, but, doubtless, the report produced a prodigious panic among the Yankees. But when Stuart was within eight miles of Alexandria, he telegraphed the government at Washington that if they did not send forward larger supplies of stores to Burnside's army, he (Stuart) would not find it worth while to intercept them.

Capt. Semmes, of the Alabama, has taken another prize—the steamer Ariel—but no gold being on board, and having 800 passengers, he released it, under bonds to pay us a quarter million dollars at the end of the war.

A large meeting has been held in New York, passing resolutions in favor of peace. They propose that New Jersey send a delegation hither to induce us to meet the United States in convention at Louisville, to adopt definitive terms of peace, on the basis of the old Union, or, that being impracticable, separation. Too late!

JANUARY 4TH.—We have nothing additional from Murfreesborough, but it is ascertained that the bridges burned by the enemy on the Virginia and Tennessee Railroad cannot be repaired in a month.

It really does seem that some potent and malign influence, resident at the capital, some high functionary, by some species of occultation, controlling the action of the government, a Talleyrand in the pay of both governments, and balancing or equalizing disasters between them to magnify his importance and increase his reward, has been controlling many events since the beginning of this war, and is still engaged in the diabolical work. It now appears that several regiments were withdrawn from the vicinity of Bristol, whose presence there was necessary for the protection of the railroad and the bridges. They were brought hither *after Lee's defeat of Burnside*, for the protection of the capital! The President was away, and Mr. Seddon was now in the War Office. But Gen. Cooper is *old* in office, and should have known better; and Gen. G. W. Smith certainly must have known better. Just suppose we had been beaten at Murfreesborough, and our communications cut, west and east and south! There would have been no escape.

It had even been proposed to take a large portion of Lee's men from him, so that he must be inevitably defeated on the Rappahannock, but Lee's resignation would have shocked the people unbearably. Great injury was done him by abstracting some 20,000 of his men by discharges, transfers, and details. Nothing but his generalship and the heroism of his men saved us from ruin. The disasters of Donelson, Newbern, Nashville, Memphis, Roanoke, New Orleans, Norfolk, etc. may be traced to the same source. But all new governments have been afflicted by a few evil-disposed leaders.

Our people in arms have upheld the State; they have successfully resisted the open assaults of the invader, and frustrated the occult machinations of the traitors in our midst. We have great generals, but what were they without great men to obey them? Generals have fallen, and divisions and brigades have fought on without them. Regiments have lost their field officers and continued the fight, and companies have maintained their position after all their commissioned officers were stricken down. The history which shall give the credit of their achievements to others will be a vile calumny. Our cause would have been ruined if it had not been for the bravery and heroism of the people—*the privates in our armies.*

There is a rumor this morning that the enemy are advancing toward Petersburg from Suffolk. If this be so, some spy, under the protection of martial law, has informed the Yankees of our defenseless condition at that place, being alarmed at the success of our brave and patriotic men in the West.

JANUARY 5TH.—We learn from Gen. Bragg that the enemy did not retire far on the 2d inst., but remain still in the vicinity of Murfreesborough. He says, however, that our cavalry are still circling the Yankees, taking prisoners and destroying stores. During the day an absurd rumor was invented, to the effect that Bragg had been beaten. We are anxious to learn the precise particulars of the battle. It is to be feared that too many of Bragg's men were ordered to reinforce Pemberton. If that blunder should prove disastrous, the authorities here will have a hornet's nest about their ears. The President arrived yesterday, and his patriotic and cheering speech at Jackson, Miss., appeared in all the papers this morning.

We hear of no fighting at Suffolk. But we have dispatches from North Carolina, stating that a storm assailed the enemy's fleet off Hatteras, *sinking the Monitor with all on board,* and so crippling the Galena that her guns were thrown overboard! This is good news—if it be confirmed.

A letter from Major Boyle, in command at Gordonsville, gives information that the smugglers and extortioners are trading tobacco (contraband) with the enemy at Alexandria. He arrested B. Nussbaum, E. Wheeler, and S. Backrack, and sent them with their wagons and goods to Gen. Winder, Richmond. But instead of being dealt with according to law, he learns that Backrack is back again, and on his way to this city *with another wagon load of goods from Yankee-land,* and will be here to-day or to-morrow. I sent the letter to the Secretary, and hope it will not be intercepted on its way to him from the front office. The Secretary never sees half the letters addressed him, or knows of one-half the attempts of persons to obtain interviews. The Assistant Secretary's duty is to dispose of the less important communications, but to exhibit his decisions.

JANUARY 6TH.—To-day we are all *down* again. Bragg has *retreated* from Murfreesborough. It is said he saved his prisoners, captured cannon, etc., but it is *not* said what became of his own wounded. The Northern papers say they captured 500 prisoners in the battle, which they claim as a victory. I do not know how to reconcile Bragg's first dispatches, and particularly the one saying he had the whole field, and would *follow* the enemy, with this last one announcing his withdrawal and retirement from the field.

Eight thousand men were taken from Bragg a few days before the battle. It was not done at the suggestion of Gen. Johnston; for I have seen an extract of a letter from Gen. J. to a Senator (Wigfall), deprecating the detachment of troops from Bragg, and expressing grave apprehensions of the probable consequences.

A letter was received from R. R. Collier, Petersburg, to-day, in favor of civil liberty, and against the despotism of martial law.

Senator Clark, of Missouri, informed me to-day that my nephew, R. H. Musser, has been made a colonel (under Hindman or Holmes), and has a fine regiment in the trans-Mississippi Department.

Lewis E. Harvie, president of the railroad, sends a communication to the Secretary (I hope it will reach him) inclosing a request from Gen. Winder to permit liquors to be transported on his road to Clover Hill. Mr. Harvie objects to it, and asks instructions from the Secretary. He says Clover Hill is the point from which the smuggling is done, and that to place it there, is equivalent to bringing it into the city.

JANUARY 7TH.—To-day I was requested to aid, temporarily, in putting in operation a new bureau, created by the military authorities, not by law, entitled the Bureau of Conscription. From conscription all future recruits must be derived. I found Gen. Rains, the chief, a most affable officer; and Lieut.-Col. Lay, his next officer, was an acquaintance. I shall not now, perhaps, see so much of the *interior* of this moving picture of Revolution; my son, however, will note important letters. It is said that Sumner's corps (of Burnside's army) has landed in North Carolina, to take Wilmington. We shall have news soon.

We are sending troops rapidly from Virginia to North Carolina.

The Northern papers say the following dispatch was sent to Washington by our raiding Stuart: "Gen. Meigs will in future please furnish better mules; those you have furnished recently are very inferior." He signed his own name.

A large body of slaves passed through the city to-day, singing happily. They had been working on the fortifications north of the city, and go to work on them south of it. They have no faith in the efficacy of Lincoln's Emancipation.

But it is different in Norfolk; 4000 enfranchised slaves marched in procession through the town the other day in a sort of frantic jubilee. They will bewail their error; and so will the Abolitionists. They will consume the enemy's commissary stores; and if they be armed, we shall get their arms.

Lee and Beauregard were telegraphed to-day in relation to the movement on Wilmington; and the President had the cabinet with him many hours.

Gen. Rains is quite certain that the fall of New Orleans was the result of treachery.

By the emancipation, Gen. Wise's county, Princess Ann, is excepted—and so are Accomac and Northampton Counties; but I have no slaves. All I ask of the invaders is to spare my timber, and I will take care of the land—and I ask it, knowing the request will never be known by them until the war is over.

JANUARY 8TH.—Gen. French writes that the enemy at Suffolk and Newbern amounted to 45,000; and this force now threatens Weldon and Wilmington, and we have not more than 14,000 to oppose them. With generalship that should suffice.

All the Virginia conscripts are ordered to Gen. Wise, under Major-Gen. Elzey. The conscripts from other States are to be taken to Gen. Lee. If the winter should allow a continuance of active operations, and the enemy should continue to press us, we might be driven nearly to the wall. We must help ourselves all we can, and, besides, invoke the aid of Almighty God!

We have nothing fresh from Bragg—nothing from Vicksburg—and that is *bad news*.

I like Gen. Rains. He comes in and sits with me every day. Col. Lay is the active business man of the bureau. The general is engaged in some experiments to increase the efficiency of small arms.

He is very affable and communicative. He says he never witnessed more sanguinary fighting than at the battle of the Seven Pines, where his brigade retrieved the fortunes of the day; for at one time it was lost. He was also at Yorktown and Williamsburg; and he cannot yet cease condemning the giving up of the Peninsula, Norfolk, etc. Gen. Johnston did that, backed by Randolph and Mallory.

We have all been mistaken in the number of troops sent to the rescue of North Carolina; but four or five regiments, perhaps 3000 men, have gone thither from Virginia. A letter from Gen. Lee, dated the 5th inst., says he has not half as many men as Burnside, and cannot spare any. He thinks North Carolina, herself, will be able to expel the Federals, who probably meditate only a marauding expedition. And he supposes Bragg's splendid victory (what did he suppose the next day?) may arrest the inroads of the enemy everywhere for a season. At this moment I do not believe we have 200,000 men in the field against 800,000! But what of that, after seeing Lee beat 150,000 with only 20,000 in action! True, it was an ambuscade.

JANUARY 9TH.—The Northern papers say the Federals have taken Vicksburg; but we are incredulous. Yet we have no reliable intelligence from thence; and it may be so. It would be a terrible blow, involving, for a time, perhaps, the loss of the Mississippi River.

But we have cheering news from Galveston, Texas. Several of our improvised gun-boats attacked the enemy's war vessels in the harbor, and after a sanguinary contest, hand to hand, our men captured the Harriet Lane, a fine United States ship of war, iron clad. She was boarded and taken. Another of the enemy's ships, it is said, was blown up by its officers, rather than surrender, and many perished. If this be Magruder's work, it will make him famous.

Our public offices are crowded with applicants for clerkships, mostly wounded men, or otherwise unfit for field duty.

How can we live here? Boarding is $60 per month, and I have six to support! They ask $1800 rent for a dwelling—and I have no furniture to put in one. Gen. Rains and I looked at one to-day, thinking to take it jointly. But neither of us is able to furnish it. Perhaps we shall take it, nevertheless.

JANUARY 10TH.—We have news from the West, which is believed to be reliable, stating that Bragg captured 6000 prisoners altogether in his late battles; took 30 cannon, 800 stand of arms, and destroyed 1500 wagons and many stores. The estimated loss of the enemy in killed and wounded is put down at 12,000. Our loss in killed and wounded not more than half that number.

To-day we have official intelligence confirming the brilliant achievement at Galveston; and it was Magruder's work. He has men under him fitted for desperate enterprises; and he has always had a penchant for desperate work. So we shall expect to hear of more gallant exploits in that section. He took 600 prisoners.

We have news also from Vicksburg, and the city was not taken; on the contrary, the enemy had sailed away. I trust this is reliable; but the Northern papers persist in saying that Vicksburg has fallen, and that the event took place on the 3d inst.

Six hundred women and children—refugees—arrived at Petersburg yesterday from the North. They permit them to come now, when famine and pestilence are likely to be added to the other horrors of war! We are doomed to suffer this winter!

JANUARY 11TH.—The message of Gov. Seymour, of New York, if I am not mistaken in its import and purposes, will have a distracting effect on the subjugation programme of the government at Washington. I shall look for riots, and perhaps rebellions and civil wars in the North.

Mr. Stanley, ycleped Governor of North Carolina, has written a letter (dated 31st December) to Gen. French, complaining that our soldiery have been guilty of taking slaves from their humane and *loyal* masters in Washington County, against their will; and demanding a restoration of them to their kind and beneficent owners, to whom they are anxious to return. Gen. French replies that he will do so very cheerfully, provided the United States authorities will return the slaves they have taken from masters loyal to the Confederate States. These may amount to 100,000. And he might have added that on the next day all—4,000,000—were to be emancipated, so far as the authority of the United States could accomplish it.

The enemy's gun-boats (two) came up the York River last week, and destroyed an oyster boat. Beyond the deprivation of oysters, pigs, and poultry, we care little for these incursions.

JANUARY 12TH.—The news of the successful defense of Vicksburg is confirmed by an official dispatch, to the effect that the enemy had departed up the Mississippi River. By the late Northern papers, we find they confess to a loss of 4000 men in the several attacks upon the town! Our estimate of their loss did not exceed that many hundred. They lost two generals, Morgan and another. We did not lose a hundred men, according to our accounts. The *Herald* (N. Y.) calls it "another Fredericksburg affair."

The estimate of the enemy's loss, at Murfreesborough, from 12,000 to 20,000, in killed, wounded, and prisoners, and ours at from four to nine thousand. Bragg says he will fight again near the same place, and his men are in high spirits.

Our men fight to *kill* now, since the emancipation doom has been pronounced. But we have had a hard rain and nightly frosts, which will put an end to campaigning during the remainder of the winter. The fighting will be on the water, or near it.

The legislature is in session, and resolutions inimical to the passport system have already been introduced. But where are State Rights now?

Congress meets to-morrow.

JANUARY 13TH.—The generals in North Carolina are importunate for reinforcements. They represent the enemy as in great force, and that Weldon, Goldsborough, Raleigh, and Wilmington are in extreme peril. Lee cannot send any, or, if he does, Richmond will be threatened again, and possibly taken.

How shall we live? Boarding ranges from $60 to $100 per month. Our landlord says he will try to get boarding in the country, and if he succeeds, probably we may keep the house we now occupy, furnished, at a rent of $1200, for a mere robin's nest of four rooms! But I hope to get the house at the corner of First and Casey, in conjunction with Gen. Rains, for $1800. It has a dozen rooms.

JANUARY 14TH.—Gen. Beauregard, some of whose forces have been taken from him and sent to the defense of Wilmington, is apprehensive that they may be lost, in the event of the enemy making a combined naval and land attack, and then Charleston and Savannah would be in great peril. Gens. Smith and Whiting call lustily for aid, and say they have not adequate means of defense.

Some 4000 more negroes have been called for to work on the fortifications near Richmond. I believe 10,000 are at work now.

A letter "by order" of the Secretary of War to Col. Godwin, in King and Queen County, written by Judge Campbell, says that blockaders are allowed to run through, provided they be not suspicious parties. The government takes what it wants at seventy-five per cent. and releases the rest. The parties are liable to have their goods confiscated by the Secretary of the Treasury, who, however, the letter proceeds to say, has never molested any one in the illicit trade—smuggling.

In Congress, yesterday, Mr. Foote called for a committee to investigate the commissary's contract with Haxhall, Crenshaw & Co., and was particularly severe on Major Ruffin, in the commissary's office, whom he understood was a partner in the flour concern.

Mr. Foote introduced a series of resolutions to-day, tempting the Northern States to make peace with us separately, excluding the New England States, and promising commercial advantages, etc. But we must treat as independent States, pledging a league with those that abandon the United States Government—offensive and defensive—and guaranteeing the navigation of the Mississippi River to the Northwestern States. They were referred to the Committee on Foreign Relations, of which he is the chairman. This is nothing.

But neither yesterday nor the day before was there a quorum of both houses; a sad spectacle in such a season of gloom. It was enlivened, however, by a communication from the Surgeon-General, proposing to send surgeons to vaccinate all the members. They declined the honor, though the small-pox is raging frightfully.

To-day a quorum was found in each house, and the President's message was sent in. I have not read it yet.

JANUARY 15TH.—The President's message is highly applauded. It is well written; but I do not perceive much substance in it, besides some eloquent reproaches of England and France for the maintenance of their neutrality, which in effect is greatly more beneficial to the United States than to us. The President essays to encourage the people to continued effort and endurance—and such encouragement is highly judicious at this dark epoch of the struggle. He says truly we have larger armies, and a better supply of arms, etc., now, than we have had at any time previously.

The President says he will, unless Congress directs differently, have all Federal officers that we may capture, handed over to the States to be dealt with as John Brown was dealt with. The Emancipation Proclamation, if not revoked, may convert the war into a most barbarous conflict.

Mr. Foote, yesterday, introduced a resolution requesting the recall of our diplomatic agents; and, after a certain time, to notify the foreign consuls to leave the conntry, no longer recognizing them in an official capacity.

A bill was introduced making Marylanders subject to conscription.

JANUARY 16TH.—Gen. Lee is in the city, doubtless to see about the pressure upon him for reinforcements in North Carolina. Gen. Smith still writes from Goldsborough for more men, with doleful forebodings if they be refused.

From Eastern Tennessee, we have bad accounts of outrages by the disloyal inhabitants, who have fled, to escape conscription, to the mountains and caves, many of them taking their families. At night they emerge from their hiding-places, and commit depredations on the secessionists.

It has been blowing a gale for two days, and there are rumors of more losses of the enemy's ships on the coast of North Carolina.

A letter was received by the government to-day from Arizona, justifying Col. Baylor for his policy of dealing with the Indians. I do not hear of any steps yet on the part of the President.

A report of the commandant at Camp Holmes, Raleigh, N. C., states that 12,000 conscripts have been received there altogether; 8000 have been sent off to regiments, 2000 detailed on government work, 500 deserted, etc.

The *Enquirer* to-day publishes the fact that a ship, with stores, merchandise, etc., has just arrived at Charleston; that six more are on the way thither, and that a steamer has successfully run the blockade from Wilmington with cotton. This notification may increase the vigilance of the blockading fleet. The *Enquirer* is also perpetually tilting with the Raleigh *Standard.* I doubt the policy of charging the leading journals in North Carolina with predilections for the Union. I believe the *Enquirer* has no settled editor now.

Mr. Foote favors the conscription of Marylanders. If such an act should be likely to pass, Gen. Winder will be beset with applications to leave the Confederacy.

JANUARY 17TH.—Gen. Lee has left the city. His troops, encamped thirty miles north of Richmond, marched northward last night. So it is his determination to cross the Rappahannock? Or is it a demonstration of the enemy to prevent him from sending reinforcements to North Carolina? We shall know speedily.

North Carolina, one would think, is soon to be the scene of carnage; and it is asked what can 16,000 men do against 60,000?

The enemy began the attack on Fort Caswell yesterday; no

result. But one of his blockaders went ashore in the storm, and we captured the officers and crew.

All the conscripts in the West have been ordered to Gen. Bragg.

Shall we starve? Yesterday beef was sold for 40 cts. per pound; to-day it is 60 cts. Lard is $1.00. Butter $2.00. They say the sudden rise is caused by the prisoners of Gen. Bragg, several thousand of whom have arrived here, and they are subsisted from the market. Thus they injure us every way. But, *n'importe*, say some; if Lincoln's Emancipation be not revoked, *but few more prisoners will be taken on either side*. That would be a barbarous war, without quarter.

I see that Col. J. W. Wall, of New Jersey, has been nominated, and I suppose will be elected, U. S. Senator. He was confined for months in prison at Fort Lafayette. I imagine the colonel is a bold, able man.

JANUARY 18TH.—It was bitter cold last night, and everything is frozen this morning; there will be abundance of ice next summer, if we keep our ice-houses.

In these times of privation and destitution, I see many men, who were never prominent secessionists, enjoying comfortable positions, and seeking investments for their surplus funds. Surely there must be some compensation in this world or the next for the true patriots who have sacrificed everything, and still labor in subordinate positions, with faith and patient suffering. These men and their families go in rags, and upon half-rations, while the others fare most sumptuously.

We are now, in effect, in a state of siege, and none but the opulent, often those who have defrauded the government, can obtain a sufficiency of food and raiment. Calico, which could once be bought for 12½ cts. per yard, is now selling at $2.25, and a lady's dress of calico costs her about $30.00. Bonnets are not to be had. Common bleached cotton shirting brings $1.50 per yard. All other dry goods are held in the same proportion. Common tallow candles are $1.25 per pound; soap, $1.00; hams, $1.00; oppossum $3.00; turkeys $4 to $11.00; sugar, brown, $1.00; molasses $8.00 per gallon; potatoes $6.00 per bushel, etc.

These evils might be remedied by the government, for there is no great scarcity of any of the substantials and necessities of life in the country, if they were only equally distributed. The difficulty is in procuring transportation, and the government monopolizes the railroads and canals.

Our military men apprehend no serious consequences from the army of negroes in process of organization by the Abolitionists at Washington. Gen. Rains says the negro cannot fight, and will always run away. He told me an anecdote yesterday which happened under his own observation. An officer, when going into battle, charged his servant to stay at his tent and take care of his property. In the fluctuations of the battle, some of the enemy's shot fell in the vicinity of the tent, and the negro, with great white eyes, fled away with all his might. After the fight, and when the officer returned to his tent, he was vexed to learn that his slave had run away, but the boy soon returned, confronting his indignant master, who threatened to chastise him for disobedience of orders. Cæsar said: "Massa, you told me to take care of your property, and dis property" (placing his hand on his breast) "is worf fifteen hundred dollars." He escaped punishment.

Some 200,000 of the Abolition army will be disbanded in May by the expiration of their terms of enlistment, and we have every reason to believe that their places cannot be filled by new recruits. If we hold out until then, we shall be able to resist at all vital points.

JANUARY 19TH.—We have rumors of fighting this morning on the Rappahannock; perhaps the enemy is making another advance upon Richmond.

There was a grand funeral to-day,—Gen. D. R. Jones's; he died of heart disease.

Gen. Bragg dispatches that Brig.-Gen. Wheeler, with his cavalry, got in the rear of Rosecrans a few days ago, and burned a railroad bridge. He then penetrated to the Cumberland River, and destroyed three large transports and bonded a fourth, which took off his paroled prisoners. After this he captured and destroyed a *gun-boat* and its armament sent in quest of him.

We have taken Springfield, Missouri.

Rosecrans sends our officers, taken at Murfreesborough, to Alton, Ill., to retaliate on us for the doom pronounced in our President's proclamation, and one of his generals has given notice that if we burn a railroad bridge (in our own country) all private property within a mile of it shall be destroyed. The black flag next.

We have no news from North Carolina.

Mr. Caperton was elected C. S. Senator by the Virginia Legisture on Saturday, in place of Mr. Preston, deceased.

An intercepted letter from a Mr. Sloane, Charlotte, N. C., to A. T. Stewart & Co., New York, was laid before the Secretary of War yesterday. He urged the New York merchant, who has contributed funds for our subjugation, to send merchandise to the South, now destitute, and he would act as salesman. The Secretary indorsed "conscript him," and yet the Assistant Secretary has given instructions to Col. Godwin, in the border counties, to wink at the smugglers. This is consistency! And the Assistant Secretary writes "by order of the Secretary of War!"

JANUARY 20TH.—The rumor of fighting on the Rappahannock is not confirmed. But Gen. Lee writes that his beeves are so poor the soldiers won't eat the meat. He asks the government to send him salt meat.

From Northern sources we learn that Arkansas Post has fallen, and that we have lost from 5000 to 7000 men there. If this be true, our men must have been placed in a man-trap, as at Roanoke Island.

Mr. Perkins, in Congress, has informed the country that Mr. Memminger, the Secretary of the Treasury, has hitherto opposed and defeated the proposition that the government buy all the cotton. Mr. M. should never have been appointed. He is headstrong, haughty, and tyrannical when he imagines he is dealing with inferiors, and he deems himself superior to the rest of mankind. But he is no Carolinian by birth or descent.

We see accounts of public meetings in New Jersey, wherein the government at Washington is fiercely denounced, and peace demanded, regardless of consequences. Some of the speakers openly predicted that the war would spread into the North, if not terminated at once, and in that event, the emancipationists would have foes to fight elsewhere than in the South. Among the participants I recognize the names of men whom I met in convention at Trenton in 1860. They clamor for the "Union as it was, the Constitution as it is," adopting the motto of my paper, the "*Southern Monitor*," the office of which was sacked in Philadelphia in April,

1861. Our government will never agree to anything short of independence. President Davis will be found inflexible on that point.

There was a rumor yesterday that France had recognized us. The news of the disaster of Burnside at Fredericksburg having certainly been deemed very important in Europe. But France has not yet acted in our behalf. We all pray for the Emperor's intervention. We suffer much, and but little progress is made in conscription. Nearly all our resources are in the field. Another year of war, and —— !

JANUARY 21ST.—Last night the rain fell in torrents, and to-day there is a violent storm of wind from the N.W. This may put an end, for a season, to campaigning on land, and the enemy's fleet at sea may be dispersed. Providence may thus intervene in our behalf.

It is feared that we have met with a serious blow in Arkansas, but it is not generally believed that so many (5000 to 7000 men) surrendered, as is stated in the Northern papers. Gen. Holmes is responsible for the mishap.

Conscription drags its slow length along. It is not yet adding many to the army. The Assistant Secretary of War, and several others, "by order of the Secretary of War," are granting a fearful number of exemptions daily. Congress, I hope, will modify the exemption bill immediately. It is believed enrolling officers, surgeons, and others are permitting thousands to remain at home "for a price." Even clerks in the War Department, it is said, are driving a lucrative business in "getting men off," who should be on duty, in this war of independence. *Young* men in the departments, except in particular cases, will not stand in good repute "when the hurly burly's done, when the battle's lost and won."

Congress is at work projecting the organization of a Supreme Court.

JANUARY 22D.—We have reliable intelligence of the sinking of the U. S. gun-boat Hatteras, in the Gulf, by the Alabama. She was iron-clad, and all the officers and crew, with the exception of five, went down.

Gen. Whiting telegraphs to-day for the use of conscripts near Wilmington, in the event of an *emergency*. Several ships have just come in safely from abroad, and it is said a large number are on the way.

Mr. Miles yesterday reported, from the Military Committee, a bill repealing the existing exemption law, and embracing all male residents between the ages of 18 and 45 years. The President, or Secretary of War, to have authority to grant exemptions in certain cases, if deemed expedient. This *ought* to give us 200,000 more men. And they will be required.

A resolution was passed demanding of the Commissary and Quartermaster-General the number of their employees capable of performing military duty. It would be well to extend the inquiry to the War Department itself.

A letter from Norfolk states that at a grand ball, in celebration of the emancipation of the negroes, Gen. Vieille opened the dance with a mulatto woman of bad character as his partner; and Mrs. V. had for her partner a negro barber.

JANUARY 23D.—The Northern papers are filled with what purports to be the intercepted correspondence of Mr. Benjamin with Messrs. Mason and Slidell. Lord John Russell is berated. The Emperor of France is charged with a design to seize Mexico as a colony, and to recognize Texas separately, making that State in effect a dependency, from which cotton may be procured as an offset to British India. He says the French Consuls in Texas are endeavoring to detach Texas from the Confederacy. If this be a genuine correspondence, it will injure the South; if it be false (if the allegations be false), it will still injure us. I have no doubt of its genuineness; and that Mr. Sanders, once the correspondent of the New York *Tribune*, was the bearer. If Texas leaves us, so may Louisiana—and the gigantic Houmas speculation may turn out well at last.

Mr. Curry has brought forward a copyright bill; Mr. Foster, of Alabama, has introduced a bill to abolish the passport system—leaving the matter to railroad conductors.

A dispatch from Gen. Bragg assures us that our cavalry are still capturing and destroying large amounts of Rosecrans's stores on the Cumberland River.

Col. Wall has been elected Senator from New Jersey. They say he is still pale and ill from his imprisonment, for opinion sake. I hope he will speak as boldly in the Senate as out of it.

I met Gen. Davis to-day (the President's nephew), just *from* Goldsborough, where his brigade is stationed. He is in fine *plumage* —and I hope he will prove a game-cock.

Major-Gen. French, in command at Petersburg, is a Northern man. Our *native* generals are brigadiers. It is amazing that all the superior officers in command near the capital should be Northern men. Can this be the influence of Gen. Cooper? It may prove disastrous!

JANUARY 24TH.—Gen. Smith writes that he deems Wilmington in a condition to resist any attacks.

The exposition of Mr. Benjamin's dispatches has created profound mortification in the community.

Another transport has been taken from the enemy in the Cumberland River. No further news from Arkansas.

There is a white flag (small-pox) within seventy yards of our house. But it is probable we must give up the house soon, as the owner is desirous to return to it—being unable to get board in the country.

Gen. Rains, who has been making a certain sort of primer, met with an accident this morning; one of them exploded in his hand, injuring his thumb and finger. He was scarcely able to sign his name to official documents to-day.

Mr. Hunter has brought forward a measure for the funding of Treasury notes, the redundant circulation having contributed to produce the present fabulous prices in the market.

In the New Jersey Legislature petitions are flowing in denunciatory of Lincoln's Emancipation scheme, which would cast into the free States a large excess of profitless population.

JANUARY 25TH.—Gen. Lee mentions, in his recent correspondence, an instance of the barbarity of some of the Yankee soldiers in the Abolition Army of the Potomac. They thrust into the Rappahannock River a poor old negro man, whom they had taken from his master, because he had the small-pox; and he would have been drowned had he not been rescued by our pickets. It is surmised that this dreadful disease prevails to an alarming extent in the Yankee army, and probably embarrasses their operations. Our men have all been vaccinated; and their recklessness of disease and death is perhaps a guarantee of exemption from affliction. Their health, generally, is better than it has ever been before.

The government at Washington has interdicted the usual exchange of newspapers, for the present. This gives rise to conjecture that Lincoln experiences grave difficulties from the adverse sentiment of his people and his armies regarding his Emancipation Proclamation. And it is likely he has met with grave losses at sea, for the invading army in North Carolina has retired back on Newbern. But the season for naval enterprises is not over, and we are prepared to expect some heavy blows before April.

The revelations in the intercepted dispatches captured with Mr. Sanders, whose father is a notorious political adventurer, may be most unfortunate. They not only show that we even were negotiating for six war steamers, but give the names of the firms in Europe that were to furnish them. The project must now be abandoned. And Louis Napoleon will be enraged at the suspicions and imputations of our Secretary of State regarding his occult policy.

Gen. Rains has invented a new primer for shell, which will explode from the slightest pressure. The shell is buried just beneath the surface of the earth, and explodes when a horse or a man treads upon it. He says he would not use such a weapon in ordinary warfare; but has no scruples in resorting to any means of defense against an army of Abolitionists, invading our country for the purpose, avowed, of extermination. He tried a few shell on the Peninsula last spring, and the explosion of only four sufficed to arrest the army of invaders, and compelled them to change their line of march.

JANUARY 26TH.—The *Northern* papers say Hooker's grand division crossed the Rappahannock, ten miles above Falmouth, several days ago.

Burnside has issued an address to his army, promising them another battle immediately.

Gen. Lee advises the government to buy all the grain in the counties through which the canal runs. He says many farmers are hoarding their provisions, for extortionate prices.

I have no house yet. Dr. Wortham had one; and although I applied first, he let Mr. Reagan, the Postmaster-General, have it. He is a member of President Davis's cabinet—and receives $6000 salary.

There is much indignation expressed by the street talkers against Mr. Benjamin and Mr. Sanders, in the matter of the intercepted dispatches: against Mr. Benjamin for casting such imputations on Napoleon and his consular agents, and for sending his dispatches by such a messenger, in the absence of the President; against Sanders for not destroying the dispatches. Many think the information was *sold* to the United States Government.

Col. Wall has made a speech in Philadelphia. He said he should take his seat in the United States Senate as an advocate of peace; and he boldly denounced the Lincoln administration.

Our official report shows that our military authorities, up to this time, have burnt 100,000 bales of cotton in Arkansas. I have not learned the amount destroyed in other States—but it is large. Gen. Lee thinks the object of the expeditions of the enemy on the Southern coast is to procure cotton, etc. The slaves can do them no good, and the torch will disappoint the marauders.

Strong and belligerent resolutions have been introduced in the United States Congress against France, for her alleged purpose to obtain dominion in Mexico. It is violative of the Monroe doctrine. And Mr. Benjamin's accusation against the consuls (embracing a French design on Texas) might seem like a covert purpose to unite both the Confederate and the United States against France—and that might resemble premeditated reconstruction. But diplomatists *must* be busy—always at their webs. President Davis would be the last man to abandon the ship Independence.

JANUARY 27TH.—It is too true that several thousand of our men were captured at Arkansas Post, and that Little Rock is now in danger.

There seems to be no probability, after all, of an immediate advance of the enemy across the Rappahannock.

But there are eight iron-clad gun-boats and ninety sail at Beaufort, North Carolina, and, it is reported, 52,000 men. Wilmington will probably be assailed.

Mr. Foote said, yesterday, if Indiana and Illinois would recede from the war, he should be in favor of aiding them with an army against Lincoln. And all the indications from the North seem to exhibit a strong sentiment among the people favoring peace. But the people are not the government, and they sink peace and reconstruction together.

Yesterday Mr. Crockett, of Kentucky, said, in the House of

Representatives, that there was a party in favor of forming a Central Confederacy (of free and slave States) between the Northern and Southern extremes. Impracticable.

To-day we have news of the bombardment of Fort McAlister, near Savannah. No result known. Now we shall have tidings every few days of naval operations. Can Savannah, and Charleston, and Wilmington be successfully defended? They may, if they will emulate the example of Vicksburg. If they fall, it will *stagger* this government—before the peace party in the North can operate on the Government of the United States. But it would not "crush the rebellion."

JANUARY 28TH.—The bombardment of Fort McAlister continued five hours yesterday, when the enemy's boats drew off. The injury to the fort can be repaired in a day. Not a man was killed or a gun dismounted. The injury done the fleet is not known. But the opinion prevails here that if the bombardment was continued to-day, the elongated shot of the enemy probably demolished the fort.

Last night and all this day it snowed incessantly—melting rapidly, however. This must retard operations by land in Virginia and probably in North Carolina.

JANUARY 29TH.—It appears from the Northern press that the enemy *did* make three attempts last week to cross the Rappahannock; but as they advanced toward the stream, the *elements* successfully opposed them. It rained, it snowed, and it froze. The gun carriages and wagons sank up to the hubs, the horses to their bodies, and the men to their knees; and so all stuck fast in the mud.

I saw an officer to-day from the army in North Carolina. He says the prospect for a battle is good, as soon as the roads admit of marching.

We have nothing further from the bombardment near Savannah. The wires may not be working—or the fort may be taken.

Gov. Vance has sent to the department a strong protest against the appointment of Col. August as commandant of conscripts in Northern Tennessee. Col. A. is a Virginian—that is the only reason. Well, Gen. Rains, who commands all the conscripts in the Confederate States, is a North Carolinian. But the War Department has erred in putting so many strangers in command of localities, where natives might have been selected. Richmond, for instance, has never yet been in the command of a Southern general.

There are indications of a speedy peace, although we are environed by sea and by land as menacingly as ever. The *Tribune* (New York) has an article which betrays much desperation. It says the only way for the United States Government to raise $300,000,000, indispensably necessary for a further prosecution of the war, is to guarantee (to the capitalists) that it will be the *last* call for a loan, and that subjugation will be accomplished in ninety days, or never. It says the war must then be urged on *furiously*, and negro soldiers sent among the slaves to produce an insurrection! If this will not suffice, then let peace be made on the best possible terms. The New York *World* denounces the article, and is for peace at once. It says if the project (diabolical) of the *Tribune* fails, it may not be possible to make peace on any terms. In this I see indications of a foregone conclusion. All over the North, and especially in the Northwest, the people are clamoring for peace, and denouncing the Lincoln Emancipation Proclamation. I have no doubt, if the war continues throughout the year, we shall have the spectacle of more Northern men fighting against the United States Government than slaves fighting against the South.

Almost every day, now, ships from Europe arrive safely with merchandise: and this is a sore vexation to the Northern merchants. We are likewise getting, daily, many supplies from the North, from blockade-runners. No doubt this is winked at by the United States military authorities, and perhaps by some of the civil ones, too.

If we are not utterly crushed before May (an impracticable thing), we shall win our independence.

JANUARY 30TH.—There is a rumor that Kentucky has voted to raise an army of 60,000 men to resist the execution of Lincoln's Emancipation Proclamation.

Fort Caswell, below Wilmington, has been casemated with iron; but can it withstand elongated balls weighing 480 pounds? I fear not. There are, however, submarine batteries; yet these may be avoided, for Gen. Whiting writes that the best pilot (one sent thither some time ago by the enemy) escaped to the hostile fleet since Gen. Smith visited North Carolina, which is embraced within his command. This pilot, no doubt, knows the location of all our torpedoes.

Nothing further from Savannah.

Mr. Adams, the United States Minister at London, writes to Mr. Seward, Secretary of State, dated 17th of October, 1862, that if the Federal army shall not achieve decisive successes by the month of February ensuing, it is probable the British Parliament will recognize the Confederate States. To-morrow is the last day of January.

I cut the following from yesterday's *Dispatch:*

"*The Results of Extortion and Speculation.*—The state of affairs brought about by the speculating and extortion practiced upon the public cannot be better illustrated than by the following grocery bill for one week for a small family, in which the prices before the war and those of the present are compared :

1860.		1863.	
Bacon, 10 lbs. at 12½c..........	$1 25	Bacon, 10 lbs. at $1..........	$10 00
Flour, 30 lbs. at 5c.............	1 50	Flour, 30 lbs. at 12½c.........	3 75
Sugar, 5 lbs. at 8c...............	40	Sugar, 5 lbs. at $1 15........	5 75
Coffee, 4 lbs. at 12½c...........	50	Coffee, 4 lbs. at $5............	20 00
Tea (green), ½ lb. at $1........	50	Tea (green), ½ lb. at $16......	8 00
Lard, 4 lbs. at 12½c.............	50	Lard, 4 lbs. at $1..............	4 00
Butter, 3 lbs. at 25c...........	75	Butter, 3 lbs. at $1 75.......	5 25
Meal, 1 pk. at 25c...............	25	Meal, 1 pk. at $1...............	1 00
Candles, 2 lbs. at 15c..........	30	Candles, 2 lbs. at $1 25.......	2 50
Soap, 5 lbs. at 10c..............	50	Soap, 5 lbs. at $1 10.........	5 50
Pepper and salt (about).........	10	Pepper and salt (about)........	2 50
Total..........................	$6 55	Total..........................	$68 25

"So much we owe the speculators, who have stayed at home to prey upon the necessities of their fellow-citizens."

We have just learned that a British steamer, with cannon and other valuable cargo, was captured by the enemy, two days ago, while trying to get in the harbor. Another, similarly laden, got safely in yesterday. We can afford to lose one ship out of three—that is, the owners can, and then make money.

Cotton sells at *seventy-five cents* per pound in the United States. So the blockade must be felt by the enemy as well as ourselves. War is a two-edged sword.

JANUARY 31ST.—We have dispatches from Charleston, to-day, which reconcile us to the loss of the cargo captured by the blockading squadron early in the week. An artillery company captured a fine gun-boat in Stone River (near Charleston) yesterday evening. She had eleven guns and 200 men.

But this morning we did better still. Our little fleet of two iron-clads steamed out of Charleston harbor, and boldly attacked the blockading fleet. We crippled two of their ships, and sunk one, completely raising the blockade, for the time being. This will frustrate some of their plans, and may relieve Wilmington.

The attack on Fort McAlister was a failure. The monitor which assaulted the fort sustained so much injury, that it had to retire for repairs.

Several blockade-runners between this and Williamsburg were arrested and sent to Gen. Winder to-day by Lieut. G. D. Wise. Gen. W. sent them to Gen. Rains. Mr. Petit and Mr. James Custis (from Williamsburg) came with them to endeavor to procure their liberation. Gen. Rains sent them back to Gen. W., with a note that he had no time to attend to such matters. Such business does not pertain to his bureau. I suppose they will be released.

Major Lear, of Texas, who was at the capture of the Harriet Lane, met on the captured steamer his mortally-wounded son, the lieutenant.

A few days ago, Lieut. Buchanan was killed on a United States gun-boat by our sharpshooters. He was the son of Admiral Buchanan, in the Confederate service, now at Mobile. Thus we are reminded of the wars of the roses—father against son, and brother against brother. God speed the growth of the Peace Party, North and South; but we must have independence.

Mr. Hunter was in our office to-day, getting the release of a son of the Hon. Jackson Morton, who escaped from Washington, where ha had resided, and was arrested here as a conscript. The Assistant Secretary of War ruled him entitled to exemption, although yesterday others, in the same predicament, were ruled into the service.

CHAPTER XXIII.

Proposed fixture of prices.—Depreciation in the North.—Gen. Hooker in command of the U. S. forces.—Lee thinks Charleston will be attacked.—Congress does nothing.—Some fears for Vicksburg.—Pemberton commands.—Wise dashes into Williamsburg.—Rats take food from my daughter's hand.—Lee wants the meat sent from Georgia to Virginia, where the fighting will be.—Gen. Winder uneasy about my Diary.—Gen. Johnston asks to be relieved in the West.

FEBRUARY 1ST.—The Virginia Legislature, now in session, has a bill under discussion for the suppression of extortion. One of the members, Mr. Anderson, read the following table of the prices of

AGRICULTURAL PRODUCE.

Before the war.		*Now.*	
White wheat, per bushel	$1 50	White wheat, per bushel	$4 50
Flour, per barrel	7 50	Flour, per barrel	22 00
Corn, per bushel	70	Corn, per bushel	3 50
Hay, per hundred	1 00	Hay, per hundred	3 50
Hides, per pound	7	Hides, per pound	40
Beef, per pound	8	Beef, per pound	50
Bacon, per pound	13	Bacon, per pound	60
Lard, per pound	15	Lard, per pound	1 00
Butter, per pound	30	Butter, per pound	1 50
Irish potatoes	1 00	Irish potatoes	5 00
Sweet potatoes	1 00	Sweet potatoes	6 00
Apple brandy	1 00	Apple brandy	15 00
Wool, per pound	30	Wool, per pound	2 00

MANUFACTURES.

Bar iron, per pound	4	Bar iron, per pound	20
Nails, per pound	4	Nails, per pound	60
Leather, sole, per pound	25	Leather, sole, per pound	2 50
" upper, per pound	33	" upper, per pound	3 50

COTTON GOODS.

Osnaburgs, per yard	10	Osnaburgs, per yard	75
Brown cotton, per yard	10	Brown cotton, per yard	75
Sheeting, per yard	15	Sheeting, per yard	1 25

WOOLEN GOODS.

Coarse jeanes	45	Coarse jeanes	4 00
Crenshaw's gray	2 00	Crenshaw's gray	28 00

MISCELLANEOUS.

Coarse shoes	$1 50	Coarse shoes	$15 00
High-quartered shoes	3 50	High-quartered shoes	25 00
Boots	7 50	Boots	60 00
Wool hats, per dozen	7 00	Wool hats, per dozen	50 00

STOCKS.

Dividends on stocks in cotton companies, worth in May, 1861, $25 to $50 per share, now from $112 to $140.

It is doubtful whether the bill will pass, as most of the members are agriculturists.

It is said and believed that several citizens from Illinois and Indiana, now in this city, have been sent hither by influential parties, to consult our government on the best means of terminating the war; or, that failing, to propose some mode of adjustment between the Northwestern States and the Confederacy, and new combination against the Yankee States and the Federal administration.

Burnside has at last been removed; and Franklin and Sumner have resigned. Gen. Hooker now commands the Federal Army of the Potomac—if it may be still called an army. Gen. R——, who knows Hooker well, says he is deficient in talent and character; and many years ago gentlemen refused to associate with him. He resigned from the army, in California, and worked a potatoe patch, Yankee like, on speculation—and failed.

FEBRUARY 2D.—After the feat at Charleston, Gen. Beauregard and Commodore Ingraham invited the consuls resident to inspect the harbor, and they pronounced the blockade raised, no United States ship being seen off the coast. Then the general and the commodore issued a proclamation to the world that the port was open. If this be recognized, then the United States will have to give sixty days' notice before the port can be closed again to neutral powers; and by that time we can get supplies enough to suffice us for a year. Before night, however, some twenty blockaders were in sight of the bar. It is not a question of right, or of might, with France and England—but of inclination. Whenever they, or either of them, shall be disposed to relieve us, it can be done.

There was a fight near Suffolk yesterday, and it is reported that our troops repulsed the enemy.

The enemy's gun-boats returned to the bombardment of Fort McAlister, and met no success. They were driven off. But still, I fear the fort must succumb.

Senator Saulsbury, of Delaware, has been arrested by the Sergeant-at-Arms of the Senate, for his denunciation of Lincoln as an "imbecile." And a Philadelphia editor has been imprisoned for alleged "sympathy with secessionists." These arrests signify more battles—more blood.

FEBRUARY 3D.—It appears that Gen. Pryor's force, 1500 strong, was attacked by the enemy, said to be 5000 in number, on the Blackwater. After some shelling and infantry firing, Gen. P. retired some eight miles, and was not pursued. Our loss was only fifty; *it is said* the enemy had 500 killed and wounded; but I know not how this was ascertained.

Gold in the North now brings 58½ cents premium. Exchange sells at $1.75. Cotton at 96 cents per pound!

They are getting up a fine rumpus in the North over the imprisonment of an editor.

To-day, when conversing with Judge Perkins in relation to having a passport system established by law, he admitted the necessity, but despaired of its accomplishment. "For," said he, "nothing can be done in Congress which has not the sanction of the Executive." He meant, I thought, from his manner and tone, that the Executive branch of the government was omnipotent, having swallowed up the functions of the other co-ordinate branches. I cannot understand this, for the Executive has but little appointing patronage, the army being completely organized, having supplementary generals, and all officers, under the grade of brigadiers, being promoted as vacancies occur.

FEBRUARY 4TH.—One of the enemy's iron-clad gun-boats has got past our batteries at Vicksburg. Gen. Pemberton says it was struck "three times." But it is through.

The enemy's presses reiterate the assertion that Gen. Longstreet is in Tennessee with his corps; and that the detachments from Gen. Lee's army amount to 75,000 men. This is evidently for the purpose to encourage Hooker's army to cross the Rappahannock. These presses must know that Gen. Lee's whole army was less than 75,000 men; that Longstreet is still with him, and that only one small brigade has been sent away to North Carolina. Well, let them come! They will be annihilated. But is it not diabolical in the New York *Post*, *Times*, etc. to urge their own people on to certain destruction? If Hooker had 300,000, he could not now come to Richmond!

We have extremely cold weather now; and, probably, the rivers in Virginia will be frozen over to-night.

FEBRUARY 5TH.—It snowed again last night. Tuesday night the mercury was 8° below zero.

A dispatch from Gen. Beauregard says sixty sail of the enemy have left Beaufort, N. C., for Charleston. A British frigate (Cadmus) has arrived at Charleston with intelligence that the Federal fleet of gun-boats will attack the city immediately; and that the British consul is ordered away by the Minister at Washington. The attack will be by sea and land. God help Beauregard in this fearful ordeal!

FEBRUARY 6TH.—Gen. Lee thinks Charleston will be assailed, and suggests that all the troops in North Carolina be concentrated near Wilmington, and he will undertake the defense of the rest of the State. Nevertheless, if the government deems it more important to have his troops sent to North Carolina, than to retain them for the defense of Richmond, he must acquiesce. But he thinks Hooker will attempt the passage of the Rappahannock, at an early day, if the weather will admit of it. In regard to the last attempt of Burnside to cross his army (when he stuck in the mud), Gen. Lee says it was fortunate for the Federals that they failed to get over. No doubt he was prepared for their reception.

Congress is doing nothing but voting money for themselves. The President (some of the members say) is their master, and they await his nod. These are his enemies.

FEBRUARY 7TH.—We have a dispatch from Texas, of another success of Gen. Magruder at Sabine Pass, wherein he destroyed a large amount of the enemy's stores.

But we are calmly awaiting the blow at Charleston, or a Savannah, or wherever it may fall. We have confidence in Beauregard.

We are more anxious regarding the fate of Vicksburg. Northern man as he is, if Pemberton suffers disaster by any default, he will certainly incur the President's eternal displeasure. Mississippi must be defended, else the President himself may feel the pangs of a refugee.

"That mercy I to others show,
That mercy show to me!"

FEBRUARY 8TH.—From intelligence received yesterday evening, it is probable the Alabama, Harriet Lane, and Florida have met off the West Indies, and turned upon the U. S. steamer Brooklyn. The account says a large steamer was seen on fire, and three others were delivering broadsides into her. The United States press thought the burning steamer was the Florida.

From Charleston or Savannah we shall soon have stirring news. They may overpower our forces, but our power there will be completely exhausted before resistance ceases. There will be no more "giving up," as with New Orleans, Norfolk, etc. Yet there is a feverish anxiety regarding Vicksburg. Pemberton permitted one iron-clad gun-boat to pass, and all our boats below are now at its mercy.

The House of Representatives, at Washington, has passed the "negro soldier bill." This will prove a "Pandora's Box," and the Federals may rue the day that such a measure was adopted.

FEBRUARY 9TH.—Gen. Lee requests that all dispatches passing between his headquarters and the War Department be in cipher. He says everything of importance communicated, he has observed, soon becomes the topic of public conversation; and thence is soon made known to the enemy.

The iron-clad gun-boat, which got past Vicksburg, has been up the Red River spreading devastation. It has taken three of our steamers, forty officers on one, and captured large amounts of stores and cotton.

Gen. Wise made a dash into Williamsburg last night, and captured the place, taking some prisoners.

Custis (my son) received a letter to-day from Miss G., Newbern, *via* underground railroad, inclosing another for her sweet-heart in the army. She says they are getting on tolerably well in the hands of the enemy, though the slaves have been emancipated. She says a Yankee preacher (whom she calls a white-washed negro) made a *speculation.* He read the Lincoln Proclamation to the negroes: and then announced that none of them had been legally married, and might be liable to prosecution. To obviate this, he proposed to marry them over, charging *only* a dollar for each couple. He realized several thousand dollars, and then returned to the North. This was a legitimate Yankee speculation; and no doubt the preacher will continue to be an enthusiastic advocate of a war of subjugation. As long as the Yankees can make money by it, and escape killing, the war will continue.

FEBRUARY 10TH.—No stirring news yet. The enemy's fleet is at Port Royal, S. C. Everywhere we are menaced with overwhelming odds. Upon God, and our own right arms, we must rely, and we do rely.

To-day, in cabinet council, it is believed it was decided to call out all conscripts under forty-five years of age. The President might have done it without consulting the cabinet.

Yesterday Mrs. Goddin, the owner or wife of the owner of the house I occupy, failing to get board in the country, and we having failed to get another house, took possession of one room of the little cottage. We have temporarily the rest: parlor, dining-room, and two chambers—one of them 8 by 11—at the rate of $800 per annum. This is low, now; for ordinary dwellings, without furniture, rent for $1800. Mr. G. has an hereditary (I believe) infirmity of the mind, and is confined by his father in an asylum. Mrs. G. has four little children, the youngest only a few weeks old. She has a white nurse, who lost her only child (died of scarlet fever) six days ago; her husband being in the army. It is a sad spectacle.

To-day beef was selling in market at *one dollar* per pound. And yet one might walk for hours in vain, in quest of a *beggar*. Did such a people ever exist before?

FEBRUARY 11TH.—There is a rumor that Major-Gen. Gustavus W. Smith has tendered his resignation.

Some idea may be formed of the scarcity of food in this city from the fact that, while my youngest daughter was in the kitchen to-day, a young rat came out of its hole and seemed to beg for something to eat; she held out some bread, which it ate from her hand, and seemed grateful. Several others soon appeared, and were as tame as kittens. Perhaps we shall have to eat them!

FEBRUARY 12TH.—Congress has not yet restricted the class of exempts, and the work of conscription drags heavily along. All under forty-five must be called, else the maximum of the four hundred regiments cannot be kept up. It reminds me of Jack Falstaff's mode of exemption. The numerous employees of the Southern Express Co. have been let off, after transporting hither, for the use of certain functionaries, sugars, etc. from Alabama. And so in the various States, enrolling and other officers are letting thousands of conscripts slip through their hands.

FEBRUARY 13TH.—There is a rumor in the papers that something like a revolution is occurring, or has occurred, in the West; and it is stated that the Federal troops demand the recall of the Emancipation Proclamation. They also object to serving with negro troops.

But we ought to look for news of terrific fighting at Savannah or Charleston. No doubt all the troops in the field (Federal) or on the water will be hurled against us before long, so as to effect as much injury as possible before defection can spread extensively, and before the expiration of the enlistments of some 200,000 men in May.

And what are we doing? But little. The acceptance of substitutes who desert, and the exemption of thousands who should be fighting for the country, employ hundreds of pens daily in this city. Alas, that so many dishonest men have obtained easy places! The President has been grossly imposed upon.

FEBRUARY 14TH.—A beautiful day. Yet Gen. Lee is giving furloughs, two to each company. If the weather should be dry, perhaps Hooker will advance: a thing desired by our people, being confident of his destruction.

The papers issued extras to-day with news from the Northwest, based upon the account of a "reliable gentleman," who has just run the blockade. He says Ohio, Kentucky, Indiana, and Illinois have resolved to meet in convention, at Frankfort, Ky., for the purpose of *seceding from the United States, and setting up a confederacy for themselves, or joining the Southern Confederacy.* I fear the "reliable gentleman" is not to be relied upon. Yet it would be well for the Western States, a just retribution to New England, *and a very great relief to us.*

Gen. Lee is urging the department to have the meat at Atlanta brought to his army without delay. It is *here* the army will be wanted.

I saw pigs to-day, not six weeks old, selling in market at $10 a piece.

I met Col. Bledsoe to-day, on a visit to the city, who told me Fenelon never tasted meat, and lived to be ninety years old. I am no Fenelon, but I shall probably have to adopt his regimen. I would barter, however, some of his years for a good supply of food. We must have peace soon, or a famine.

FEBRUARY 15TH.—Already, as if quite certain that the great Northwest would speedily withdraw from the Eastern United States, our people are discussing the eventualities of such a momentous occurrence. The most vehement opposition to the admission of any of the non-slaveholding States, whose people have invaded our country and shed the blood of our people, into this Confederacy, is quite manifest in this city. But Virginia, "the Old Mother," would, I think, after due hesitation, take back her erring children, Ohio, Illinois, Indiana, and perhaps one or two more, if they earnestly desired to return to her parental protection.

Some of the Cotton States might revolt at such a project, and even the cabinet might oppose the scheme of adding several powerful free States to the Confederacy; but it would not all suffice to prevent it, if they desire to join us. It is true, the constitution would have to be modified, for it is not to be supposed that slaves would be held in any of the States referred to; but then slavery would be recognized by its proper term, and ample guarantees would be agreed upon by the great free States which abandon the United States on the issue of emancipation.

Ohio, Indiana, and Illinois, added to the thirteen Confederate States, would speedily constitute us a people of sufficient military power to defy the menaces of the arms of the greatest powers of the earth; and the commercial and agricultural prosperity of the country would amaze the world.

I am of the opinion that Virginia, Maryland, Delaware, Kentucky, North Carolina, Tennessee, Arkansas, and Missouri would form a league of union with Ohio, Illinois, and Indiana, even if the rest of the Southern States were to reject the alliance. But who can foresee the future through the smoke of war, and amid the clash of bayonets? Nevertheless, division and subdivision would *relieve all of the burden of debt, for they would repudiate the greater part, if not the whole, of the indebtedness of both the present governments, which has been incurred in ravaging the country and cutting each other's throats.* The cry will be: "We will not pay the price of blood—for the slaughter of our brothers!"

FEBRUARY 16TH.—Another gun-boat has got past Vicksburg. But three British steamers have run into Charleston with valuable cargoes.

Gen. Lee is now sending troops to Charleston, and this strengthens the report that Hooker's army is leaving the Rappahannock. They are probably crumbling to pieces, under the influence of the peace party growing up in the North. Some of them, however, it is said, are sent to Fortress Monroe.

Our Bureau of Conscription ought to be called the Bureau of Exemption. It is turning out a vast number of exempts. The Southern Express Company bring sugar, partridges, turkeys, etc. to the potential functionaries, and their employees are exempted during the time they may remain in the employment of the company. It is too bad!

I have just been reperusing Frederick's great campaigns, and find much encouragement. Prussia was not so strong as the Confederate States, and yet was environed and assailed by France, Austria, Russia, and several smaller powers simultaneously. And yet Frederick maintained the contest for seven years, and finally triumphed over his enemies. The preponderance of numbers against him in the field was greater than that of the United States against us; and Lee is as able a general as Frederick. Hence we should never despair.

FEBRUARY 17TH.—Gen. Lee is *not* sending troops to Charleston. He is sending them *here* for the defense of Richmond, which is now supposed to be the point of attack, by land and by water, and on both sides of the James River. Well, they have striven to capture this city from every point of the compass but one—the south side. Perhaps they will make an attempt from that direction; and I must confess that I have always apprehended the most danger from that quarter. But we shall beat them, come whence they may!

FEBRUARY 18TH.—Mr. H——s, another of Gen. Winder's detectives, has gone over to the enemy. He went on a privateering cruise from Wilmington; the vessel he sailed in captured a brig, and H——s was put in command of the prize, to sail into a Confederate port. Instead of this, however, H——s sailed away for one of the West India islands, and gave up his prize to Com. Wilkes, of the United States Navy.

One or two of the regiments of Gen. Lee's army were in the city last night. The men were pale and haggard. They have but a quarter of a pound of meat per day. But meat has been ordered from Atlanta. I hope it is abundant there.

All the necessaries of life in the city are still going up higher in price. Butter, $3 per pound; beef, $1; bacon, $1.25; sausage-meat, $1; and even liver is selling at 50 cents per pound.

By degrees, quite perceptible, we are approaching the condition of famine. What effect this will produce on the community is to be seen. The army must be fed or disbanded, or else the city must be abandoned. How we, "the people," are to live is a thought of serious concern.

Gen. Lee has recommended that an appeal be made to the people to bring food to the army, to feed their sons and brothers; but the Commissary-General opposes it; probably it will not be done. No doubt the army could be half fed in this way for months. But the "red tape" men are inflexible and inscrutable. Nevertheless, the commissaries and quartermasters are getting rich.

FEBRUARY 19TH.—The resignation of Gen. Gustavus W. Smith has been accepted by the President. It was well done—the acceptance, I mean. Who will Gen. Winder report to now? Gen. Winder has learned that I am keeping a diary, and that some space in it may be devoted to the history of martial law. He said to Capt. Warner, his commissary of prisons, that he would patronize it. The captain asked me if Gen. Winder's rule was not dwelt upon in it. I said doubtless it was; but that I had not yet revised it, and was never in the habit of perusing my own works until they were completed. Then I carefully corrected them for the press.

Major-Gen. Pickett's division marched through the city to-day for Drewry's Bluff. Gen. Lee writes that this division can beat the army corps of Hooker, supposed to be sent to the Peninsula. It has 12,000 men—an army corps 40,000. Brig.-Gen. Hood's division is near the city, on the Chickahominy. Gen. Lee warns the government to see that Gens. French and Pryor be vigilant, and to have their scouts closely watching the enemy at Suffolk. He thinks, however, the main object of the enemy is to take Charleston; and he suggests that every available man be sent thither. The rest of his army he will keep on the Rappahannock, to watch the enemy still remaining north of that river.

I sent a communication to the President to-day, proposing to reopen my register of "patriotic contributions" to the army, for they are suffering for meat. I doubt whether he will agree to it. If the war be prolonged, the appeal must be to the people to feed the army, or else it will dissolve.

FEBRUARY 20TH.—We have exciting news from the West. The iron-shod gun-boat, Queen of the West, which run past Pemberton's batteries some time since, captured, it appears, one of our steamers in Red River, and then compelled our pilot to steer the Queen of the West farther up the river. The heroic pilot ran the boat under our masked batteries, and then succeeded in escaping by swimming. The Queen of the West was forced to surrender. This adventure has an exhilarating effect upon our spirits.

Hon. James Lyons sent to the President to-day a petition, signed by a majority of the members of Congress, to have me appointed major in the conscription service.

FEBRUARY 21ST.—Major-Gen. Hood's division passed through the city to-day, and crossed over the river. I hope an attack will be made at Suffolk. It is too menacing a position to allow the invader to occupy it longer.

No attack on Charleston yet, and there is a rumor that the command of the expedition is disputed by Foster and Hunter. If it hangs fire, it will be sure to miss the mark.

FEBRUARY 22D.—This is the anniversary of the birth of Washington, and of the inauguration of President Davis, upon the installation of the permanent government of the Confederate States. It is the ugliest day I ever saw. Snow fell all night, and was falling fast all day, with a northwest wind howling furiously. The snow is now nearly a foot deep, and the weather very cold.

My communication to the President, proposing an appeal to the people to furnish the army with meat and clothing (voluntary contributions), was transmitted to the Secretary of War yesterday, without remark, other than the simple reference. The plan will not be adopted, in all probability, for the Secretary will consult the Commissary and Quartermaster-General, and they will oppose any interference with the business of their departments. Red tape will win the day, even if our cause be lost. Our soldiers must be fed and clothed according to the "rules and regulations," or suffer and perish for the want of food and clothing!

I have some curiosity to learn what the President has indorsed, or may indorse, on the paper sent him by Mr. Lyons, signed by half the members of Congress. Will he simply refer it to the Secretary? Then what will the Secretary do? My friends in Congress will likewise be curious to learn the result.

FEBRUARY 23D.—I saw a letter from Gen. Lee to-day, suggesting to the government on appeal to the Governors of the States to aid more directly in recruiting the armies. He says the people habitually expect too much from the troops now in the field; that because we have gained many victories, it does not follow that we shall always gain them; that the legitimate fruits of victory have hitherto been lost, for the want of numbers on our side; and, finally, that all those who fail to go to the field at such a momentous period as this, are guilty of the blood of the brave soldiers who perish in the effort to achieve independence.

This would be contrary to the "rules and regulations" as understood by the Adjutant and Inspector-General (a Northern man), and no doubt the Secretary of War and the President will reject the plan.

The petition of forty members of Congress in my behalf came from Mr. Seddon, the Secretary, to our bureau to-day. He asks the superintendent if there is a necessity for such an officer, one whose rank is equal to that of a commandant of a camp of instruction. He says important services only should require the appointment of such an officer. Well, Gen. Rains recommended it. I know not whether he can say more. I shall not get it, for Congress has but little influence, just now.

FEBRUARY 24TH.—Gen. Longstreet is now in command of Gen. Smith's late department, besides his own corps. Richmond is safe.

Our papers contain a most astonishing speech purporting to have been delivered by Mr. Conway, in the United States Congress.

Mr. C. is from Kansas, that hot-bed of Abolitionism. He is an avowed Abolitionist; and yet he advocates an immediate suspension of hostilities, or at least that the Federal armies and fleets be ordered to act on the defensive; that the independence of the Confederate States be recognized, upon the basis of a similar tariff; free-trade between the North and South; free navigation of the Mississippi, and co-operation in the maintenance of the Monroe doctrine. I like the indications apparent in this speech. Let us have a suspension of hostilities, and then we can have leisure to think of the rest. No doubt the peace party is growing rapidly in the United States; and it may be possible that the Republicans mean to beat the Democrats in the race, by going beyond them on the Southern question. The Democrats are for peace and Union; the Republicans may resolve to advocate not only peace, *but secession.*

FEBRUARY 25TH.—On the 18th inst. the enemy's battery on the opposite side of the Mississippi River opened on Vicksburg. The damage was not great; but the front of the town is considered untenable.

The Conscription bill has passed the United States Senate, which will empower the President to call for 3,000,000 men. "Will they come, when he does call for them?" That is to be seen. It may be aimed at France; and a war with the Emperor might rouse the Northern people again. Some of them, however, have had enough of war.

To-day I heard of my paper addressed to the President on the subject of an appeal to the people to send food to the army. He referred it to the Commissary-General, Col. Northrop, who sent it to the War Department, with an indorsement that as he had no acquaintance with that means of maintaining an army (the patriotic contributions of the people), he could not recommend the adoption of the plan. Red tape is mightier than patriotism still. There may be a change, however, for Gen. Lee approves the plan.

FEBRUARY 26TH.—We have good news from Vicksburg to-day. The Queen of the West, lately captured by us, and another gun-boat, attacked the Indianola, the iron-clad Federal gun-boat which got past our batteries the other day, and, after an engagement, sunk her. We captured all the officers and men.

FEBRUARY 27TH.—No news from any quarter to-day.

Gen. Joseph E. Johnston is discontented with his command in the West. The armies are too far asunder for co-operative action; and, when separated, too weak for decisive operations. There is no field there for him, and he desires to be relieved, and assigned to some other command.

I was surprised to receive, to-day, the following very official letter from the Secretary of War:

"RICHMOND, VA., Feb. 27th, 1863.

"J. B. JONES, ESQ.

"SIR:—The President has referred your letter of the 19th inst. to this department.

"In reply, you are respectfully informed that it is not deemed judicious, unless in the last extremity, to resort to the means of supply suggested. The patriotic motives that dictated the suggestion are, however, appreciated and acknowledged.

"Your obedient servant,

"JAMES A. SEDDON,

"*Secretary of War.*"

CHAPTER XXIV.

Removed into Clay Street.—Gen. Toombs resigned.—Lincoln dictator.—He can call 3,000,000 of men.—President is sick.—His office is not a bed of roses.—Col. Gorgas sends in his oath of allegiance.—Confederate gold $5 for $1.—Explosion of a laboratory.—Bad weather everywhere.—Fighting on the Mississippi River.—Conflict of views in the Conscription Bureau.—Confederate States currency $10 for $1.—Snow a foot deep, but melting.—We have no negro regiments in our service.—Only 6000 conscripts from East Tennessee.—How seven were paroled by one.—This is to be the crisis campaign.—Lee announces the campaign open.

MARCH 1ST.—To-morrow we remove to new quarters. The lady's husband, owning cottage, and who was confined for seven months among lunatics, has returned, and there is not room for two families. Besides, Mrs. G. thinks she can do better taking boarders, than by letting the house. What a mistake! Beef sold yesterday for $1.25 per pound; turkeys, $15. Corn-meal $6 per bushel, and all other articles at the same rates. No salaries can board families now; and soon the expense of boarding will exceed the incomes of unmarried men. Owners and tenants, unless engaged in lucrative business, must soon vacate their houses and leave the city.

But we have found a house occupied by three widows in Clay Street. They have no children. They mean to board soon among their relatives or friends, and then we get the house; in the mean time, they have fitted up two rooms for us. We should have gone yesterday, but the weather was too bad. The terms will not exceed the rent we are now paying, and the house is larger. I espied several fruit trees in the back yard, and a space beyond, large enough for a smart vegetable garden. How delighted I shall be to cultivate it myself! Always I have visions of peas, beans, radishes, potatoes, corn, and tomatoes of my own raising! God bless the widows sent for our relief in this dire necessity!

Met Judge Reagan yesterday, just from the Council Board. I thought he seemed dejected. He said if the enemy succeeded in getting command of the Mississippi River, the Confederacy would be "cut in two;" and he intimated his preference of giving up Richmond, if it would save Texas, etc. for the Confederacy. Texas is his adopted State.

March 2d.—The enemy burnt the steamship Nashville on Saturday near Savannah. She was employed taking provisions to Fort McAlister. I think it was destroyed by an incendiary shell.

There is a rumor to-day of the burning of railroad bridges between this and Fredericksburg.

I signed an agreement to-day with Mr. Malsby to publish my new "Wild Western Scenes." He is to print 10,000 copies, which are to retail at $2; on this he pays me 12½ per cent. or 25 cents for every copy sold; $2500 if the whole are sold. He will not be able to get it out before May.

We moved into the west end of Clay Street to-day, and like the change. There are no children here except our own. The house is a brick one, and more comfortable than the frame shell we abandoned.

March 3d.—We like our new quarters—and the three Samaritan widows, without children. They lend us many articles indispensable for our comfort. It is probable they will leave us soon in the sole occupancy of the house. There is ground enough for a good many vegetables—and meat is likely to be scarce enough. Bacon is now $1.37½ cts. per pound, and flour $30 per barrel. The shadow of the gaunt form of famine is upon us! But the pestilence of small-pox is abating.

We have now fine March weather; but the floods of late have damaged the railroad bridges between this and Fredericksburg. The Secretary of War requested the editors, yesterday, to say nothing of this. We have no news from the West or from the Southeast—but we shall soon have enough.

The United States Congress has passed the Conscription Act. We shall see the effect of it in the North; I predict civil war there; and that will be our "aid and comfort."

Gen. Toombs has resigned; and it is said Pryor has been made a major-general. Thus we go up and down. The President has issued a proclamation for prayer, fasting, etc., on the twenty-seventh of this month. There will certainly be fasting—and prayer also. And God *has* helped us, or we should have been destroyed ere this.

March 4th.—The enemy bombarded Fort McAlister again yesterday, several gun-boats opening fire on it. It lasted all day; during which one of the iron-clads retired, perhaps injured. We had only two men wounded and one gun (8 in. columbiad) dismounted. The fort was but little injured.

Recent Northern papers assert that their gun-boats have all passed through the canal opposite Vicksburg. This is not true—yet.

Lincoln is now Dictator, his Congress having given him power to call out all the male population between the ages of twenty and thirty-five years, and authority to declare martial law whenever he pleases. The *Herald* shouts for Lincoln—of course. We must fight and pray, and hope for revolution and civil war in the North, which may occur any day.

Our cavalry, under Gen. Jones, has done some brilliant skirmishing recently in the vicinity of Winchester; and as soon as the March winds dry the earth a little, I suppose Hooker will recommence the "On to Richmond." We shall be weaker the next campaign, but our men are brave.

March 5th.—Yesterday the government seized the flour in the

mills and warehouses; and now the price has risen from $30 to $40 per barrel. I wrote to the Commissary, in view of the dissatisfaction of the people, and to prevent disturbances, advising him to seize the 5000 barrels in the hands of the small speculators, and to allow so many pounds per month to each inhabitant, at the rate paid by government. This would be beneficent and popular, confining the grumblers to the extortioners. But he will not do it, as the Constitution only provides for impressments for the public use.

Our dinner to-day (for seven, for the servant has an equal share) consisted of twelve eggs, $1.25; a little corn bread, some rice and potatoes. How long shall we have even this variety and amount? Bad beef in market, this morning, sold at $1.25 per pound.

After bombarding Fort McAlister on the 3d inst. and all night, the enemy's fire ceased. The fort was not much injured, says the dispatch. There is a rumor to-day that the fort has been reduced—but no one believes it.

Gen. Van Dorn has had a fight in Tennessee, killing and wounding 1000 and capturing 2600 prisoners. Our loss is said to have been heavy.

Gen. Lee writes that now, since Lincoln may call out 3,000,000 men, and has $900,000,000 voted him, we must put out all our strength, if we expect to keep the field. We shall certainly have an exciting time. But there may be use for some of the Federal troops in the North! If not, I apprehend that Richmond must withstand another siege and assault. It is said they have dropped the "Constitution and the Union" in the United States, and raised the cry of the "NATION" and the "FLAG." This alarms me. If they get up a new sensation, they will raise new armies.

Gold is selling at a premium of $4.25 in Confederate notes.

We bought a barrel of flour to-day (that is, my wife paid for one not yet delivered), from a dealer who was not an extortioner, for the moderate sum of $28.00. This, with what we have on hand, ought to suffice until the growing wheat matures.

For *tea* we had meal coffee, and corn cakes without butter. But we had a *half-pint* of molasses (for seven) which cost 75 cts. The gaunt specter is approaching nearer every day!

Every morning there is a large crowd of Irish and Germans besieging Gen. Winder's office for passports to go North. Is it famine they dread, or a desire to keep out of the war? Will they not be conscripted in the North? They say they can get consular protection there.

MARCH 6TH.—I have meditated on this day, as the anniversary of my birth, and the shortening lapse of time between me and eternity. I am now fifty-three years of age. Hitherto I have dismissed from my mind, if not with actual indifference, yet with far more unconcern than at present, the recurring birthdays which plunged me farther in the vale of years. But now I cannot conceal from myself, if so disposed, that I am getting to be an old man. My hair is gray—but nevertheless my form is still erect, and my step is brisk enough. My fancies, tastes, and enjoyments have not changed perceptibly; and I can and often do write without glasses. I desire to live after this war is over, if it be the will of God—if not, I hope to exist in a better world.

We have no news of interest to-day. A letter says the non-combatants, even the women and children, heedless of danger, were voluntary spectators of the bombardment of Vicksburg the other day. The shells often exploded near them, and behind them, but the fascination was so great that they remained on the ground; even one had an arm carried away by a ball! Can such a people be subjugated?

Houses (furnished) are beginning to be offered more plentifully than ever before; their occupants and owners finding their ordinary incomes insufficient for subsistence. I suppose they mean to find in the country an escape from famine prices prevailing in the city.

There is a rumor this evening of the fall of Vicksburg; but that rumor has been whispered here several times during the last few months. No one believes it. When Vicksburg falls, many an invader will perish in its ruins.

MARCH 7TH.—The President is sick, and has not been in the Executive Office for three days. Gen. Toombs, resigned, has published a farewell address to his brigade. He does not specify of what his grievance consists; but he says he cannot longer hold his commission with honor. The President must be aware of his perilous condition. When in adversity, some of those he has trusted, discuss the bases of reconstruction; and when we are prosperous, others, in similar positions, agitate the question of reorganization—the motive of both being his ruin. But I suppose he has calculated these contingencies, and never anticipated paving a bed of roses to recline upon during the terrible, and sometimes doubtful struggle for independence.

The rumor that Vicksburg had fallen is not confirmed; on the contrary, the story that the Indianola, captured from the enemy, and reported to have been blown up, was unfounded. We have Gen. Pemberton's official assurance of this.

Col. Gorgas, Chief of Ordnance, a Pennsylvanian, sent into the department to-day, with a request that it be filed, his oath of allegiance to this government, and renunciation of that of the United States, and of his native State. This would indicate that the location of his nativity has been the subject of remark. What significance is to be attributed to this step at this late day, I know not, and care not. An error was committed in placing Northern men in high positions to the exclusion of Southern men, quite as capable of filling them.

MARCH 8TH.—Judge Meredith's opinion, that foreigners, Marylanders, and others, who have served in the army, have become domiciled, and are liable to conscription, has produced a prodigious commotion. Gen. Winder's door is beset with crowds of eager seekers of passports to leave the Confederacy; and as these people are converting their Confederate money into gold, the premium on specie has advanced.

Judge Campbell, Assistant Secretary of War, has decided that Judge Meredith's opinion is not authority; and hence his son-in-law, Lieut.-Col. Lay, who at present wields the Conscription Bureau, acts accordingly. But Gen. Rains has a contrary opinion; and he intended to see the President yesterday, who is understood to coincide with Judge Meredith. It is also alleged that Secretary Seddon concurs in this opinion; and if this be the case, an explosion is imminent—for Judge Campbell must have given instructions "by order of the Secretary," without the Secretary's knowledge or consent.

I advised the general to see the President and Secretary once a week, and not rely upon verbal instructions received through a subordinate; he said the advice was good, and he should follow it. But he is much absorbed in his subterrene batteries.

MARCH 9TH.—We have no news to-day. But the next act of

this terrible drama is near at hand. The Northern papers have reports of the fall of Vicksburg and Charleston. Unfounded. They also say 22,000 men have deserted from the Army of the Potomac. This is probably true.

There is much denunciation of the recent seizure of flour; but this is counteracted by an appalling intimation in one of the papers that unless the army be subsisted, it will be withdrawn from the State, and Virginia must fall into the hands of the enemy. The loss of Virginia might be the loss of the Confederacy.

March 10th.—No war news of importance.

Just at this time there is a large number of persons passing to and from the North. They are ostensibly blockade-runners, and they do succeed in bringing from the enemy's country a large amount of goods, on which an enormous profit is realized. The Assistant Secretary of War, his son-in-law, Lt.-Col. Lay, the controlling man in the Bureau of Conscription, and, indeed, many heads of bureaus, have received commodities from Maryland, from friends running the blockade. Gen. Winder himself, and his Provost Marshal Griswold (how much that looks like a Yankee name!), and their police detectives, have reaped benefit from the same source. But this intercourse with the enemy is fraught with other matters. Communications are made by the disloyal to the enemy, and our condition—bad enough, heaven knows!—is made known, and hence the renewed efforts to subjugate us. This illicit intercourse, inaugurated under the auspices of Mr. Benjamin, and continued by subsequent Ministers of War, may be our ruin, if we are destined to destruction. Already it has unquestionably cost us thousands of lives and millions of dollars. I feel it a duty to make this record.

To-day we have a violent snow-storm—a providential armistice.

It has been ascertained that Hooker's army is still near the Rappahannock, only some 20,000 or 30,000 having been sent to the Peninsula and to Suffolk. No doubt he will advance as soon as the roads become practicable. If Hooker has 150,000 men, and advances soon, Gen. Lee cannot oppose his march; and in all probability we shall again hear the din of war, from this city, in April and May. The fortifications are strong, however, and 25,000 men may defend the city against 100,000—provided we have subsistence. The great fear is famine. But hungry men will fight desperately. Let the besiegers beware of them !

We hope to have nearly 400,000 men in the field in May, and I doubt whether the enemy will have over 500,000 veterans at the end of that month. Their new men will not be in fighting condition before July. We may cross the Potomac again.

MARCH 11TH.—Gen. Fitzhugh Lee has made a dash into Fairfax (near Washington) a day or two ago, and captured the Federal Gen. Slaughter and other officers, in their beds.

Last night one of the government warehouses in this city was burnt. It is supposed to have been the work of an incendiary traitor; perhaps in retaliation for the recent impressment of flour. Yesterday the lower house of Congress passed a resolution restricting impressments. This has a bad aspect.

The Bureau of Conscription, to-day, under the direction of Col. Lay, decided that all clerks in the departments, appointed subsequent to the eleventh of October last, are liable to be enrolled for service. Yet the colonel himself has a clerk appointed in January last.

Gold sells at $5 in Confederate States notes for one; U. S. Treasury notes are at a premium here of $2.50. Even the notes of our State banks are at 60 per cent. premium over Confederate notes. This is bad for Mr. Memminger. An abler financier would have worked out a different result.

All the patriotism is in the army; out of it the demon avarice rages supreme. Every one seems mad with speculation; and the extortioners prey upon every victim that falls within their power. Nearly all who sell are extortioners. We have at the same time, and in the same community, spectacles of the most exalted virtue and of the most degrading vice.

Col. Mattel, the former commandant of conscripts for North Carolina, who was wounded at Kinston, and yet was superseded by Col. Lay's friend, Col. August, is now to be restored, and Col. A. relieved. Upon this Col. L. has fallen sick.

Mr. Duffield, whom Col. Lay and Mr. Jacques had appointed A. A. G. over me, has not yet, for some cause, got his commission. The Secretary or some one else may have "intervened."

MARCH 12TH.—To-day we have no army news.

Mr. Richard Smith issued the first number of *The Sentinel*

yesterday morning. Thus we have five daily morning papers, all on half sheets. *The Sentinel* has a biography of the President, and may aspire to be the "organ."

John Mitchel, the Irishman, who was sentenced to a penal colony for disturbances in Ireland, some years ago, is now the leading editor of the *Enquirer*. He came hither from the North recently. His "compatriot," Meagher, once lived in the South and advocated our "institutions." He now commands a Federal brigade. What Mitchel will do finally, who knows? My friend R. Tyler, probably, had something to do with bringing him here. As a politician, however, he must know there is no Irish element in the Confederate States. I am sorry this Irish editor has been imported.

The resignation of Gen. Toombs is making some sensation in certain circles. He was among the foremost leaders of the rebellion. He was Secretary of State, and voluntarily resigned to enter the army. I know not precisely what his grievance is, unless it be the failure of the President to promote him to a higher position, which he may have deemed himself entitled to, from his genius, antecedents, wealth, etc. But it is probable he will cause some disturbance. Duff Green, who is everywhere in stormy times, told me to-day that Gen. Toombs would be elected Governor of Georgia this fall, and said there were intimations that Georgia might make peace with the United States! This would be death to the government—and destruction to Toombs. It must be a mistake. He cannot have any such design. If he had, it would be defeated by the people of Georgia, though they sighed for peace. Peace is what all most desire—but not without independence. Some there are, in all the States, who would go back into the Union, for the sake of repose and security. But a majority would not have peace on such terms.

Still, it behooves the President to be on his guard. He has enemies in the South, who hate him much.

MARCH 13TH.—To-day a great calamity occurred in this city. In a large room of one of the government laboratories an explosion took place, killing instantly five or six persons, and wounding, it is feared fatally, some thirty others. Most of them were little indigent girls!

MARCH 14TH.—Gen. Pemberton writes that he has 3000 hogsheads of sugar at Vicksburg, which he retains for his soldiers to subsist on when the meat fails. Meat is scarce there as well as here. Bacon now sells for $1.50 per pound in Richmond. Butter $3. I design to cultivate a little garden 20 by 50 feet; but fear I cannot get seeds. I have sought in vain for peas, beans, corn, and tomatoes seeds. Potatoes are $12 per bushel. Ordinary chickens are worth $3 a piece. My youngest daughter put her earrings on sale to-day—price $25; and I think they will bring it, for which she can purchase a pair of shoes. The area of subsistence is contracting around us; but my children are more enthusiastic for independence than ever. Daily I hear them say they would gladly embrace death rather than the rule of the Yankee. If all our people were of the same mind, our final success would be certain.

This day the leading article in the *Examiner* had a striking, if not an ominous conclusion. Inveighing against the despotism of the North, the editor takes occasion likewise to denounce the measure of impressment here. He says if our Congress should follow the example of the Northern Congress, and invest our President with dictatorial powers, a reconstruction of the Union might be a practicable thing; for our people would choose to belong to a strong despotism rather than a weak one—the strong one being of course the United States with 20,000,000, rather than the Confederate States with 8,000,000. There may be something in this, but we shall be injured by it; for the crowd going North will take it thither, where it will be reproduced, and stimulate the invader to renewed exertions. It is a dark hour. But God disposes. If we deserve it, we shall triumph; if not, why should we?

But we cannot fail without more great battles; and who knows what results may be evolved by them? Gen. Lee is hopeful; and so long as we keep the field, and he commands, the foe must bleed for every acre of soil they gain.

MARCH 15TH.—Another cold, disagreeable day. March so far has been as cold and terrible as a winter month.

MARCH 16TH.—Gen. Hill is moving toward Newbern, N. C., and may attack the enemy there.

The weather continues dreadful—sleeting; and movements of armies must perforce be stayed. But the season of slaughter is approaching.

There was an ominous scantiness of supply in the market this morning, and the prices beyond most persons—mine among the rest.

Col. Lay got turkeys to-day from Raleigh; on Saturday partridges, by the Express Company. Fortunate man!

MARCH 17TH.—On Saturday, the enemy's lower Mississippi fleet attacked our batteries at Port Hudson. The result reported is that only one of their gun-boats got past, and that in a damaged condition. The frigate Mississippi, one of the best war steamers of the United States, was burned, and the rest retired down the river, badly repulsed. We sustained no loss.

To-day, the Secretary of War sent in a paper indorsing Judge Meredith's opinion in regard to foreigners who have accepted service in our country, viz., that they are liable to conscription. This is in the teeth of the decision of the Assistant Secretary, Judge Campbell, Col. Lay's father-in-law, and upon which the bureau has been acting, although Gen. Rains, the Superintendent, permitted it with reluctance, upon the assurance of Col. L. that such was the will of the department. This business may produce an explosion.

I walked with Gen. Rains this afternoon in Capitol Square. He is annoyed at the action of Col. Lay in following the instructions of the Assistant Secretary of War in regard to foreigners. The decision had not the sanction of the Secretary of War, Mr. Seddon. He thinks *several thousand* men may have been permitted to escape military service by it. He intended to lay Judge Campbell's decision before the President, but it disappeared very mysteriously from his desk. And to-day it reappeared just as mysteriously. And, simultaneously, and quite as mysteriously, a paper appeared, signed by Mr. Seddon, Secretary of War, suggesting that the bureau act in conformity with Judge Meredith's opinion, directly in the teeth of Mr. Assistant Secretary Campbell's decision! And it was dated March 13th, full four days before. What delayed it, and who brought it, no one seemed to know. Col. Lay suggested that it be sent back, with an indorsement that the bureau had been already acting under the decision of Judge Campbell (just the reverse of the opinion), Assistant Secretary of War, "by order of the Secretary of War."

To this Gen. R. demurred, and said the bureau would conform

its action to Mr. Seddon's suggestions; and he charged a clerk to preserve *that* paper. Col. L. grumbled awfully at Mr. Seddon's off-hand decision, without mature reflection.

Gen. Stewart (of Maryland) was at the office a short time before, and advocated Mr. Seddon's views; for he knew how many Marylanders would be embraced in the decision, as well as other foreigners.

Lieut.-Col. A. C. Jones, Assistant Adjutant-General, had, in the name of the bureau, notified Gen. Winder, this morning, that Marylanders, etc. were not liable to bear arms for the South after being in the service two years!

The general says he will have all the commandants of conscripts written to immediately; and that he will have an interview with the Secretary of War in relation to the matter.

Every man we can put in the field is demanded; and many fear we shall not have a sufficient number to oppose the overwhelming tide soon to be surging over the land. At such a crisis, and in consideration of all the circumstances attending this matter, involving the loss of so many men, one is naturally startled at Judge Campbell's conduct.

MARCH 18TH.—I sent an extract from my Diary of yesterday to the Hon. T. H. Watts, Minister of Justice. I know not whether he will appreciate its importance; but he has professed friendship for me.

The city is in some excitement to-day, for early this morning we had intelligence of the crossing of the Rappahannock by a portion of the Federal army. During the day the division of Hood defiled through the streets, at a quick pace, marching back to Lee's army. But the march of troops and the rumbling of artillery have ceased to be novel spectacles to our community. Some aged ladies ran out as they passed, calling the bronzed Texans their "children," and distributed loaves of bread and other food among them. I never saw a merrier set than these brave soldiers, who have been through the "fire and the flood" numberless times. Some of them had three or four loaves on their bayonets.

Gen. Lee himself left early this morning, on an extra train, having been "caught napping" here, the first time. The enemy crossed the river yesterday.

But during the day a dispatch was received from Gen. J. E. B.

Stuart (cavalry), stating that he had attacked the enemy on this side of the river, and beaten him back, forcing him to recross with loss. The particulars of the fight were not stated; but it is believed we lost a brigadier-general, killed.

MARCH 19TH.—Snowing. It is estimated that we lost 250 men, killed, wounded, and taken, in the fight on the Rappahannock; the enemy's loss is not known, but certainly was heavy, since they were defeated, and fled back, hotly pursued.

Confederate money still depreciates, in spite of the funding act. Some of the brokers are demanding ten dollars Confederate notes for one in gold! That is bad, and it may be worse.

The enemy are advancing from Corinth, and there are not sufficient troops to resist them. Gen. Johnston says if men are taken from Bragg, his army may be destroyed; and none can be ordered from Mobile, where there are only 2500 for land defense.

MARCH 20TH.—The snow is eight inches deep this morning, and it is still falling fast.

Not a beggar is yet to be seen in this city of 100,000 inhabitants!

Hood's division, mostly Texans, whose march to the Rappahannock was countermanded when it was ascertained that the enemy had been beaten back across the river, were all the morning defiling through Main Street, in high spirits, and merrily snowballing each other. And these men slept last night out in the snow without tents! Can such soldiers be vanquished?

Yesterday Floyd's division of State troops were turned over to the Confederacy—only about 200!

We have no further particulars of the fight on the Rappahannock; we know, however, that the enemy were beaten, and that this snow-storm must prevent further operations for many days. Several Eastern Shore families, I learn, are about to return to their homes. This is no place for women and children, who have homes elsewhere. We are all on quarter-rations of meat, and but few can afford to buy clothing at the present prices.

MARCH 21ST.—The snow is nearly a foot deep this morning, as it continued to fall all night, and is falling still. It grows warmer, however.

But we now learn that the Indianola *was* destroyed in the Mississippi by the officers, upon the appearance of a simulated gun-boat sent down, without a crew! This was disgraceful, and some one should answer for it.

Col. Godwin writes from King and Queen County, that many of the people there are deserting to the enemy, leaving their stock, provisions, grain, etc., and he asks permission to seize their abandoned property for the use of the government. Mr. Secretary Seddon demands more specific information before that step be taken. He intimates that they may have withdrawn to avoid conscription.

MARCH 22D.—It was thawing all night, and there is a heavy fog this morning. The snow will disappear in a few days.

A very large number of slaves, said to be nearly 40,000, have been collected by the enemy on the Peninsula and at adjacent points, for the purpose, it is supposed, of co-operating with Hooker's army in the next attempt to capture Richmond.

The snow has laid an embargo on the usual slight supplies brought to market, and all who had made no provision for such a contingency are subsisting on very short-commons. Corn-meal is selling at from \$6 to \$8 per bushel. Chickens \$5 each. Turkeys \$20. Turnip greens \$8 per bushel. Bad bacon \$1.50 per pound. Bread 20 cts. per loaf. Flour \$38 per barrel,—and other things in proportion. There are some pale faces seen in the streets from deficiency of food; but no beggars, no complaints. We are all in rags, especially our underclothes. This for liberty!

The Northern journals say we have negro regiments on the Rappahannock and in the West. This is utterly untrue. We have no armed slaves to fight for us, nor do we fear a servile insurrection. We are at no loss, however, to interpret the meaning of such demoniac misrepresentations. It is to be seen of what value the negro regiments employed against us will be to the invader.

MARCH 23D.—The snow has nearly disappeared, and the roads are very bad. No food is brought to the market, and such as may be found in the city is held at famine prices.

I saw a letter to-day from Bishop Lay, in Arkansas. He says affairs in that State wear a dark and gloomy aspect. He thinks the State is lost.

Gen. Beauregard writes the Hon. Mr. Miles that he has not men enough, nor heavy guns enough, for the defense of Charleston.

If this were generally known, thousands would despair, being convinced that those charged with the reins of power are incompetent, unequal to the crisis, and destined to conduct them to destruction rather than independence.

MARCH 24TH.—Judge Lyons has granted an injunction, arresting the impressment of flour by the Secretary of War, and Congress is debating a bill which, if passed, will be a marked rebuke to the government.

Notwithstanding the wishes of the Secretary of War, the President, and Gen. Rains, Lt.-Col. Lay is *still* exempting Marylanders, and even foreigners who have bought real estate, and resided for years in this country, if they have "not taken the oath of domicile."

In Eastern Tennessee, 25,500 conscripts were enrolled, and yet only 6000 were added to the army. The rest were exempted, detailed, or deserted. Such is the working of the Conscription Act, fettered as it is by the Exemption Law, and still executed under Judge Campbell's decision. Gen. Rains has the title, but does not execute the functions of Superintendent of the Bureau of Conscription. The President has been informed of everything.

MARCH 25TH.—We have no news to-day, excepting the falling back of Rosecrans from Murfreesborough, and a raid of Morgan and capture of a train of cars. Rosecrans means, perhaps, to aid in the occupation of the Mississippi River. It will be expensive in human life.

Although our conscription is odious, yet we are collecting a thousand per week. The enemy say they will crush the rebellion in ninety days. In sixty days half their men will return to their homes, and then we may take Washington. God knows, but man does not, what will happen.

MARCH 26TH.—We have dispatches (unofficial) from the West, stating that one of the enemy's gun-boats has been sunk in attempting to pass Vicksburg, and another badly injured. Also that an engagement has occurred on the Yazoo, the enemy having several gun-boats sunk, the rest being driven back.

It snowed a little this morning, and is now clear and cold.

Mr. Seddon is vexed at the unpopularity of the recent impressments by his order. It was an odious measure, because it did not go far enough and take all, distributing enough among the people to crush the extortioners.

MARCH 27TH.—This is the day appointed by the President for fasting and prayers. Fasting in the midst of famine! May God save this people! The day will be observed throughout the Confederacy.

The news from the West, destruction of more of the enemy's gun-boats, seems authentic. So far we have sustained no disasters this spring, the usual season of success of the enemy by water.

Mr. G. W. Randolph was the counsel of the speculators whose flour was impressed, and yet this *man*, when Secretary of War, ordered similar impressments repeatedly. "Oh, man! dressed in a little brief authority," etc.

Mr. Foote has brought forward a bill to prevent trading with the enemy. Col. Lay even gets his pipes from the enemy's country. Let Mr. Foote smoke that!

A gentleman said, to-day, if the Yankees only knew it, they might derive all the benefits they seek by the impracticable scheme of subjugation, without the expenditure of human life, by simply redoubling the blockade of our ports, withdrawing their armies to the borders, and facilitating trade between the sections. We would not attack them in their own country, and in a month millions of their products would be pouring into the South, and cotton, tobacco, etc. would go to the North in vast quantities. I wonder the smart Yankee never thinks of this! Let both sides give passports freely, and an unlimited intercourse would be immediately established.

MARCH 28TH.—We have nothing additional or confirmatory from the West. A letter from Gen. Beauregard states that he has but 17,000 men in South Carolina, and 10,000 in Georgia, 27,000 in all. He asks more, as he will be assailed, probably, by 100,000 Federals. The President refers this important letter to the Secretary of War, simply with the indorsement, "this is an exact statement of affairs in South Carolina and Georgia."

Col. Lay predicts that we shall be beaten in thirty days, or else we shall then be in the way of beating the enemy. A safe prediction—but what is his belief? This deponent saith not. There will be fearful odds against us, and yet our men in the field fear nothing.

We are sending Napoleons up to Lee. But the weather, which has been fine for the last two days, is wet again. If Hooker makes a premature advance, he will be sure to "march back again."

An amusing letter was received from an officer in Tennessee to-day. He was taken prisoner by seven Federals when straying some distance from camp, and subsequently hearing the men express some anxiety to be at home again with their families, gave them some brandy which he happened to possess. He then suggested a plan by which they might return to their homes, viz., to become his prisoners, and being paroled by him. After consultation, they agreed to it, and released him. He then paroled them, giving them the usual certificates to exhibit to their officer, and so, taking another drink, they pursued their different ways. If this disposition prevails extensively among the Western Federals, we may look for speedy results in that quarter. Rosecrans may lose his laurels in a most unexpected manner.

MARCH 29TH.—No news. Yet a universal expectation. What is expected is not clearly defined. Those who are making money rapidly no doubt desire a prolongation of the war, irrespective of political consequences. But the people, the majority in the United States, seem to have lost their power. And their representatives in Congress are completely subordinated by the Executive, and rendered subservient to his will. President Lincoln can have any measure adopted or any measure defeated, at pleasure. Such is the irresistible power of enormous executive patronage. He may extend the sessions or terminate them, and so, all power, for the time being, reposes in the hands of the President.

A day of reckoning will come, for the people of the United States will resume the powers of which the war has temporarily dispossessed them, or else there will be disruptions, and civil war will submerge the earth in blood. The time has not arrived, or else the right men have not arisen, for the establishment of despotisms.

Everything depends upon the issues of the present campaign, and upon them it may be bootless to speculate. No one may foretell the fortunes of war—I mean where victory will ultimately perch in this frightful struggle. We are environed and invaded by not less than 600,000 men in arms, and we have not in the field more than 250,000 to oppose them. But we have the advantage of occupying the interior position, always affording superior facilities for concentration. Besides, our men *must* prevail in combat, or lose their property, country, freedom, everything,—at least this is their conviction. On the other hand, the enemy, in yielding the contest, may retire into their own country, and possess everything they enjoyed before the war began. Hence it may be confidently believed that in all the battles of this spring, when the numbers are nearly equal, the Confederates will be the victors, and even when the enemy have superior numbers, the armies of the South will fight with Roman desperation. The conflict will be appalling and sanguinary beyond example, provided the invader stand up to it. That much is certain. And if our armies are overthrown, we may be no nearer peace than before. The paper money would be valueless, and the large fortunes accumulated by the speculators, turning to dust and ashes on their lips, might engender a new exasperation, resulting in a regenerated patriotism and a universal determination to achieve independence or die in the attempt.

MARCH 30TH.—Gen. Bragg dispatches the government that Gen. Forrest has captured 800 prisoners in Tennessee, and several thousand of our men are making a successful raid in Kentucky.

Gen. Whiting makes urgent calls for reinforcements at Wilmington, and cannot be supplied with many.

Gen. Lee announces to the War Department that the spring campaign is now open, and his army may be in motion any day.

Col. Godwin (of King and Queen County) is here trying to prevail on the Secretary of War to put a stop to the blockade-runners, Jews, and spies, daily passing through his lines with passports from Gens. Elzey and Winder. He says the persons engaged in this illicit traffic are all extortioners and spies, and $50,000 worth of goods from the enemy's country pass daily.

Col. Lay still repudiates Judge Meredith's decision in his instructions to the Commandants of Camps of Instruction. Well, if we have a superabundance of fighting men in the field, the foreign-born denizens and Marylanders can remain at home and make money while the country that protects them is harried by the invader.

The gaunt form of wretched famine still approaches with rapid strides. Meal is now selling at $12 per bushel, and potatoes at $16. Meats have almost disappeared from the market, and none but the opulent can afford to pay $3.50 per pound for butter. *Greens*, however, of various kinds, are coming in; and as the season advances, we may expect a diminution of prices. It is strange that on the 30th of March, even in the "sunny South," the fruit-trees are as bare of blossoms and foliage as at mid-winter. We shall have fire until the middle of May,—six months of winter!

I am spading up my little garden, and hope to raise a few vegetables to eke out a miserable subsistence for my family. My daughter Ann reads Shakspeare to me o' nights, which saves my eyes.

MARCH 31ST.—Another stride of the grim specter, and corn-meal is selling for $17 per bushel. Coal at $20.50 per ton, and wood at $30 per cord. And at these prices one has to wait several days to get either. Common tallow candles are selling at $1 per pound. I see that some furnished houses are now advertised for rent; and I hope that all the population that can get away, and subsist elsewhere, will leave the city.

The lower house of Congress has passed a most enormous tax bill, which I apprehend cannot be enforced, if it becomes a law. It will close half the shops—but that may be beneficial, as thousands have rushed into trade and become extortioners.

I see some batteries of light artillery going toward Petersburg. This is to be used against the enemy when he advances in that direction from Suffolk. No doubt another attempt will be made to capture Richmond. But Lee knows the programme, I doubt not.

CHAPTER XXV.

Symptoms of bread riots.—Lee forming depots of provisions near the Rappahannock.—Beauregard ready to defend Charleston.—He has rebuffed the enemy severely.—French and British advancing money on cotton.—The Yankees can beat us in bargaining.—Gen. Lee anxious for new supplies.—The President appeals to the people to raise food for man and beast.—Federal and Confederate troops serenading each other on the Rappahannock.—Cobbler's wages $3000 per annum.—Wrangling in the Indian country.—Only 700 conscripts per month from Virginia.—Longstreet at Suffolk.—The President's well eye said to be failing.—A "reconnoissance!"—We are planting much grain.—Picking up pins.—Beautiful season.—Gen. Johnston in Tennessee.—Longstreet's successes in that State.—Lee complains that his army is not fed.—We fear for Vicksburg now.—Enemy giving up plunder in Mississippi.—Beauregard is busy at Charleston.—Gen. Marshall, of Kentucky, fails to get stock and hogs.—Gen. Lee calls for Longstreet's corps.—The enemy demonstrating on the Rappahannock.

APRIL 1ST.—It is said we have taken Washington, a village in North Carolina. And it is represented that large supplies of meat, etc. can be taken from thence and the adjacent counties.

Every day we look for important intelligence from Charleston, and from the West.

Mr. Seddon, the Secretary of War, has receded from his position in regard to resident aliens.

APRIL 2D.—This morning early a few hundred women and boys met as by concert in the Capitol Square, saying they were hungry, and must have food. The number continued to swell until there were more than a thousand. But few men were among them, and these were mostly foreign residents, with exemptions in their pockets. About nine A.M. the mob emerged from the western gates of the square, and proceeded down Ninth Street, passing the War Department, and crossing Main Street, increasing in magnitude at every step, but preserving silence and (so far) good order. Not knowing the meaning of such a procession, I asked a pale boy where they were going. A young woman, seemingly emaciated, but yet with a smile, answered that they were going to find something to eat. I could not, for the life of me, refrain from expressing the hope that they might be successful; and I remarked they were going in the right direction to find plenty in the hands of the extortioners. I did not follow, to see what they did; but I learned an hour after that they marched through Cary Street, and entered diverse stores of the speculators, which they proceeded to empty of their contents. They impressed all the carts and drays in the street, which were speedily laden with meal, flour, shoes, etc. I did not learn whither these were driven; but probably they were rescued from those in charge of them. Nevertheless, an immense amount of provisions, and other articles, were borne by the mob, which continued to increase in numbers. An eye-witness says he saw a boy come out of a store with a hat full of money (notes); and I learned that when the mob turned up into Main Street, when all the shops were by this time closed, they broke in the plate-glass windows, demanding silks, jewelry, etc. Here they were incited to pillage valuables, not necessary for subsistence, by the class of residents (aliens) exempted from military duty by Judge Campbell, Assistant Secretary of War, in contravention of Judge Meredith's decision. Thus the work of spoliation went on, until the military appeared upon the scene, summoned by Gov. Letcher, whose term of service is near its close. He had the Riot Act read (by the mayor), and then threatened to fire on the mob. He gave them five minutes' time to disperse in, threatening to use military force (the city battalion being present) if they did not comply with the demand. The timid women fell back, and a pause was put to the devastation, though but few believed he would venture to put his threat in execution. If he had done so, he would have been hung, no doubt.

About this time the President appeared, and ascending a dray, spoke to the people. He urged them to return to their homes, so that the bayonets there menacing them might be sent against the common enemy. He told them that such acts would bring *famine* upon them in the only form which could not be provided against, as it would deter people from bringing food to the city. He said he was willing to share his last loaf with the suffering people (his best horse had been stolen the night before), and he trusted we would all bear our privations with fortitude, and continue united against the Northern invaders, who were the authors of all our sufferings. He seemed deeply moved; and indeed it was a frightful spectacle, and perhaps an ominous one, if the government does not remove some of the quartermasters who have contributed very much to bring about the evil of scarcity. I mean those who have allowed transportation to forestallers and extortioners.

Gen. Elzey and Gen. Winder waited upon the Secretary of War in the morning, asking permission to call the troops from the camps near the city, to suppress the women and children by a summary process. But Mr. Seddon hesitated, and then declined authorizing any such absurdity. He said it was a municipal or State duty, and therefore he would not take the responsibility of interfering in the matter. Even in the moment of aspen consternation, he was still the politician.

I have not heard of any injuries sustained by the women and children. Nor have I heard how many stores the mob visited; and it must have been many.

All is quiet now (three P.M.); and I understand the government is issuing rice to the people.

APRIL 3D.—Gen. D. H. Hill writes from North Carolina that the business of conscription is miserably mismanaged in that State. The whole business, it seems, has resolved itself into a machine for making money and putting pets in office.

No account of yesterday's riot appeared in the papers to-day, for obvious reasons. The mob visited most of the shops, and the pillage was pretty extensive.

Crowds of women, Marylanders and foreigners, were standing at the street corners to-day, still demanding food; which, it is said, the government issued to them. About midday the City Battalion was marched down Main Street to disperse the crowd.

Congress has resolved to adjourn on the 20th April. The tax bill has not passed both Houses yet.

Gen. Blanchard has been relieved of his command in Louisiana. He was another general from Massachusetts.

APRIL 4TH.—It is the belief of some that the riot was a premeditated affair, stimulated from the North, and executed through the instrumentality of emissaries. Some of the women, and others, have been arrested.

We have news of the capture of another of the enemy's gun-boats, in Berwick Bay, Louisiana, with five guns. It is said to have been done by *cavalry*.

A dispatch just received from Charleston states that the enemy's monitors were approaching the forts, seven in number, and that the attack was commencing. This is *joyful* news to our people, so confident are they that Gen. Beauregard will beat them.

April 5th.—Snow fell all night, and a depth of several inches covers the earth this morning. It will soon melt, however, as it is now raining. The Northern invaders who anticipate a pleasant sojourn during the winter and spring in this climate, have been very disagreeably disappointed in these expectations.

A surgeon was arrested yesterday for saying there was "a power behind the throne greater than the throne." Upon being asked by the mayor what power he alluded to, he answered "the people." He was released.

April 6th.—It seems that it was a mistake about the enemy's monitors approaching the forts in Charleston harbor; but the government has dispatches to the effect that important movements are going on, not very distant from Charleston, the precise nature of which is not yet permitted to transpire.

Generals Johnston and Bragg write that Gen. Pillow has secured ten times as many conscripts, under their orders, as the bureau in Richmond would have done. Judge Campbell, as Assistant Secretary of War, having arrested Gen. P.'s operations, Generals J. and B. predict that our army in Tennessee will begin, immediately, to diminish in numbers.

The rails of the York River Railroad are being removed to-day toward Danville, in view of securing a connection with the N. C. Central Road. It seems that the government thinks the enemy will again possess the York River Railroad, but it cannot be possible a retreat *out of Virginia* is meditated.

April 7th.—Nothing definite has transpired at Charleston, or if so, we have not received information of it yet.

From the West, we have accounts, from Northern papers, of the failure of the Yankee Yazoo expedition. That must have its effect.

Judge Campbell, Assistant Secretary of War, has decided in one instance (page 125, E. B. Conscript Bureau), that a paroled political prisoner, returning to the South, is not subject to conscription. This is in violation of an act of Congress, and general orders. It appears that grave judges are not all inflexibly just, and immaculately legal in their decisions. Col. Lay ordered the commandant of conscripts (Col. Shields) to give the man a protection, without any reason therefor.

It is now said large depots of provisions are being formed on the Rappahannock. This does not look like an indication of a retrograde movement on the part of Gen. Lee. Perhaps he will *advance.*

This afternoon dispatches were received from Charleston. Notwithstanding all the rumors relative to the hostile fleet being elsewhere, it is now certain that all the monitors, iron-clads, and transports have succeeded in passing the bar, and at the last accounts were in readiness to begin the attack. And Beauregard was prepared to receive it. To-morrow we shall have exciting intelligence. If we are to believe what we hear from South Carolinians, recently from Charleston (I do believe it), *Charleston* will not be taken. If the ground be taken, it will not be Charleston. If the forts fall, and our two rams be taken or destroyed, the defenders will still resist. Rifle-pits have been dug in the streets; and if driven from these, there are batteries beyond to sweep the streets, thus involving the enemy and the city in one common ruin.

APRIL 8TH.—We learn to-day that the enemy bombarded our forts at Charleston, yesterday, two hours and a half. But few of our men were injured, and the forts sustained no damage of consequence. On the other hand, several of the iron-clads and monitors of the enemy were badly crippled; one of the latter, supposed to be the Keokuk, was sunk. Since then the bombardment has not been renewed. But no doubt the enemy will make other efforts to reduce a city which is the particular object of their vengeance. Every one is on the *qui vive* for further news from Charleston. Success there will make Beauregard the most popular man in the Confederacy, Lee excepted.

Speculation is running wild in this city; and the highest civil and military officers are said to be engaged, directly or indirectly, in the disgraceful business of smuggling. Mr. Memminger cannot be ignorant of this; and yet these men are allowed to retain their places.

April 9th.—Nothing additional has occurred at Charleston, the enemy not having renewed the attack. At Vicksburg all was quiet, and the enemy abandoning their canal. Such news must have a depressing effect upon the North. They will see that their monitors and iron-clads have lost their terrors. They have lost some twenty war steamers within the last few months; and how many of their merchantmen have been destroyed on the ocean, we have no means of knowing.

British and French capitalists have taken a cotton loan of $15,000,000, which is now selling at a premium of four per cent. in those countries. Our government can, if it will, soon have a navy of Alabamas and Floridas.

But we are in danger of being sold to the enemy by the blockade-runners in this city. High officers, civil and military, are said, perhaps maliciously, to be engaged in the unlawful trade hitherto carried on by the Jews. It is said that the flag of truce boats serve as a medium of negotiations between official dignitaries here and those at Washington; and I have no doubt many of the Federal officers at Washington, for the sake of lucre, make no scruple to participate in the profits of this treasonable traffic. They can beat us at this game: cheat us in bargaining, and excel us in obtaining information as to the number and position of troops, fortifications, etc.

April 10th.—We are not informed of a renewal of the attack on Charleston. It is said our shot penetrated the turret of the Keokuk, sunk.

In New York they have been exulting over the capture of Charleston, and gold declined heavily. This report was circulated by some of the government officials, at Washington, for purposes of speculation.

Col. Lay announced, to-day, that he had authority (oral) from Gen. Cooper, A. and I. G., to accept Marylanders as substitutes. Soon after he ordered in two, in place of Louisianian sutlers, whom he accompanied subsequently—I know not whither. But this verbal authority is in the teeth of published orders.

April 11th.—Gen. Beauregard telegraphs that Gen. Walker has destroyed another Federal gun-boat in Coosa River. They are looking for a renewal of the attack on Charleston, and are ready for it.

Gen. Lee writes that he is about sending a cavalry brigade into Loudon County to bring off commissary's and quartermaster's stores. This will frighten the people in Washington City! He also writes that, unless the railroads be repaired, so as to admit of speedier transportation of supplies, he cannot maintain his present position much longer.

The President has published a proclamation, to-day, appealing to the patriotism of the people, and urging upon them to abstain from the growth of cotton and tobacco, and raise food for man and beast. Appended to this is a plan, "suggested by the Secretary of War," to obtain from the people an immediate supply of meat, etc. in the various counties and parishes. This is *my* plan, so politely declined by the Secretary! Well, if it will benefit the government, the government is welcome to it; and Mr. Seddon to the credit of it.

APRIL 12TH.—Gen. Van Dorn, it is reported, has captured or destroyed another gun-boat in the West.

Night before last another riot was looked for in this city by the mayor, and two battalions of Gen. Elzey's troops were ordered into the city. If the President could only see the necessity of placing this city under the command of a native Southern general, he might avoid much obloquy. The Smiths, Winders, and Elzeys, who are really foreigners, since the men from their States are not liable to conscription (vide Judge Campbell's decision), are very obnoxious to the people. Virginians can never be reconciled to the presence of a mercenary Swiss guard, and will not submit to imported masters.

Notwithstanding the *Enquirer* urges it, and Mr. Barksdale, of Mississippi, persistently advocates it, Congress still refuses to confer additional powers on the President. Twice, within the last week, Congress has voted down the proposition to clothe the President with power to suspend the writ of *habeas corpus*. Congress has likewise refused to reconsider the vote postponing the consideration of the bill to create a Court of Claims. Judge S—— was here, working for it; but was doomed to disappointment.

A few nights since a full Federal band came within a hundred yards of our men, the Rappahannock only separating them, and played "Dixie." Our men cheered them lustily. Then they played

"Yankee Doodle," when the Yankees cheered. After this they played "Home, sweet Home!" and all parties cheered them. There may be something significant in this. The pickets have orders not to fire on each other, when no demonstration is in progress.

Our members of Congress get salaries of $2750. A cobbler (free negro), who mends shoes for my family, told me yesterday that he earned $10 per day, or $3000 per annum.

A pair of pantaloons now costs $40; boots, $60; and so on.

We have warm weather at last, and dry. Armies will soon be in motion.

Our government and people seem now to despair of European intervention. But the President says our armies are more numerous, and better armed and disciplined than at any period during the war. Hence the contest will be maintained indefinitely for independence. With these feelings the third year of the war opens. May God have mercy on the guilty men who determine more blood shall be shed. The South would willingly cease the sanguinary strife, if the invader would retire from our territory; but just as willingly will she fight hereafter as heretofore, so long as a foeman sets foot upon her soil. It must soon be seen with what alacrity our people will rush to the battle-field!

April 13th.—The Federal monitors, gun-boats, and transports no more menace the City of Charleston! The fleet has sailed away, several of the iron-clads towed out of the harbor being badly damaged. But before leaving that part of the coast, the Yankees succeeded in intercepting and sinking the merchant steamer Leopard, having 40,000 pairs of shoes, etc. on board for our soldiers. It is supposed they will reappear before Wilmington; our batteries there are ready for them.

Gen. Wise assailed the enemy on Saturday, at Williamsburg, captured the town, and drove the Federals into their fort—Magruder.

The President was ill and nervous on Saturday. His wife, who lost her parent at Montgomery, Ala., a month ago, and who repaired thither, is still absent.

Congress still refuses to clothe the President with dictatorial powers.

Senator Oldham, of Texas, made a furious assault on the Secretary of War, last Saturday. He says Senators, on the most urgent public business, are subjected to the necessity of writing their names on a slate, and then awaiting the pleasure of some lackey for permission to enter the Secretary's office. He was quite severe in his remarks, and moved a call on the President for certain information he desired.

The *Sentinel* abuses Congress for differing with the President in regard to the retention of diplomatic agents in London, etc. And the *Enquirer*, edited by John Mitchel, the fugitive Irishman, opens its batteries on the *Sentinel*. So we go.

APRIL 14TH.—We have nothing additional from Gen. Wise's expedition against Williamsburg; but it was deprecated by our people here, whose families and negroes have been left in that vicinity. They argue that we cannot hold the town, or any portion of the Peninsula in the neighborhood; and when the troops retire, the enemy will subject the women and children to more rigorous treatment, and take all the slaves.

We have news from Tennessee, which seems to indicate that Gen. Van Dorn has been beaten, losing a battery, after a sanguinary battle of several hours. Van Dorn had only cavalry—7000. This has a depressing effect. It seems that we lose all the battles of any magnitude in the West. This news may have been received by the President in advance of the public, and hence his indisposition. We shall have news now every day or so.

Albert Pike is out in a pamphlet against Gens. Holmes and Hindman. He says their operations in Arkansas have resulted in reducing our forces, in that State, from forty odd thousand to less than 17,000. It was imprudent to publish such a statement. Albert Pike is a native Yankee, but he has lived a long time in the South.

Gov. Vance is furious at the idea of conscribing magistrates, constables, etc. in North Carolina. He says it would be an annihilation of State Rights—nevertheless, being subject to militia duty by the laws of the State, they are liable under the Act of Conscription.

Well, we are getting only some 700 conscripts per month in Virginia—the largest State! At this rate, how are we to replenish the ranks as they become thinned in battle? It is to be hoped the enemy will find the same difficulty in filling up their regiments, else we have rather a gloomy prospect before us. But God can and will save us if it be His pleasure.

APRIL 15TH.—There is a dispatch, unofficial, from the West, contradicting the news of the defeat of Van Dorn. On the Cumberland River, another dispatch says, we have met with new successes, capturing or destroying several more gun-boats. And Wheeler has certainly captured a railroad train in the rear of the enemy, containing a large sum of Federal money, and a number of officers.

We have nothing from the South, except a letter from Gen. Whiting, in regard to some demonstration at Bull Bay, S. C.

Major Griswold, Provost Marshal, is now himself on trial before a court-martial, for allowing 200 barrels of spirits to come into the city. He says he had an order from the Surgeon-General; but what right had he to give such orders? It is understood he will resign, irrespective of the decision of the court.

Congress, yesterday (the House of Representatives), passed a series of resolutions, denying the authority of the government to declare martial law, such as existed in this city under the administration of Gen. Winder. It was a great blunder, and alienated thousands.

We have a seasonable rain to-day.

APRIL 16TH.—The Federal papers have heard of the failure to take Charleston, and the sinking of the Keokuk; and yet they strive to mollify the disaster, and represent that but little damage was sustained by the rest of the fleet. Those that escaped, they say, have proved themselves invulnerable. The Keokuk had ninety shots on the water line. No wonder it sunk!

Gen. Longstreet has invested Suffolk, this side of Norfolk, after destroying one gun-boat and crippling another in the Nansemond River. Unless the enemy get reinforcements, the garrison at Suffolk may be forced to surrender. Perhaps our general may storm their works!

I learn, to-day, that the remaining eye of the President is failing. Total blindness would incapacitate him for the executive office. A fearful thing to contemplate!

APRIL 17TH.—From the Northern papers we learn that the defeat at Charleston is called by the enemy a RECONNOISSANCE.

This causes us much merriment here; McClellan's defeat was called a "strategical movement," and "change of base."

We have some rumors to-day, to the effect that Gen. Hill is likely to take Washington and Newbern, N. C.; Gen. Longstreet, Suffolk; and Gen. Wise, Fort Magruder, and the Peninsula—he has not troops enough.

Gold advanced 7 per cent. in New York when the news of the "reconnoissance" reached that city.

We are planting almost every acre in grain, to the exclusion of cotton and tobacco—resolved never to be *starved*, nor even feel a scarcity of provisions in future. We shall be cutting wheat in another month in Alabama and other States.

Among the other rumors, it is said Hooker is falling back toward Washington, but these are merely rumors.

The President is in a very feeble and nervous condition, and is really threatened with the loss of sight altogether. But he works on; and few or no visitors are admitted. He remains at his dwelling, and has not been in the executive office these ten days.

Col. Lay was merry again to-day. He ordered in another foreign substitute (in North Carolina).

Pins are so scarce and costly, that it is now a pretty general practice to stoop down and pick up any found in the street. The boarding-houses are breaking up, and rooms, furnished and unfurnished, are rented out to messes. One dollar and fifty cents for beef, leaves no margin for profit, even at $100 per month, which is charged for board, and most of the boarders cannot afford to pay that price. Therefore they take rooms, and buy their own scanty food. I am inclined to think provisions would not be deficient, to an alarming extent, if they were equally distributed. Wood is no scarcer than before the war, and yet $30 per load (less than a cord) is demanded for it, and obtained.

The other day Wilmington *might* have been taken, for the troops were sent to Beauregard. Their places have since been filled by a brigade from Longstreet. It is a monstrous undertaking to attempt to subjugate so vast a country as this, even with its disparity of population. We have superior facilities for concentration, while the invader must occupy, or penetrate the outer lines of the circumference. Our danger is from within, not from without. We are distressed more by the extortioners than by the enemy. Eternal infamy on the heads of speculators in articles of prime necessity! After the war, let them be known by the fortunes they have amassed from the sufferings of the patriots and heroes! —the widows and orphans!

This day is the anniversary of the secession of Virginia. The government at Washington did not believe the separation would last two years! Nor do they believe now, perhaps, that it will continue two years longer.

APRIL 18TH.—We have nothing more from the Peninsula, Suffolk, N. C., or South Carolina; but it is rumored that the enemy's gun-boats (seven or eight) have passed down the Mississippi in spite of our batteries at Vicksburg, which sunk one of them. If this be true, it is bad news.

We have lovely weather now, and vegetation shows signs of the return of the vernal season. We shall soon have blossoms and roses in abundance, and table vegetables too, to dispel the fears of famine. But we shall also have the horrid sounds of devastating war; and many a cheerful dame and damsel to-day, must soon put on the weeds of mourning.

Gen. Jos. E. Johnston has assumed the command of the army of Tennessee. Gen. Howell Cobb is preparing for the defense of Florida. We do not hear a word from Lee or Jackson—but this is the ominous silence preceding their decisive action.

Bacon fell to-day from $2 to $1.50 per pound, and butter from $3.50 to $3.25; potatoes are $16 per bushel. And yet they say there is no scarcity in the country. Such supplies are hoarded and hidden to extort high prices from the destitute. An intelligent gentleman from North Carolina told me, to-day, that food was never more abundant in his State; nevertheless, the extortioners are demanding there very high prices.

This evening we have dispatches (unofficial) confirmatory of the passing of Vicksburg by the enemy's gun-boats. One of them was destroyed, and two disabled, while five got by uninjured. This is not cheering. No doubt an attack by land will be made, by superior numbers, and blood will gush in streams!

It is now said that Longstreet has captured two gun-boats in the Nansemond, and taken 600 prisoners; and that the Yankees in Norfolk have been thrown into great commotion. The general in command there, Veillé, has adopted very stringent measures to keep the people sympathizing with our cause in subjection. Perhaps he fears an outbreak.

The weather continues fine, and we must soon have important operations in the field.

APRIL 19TH, SUNDAY.—It is now said Longstreet captured two transports, instead of gun-boats, and 600 prisoners.

Mr. Benjamin reports that the enemy's gun-boats, which passed Vicksburg, have recaptured the Queen of the West! It must be so, since he says so.

Mr. Baldwin, the other day, in Congress, asserted a fact, on his own knowledge, that an innocent man had been confined in prison nearly two years, in consequence of a mistake of one of Gen. Winder's subordinates in writing his name, which was Simons; he wrote it Simmons!

APRIL 20TH.—We have nothing definite from Suffolk, or from Washington, N. C.

But we have Northern accounts of their great disaster at Charleston. It appears that during the brief engagement on the 7th inst., all their monitors were so badly damaged that they were unable to prolong or to renew the contest. They will have to be taken to New York for repairs; and will not go into service again before autumn. Thus, after nearly a year's preparation, and the expenditure of $100,000,000, all their hopes, so far as Charleston is concerned, have been frustrated in a few brief hours, under the fire of Beauregard's batteries. They complain that England furnished us with the steel-pointed balls that penetrated their iron turrets. To this there can be no objection; indeed it may be productive of good, by involving the Abolitionists in a new quarrel: but it is due to candor to state that the balls complained of were manufactured in this city.

It was a Federal account of the retaking the Queen of the West, reported by Mr. Benjamin; and hence, it is not generally believed.

It is thought by many that Hooker will change his base from the Rappahannock to the Pamunky, embarking his army in transports. If this be so, we shall again have the pleasure of hearing the thunders of battle, this summer, in Richmond.

Gen. Lee has been quite ill, but is now recovering.

APRIL 21ST.—Gen. Longstreet lost, it is said, two 32-pounder guns yesterday, with which he was firing on the enemy's gunboats. A force was landed and captured the battery.

Gen. Lee writes that his men have each, daily, but a quarter pound of meat and 16 ounces of flour. They have, besides, 1 pound of rice to every ten men, two or three times a week. He says this may keep them *alive;* but that at this season they should have more generous food. The scurvy and the typhoid fever are appearing among them. Longstreet and Hill, however, it is hoped will succeed in bringing off supplies of provision, etc.—such being the object of their demonstrations.

Gen. Wise has fallen back, being ordered by Gen. Elzey not to attempt the capture of Fort Magruder—a feat he could have accomplished.

April 22d.—The President is reported to be very ill to-day—dangerously ill—with inflammation of the throat, etc. While this is a source of grief to nearly all, it is the subject of secret joy to others. I am sure I have seen some officers of rank to-day, not *fighting* officers, who sincerely hope the President will not recover. He has his faults, but upon the whole is no doubt well qualified for the position he occupies. I trust he will recover.

The destruction of the Queen of the West, and of another of our steamers, is confirmed. Is not Pemberton and Blanchard responsible?

The loss of two guns and forty men the other day, on the Nansemond, is laid at the door of Major-Gen. French, a Northern man! Can it be Gen. Cooper (Northern) who procures the appointment of so many Northern generals in our army?

I cut the following from the *Dispatch* of yesterday:

Produce, etc.—Bacon has further declined, and we now quote $1.25 to $1.30 for hog-round; butter, $2.25 to $3 per pound; beans in demand at $20 per bushel. Corn is lower—we quote at $6 to $6.50 per bushel; corn meal, $7 to $9 per bushel—the latter figure for a limited quantity; candles, $3.50 to $3.75 per pound; fruit—dried apples, $10 to $12; dried peaches, $15 to $18 per bushel; flour—superfine, $31 to $32; extra, $34; family, $36; hay is in very small supply—sales at $15 per cwt.; lard, $1.65 to $1.70 per pound; potatoes—Irish, $8 to $10; sweet, $10 to $11 per bushel; rice, 25 to 33 cents per pound; wheat, $6.50 to $7 per bushel.

Groceries.—Sugars have a declining tendency: we quote brown at $1.15 to $1.25; molasses, $9 to $10 per gallon; coffee, $4 to $4.50; salt, 45 cents per pound; whisky, $28 to $35; apple brandy, $24 to $25; French brandy, $65 per gallon.

April 23d.—The President's health is improving. His eye is better; and he would have been in his office to-day (the first time for three weeks) if the weather (raining) had been fine.

The expenses of the war amount now to $60,000,000 per month, or $720,000,000 per annum. This enormous expenditure is owing to the absurd prices charged for supplies by the farmers, to save whose slaves and farms the war is waged, in great part. They are charging the government $20 per hundred weight, or $400 per ton for hay! Well, we shall soon see if they be reluctant to pay the taxes soon to be required of them—one-tenth of all their crops, etc. If they refuse to pay, then what will they deserve?

April 24th.—We lost five fine guns and over a hundred men on the Nansemond; and we learn that more of the enemy's gun-boats and transports have passed Vicksburg! These are untoward tidings. Gens. Pemberton and French are severely criticised.

We had a tragedy in the street to-day, near the President's office. It appears that Mr. Dixon, Clerk of the House of Representatives, recently dismissed one of his under clerks, named Ford, for reasons which I have not heard; whereupon the latter notified the former of an intention to assault him whenever they should meet. About two P.M. they met in Bank Street; Ford asked Dixon if he was ready; and upon an affirmative response being given, they both drew their revolvers and commenced firing. Dixon missed Ford, and was wounded by his antagonist, but did not fall. He attempted to fire again, but the pistol missed fire. Ford's next shot missed D. and wounded a man in Main Street, some seventy paces beyond; but his next fire took effect in Dixon's breast, who fell and expired in a few moments.

Many of our people think that because the terms of enlistment of so many in the Federal army will expire next month, we shall not have an active spring campaign. It may be so; but I doubt it. Blood must flow as freely as ever!

April 25th.—We have bad news from the West. The enemy (cavalry, I suppose) have penetrated Mississippi some 200 miles, down to the railroad between Vicksburg and Meridian. This is in the rear and east of Vicksburg, and intercepts supplies They destroyed two trains. This dispatch was sent to the Secretary of War by the President without remark. The *Enquirer* this morning contained a paragraph stating that Gen. Pemberton was exchanging civilities with Gen. Sherman, and had sent him a beautiful bouquet! Did he have any conception of the surprise the enemy was executing at the moment? Well, Mississippi is the President's State, and if he is satisfied with Northern generals to defend it, he is as likely to be benefited as any one else.

Gen. Beauregard is urging the government to send more heavy guns to Savannah.

I saw an officer to-day just from Charleston. He says none of the enemy's vessels came nearer than 900 yards of our batteries, and that the Northern statements about the monitors becoming entangled with obstructions are utterly false, for there were no obstructions in the water to impede them. But he says one of the monitors was directly over a torpedo, containing 4000 pounds of powder, which we essayed in vain to ignite.

APRIL 26TH.—This being Sunday I shall hear no news, for I will not be in any of the departments.

There is a vague understanding that notwithstanding the repulse of the enemy at Charleston, still the Federal Government collects the duties on merchandise brought into that port, and, indeed, into all other ports. These importations, although purporting to be conducted by British adventurers, it is said are really contrived by Northern merchants, who send hither (with the sanction of the Federal Government, by paying the duty in advance) British and French goods, and in return ship our cotton to Liverpool, etc., whence it is sometimes reshipped to New York. The duties paid the United States are of course paid by the consumers in the Confederate States, in the form of an additional per centum on the prices of merchandise. Some suppose this arrangement has the sanction of certain members of our government. The plausibility of this scheme (if it really exists) is the fact that steamers having munitions of war rarely get through the blockading fleet without trouble, while those having only merchandise arrive in safety almost daily. Gen. D. Green intimates that Mr. Memminger, and Frazer & Co., Charleston, are personally interested in the profits of heavy importations.

APRIL 27TH.—A dispatch from Montgomery, Ala., states that the enemy have penetrated as far as Enterprise, Miss., where we had a small body of troops, conscripts. If this be merely a raid, it is an extraordinary one, and I feel some anxiety to learn the conclusion of it. It is hard to suppose a small force of the enemy would evince such temerity. But if it be supported by an army, and the position maintained, Vicksburg is doomed. We shall get no more sugar from Louisiana.

APRIL 28TH.—The enemy's raid in Mississippi seems to have terminated at Enterprise, where we collected a force and offered battle, but the invaders retreated. It is said they had 1600 cavalry and 5 guns, and the impression prevails that but few of them will ever return. It is said they sent back a detachment of 200 men some days ago with their booty, watches, spoons, jewelry, etc. rifled from the habitations of the non-combating people.

I saw Brig.-Gen. Chilton to day, Chief of Gen. Lee's Staff. He says, when the time comes, Gen. Lee will do us all justice. I asked him if Richmond were safe, and he responded in the affirmative.

I am glad the Secretary of War has stopped the blockade-running operations of Gen. Winder and Judge Campbell, Assistant Secretary of War. Until to-day, Gen. W. issued many passports which were invariably approved by Judge Campbell, but for some cause, and Heaven knows there is cause enough, Mr. Secretary has ordered that no more passports be granted Marylanders or foreigners to depart from the Confederacy. I hope Mr. S. will not "back down" from this position.

To-day I returned to the department from the Bureau of Conscription, being required at my old post by Mr. Kean, Chief of the Bureau of War, my friend, Jacques, being out of town with a strangury. Thus it is; when Congress meets I am detailed on service out of the department, and when Congress adjourns they send for me back again. Do they object to my acquaintance with the members?

A few weeks ago I addressed the President a letter suggesting that an alphabetical analysis be made of letter and indorsement books, embracing principles of decisions, and not names. This I did for the Bureau of Conscription, which was found very useful. Precedents could thus be readily referred to when, as was often the case, the names of parties could not be recollected. It happened, singularly enough, that this paper came into my hands with forty-nine others to-day, at the department, where I shall wholly remain hereafter. The President seemed struck with the idea, and indorsed a reference on it to the "State, Treasury, War, and Navy Departments," and also to the Attorney-General. I shall be curious to know what the Secretary thinks of this plan. No matter what the Secretary of War thinks of it; he declined my plan of deriving supplies directly from the people, and then adopted it.

APRIL 29TH.—Gen. Beauregard is eager to have completed the "Torpedo Ram," building at Charleston, and wants a "great gun" for it. But the Secretary of the Navy wants all the iron for *mailing* his gun-boats. Mr. Miles, of South Carolina, says the ram will be worth two gun-boats.

The President of the Manassas Gap Railroad says his company is bringing all its old iron to the city. Wherefore?

The merchants of Mobile are protesting against the impressment by government agents of the sugar and molasses in the city. They say this conduct will double the prices. So Congress did not and cannot restrain the military authorities.

Gen. Humphrey Marshall met with no success in Kentucky. He writes that none joined him, when he was led to expect large accessions, and that he could get neither stock nor hogs. Alas, poor Kentucky! The brave hunters of former days have disappeared from the scene.

The Secretary of War was not *permitted* to see my letter which the President referred to him, in relation to an alphabetical analysis of the decisions of the departments. The *Assistant* Secretary, Judge Campbell, and the young Chief of the Bureau of War, sent it to the Secretary of the Navy, who, of course, they knew had no decisions to be preserved. Mr. Kean, I learn, indorsed a hearty approval of the plan, and said he would put it in operation in the War Office. But he said (with his concurrence, no doubt) that *Judge Campbell* had suggested it some time before. Well, that may be; but I first suggested it a year ago, and before either Mr. K. or Judge Campbell were in office. Office makes curious changes in men! Still, I think Mr. Seddon badly used in not being permitted to see the communications the President sends him. I have the privilege, and will use it, of sending papers directly to the Secretary.

Gen. Lee telegraphs the President to-day to send troops to Gordonsville, and to hasten forward supplies. He says Lt.-Gen. Longstreet's corps might now be sent from Suffolk to him. Something of magnitude is on the tapis, whether offensive or defensive, I could not judge from the dispatch.

We had hail this evening as large as pullets' eggs.

The Federal papers have accounts of brilliant successes in Louisiana and Missouri, having taken 1600 prisoners in the former State and defeated Price at Cape Girardeau in the latter. Whether these accounts are authentic or not we have no means of knowing yet. We have nothing further from Mississippi.

It is said there is some despondency in Washington.

Our people will die in the last ditch rather than be subjugated and see the confiscation of their property.

APRIL 30TH.—The enemy are advancing across the Rappahannock, and the heavy skirmishing which precedes a battle has begun. We are sending up troops and supplies with all possible expedition. Decisive events are looked for in a few days. But if all of Longstreet's corps be sent up, we leave the southern approach to the city but weakly defended. Hooker must have overwhelming numbers, else he would not venture to advance in the face of Lee's army! Can he believe the silly tale about our troops being sent from Virginia to the Carolinas? If so, he will repent his error.

We hear of fighting in Northwestern Virginia and in Louisiana, but know not the result. The enemy have in possession all of Louisiana west of the Mississippi River. This is bad for us,—sugar and salt will be scarcer still. At Grand Gulf our batteries have repulsed their gun-boats, but the battle is to be renewed.

The railroad presidents have met in this city, and ascertained that to keep the tracks in order for military purposes, 49,500 tons of rails must be manufactured per annum, and that the Tredegar Works here, and the works at Atlanta, cannot produce more than 20,000 tons per annum, even if engaged exclusively in that work! They say that neither individual nor incorporated companies will suffice. The government must manufacture iron or the roads must fail!

A cheering letter was received from Gov. Vance to-day, stating that, upon examination, the State (North Carolina) contains a much larger supply of meat and grain than was supposed. The State Government will, in a week or so, turn over to the Confederate Government 250,000 pounds of bacon, and a quantity of corn; and as speculators are driven out of the market, the Confederate States agents will be able to purchase large supplies from the people, who really have a considerable surplus of provisions. He attributes this auspicious state of things to the cessation of arbitrary impressments.

CHAPTER XXVI.

Lee snuffs a battle in the breeze.—Hooker's army supposed to be 100,000 men.—Lee's perhaps 55,000 efficient.—I am planting potatoes.—Part of Longstreet's army gone up.—Enemy makes a raid.—Great victory at Chancellorville.—Hot weather.—Our poor wounded coming in streams, in ambulances and on foot.—Hooker has lost the game.—Message from the enemy.—They ask of Lee permission to bury their dead.—Granted, of course.—Hooker fortifying.—Food getting scarce again.—Gen. Lee's thanks to the army.—Crowds of prisoners coming in.—Lieut.-Gen. Jackson dead.—Hooker's raiders "hooked" a great many horses.—Enemy demand 500,000 more men.—Beauregard complains that so many of his troops are taken to Mississippi.—Enemy at Jackson, Miss.—Strawberries.—R. Tyler.—My cherries are coming on finely.—Ewell and Hill appointed lieutenant-generals.—President seems to doubt Beauregard's veracity.—Hon. D. M. Lewis cuts his wheat to morrow, May 28th.—Johnston says our troops are in fine spirits around Vicksburg.—Grant thunders on.—Plan of servile insurrection.

MAY 1ST.—Gov. Vance writes that Gen. Hill desires him to call out the militia, believing the enemy, balked in the attempt on Charleston, will concentrate their forces against North Carolina. But the Governor is reluctant to call the non-conscripts from the plow in the planting season. He thinks the defense of North Carolina has not been adequately provided for by the government, and that his State has been neglected for the benefit of others. He asks heavy guns; and says half the armament hurled against Charleston would suffice for the capture of Wilmington.

A protest, signed by the thousands of men taken at Arkansas Post, now exchanged, against being kept on this side of the Mississippi, has been received. The protest was also signed by the members of Congress from Texas, Louisiana, Arkansas, and Missouri.

Capt. Causey, of the Signal Corps, writes that there are only a few battalions of the enemy on the Peninsula; but that rations for 40,000 men are sent to Suffolk.

Gen. Lee announces the crossing of the Rappahannock at Port Royal (which the Yankees pillaged) and at places above Fredericksburg. Gen. Stuart is hovering on their flank. A great battle may happen any moment.

L. E. Harvey, president of Richmond and Danville Railroad, asks for details to repair locomotives, else daily trains (freight) must be reduced to tri-weekly trains—and then the army cannot be sustained in Virginia.

Hon. Mr. Garnett asked (and obtained) permission for a Mr. Hurst (Jew?) to pass our lines, and bring Northern merchandise to Richmond for sale. He vouches for his loyalty to Virginia. Congress has before it a bill rendering this traffic criminal.

MAY 2D.—The awful hour, when thousands of human lives are to be sacrificed in the attempt to wrest this city from the Confederate States, has come again. Now parents, wives, sisters, brothers, and little children, both in the North and in the South, hold their breath in painful expectation. At the last accounts the two armies, yesterday, were drawn up in battle array, facing each other. No water flowed between them, the Northern army being on this side of the Rappahannock. We have no means of knowing their relative numbers; but I suspect Gen. Hooker commands more than 100,000 men, while Gen. Lee's army, perhaps, does not exceed 55,000 efficients.

Accounts by passengers, and reports from the telegraph operators at the northern end of the line, some ten or twelve miles this side of the armies, indicate that the battle was joined early this morning. Certainly heavy cannonading was heard. Yet nothing important transpired up to 3 P.M., when I left the department, else I should have known it. Still, the battle may be raging, without, as yet, decisive result, and the general may not have leisure to be dictating dispatches.

Yet the heavy artillery may be only the preliminary overture to the desperate engagement; and it seems to me that several days might be spent in manœuvring into position before the shock of arms occurs, which will lay so many heads low in the dust.

But a great battle seems inevitable. All the world knows the fighting qualifications of Gen. Lee, and the brave army he commands; and Gen. Hooker will, of course, make every effort to sustain his reputation as "fighting Joe." Besides, he commands, for the first time, an army: and knows well that failure to fight, or failure to win, will consign him to the same disgrace of all his predecessors who have hitherto commanded the "Army of the Potomac."

It is certain that a column of Federal cavalry, yesterday, cut the Central Railroad at Trevillian's depot, which prevents communication with Gordonsville, if we should desire to send heavy stores thither. And some suppose Lee is manœuvring to get in the rear of Hooker, which would place the enemy between him and Richmond! He could then cut off his supplies, now being drawn by wagons some twenty or thirty miles, and spread alarm even to Washington. But, then, how would it be with Richmond, if Hooker should accept the position, and if the force at Suffolk should advance on the south side of the river, and gun-boats and transports were to come, simultaneously, up the York and James? Has Hooker the genius to conceive such a plan? Suppose it were so, and that he has shipped his supplies from the Potomac—the supplies which Stuart expects to capture—with the desperate resolution, abandoning his base on the Rappahannock, to force a junction with the heavy detachments south and east of this city? A Napoleon would get Richmond—*but then Lee might get Washington!* Longstreet's corps is somewhere in transitu between Petersburg and Gordonsville, and would no doubt be ordered here, and it might arrive in time. Our defenses are strong; but at this moment we have only Gen. Wise's brigade, and a few battalions at the batteries, to defend the capital—some 5000 in all.

This is mere speculation, to be succeeded speedily by awful facts. The inhabitants here do not doubt the result, although there is a feverish anxiety to get intelligence. There is no such thing as fear, in this community, of personal danger, even among the women and children; but there is some alarm by the opulent inhabitants, some of whom, for the sake of their property, would submit to the invader. One thing is pretty certain, Richmond will not fall by assault without costing the lives of 50,000 men, which is about equal to its population in ordinary times.

Well, I am planting potatoes in my little garden, and hope to reap the benefit of them. I pay 50 cts. per quart for seed potatoes, and should be chagrined to find my expenditure of money and labor had been for the benefit of the invader! Yet it may be so; and if it should be, still there are other little gardens to cultivate where we might fly to. We have too broad and too long a territory in the revolted States to be overrun and possessed by the troops of the United States.

MAY 3D.—We have no further news from the army, except the usual skirmishing. A number of our wounded arrived last evening. An officer reports that, from what he could see of the enemy's conduct, the soldiers do not come to the point with alacrity. He thinks they fight with reluctance, and are liable to be routed any hour by inferior numbers.

Troops were sent up in special trains last night, and also this morning. These are some of the regiments which Gen. D. P. Hill had in North Carolina; and hence the complaints of Gov. Vance, that his State did not have its just proportion of the protection of the government. Of Longstreet's movements, I am not advised. But there will be news enough in a few days.

The President's health is still precarious, and he is still threatened with the loss of his remaining eye.

The Vice-President was in my office yesterday, and told me his health is quite as good as usual. One would suppose him to be afflicted with all manner of diseases, and doomed to speedy dissolution; but, then, he has worn this appearance during the last twenty years. His eyes are magnificent, and his mind is in the meridian of intellectual vigor.

There has been some commotion in the city this afternoon and evening, but no painful alarm, produced by intelligence that the enemy's cavalry, that cut the road at Trevillian's depot, had reached Ashland and destroyed the depot. Subsequent rumors brought them within eight miles of the city; and we have no force of any consequence here. The account was brought from Ashland by a

Mr. Davis, who killed his horse in riding eighteen miles in one hour and a half.

Later in the day a young man, sixteen years old (Shelton), reached the city from Hanover on a United States horse, the enemy having foraged on his father's farm and taken his blooded steed. He says, when he escaped from them (having been taken prisoner this morning) 1500 were at his father's place, and three times as many more, being 6000 in all, were resting a short distance apart on another farm; but such ideas of numbers are generally erroneous. They told him they had been in the saddle five days, and had burnt all the bridges behind them to prevent pursuit. It was after this that they cut the road at Ashland. They professed to have fresh horses taken from our people, leaving their own. I think they will disappear down the Pamunky, and of course will cut the Central and York River Roads, and the wires. Thus communication with Lee's army is interrupted!

The Fredericksburg train, of course, failed to arrive to-day at 6 P.M.; and it is rumored there were 700 of our wounded in it, and that a great battle was fought yesterday by Lee. These are rumors.

MAY 4TH.—This morning early the *tocsin* sounded, and the din, kept up for several hours, intensified the alarm. The presence of the enemy would not have produced a greater effect. But, in truth, the enemy were almost in sight of the city. Hon. James Lyons told me they were within a mile and a half of his house, which is about that distance from the city. Thousands of men, mostly old men and employees of the government, were instantly organized and marched to the batteries.

But the alarm subsided about 10 A.M. upon information being received that the enemy were flying before Gen. Wise down the Peninsula.

After this the following dispatch was received from Gen. Lee:

"MILFORD, May 3d, 1863.

"PRESIDENT DAVIS.

"Yesterday Gen. Jackson, with three of his divisions, penetrated to the rear of the enemy, and drove him from all his positions, from the Wilderness to within one mile of Chancellorville. He was engaged at the same time, in front, by two of Longstreet's divisions.

This morning the battle was renewed. He was dislodged from all his positions around Chancellorville, and driven back toward the Rappahannock, over which he is now retreating.

"Many prisoners were taken, and the enemy's loss, in killed and wounded, large.

"We have again to thank Almighty God for a great victory.

"I regret to state that Gen. Paxton was killed. Gen. Jackson severely, and Generals Heth and A. P. Hill slightly, wounded.

(Signed) "R. E. LEE, *General.*"

Enough is known to raise the spirits of all. Gen. Lee gives thanks to God "for a great victory;" and he never misleads, never exaggerates.

My son Custis got a musket and marched in one of the companies—I have not learned which—for the defense of the city. It is a sultry day, and he will suffer.

The President was driven out in a light open carriage after the reception of Gen. Lee's dispatch, and exhibited the finest spirits. He was even diverted at the zeal of the old men and boys marching out with heavy muskets to the batteries.

Brig.-Gen. Pryor, who has been under arrest (I know not for what offense), volunteered in a company of horse, and galloped away with the rest in pursuit of the enemy.

MAY 5TH.—To-day the excitement was quite as great as ever, for bodies of the enemy are still in the vicinity. They are like frightened quails when the hawks are after them, skurrying about the country in battalions and regiments. Fitzhugh Lee defeated one of their parties, and reports that the entire calvary force of Hooker, in anticipation of certain victory, had been detached in the rear of Lee's army. This force comprises twenty-eight regiments, or 15,000 mounted men! Now that Hooker is defeated—our operator at Guiney's station dispatches to-day that it is reported there, and believed, that Hooker and his staff are prisoners—it may be reasonably doubted whether one-half of this wild cavalry will escape. It was the mad pranks of a desperate commander. Hooker cast all upon the hazard of the die—and lost.

Among the mad pranks of the enemy, they sent a message over the wires to-day from Louisa County, I believe, to this purport: "For Heaven's sake, come and take us. We are broken down, and will surrender."

They captured an engine sent out yesterday to repair the road. The white men escaped, leaving two free negroes. The Yankees made the negroes put on a full head of steam, and run the locomotive into the river.

One of the enemy was taken sleeping at one of our city batteries near the river.

My friend, Dr. Powell, on the Brooke Turnpike, sent his little son, mounted on his finest horse, on an errand to a neighbor. The lad fell in with, as he called them, "some Yankee Dutchmen," who presented their pistols and made him dismount. They took his horse and allowed him to return.

At the hour we were dining yesterday, the enemy were within two and a half miles of us on the Brooke road, and might have thrown shell into this part of the city.

Col. D. J. Godwin writes a long letter to the Secretary of War, from King and Queen Counties, concerning the great number of suspicious persons continually passing our lines into those of the enemy, with passports from this city; and the great injury done by the information they give. Unquestionably they have not only given information, but have furnished guides to the many regiments of cavalry now skurrying through the country. But the Baltimore Plug Uglies, under the protection of Gen. Winder, are the masters, now Mr. Secretary Seddon has yielded again.

A letter was received from Gen. J. E. Johnston to-day. He is too unwell to take the field, and suggests, if it be desirable to be in regular communication with Gen. Bragg, that the President send out a *confidential* officer. He says the army is suffering for meat, and if it retires into East Tennessee, supplies must be obtained from its flanks instead of from its rear, which would be dangerous. The letter was dated a week ago, and gives no indications of a battle. The general says he is exchanging sugar for bacon; but condemns the practice of allowing our people to sell cotton to the enemy for supplies. In my opinion none but government cotton should be exchanged for subsistence. He says the people are subjugated by trade. He suggests that our men when paroled, and not exchanged, may do duty otherwise than in arms—as is practiced by the enemy.

H. D. Bird, general superintendent of the railroad, writes from Petersburg that the movements of cars with ammunition, etc. are thrown into confusion by the neglect of telegraph agents in giving timely notice. *This* is an unfortunate time for confusion. I sent the letter to the Secretary, and know that it was not "filed" on the way to him.

A communication came in to-day from the Committee of Safety at Mobile, Ala., charging that J. S. Clark, Wm. G. Ford, and —— Hurt, have been shipping cotton to New Orleans, after pretending to clear it for Nassau. It says Mr. Clarke was an intimate crony of Gen. Butler's speculating brother. It also intimates that the people believe the government here winks at these violations of the act of Congress of April, 1862.

Very curiously, a letter came from the Assistant Secretary's room to-day for "file," which was written April 22d, 1861, by R. H. Smith to Judge Campbell—a private letter—warning him not to come to Mobile, as nothing was thought of but secession, and it was believed Judge C. had used his influence with Mr. Seward to prevent secession. The writer deprecates civil war. And quite as curiously, the *Examiner* to-day contains what purports to be Admiral Buchanan's correspondence with the Lincoln government, two letters, the first in April, 1861, tendering his resignation, and the last on May 4th, begging, if it had not been done already, that the government would not accept his resignation.

MAY 6TH.—The excitement has subsided, as troops come pouring in, and many improvised cavalry companies go out in quest of the fox—who has vanished we know not exactly whither.

It is believed we have taken 15,000 or 20,000 prisoners, and that the enemy's killed, wounded, and prisoners must reach the appalling number of 40,000.

On Sunday, the enemy opposite Fredericksburg sent over a flag, asking permission to bury their dead. This was granted. But when they came—two corps under Gen. Sedgwick came over and fell upon our few regiments in the vicinity. So goes the story. Then, it is said, when Gen. Lee ordered two of our divisions to drive Sedgwick back, the men, learning the enemy with the flag of truce had given no quarter to their comrades, refused to fight unless permitted to retaliate in *kind*. This was promised them; and then their charge was irresistible, never pausing until the Yankees were hurled back across the river. No prisoners were taken. However this may be, Gen. Lee sends the following to the President:

"[Received by telegraph from Guiney's Depot.]

"HEADQUARTERS, 10 o'clock A M.,
"May 5, 1863.

"TO HIS EXCELLENCY, PRESIDENT DAVIS.

"At the close of the battle of Chancellorville, on Sunday, the enemy was reported advancing from Fredericksburg in our rear.

"Gen. McLaws was sent back to arrest his progress, and repulsed him handsomely that afternoon. Learning that this force consisted of two corps, under Gen. Sedgwick, I determined to attack it, and marched back yesterday with Gen. Anderson, and uniting with Gens. McLaws and Early in the afternoon, succeeded by the blessing of Heaven in driving Gen. Sedgwick over the river. We have reoccupied Fredericksburg, and no enemy remains south of the Rappahannock in its vicinity.

"(Signed) R. E. LEE, *General.*"

Another dispatch from Gen. Lee says Hooker is still on this side of the river, at United States Ford, *fortifying.*

Gen. Longstreet is now closeted with the Secretary of War. No doubt his entire corps will immediately rejoin Lee.

Jackson was wounded (his arm has been amputated) before the great battle was fought, by our own men, in the gloom of the evening, supposing him a Federal officer. He was reconnoitering in front of the line.

S. S. H—— writes to the department, proposing to send an emissary to the North, to organize secret societies to destroy the enemy's stores, ships, railroad bridges, etc. by an unexplained process.

Tillman, Griffin & Co. write to Judge Campbell to obtain them permission to trade with Mexico. Does this mean trading cotton with the enemy? I know not whether the request was granted.

Mr. Benjamin, Secretary of State, writes to the Secretary to-day for permission for some of his Louisiana friends to leave the country in a government steamer.

It is said that the government at Washington is ordering their troops from North Carolina and other places on the Southern seaboard towards Washington, and to reinforce Hooker—or Hooker's army. I think Hooker himself will go the way of all general flesh that fails.

The President sent to the War Department fifty-five letters to-day, written to him on various subjects, but mostly asking appointments. He had read them, and several had indorsed on them, in his own hand, what he wished done in the premises. So he has not lost his sight. He still attends to business at his dwelling, and has not been in his office for more than a month.

Secretary Seddon is gaunt and emaciated, with long straggling hair, mingled gray and black. He looks like a dead man galvanized into muscular animation. His eyes are sunken, and his features have the hue of a man who had been in his grave a full month. But he is an orator, and a man of fine education—but in bad health, being much afflicted with neuralgia. His administrative capacity will be taxed by the results.

MAY 7TH.—A scout came in to-day with the vexatious intelligence that a body of hostile cavalry is still in Louisa County. And later in the day we have information that the Mattapony bridge was burned last night! Thus again is communication interrupted between Gen. Lee and the city! Our wounded cannot be brought to the hospitals here, nor supplies sent to them! It really does seem as if an organization of Union men here were co-operating with the enemy, else they never could disappear and reappear so often with impunity. Every one is asking what Gens. Elzey and Winder are doing—and echo answers, WHAT?

There is a great pressure for passports to leave the country. Mr. Benjamin writes an indignant letter to the Secretary against Gen. Whiting, at Wilmington, for detaining a Mr. Flanner's steamer, laden with cotton for some of the nationalities—Mr. B. intimates a foreign or neutral power. But when once away from our shore, many of these vessels steer for New York, depositing large sums "for those whom it may concern."

Mr. J. B. Campbell, attorney for J. E. Hertz (Jew), writes a long letter to "J. A. Campbell, Assistant Secretary of War," urging the payment of the slight sum of $25,200 for ninety kegs of bicarbonate of soda seized by the agent of the department! The true value is about $250!

At two o'clock this afternoon a note was received by the Secretary of War from Lieut.-Gen. Longstreet (still in the city), stating that the President last night desired him to go to Gen. Lee immediately; but the general, during the day, has become convinced that he should not leave the city until communications are re-established with Gen. Lee, and the city in a condition of defense against the sudden dash of one or two columns of the enemy—an event, he thinks, meditated by the Yankees! And the persistency of the Federal cavalry in hanging round the city in spite of all the generals here, and the many companies, battalions, and regiments vainly sent out in quest of them, would seem to indicate such purpose.

But the raids in the West don't seem to flourish so well. We have an official dispatch from Gen. Bragg, stating that Gen. Forrest has captured 1600 of the enemy's cavalry in a body, near Rome, Georgia.

There are amusing scenes among the horrors of war, as the following, taken from a paper to-day, shows:

"*Taking the Oath under Protest.*—A few weeks ago a laughable incident occurred in the neighborhood of Nashville, which is worthy of record. A saucy, dashing young girl, of the Southern persuasion, was, with a number of other ladies, brought into the presence of Gen. Rosecrans, in order that their Southern ardor might be checked by the administration of the oath of loyalty. The bold, bright-eyed Juno in question, objected to take the oath, saying that her mother had taught her that it was unlady-like to swear; her sense of morality forbid her to swear, and swear she could and would not. The officer insisted that the lady *must* take an oath before she left his presence.

"'Well, general,'" said bright eyes, 'if I must swear, I will; but all sins of the oath must rest on your shoulders, for I swear on your compulsion: "G—d d—m every Yankee to h—l!'"

"And the defiant beauty tossed her dark curls and swept out of the presence unmolested."—*Nashville Union.*

7 O'CLOCK P.M. The report that the bridge over the Mattapony had been burned by the enemy was false—invented probably by a spy or emissary, who, has enjoyed the freedom of the city under the Dogberrys and Vergises imported hither to preserve the government. A number of trains containing our wounded men, guarded by a detachment of troops, have arrived at the Fredericksburg depot. An officer just arrived from the army says we have taken 15,000 prisoners. If this be so, the loss of the enemy during the week in Virginia will not be less than 40,000. Our loss in

killed and wounded is estimated at from 8 to 10,000—we lost a few hundred prisoners. We have taken, it is said, 53 guns, and lost 14.

I think the reports to-day of squadrons of the enemy's cavalry seen in the surrounding counties are not reliable—they were probably our own men in quest of the enemy.

MAY 8TH.—To-day the city is in fine spirits. Hooker had merely thrown up defenses to protect his flight across the river. The following dispatch was received last night from Gen. Lee:

"CHANCELLORVILLE, May 7th, 1863.

"TO HIS EXCELLENCY, PRESIDENT DAVIS.

"After driving Gen. Sedgwick across the Rappahannock, on the night of the 4th inst., I returned on the 5th to Chancellorville. The march was delayed by a storm, which continued all night and the following day. In placing the troops in position on the morning of the 6th, to attack Gen. Hooker, it was ascertained he had abandoned his fortified position. The line of skirmishers was pressed forward until they came within range of the enemy's batteries, planted north of the Rappahannock, which, from the configuration of the ground, completely commanded this side. His army, therefore, escaped with the loss of a few additional prisoners.

"(Signed) R. E. LEE, *General.*"

Thus ends the career of Gen. Hooker, who, a week ago, was at the head of an army of 150,000 men, perfect in drill, discipline, and all the muniments of war. He came a confident invader against Gen. Lee at the head of 65,000 "butternuts," as our honest poor-clad defenders were called, and we see the result! An active campaign of less than a week, and Hooker is hurled back in disgrace and irreparable disaster! Tens of thousands of his men will never live to "fight another day"—and although the survivors did "run away," it is doubtful whether they can be put in fighting trim again for many a month.

And the raiding cavalry have not been heard from to-day. If they be not back on the north side of the Rappahannock by this time, it is probable they will reach Richmond in a few days without arms, and on foot.

Gens. Hood's and Pickett's divisions (Longstreet's corps) are now passing through the city—perhaps 15,000 of the best fighting men in the South. Oh, what wisdom and foresight were evinced by Gen. Lee, when, some ten days ago, he telegraphed the President to send him Longstreet's corps, via Gordonsville! It was referred to the Secretary of War, who consulted with Gen. Cooper—and of course it was not done. This corps was not in the battle. If it had been on the field, Hooker's destruction would have been speedy and complete; and his routed regiments would have been followed to the very gates of the Federal capital. As it was, Lee lost a day in driving Sedgwick back—and then Hooker "escaped," as Lee expresses it.

I do not understand the Assistant Secretary of War's official correspondence. He sent in the other day a letter addressed to him two years ago to be filed—and to-day an envelope addressed to him as Assistant Secretary by Mr. Benjamin, Secretary of State, merely covering a letter (sealed) for R. S. Bunkee, Mobile, Alabama. Well, it is filed.

The pressure for permits to leave the Confederacy is not renewed to-day. Judge Campbell will not have so many passports to "approve," and I trust confidence in the permanency of the Confederacy will be unshaken. How must they feel who, in anticipation of Lee's defeat, had received, in advance, a pardon from the powers at Washington!

Col. Lay was in to-day; he thinks the North will be cheered a little by their capture of Grand Gulf, in the West. But that is not Vicksburg, or Charleston, or Richmond.

We have had short allowance of food yesterday and to-day; the country people being afraid to come to market, lest their horses should be seized to go in quest of the enemy's cavalry. My family dined to-day on eight fresh herrings, which cost two dollars.

The trains from Fredericksburg brought down several hundred Federal officers; among them was a general, a large number of colonels, lieutenant-colonels, majors, captains, etc. These, when exchanged, as I suppose they will be—for victory makes our government magnanimous—may, if they choose, deny the report that the raiding cavalry destroyed the railroad.

Now what will the *Tribune* say? It did say, a few months ago, that if the effort to crush the rebellion failed this spring, it would be useless to prolong the war—and that peace should be made on the best practicable terms. Since the beginning of the war, I doubt not 500,000 men have been precipitated upon Virginia. Where are they now? In the third year of the war, we see "the finest army the world ever saw," overthrown by about half its numbers, and in full retreat toward its own frontier. Perhaps 100,000 invaders have found bloody graves in Virginia—and an equal number have died of their wounds, or from disease contracted in this State. The number of maimed and disabled must also be 100,000—and yet Richmond is not taken, or likely to be. To invade and subjugate a vast territory, inhabited by millions of warlike people, the assailants must always have four times as many men as the assailed; therefore we stand on an equal footing with the United States in this war, and they may, if they be insane enough, protract it indefinitely, and in the end reap no substantial benefit. On the contrary, the fortune of war may shift the scene of devastation to their own homes. Perhaps Lee may follow up this blow until he enters Pennsylvania.

MAY 9TH.—The papers contain the following order from Gen. Lee:

"HEADQUARTERS ARMY NORTHERN VIRGINIA,
"May 7th, 1863.

"GENERAL ORDERS NO. 59.

"With heartfelt gratification, the General Commanding expresses to the army his sense of the heroic conduct displayed by officers and men, during the arduous operations in which they have just been engaged.

"Under trying vicissitudes of heat and storm, you attacked the enemy, strongly intrenched in the depths of a tangled wilderness, and again on the hills of Fredericksburg, fifteen miles distant, and by the valor that has triumphed on so many fields, forced him once more to seek safety beyond the Rappahannock. While this glorious victory entitles you to the praise and gratitude of the nation, we are especially called upon to return our grateful thanks to the only Giver of victory for the signal deliverance He has wrought.

"It is, therefore, earnestly recommended that the troops unite on Sunday next in ascribing to the Lord of hosts the glory due unto His name.

"Let us not forget in our rejoicing the brave soldiers who have fallen in defense of their country; and while we mourn their loss, let us resolve to emulate their noble example.

"The army and the country alike lament the absence for a time of one to whose bravery, energy, and skill they are so much indebted for success.

"The following letter from the President of the Confederate States is communicated to the army as an expression of his appreciation of its success:

"'I have received your dispatch, and reverently unite with you in giving praise to God for the success with which He has crowned our arms.

"'In the name of the people, I offer my cordial thanks to yourself and the troops under your command for this addition to the unprecedented series of great victories which your army has achieved.

"'The universal rejoicing produced by this happy result will be mingled with a general regret for the good and the brave who are numbered among the killed and wounded.'

"R. E. LEE, *General.*"

The losses on either side are not yet relatively ascertained. Ours, in killed, wounded, and prisoners, will probably reach 10,000. We have taken about 10,000 prisoners; the enemy's killed and wounded is thought to be 15,000 to 20,000. We have taken about fifty guns—and it is said 40,000 small arms, in good order. They did not have leisure to destroy them as on former occasions. It was a complete and stunning defeat.

Gen. Jackson remains near Fredericksburg, and is doing well since the amputation of his (left) arm. The wound was received, during the battle by moonlight, from his own men, who did not recognize their beloved general.

A letter was received to-day from Gen. Whiting at Wilmington, who refuses to permit the "Lizzie" to leave the port, unless ordered to do so. He intimates that she trades with the enemy. And yet Mr. Benjamin urges the Secretary to allow her to depart! Commodore Lynch also writes that the detention of the "Lizzie" is a prudential measure, as it is the only steamer in port that could conduct our unfinished gun-boat to a place of safety, should the enemy's fleet make a sudden attack on the city.

The President (who still absents himself from the Executive Office, his health being precarious) writes the Secretary to consult Gen. Lee before detaching Gen. Jenkins's cavalry brigade from the West. It would have been better if Gen. Lee's advice had been taken in regard to Gen. Longstreet.

The men from the garrison at Drewry's Bluff, and the crew from the steamer Richmond, were taken away to man the batteries around the city. The President requests the Secretary to order them back at the earliest moment practicable. It would be an ugly picture if our defenses at Drewry's Bluff were surprised and taken by a sudden dash of the enemy up James River.

The raid of the enemy's cavalry, after all, did little or no permanent injury to the roads or canal. They are all in operation again.

It is said Lincoln has called for 500,000 more men. Numbers have now no terror for the Southern people. They are willing to wage the war against quadruple their number.

MAY 10TH.—Detachments of Federal troops are now marching into the city every few hours, guarded by (mostly) South Carolinians, dressed in home-spun, dyed yellow with the bark of the butternut-tree. Yesterday evening, at 7 o'clock, a body of 2000 arrived, being marched in by way of the Brooke Pike, near to my residence. Only 200 Butternuts had them in charge, and a less number would have sufficed, for they were extremely weary. Some of them, however, attempted to be humorous.

A young officer asked one of the spectators if the "Libby" (the prison) was the best house in the city to put up at. He was answered that it was the best *he* would find.

Another passed some compliment on a mulatto wench, who replied: "Go long, you nasty Abolition Yankee."

One of our soldiers taken at Arkansas Post, just exchanged, walked along with the column, and kept repeating these words: "Now you know how *we* felt when you marched us through your cities."

But generally a deep silence was maintained, and neither insult nor indignity offered the fallen foe. Other columns are on the way —and how they are to be subsisted is a vexatious question.

The Washington papers of the day preceding the first battle contain Hooker's address to his army—how different from Lee's! It is short, though:

"HEADQUARTERS ARMY OF THE POTOMAC,
"Camp near Falmouth, April 30th.

"GENERAL ORDERS NO. 47.

"It is with heartfelt satisfaction that the Commanding General announces to the army that the operations of the last three days have determined that our enemy must either ingloriously fly or come out from behind his defenses and give us battle on our own ground, where certain destruction awaits him. The operations of the 15th, 11th, and 12th corps have been a succession of splendid achievements.

"By command of MAJ.-GEN. HOOKER.

"S. WILLIAMS, *Ass't. Adj't.-Gen.*"

Another column of between twelve and fifteen hundred prisoners marched in this afternoon. It is said a copy of the New York *Herald* is in town, which acknowledges Hooker's loss to be fully 40,000. There are rumors, also, that our army in Tennessee has gained a great victory. Rumors from the West have hitherto been so very unreliable, that I shall wait patiently for the confirmation of any reports from that quarter.

MAY 11TH.—Lieut.-Gen. J. T. Jackson died at 3 P.M. yesterday. His remains will arrive in the city at 5 P.M. this afternoon. The flags are at half-mast, and all the government offices and even places of business are closed. A multitude of people, mostly women and children, are standing silently in the streets, awaiting the arrival of the hero, destined never again to defend their homes and honor.

A letter from Gen. Lee says, emphatically, that if cavalry be not brought from North Carolina and the South, the enemy's cavalry will be enabled to make raids almost anywhere without molestation. I recollect distinctly how he urged the Secretary of War (Randolph), months ago, to send to Texas for horses, but it was not attended to—and now we see the consequences.

The exchanged prisoners here, taken at Arkansas Post, are ordered to the Mississippi. Gen. Longstreet urged the Secretary to send them off, if that were their destination, without a moment's delay, several days ago—else they would be too late to participate in the campaign.

Northern papers set down Hooker's loss at 20,000, a modest figure, subject to revision.

The Federal Secretary of War has issued a statement to mollify the panic. He is bound to acknowledge that, whereas Hooker advanced upon Lee across the river, he is now, after the battle, back again, where he started from. But he says not more than a third of the army was engaged; and as 30,000 reinforcements have been sent from Washington, and as many from Suffolk, the army will soon be as strong as ever, and in condition for another advance—and defeat.

But what credit can we attach to such statements, since McClellan, under oath, said that he had ninety odd thousand men at the battle of Sharpsburg, 75,000 of whom only were actually engaged, while Lee had 100,000? We *know* that he did not have 40,000 engaged!

Gen. Van Dorn is dead—being killed by a man whose peace he had ruined.

More applications for passports to leave the country are coming in—and they are "allowed" by the Assistant Secretary of War. How could he refuse, since his own family (at least a portion of it) have enjoyed the benefits of sojourning in the North since the war began?

A letter was received to-day from Mr. Ranney, president of the N. C., Jackson, and Great Northern Railroad Co., asking the protection of government from harm for violations of the Act of Congress of April 19th, 1862, prohibiting the transportation of cotton within the enemy's lines. He incloses a number of peremptory orders from Lieut.-Gen. Pemberton, dated January 19th, February 16th and 19th, to take large amounts of cotton into the enemy's lines for S. J. Josephs (Jew?), and for Messrs. Clarke, Ford, and Hust, etc. etc. He says Gen. P. threatened to seize the road if he did not comply, and asserted that he had authority from the Secretary of War to issue the orders. One of these orders was from Gov. Pettus, for a small lot not more than fifty bales, to be exchanged for salt. This was authorized by the President, who most positively forbid the others. The letter from Gen. Johnston the other day said this traffic was subjugating the people. Was that "allowed" to reach the Secretary and the President? I know not; it has not yet passed through my hands from the President back to the department.

May 12th.—The departments and all places of business are still closed in honor of Gen. Jackson, whose funeral will take place to-day. The remains will be placed in state at the Capitol, where the people will be permitted to see him. The grief is universal, and the victory involving such a loss is regarded as a calamity.

The day is bright and excessively hot; and so was yesterday.

Many letters are coming in from the counties in which the enemy's cavalry replenished their horses. It appears that the government has sent out agents to collect the worn-down horses left by the enemy; and this is bitterly objected to by the farmers. It is the corn-planting season, and without horses, they say, they can raise no crops. Some of these writers are almost menacing in their remarks, and intimate that they are about as harshly used, in this war, by one side as the other.

To-day I observed the clerks coming out of the departments with chagrin and mortification. Seventy-five per cent. of them ought to be in the army, for they are young able-bodied men. This applies also to the chiefs of bureaus.

The funeral was very solemn and imposing, because the mourning was sincere and heartfelt. There was no vain ostentation. The pall bearers were generals. The President followed near the hearse in a carriage, looking thin and frail in health. The heads of departments, two and two, followed on foot—Benjamin and Seddon first—at the head of the column of young clerks (who ought to be in the field), the State authorities, municipal authorities, and thousands of soldiers and citizens. The war-horse was led by the general's servant, and flags and black feathers abounded.

Arrived at the Capitol, the whole multitude passed the bier, and gazed upon the hero's face, seen through a glass in the coffin.

Just previous to the melancholy ceremony, a very large body of prisoners (I think 3500) arrived, and were marched through Main Street, to the grated buildings allotted them. But these attracted slight attention,—Jackson, the great hero, was the absorbing thought. Yet there are other Jacksons in the army, who will win victories,—no one doubts it.

The following is Gen. Lee's order to the army after the intelligence of Gen. Jackson's death:

"HEADQUARTERS ARMY NORTHERN VA.,
"May 11th, 1863.

"GENERAL ORDERS NO. 61.

"With deep grief the Commanding General announces to the army the death of Lieut.-Gen. T. J. Jackson, who expired on the 10th inst., at 3½ P.M. The daring, skill, and energy of this great and good soldier, by the decree of an all-wise Providence, are now lost to us. But while we mourn his death, we feel that his spirit still lives, and will inspire the whole army with his indomitable courage and unshaken confidence in God as our hope and our strength. Let his name be a watchword to his corps, who have followed him to victory on so many fields. Let officers and soldiers emulate his invincible determination to do everything in the defense of our beloved country.

"R. E. LEE, *General.*"

The Letter of Gen. Lee to Gen. Jackson.

The letter written by Gen. Lee to Gen. Jackson before the death of the latter is as follows:

"CHANCELLORVILLE, May 4th.

"GENERAL:—

"I have just received your note informing me that you were wounded. I cannot express my regret at the occurrence. Could I have dictated events, I should have chosen for the good of the country to have been disabled in your stead.

"I congratulate you upon the victory which is due to your skill and energy.

"Most truly yours,
"R. E. LEE.

"*To Gen. T. J. Jackson.*"

"The nation's agony," as it is termed in a Washington paper, in an appeal for 500,000 more men, now demands a prompt response from the people. And yet that paper, under the eye and in the interest of the Federal Government, would make it appear that "the Army of the Potomac" has sustained no considerable disaster. What, then, constitutes the "nation's agony"? Is it the imminency of war with England? It may be, judging from the debates in Parliament, relating to the liberties the United States have been taking with British commerce. But what do they mean by the "*nation?*" They have nothing resembling a homogeneous race in the North, and nearly a moiety of the people are Germans and Irish. How ridiculous it would have been even for a Galba to call his people the Roman *nation!* An idiot may produce a conflagration, but he can never rise to the dignity of a high-minded man. Yet that word "Nation" may raise a million Yankee troops. It is a "new thing."

The Northern papers say Charleston is to be assailed again immediately; that large reinforcements are going to Hooker, and that they captured *six or eight thousand prisoners* in their flight on the Rappahannock. All these fictions are understood and appreciated here; but they may answer a purpose in the North, by deceiving the people again into the belief that Richmond will certainly fall the next time an advance is made. And really, where we see such extravagant statements in the Federal journals, after a great battle, we are much rejoiced, because we know them to be unfounded, and we are led to believe our victory was even greater than we supposed it to be.

MAY 13TH.—Col. Gorgas, Chief of the Bureau of Ordnance, sent in to-day a report of the arms captured in the recent battle. It appears from his statement that, so far, only eight guns have been found, taken from the enemy, while we lost ten. Thus, it would appear, our papers have been "lying," in regard to that item, as well as the Northern papers about the number of prisoners lost and taken. But, so far, we have collected 12,000 of the enemy's small arms left upon the field, and 8000 of our own, indicating the number of our killed and wounded. But the New York journals say we captured only 1700 prisoners; whereas, up to this time, more than 6000 have arrived in Richmond; 5000 of whom leave to-day, paroled until exchanged. I doubt whether we lost 2000 prisoners in the battle.

The Philadelphia *Press*, just received, charges the government at Washington with circulating false reports, and is now convinced Hooker met with a most crushing defeat.

It is rumored the enemy are disembarking troops at the White House, York River. If this be so, it is to prevent reinforcements being sent to Lee.

The Governor of Alabama declares that Mobile is neglected, and says he will continue to protest against the failure of the government to make adequate preparations for the defense of the city.

I saw Gen. Wise to-day. He seems weather-beaten, but hardy.

MAY 14TH.—We have been beaten in an engagement near Jackson, Miss., 4000 retiring before 10,000. This is a dark cloud over the hopes of patriots, for Vicksburg is seriously endangered. Its fall would be the worst blow we have yet received.

Papers from New York and Philadelphia assert most positively, and with circumstantiality, that Hooker recrossed the Rappahannock since the battle, and is driving Lee toward Richmond, with which his communications have been interrupted. But this is not all: they say Gen. Keyes marched a column up the Peninsula, and took Richmond itself, over the Capitol of which the Union flag "is now flying." These groundless statements will go out to Europe, and may possibly delay our recognition. If so, what may be the consequences when the falsehood is exposed? I doubt the policy of any species of dishonesty.

Gov. Shorter, of Alabama, demands the officers of Forrest's captives for State trial, as they incited the slaves to insurrection.

Mr. S. D. Allen writes from Alexandria, La., that the people despair of defending the Mississippi Valley with such men as Pemberton and other hybrid Yankees in command. He denounces the action also of quartermasters and commissaries in the Southwest.

A letter from Hon. W. Porcher Miles to the Secretary of War gives an extract from a communication written him by Gen. Beauregard, to the effect that Charleston must at last fall into the hands of the enemy, if an order which has been sent there, for nearly all his troops to proceed to Vicksburg, be not revoked. There are to be left for the defense of Charleston only 1500 exclusive of the garrisons!

MAY 15TH.—The Tredegar Iron Works and Crenshou's woolen factory were mostly destroyed by fire last night! This is a calamity.

We have also intelligence of the occupation of Jackson, Miss., by the enemy. Thus they cut off communication with Vicksburg, and that city may be doomed to fall at last. The President is at work again at the Executive Office, but is not fully himself yet.

The Secretary of War dispatched Gen. Lee a day or two ago, desiring that a portion of his army, Pickett's division, might be sent to Mississippi. Gen. Lee responds that it is a dangerous and doubtful expedient; *it is a question between Virginia and Mississippi; he will send the division off without delay, if still deemed necessary.* The President, in sending this response to the Secretary, says it is just such an answer as he expected from Lee, and he approves it. Virginia will not be abandoned.

Gens. Lee, Stuart, and French were all at the War Department to-day. Lee looked thinner, and a little pale. Subsequently he and the Secretary of War were long closeted with the President.

Gen. Schenck (Federal) has notified Gen. W. E. Jones, that our men taken dressed in Federal uniform will not be treated as prisoners of war, but will be tried and punished as spies, etc. The President directed the Secretary of War to-day to require Gen. Lee to send an order to the commander of the Federal army, that accouterments and clothing will be deemed subjects of capture, and if our men are treated differently than prisoners of war, when taken, we will retaliate on the prisoners in our possession.

Gen. Longstreet censured Gen. French for his conduct before Suffolk, and the Secretary of War proposed that French be relieved, and sent before a court of inquiry. The President vetoed this, saying such courts were nuisances, and would not have him molested at this critical moment.

Gen. D. H. Hill writes that desertions in North Carolina are alarmingly frequent; that deserters will soon be in arms; that papers and factions exist there in favor of reconstruction, laboring to convince the people that the State has been neglected by the Confederate States Government, and he suggests summary punishments. The President directs the Secretary to correspond with Gov. Vance on the subject.

Mr. Benjamin has had some pretty passports printed. He sends one to Assistant Secretary Campbell for a Mr. Bloodgood and son to leave the Confederate States. I hope there is no *bad* blood in this incessant intercourse with persons in the enemy's country. Just at this crisis, if so disposed, any one going thither might inflict incalculable injury on the cause of Southern independence.

May 16th.—It appears, after the consultation of the generals and the President yesterday, it was resolved not to send Pickett's division to Mississippi, and this morning early the long column march through the city northward. Gen. Lee is now stronger than he was before the battle. Gen. Pickett himself, with his long, black ringlets, accompanied his division, his troops looking like fighting veterans, as they are. And two fine regiments of cavalry, the 2d and 59th North Carolina Regiments, passed through the city this morning likewise.

A letter was received from Gen. Beauregard to-day, again protesting against the movement of so many of his troops to Mississippi; 5000 on the 5th, and more than 5000 on the 10th instant. He makes an exhibit of the forces remaining in South Carolina and Georgia—about 4000 infantry, 5000 cavalry, and 6000 artillery, some 15,000 in all. He says the enemy is still on the coast, in the rivers, and on the islands, and may easily cut his communications with Savannah; and they have sufficient numbers to take Charleston, in all probability, without passing the forts. He says information of his weakness is sure to be communicated to the enemy—and I think so too, judging from the number of passports "allowed" by Judge Campbell and Mr. Benjamin!

There is some purpose on the part of Gen. Lee to have a raid in the enemy's country, surpassing all other raids. If he can organize two columns of cavalry, 5000 each, to move in parallel lines, they may penetrate to the Hudson River; and then the North will discover that it has more to lose by such expeditions than the South. Philadelphia, even, may be taken.

To-day, the regular train on the Fredericksburg road came back to the city, the conductor being in a terrible fright, and reporting that the enemy were again at Ashland. But it turned out that the troops there were our men! It is not probable the enemy's cavalry will soon approach Richmond again.

MAY 17TH.—The last few days have been cool and dry; fine weather for campaigning. And yet we hear of no demonstrations apparently, though I believe Lee's army is moving.

Mr. Lamar, of Savannah (formerly president of the Bank of the Republic, New York), writes that he and others are organizing an Exporting and Importing Company, and desires the government to take an interest in it. So far the heads of bureaus decline, and of course the Secretary will do nothing. But the

Secretary has already engaged with Mr. Crenshaw in a similar enterprise, and so informed Mr. Mason, at London.

About 10 A.M., some 2500 men of all arms arrived at "double quick," having left Ashland, eighteen miles distant, at 5 o'clock this morning. That was brisk marching. The guns were sent down on the railroad. The government has information that Gen. Keyes, with a full division of infantry and a brigade of cavalry, had marched up to West Point, to threaten Richmond. The troops, however, which arrived from Ashland, had been taken from the batteries here, and did not belong to Gen. Lee's army.

Messrs. Davenport & Co., Mobile, charge Gen. Buckner with permitting 1000 bales of cotton to be shipped to New Orleans.

The president of the Fredericksburg Road states, in a letter to the Secretary, that, after the battle, by military authority, the cars were appropriated by the Federal officers (prisoners), while our wounded soldiers had to remain and await the return of the trains.

Hon. Mr. Dargin, of Alabama, writes to the Secretary, to procure from the President a disavowal of the "organship" of the *Enquirer*, as that paper, under the belief that it speaks for the government, is likely to inflict much mischief on the country. He alluded to the bitter articles against the Democrats and peace men of the North, who would soon have been able to embarrass, if not to check the operations of the Republican war party. He says now, that they will write against us, and deal destruction wherever they penetrate the land.

MAY 19TH.—A dispatch from Gen. Johnston says a battle has been fought between Pemberton and Grant, between Jackson and Vicksburg, Mississippi, which lasted nine hours. Pemberton was *forced back*. This is all we know yet.

Another letter, from Hon. W. Porcher Miles, remonstrating against the withdrawal of Beauregard's troops, was received today. He apprehends the worst consequences.

The government is buying 5000 bales of cotton for the Crenshaw scheme. Jas. R. Crenshaw, of this city, is at Charleston on this business. Why not arrange with Lamar?

Gov. Shorter forwards another strongly written memorial from Mobile, against the traffic of cotton with the enemy, and, indeed, against all blockade-running.

Gov. Jno. Milton, of Florida, also writes a powerful denunciation of the illicit traffic, which it seems the policy of the government has been to encourage. They all say this traffic is doing the work of subjugation more effectually than the arms of the enemy.

The President is too ill again to come to the Executive Office. His messenger, who brought me some papers this morning, says he is in a "decline." I think he has been ill every day for several years, but this has been his most serious attack. No doubt he is also worried at the dark aspects in his own State—Mississippi.

If Vicksburg falls, and the Valley be held by the enemy, then the Confederacy will be curtailed of half its dimensions. Texas, Louisiana, Mississippi, Arkansas, Missouri, Arizona, New Mexico, all the Indian country, Kentucky, half of Tennessee, one-third of Virginia, Eastern North Carolina, and sundry islands, etc. of South Carolina, Georgia, and Florida, will be wrested from us. What will remain of the Confederacy? Two-thirds of Virginia, half of Tennessee, the greater part of North Carolina, South Carolina, Georgia, and the whole of Alabama,—less than six States! But still the war will go on, as long as we have brave armies and great generals, whether the President lives or dies.

MAY 20th.—Reports from the West say we lost 3000 and the enemy 6000 men in the battle of the 15th inst., when Pemberton fell back over the Black River. Our forces numbered only 12,000, Grant's three times that number. Something decisive must occur before Vicksburg in a few days.

Mr. J. W. Henry writes from New's Ferry, that parties of cavalry, going about the country, professing to belong to our Gen. Stuart's corps, are probably Yankee spies making observations preparatory for another raid. The city councils are organizing the citizens for local defense, thinking it probable another dash may be made.

Gen. Dix threatens to hang the citizens of Williamsburg if they co-operate with Gen. Wise in his frequent attacks on the Federals. Gen. Wise replies, threatening to hang Gen. Dix if he carries his threat into execution, and should fall into his hands, in a more summary manner than John Brown was hung for making his raid in Virginia.

Butter is worth $4 per pound. A sheep is worth $50. A cow $500.

MAY 21ST.—There was a rumor on the street last night that Gen. Johnston had telegraphed the President that it would be necessary to evacuate Vicksburg. This has not been confirmed to-day, and I do not believe it. It would be irremediably disastrous.

Mr. N. S. Walker writes from Bermuda, May 11th, 1863, that seventeen additional British regiments have been ordered to Canada. A large amount of ordnance and ordnance stores, as well as several war steamers, have likewise been sent thither. He states, moreover, that United States vessels are having their registers changed. Does this really mean war?

Strawberries were selling in market this morning at $4 for less than a pint. Coal $25 per load, and wood $30 per cord.

MAY 22D.—A letter from Gen. Howell Cobb, declining the offer of the Secretary of War, of the position of Quartermaster-General, was received to-day. His wife is ill, and he prefers to remain with her; besides, he doubts his qualifications—he, who was Secretary of the Treasury of the United States! He says, moreover, referring to the imperfect ordnance stores of his brigade, that there can be no remedy for this so long as Col. G. is the Chief of the Bureau of Ordnance. So Col. Myers is to be disposed of at last, and Col. G. has but an uncertain tenure.

We have sad rumors from Vicksburg. Pemberton, it is said, was flanked by Grant, and lost 30 guns, which he abandoned in his retreat. Where Johnston is, is not stated. But, it is said, Vicksburg is closely invested, and that the invaders are closing in on all sides. There is much gloom and despondency in the city among those who credit these unofficial reports. It would be a terrible blow, but not necessarily a fatal one, for the war could be prolonged indefinitely.

I met with Robt. Tyler to-day, who offers to wager something that Gen. Stuart will be in Philadelphia in a fortnight, and he said there was a proposition to stop the publication of newspapers, if the President would agree to it, as they gave information to the enemy, and at such a time as this did no good whatever. He thinks they are on the eve of revolution in the North, and referred to Gov. Seymour's letter, read at a public meeting in New York.

MAY 23D.—The reports from Mississippi have not been confirmed by official dispatches, and it is understood that the President remarked yesterday, at dinner, that he was satisfied with the condition of affairs in that State. If this be so, Vicksburg must not only be still in our possession, but likely to be held by us at the end of this campaign. The President, I know, feels a peculiar interest in that State, and I learn by a letter from Tennessee, that on the 9th inst. troops left McMinnville for the rescue of Vicksburg—a Texas brigade.

Cavalry continue to pass through this city from the south, while infantry are passing to the south. These movements will puzzle the spies, who are daily, and without difficulty, obtaining passports to leave the Confederate States.

We have Northern papers to-day, containing Gen. Hooker's grandiloquent address to his army, a few days after his flight. I preserve it here for the inspection of the future generation, and to deter other generals from the bad policy of publishing false statements.

"[Copy.]

"HEADQUARTERS ARMY OF THE POTOMAC,
"May 6th, 1863.

"GENERAL ORDERS NO 49.

"The Major-General commanding tenders to this army his congratulations on its achievements of the last seven days. If it has not accomplished all that was expected, the reasons are well known to the army. It is sufficient to say they were of a character not to be foreseen or prevented by human sagacity or resources. In withdrawing from the south bank of the Rappahannock, before delivering a general battle to our adversaries, the army has given renewed evidence of its confidence in itself, and its fidelity to the principles it represents.

"In fighting at a disadvantage we would have been recreant to our trust, to ourselves, our cause, and our country. Profoundly loyal and conscious of its strength, the Army of the Potomac will give or decline battle whenever its interest or honor may demand. It will also be the guardian of its own history and its own honor. By our celerity and secrecy of movement our advance and passage of the rivers were undisputed, and on our withdrawal not a rebel returned to follow. The events of the last week may swell with pride the hearts of every officer and soldier of this army. We have added new laurels to its former renown. We have made long marches, crossed rivers, surprised the enemy in his intrenchments, and whenever we have fought we have inflicted heavier blows than we have received.

"We have taken from the enemy five thousand prisoners and fifteen colors, captured and brought off seven pieces of artillery, and placed *hors du combat* eighteen thousand of his chosen troops. We have destroyed his depots filled with vast amounts of stores, damaged his communications, captured prisoners within the fortifications of his capital, and filled his country with fear and consternation. We have no other regret than that caused by the death of our brave companions; and in this we are consoled by the conviction that they have fallen in the holiest cause ever submitted to the arbitrament of battle.

"By command of

"(Signed) MAJOR-GENERAL HOOKER.

"S. WILLIAMS, A.A.G."

To-day we have another official report from the Chief of Ordnance of the fruits of our victory, as far as they have been gathered, though the whole field has not been carefully gleaned, which I append as a commentary on the statements of Hooker.

Five twelve-pounder Napoleons; 7 three-inch rifled guns; 1 Parrott gun, ten-pounder; 9 caissons; 4 rear parts of caissons; 3 battery wagons; 2 forges; 1500 rounds artillery ammunition; large lot of artillery harness; large lot of wheels, axles, ammunition chests, etc.; 16,500 muskets and rifles; 4000 cap pouches; 11,500 haversacks, and 300,000 rounds infantry ammunition. The report says thousand of our soldiers helped themselves on the field to better arms, etc., which cannot be computed.

Now for the prisoners. To-day the last lot taken by Hooker arrived by flag of truce boat, making in all just 2700. We have already sent off 7000 prisoners taken from him, and 1000 are yet to go. Our killed, wounded, and missing amount to but little over 8000. Hooker's killed and wounded are admitted by the Northern papers to be 20,000, and some say his entire loss was fully 40,000. So much for his march over the Rappahannock and his flight back again. If he is not satisfied, Lee will try him again.

MAY 24TH, SUNDAY.—We have had a fortnight of calm, dry, and warm weather. There is a hazy atmosphere, and the sun rises and sets wearing a blood-red aspect. At night the moon, dimly and indistinctly seen (now a crescent), has a somber and baleful appearance. This is strange at this season of the year; it is like Indian summer in May. The ground is dry and crusted, and apprehensions are felt for the crops, unless we have rain in a few days. My poor little garden has suffered for moisture, but the area is so small I am enabled to throw water over it in the evening. My beets, tomatoes, early potatoes, and lettuce look pretty well, though not so far advanced, in consequence of the late spring, as I have seen them in Burlington. But they are a great comfort to me. I work them, water them, and look at them, and this is what the French would call a *distraction*. I have abundance of roses,—this is the city of roses. And my cherries are coming on finely,—I know not yet what kind they are; but it relieves the eye to gaze on them. And then my neighbor has a pigeon-house, and the birds come into my yard and are fed by my daughters, being pretty and tame. I sit for hours watching them.

Alas! this cruel war! But independence will be ample compensation. Our posterity will thank us for our sacrifices and sufferings. Yet all do not suffer. The Gil Blases, by their servility and cringing to their patrons, the *great* men in power, and only great because they have patronage to bestow, which is power, are getting rich. Even adroit clerks are becoming wealthy. They procure exemptions, discharges, and contracts for the speculators for heavy bribes, and invest the money immediately in real estate, having some doubts as to its ultimate redemption, and possibly indifferent as to the fate of the country, so that their own prosperity be secure. After the war the rascals and traitors will be rich, and ought to be marked and exposed.

MAY 25TH.—Dispatches from the West inform us that three attempts to carry the city of Vicksburg by assault have been repulsed with heavy loss. Johnston is on the enemy's flank and rear, engendering a new army with rapidity, and if the garrison can hold out a little while, the city may be safe.

Gens. Ewell and A. P. Hill have been made lieutenant-generals, and will command Jackson's corps. It appears that the Senate has not yet confirmed Hardee, Holmes, and Pemberton.

The Washington correspondent of the New York *Commercial Advertiser* says Hooker's loss in killed and wounded amounted to "over 23,000 men, and he left 24 guns on the other side of the Rappahannock." We got 8000 prisoners, which will make the loss 31,000 men, and it is said the stragglers, not yet collected, amount to 10,000 men! Only 13 guns fell into our hands, the rest fell—into the river!

MAY 26TH.—Reliable information of hard fighting at Vicksburg; but still, so far as we know, the garrison of the invested city has repulsed every assault made upon it. The enemy's losses are said to be very heavy. Something decisive must occur there soon, and I hope something calamitous to the enemy.

The President and the cabinet have been in council nearly all day. Can they have intelligence from the West, not yet communicated to the public?

We learn from Newbern, N. C., that gray-haired old men, women, and children, who refused to take the oath of allegiance, have been driven from their homes, on foot, despoiled of their property. Among these I see the names of the Misses Custis, cousins of my wife. Gen. Daniels, commanding our forces at Kinston, sent out wagons and ambulances to convey them within our lines. They were on foot.

MAY 27TH.—Gen. Beauregard's statement of the number of his troops, after 10,000 had been ordered to Mississippi, with urgent appeals for the order to be countermanded, came back from the President to-day, to whom it had been referred by Mr. Secretary Seddon. The President indorsed, characteristically, that the statement did not agree in numbers with a previous one, and asked the Secretary to note the discrepancy! This was all.

The president of the Seaboard Railroad requests the Secretary to forbid the common use of the bridge over the Roanoke at Weldon, the tracks being planked, to be used in case of a hasty retreat; the loss might be great, if it were rendered useless. It is 1760 feet long, and 60 feet high.

Mr. John Minor Botts is here in difficulty, a negro being detected bearing a letter from him to the enemy's camp. The letter asked if no order had come from Washington, concerning the restoration of his slaves taken away (he lives on the Rappahannock) by Hooker's men; and stating that it was hard for him to be insulted and imprisoned by the Confederate States—and deprived of his property by the United States—he a *neutral.* Gen. F. Lee thought he ought not to be permitted to remain in proximity to the enemy, and so sent him on to Richmond. He was to see the Secretary to-day.

Hon. D. M. Lewis, Sparta, Ga., writes that he will cut his wheat on the 28th (to-morrow), and both for quality and quantity he never saw it equaled. They have new flour in Alabama; and everywhere South the crops are unprecedented in amount.

To-morrow is election day. For Congress, Col. Wickham, who voted against secession, opposes Mr. Lyons. But he has *fought* since!

We have a letter from Gen. Jos. E. Johnston, dated at Calhoun, Miss., 16th inst. He says the enemy on the railroad at Clinton numbered 25,000. We got our baggage out of Jackson before it was abandoned. Pemberton marched to Edward's Station with 17,000 men. Gen. Johnston himself had 7500, and some 15,000 more were on the way to him. We had 3000 at Port Hudson—being over 40,000 which he meant to concentrate immediately. I think Vicksburg ought to be safe.

Our government has been notified that, if we execute the two officers (selected by lot) in retaliation for the execution of two of our officers in Kentucky, two men will be shot or hung by the enemy. Thus the war will be still more terrible!

Vallandigham has been sent to Shellbyville, within our lines. I think our people ought to give him a friendly greeting.

MAY 28TH.—There is some animation at the polls, this being election day. It is said Mr. Wickham, who for a long time, in the Convention, voted against the secession of Virginia, is leading Mr. Lyons, an original secessionist, and will probably beat him. And Flournoy, an old Whig politician, will probably be elected governor.

A dispatch from Gen. Johnston, dated yesterday, says in every fight, so far, around Vicksburg, our forces have been successful, and that our soldiers are in fine spirits.

Papers from the North have, in great headings, the word VICTORY, and announce that the Stars and Stripes are floating over the City of Vicksburg! They likewise said their flag was floating over the Capitol in this city. If Vicksburg falls, it will be a sad day for us; if it does not fall, it will be a sad day for the war party of the United States. It may be decisive, one way or the other. If we beat them, we may have peace. If they beat us—

although the war will not and cannot terminate—it may degenerate into a guerrilla warfare, relentless and terrible!

MAY 29TH.—A dispatch from Gen. Johnston, dated 27th inst., says fighting at Vicksburg had been in progress ever since the 19th instant, and that our troops have been invariably successful in repulsing the assults. Other dispatches say the unburied dead of the enemy, lying in heaps near our fortifications, have produced such an intolerable stench that our men are burning barrels of tar without their works.

But still all is indefinite. Yet, from the persistent assaults of the enemy it may be inferred that Grant is inspired with the conviction that it is necessary for him to capture Vicksburg immediately, and before Johnston collects an army in his rear. A few days may produce a decisive result.

Hon. E. S. Dargan, Mobile, Ala., writes that it is indispensable for our government to stipulate for aid from Europe at the earliest moment practicable, even if we must agree to the gradual emancipation of the slaves. He says the enemy will soon overrun the Southwestern States and prevent communication with the East, and then these States (Eastern) cannot long resist the superior numbers of the invaders. Better (he thinks, I suppose) yield slavery, and even be under the protection of a foreign government, than succumb to the United States.

The enemy, wherever they have possession in the South, have adopted the policy of sending away (into the Confederate States) all the inhabitants who refuse to take the oath of allegiance. This enables them to appropriate their property, and, being destitute, the wanderers will aid in the consumption of the stores of the Confederates. A Mr. W. E. Benthuisen, merchant, sent from New Orleans, telegraphs the President for passports for himself and family to proceed to Richmond. The President intimates to the Secretary of War that many similar cases may be looked for, and he thinks it would be better for the families to be dispersed in the country than congregated in the city.

The following are the *wholesale* prices to-day:

"PRODUCE, PROVISIONS, ETC.—The quotations given are wholesale. Wheat—nothing doing—we quote it nominal at \$6.50 to \$7; corn, very scarce, may be quoted at \$9 to \$10; oats, \$6 to \$6.50 per bushel; flour—superfine, \$32, extra, \$34, family, \$37 per barrel;

corn-meal, $11 per bushel; bacon, hoground, $1.45 to $1.50—a strictly prime article a shade higher; butter, $2.50 to $3 per pound; lard, $1.50 to $1.60; candles, $2.75 to $3 for tallow, $5 for adamantine; dried fruit—apples, $10 to $12, peaches, $15 to $18 per bushel; eggs, $1.40 to $1.50 per dozen; beans, $18 to $20; peas, $15 to $18 per bushel; potatoes, $8 to $10 per bushel; hay and sheaf-oats, $10 to $12 per cwt.; rice, 18 to 20 cents per pound; salt, 45 to 50 cents per pound; soap, 50 to 60 cents per pound for hard country.

"LEATHER.—Market unsettled. We quote as follows: Sole, $3.50 to $4 per pound; harness, $4 to $4.25; russett and wax upper, $5 to $5.50; wax kip skins, $6 per pound; calf skins, $300 to $325 per dozen.

"LIQUORS.—We continue to quote apple brandy at $23 to $25; whisky, $28 to $32; French brandy—common, $45, genuine, $80 per gallon.

"GROCERIES.—Brown sugar, $1.40 to $1.55 per pound—no clarified or crushed offering; molasses, $10.50 to $11 per gallon; coffee, $3.75 to $4 per pound; tea, $8.50 to $10 per pound."

MAY 30TH.—The newspapers have a dispatch, to-day, from Jackson, Miss., which says the enemy have fallen back from the position lately occupied by them in front of Vicksburg. It adds, that they will be forced to retire to the Big Black River, for want of water. Gen. G. A. Smith, who is here, and who resigned because he was not made lieutenant-general instead of Pemberton, says he "don't know how to read this dispatch." Nevertheless, it is generally believed, and affords much relief to those who appreciate the importance of Vicksburg.

Mr. Botts was offered $500 in Confederate States notes, the other day, for a horse. He said he would sell him for $250 in gold, but would not receive Confederate notes, as the South would certainly be conquered, and it was merely a question of time. This information was communicated to the Secretary of War to-day, but he will attach no importance to it.

Among the papers sent in by the President, to-day, was a communication from Gov. Vance, of North Carolina, inclosing a letter from Augustus S. Montgomery, of Washington City, to Major-Gen. Foster, Newbern, N. C., found in a steamer, captured the other day by our forces, in Albemarle and Chesapeake Canal. It informed Gen. F. that a plan of servile insurrection had been adopted, and urged his co-operation. All the Yankee generals in the South would co-operate: they were to send smart negroes from the camps among the slaves, with instructions to rise simultaneously at night on the 1st August. They were to seize and destroy all railroad bridges, cut the telegraph wires, etc., and then retire into the swamps, concealing themselves until relieved by Federal troops. It is said they were to be ordered to shed no blood, except in self-defense, and they were not to destroy more private property than should be unavoidable. The writer said the corn would be in the roasting-ear, and the hogs would be running at large, so that the slaves could easily find subsistence.

The President thanked Gov. Vance for this information, and said our generals would be made acquainted with this scheme; and he commended the matter to the special attention of the Secretary of War, who sent it to Gen. Lee.

MAY 31ST.—The commissioners, appointed for the purpose, have agreed upon the following schedule of prices for the State of Virginia, under the recent impressment act of Congress; and if a large amount of supplies be furnished at these prices—which are fifty, sometimes one hundred per cent. lower than the rates private individuals are paying—it will be good proof that all patriotism is not yet extinct:

"Wheat, white, per bushel of 60 pounds, $4.50; flour, superfine, per barrel of 196 pounds, $22.50; corn, white, per bushel of 56 pounds, $4; unshelled corn, white, per bushel of 56 pounds, $3.95; corn-meal, per bushel of 50 pounds, $4.20; rye, per bushel of 56 pounds, $3.20; cleaned oats, per bushel of 32 pounds, $2; wheat-bran, per bushel of 17 pounds, 50 cents; shorts, per bushel of 22 pounds, 70 cents; brown stuff, per bushel of 28 pounds, 90 cents; ship stuff, per bushel of 37 pounds, $1.40; bacon, hoground, per pound, $1; salt pork, per pound, $1; lard, per pound, $1; horses, first class, artillery, etc., average price per head, $350; wool, per pound, $3; peas, per bushel of 60 pounds, $4; beans, per bushel of 69 pounds, $4; potatoes, Irish, per bushel of 69 pounds, $4; potatoes, sweet, per bushel of 69 pounds, $5; onions, per bushel of 60 pounds, $5; dried peaches, peeled, per bushel of 38 pounds, $8; dried peaches, unpeeled, per bushel of 38 pounds, $4.50; dried apples, peeled, per bushel of 28 pounds, $3."

CHAPTER XXVII.

Vicksburg refuses to surrender to Grant.—Spiritualism at the White House.—Lee is pushing a little northward.—It is said Grant has lost 40,000 men.—He is still pounding Vicksburg.—Petty military organizations.—Mr. Randolph busy.—Foolish passport rules.—Great battle imminent, but speculation may defeat both sides.—Early's victory.—We have only supplies of corn from day to day.—Chambersburg struck.—Col. Whiting complains of blockade running at Wilmington.—False alarm.—Grant still before Vicksburg.

JUNE 1ST.—Nothing decisive from Vicksburg. It is said Northern papers have been received, of the 29th May, stating that their Gen. Grant had been killed, and Vicksburg (though at first prematurely announced) captured. We are not ready to believe the latter announcement.

Mr. Lyons has been beaten for Congress by Mr. Wickham.

It is said the brigade commanded by Gen. Barton, in the battle near Vicksburg, broke and ran twice. If that be so, and their conduct be imitated by other brigades, good-by to the Mississippi Valley!

Our people everywhere are alive to the expected raid of the enemy's cavalry, and are organizing the men of non-conscript age for defense.

One of our pickets whistled a horse, drinking in the Rappahannock, and belonging to Hooker's army, over to our side of the river. It was a very fine horse, and the Federal Gen. Patrick sent a flag demanding him, as he was not captured in battle. Our officer sent back word he would do so with pleasure, if the Yankees would send back the slaves and other property of the South not taken in battle. There it ended—but we shall probably soon have stirring news from that quarter.

The Baltimore *American* contains the proceedings of the City Council, justifying the arrest of Vallandigham.

JUNE 2D.—We have a dispatch from Mississippi, stating that on Thursday last Grant demanded the surrender of Vicksburg in three days. He was answered that fifteen minutes were not asked; that the men were ready to die—but would never surrender. This was followed by another assault, in which the enemy lost great numbers, and were repulsed—as they have been in every subsequent attempt to take the town.

A letter from our agent in London says H. O. Brewer, of Mobile, advanced £10,000 in March last, to buy a steamer for the use of the Confederate States.

Gen. Whiting writes from Wilmington, that a captured mail furnishes the intelligence that the enemy have thirty-one regiments at Newbern, and he apprehends they will cut the railroad at Goldsborough, as we have but two small brigades to resist them. Then they may march against Wilmington, where he has not now sufficient forces to man his batteries. The general says he is quite sure that individual blockade-runners inform the enemy of our defenseless points, and inflict incalculable injury. He desires the Secretary to lay his letter before the President.

A circular from the Bureau of Conscription to the commandants of conscripts says, the Assistant Secretary of War (Judge Campbell) suggests that overseers and managers on farms be disturbed as little as possible just at this time, for the benefit of the crops. But what good will the crops do, if we be subjugated in the mean time? I thought every man was needed, *just at this time*, on the field of battle.

The President rides out (on horse) every afternoon, and sits as straight as an English king could do four centuries ago.

June 3d.—Gen. Lee communicates to the department to-day his views of the Montgomery letter to Gen. Forrest, a copy of which was sent him by Governor Vance. He terms it "diabolical." It seems to have been an official letter, superscribed by "C. Marshall, Major and A. A. G." Gen. Lee suggests that it be not published, but that copies be sent to all our generals.

Hon. R. M. T. Hunter urges the Secretary, in a lengthy letter, to send a cavalry brigade into Essex and the adjacent counties, to protect the inhabitants from the incursions of the "Yankees." He says a government agent has established a commissary department within six miles of his house, and it will be sure to be destroyed if no force be sent there adequate to its defense. He says, moreover, if our troops are to operate only in the great armies facing the enemy, a few hostile regiments of horse may easily devastate the country without molestation.

Gov. Vance writes a most indignant reply to a letter which, it seems, had been addressed to him by the Assistant Secretary of War, Judge Campbell, in which there was an intimation that the judicial department of the State government "lent itself" to the work of protecting deserters, etc. This the Governor repels as untrue, and says the judges shall have his protection. That North Carolina has been wronged by calumnious imputations, and many in the army and elsewhere made to believe she was not putting forth all her energies in the work of independence. He declares that North Carolina furnished more than half the killed and wounded in the two great battles on the Rappahannock, in December and May last.

By the Northern papers we see the President of the United States, his wife, and his cabinet are amusing themselves at the White House with Spiritualism.

June 4th.—To-day we have characteristic unintelligible dispatches from Mississippi. They say, up to third instant, yesterday, everything is encouraging; but the Memphis papers say Grant's losses have not been so large as was supposed. Then it is reported that Grant has retired to Grand Gulf. Yet it is expected the town will be stormed in twenty-four hours!

When Grant leaves Vicksburg, our generals will pursue, and assume the aggressive in more directions than one. Lee has some occult object in view, which must soon be manifest.

Major-Gen. D. H. Hill writes that if the enemy penetrates to the railroad, a great many men in North Carolina will welcome them, and return to their allegiance to the United States. The general wants Ranseur's brigade sent him. He says Mr. Warren, one of the governor's council, in a recent speech remarked, if the enemy got the railroad, it would be a question whether they should adhere to the Confederate States or to the United States. Does the general mean to alarm the authorities here?

After a month of dry weather, we have just had a fine rain, most refreshing to the poor kitchen vegetables in my little garden, which I am cultivating with careful assiduity in hopes of saving some dollars in the items of potatoes, tomatoes, beets, etc.

The crops of wheat, etc. south of Virginia, mature and maturing, are *perfect* in quality and unprecedented in quantity.

JUNE 5TH.—More unofficial dispatches from the Mississippi. It is said Kirby Smith has defeated the enemy at Port Hudson; but how could his army get over the river? It is also stated that Grant's losses have been 40,000, and ours 5000. Who could have computed them? But they go on to say nothing has been heard from Vicksburg since Sunday, four days previously; and that heavy firing was heard still on Thursday.

Lee's army is in motion—that means something; and it is generally believed that Stuart is out on a raid into the enemy's country.

Mr. M. A. Malsby, a Georgian, disabled by a wound in the first battle of Manassas, has published *one-half* of my new "Wild Western Scenes;" the balance to appear when he can get paper. He publishes 5000 copies of about 130 pages. The paper costs nearly one dollar per pound, over $40 per ream. The printing costs $2 per 1000 ems. But then he retails the pamphlet at $1.25, and pays me 12½ cents copyright on each number sold.

JUNE 6TH.—We have not even a rumor to-day from Mississippi. The *Examiner* has made a pretty severe attack on Judge Campbell, Assistant Secretary of War, for the great number of persons he has "allowed" to pass into the enemy's country. It does not attribute the best motives to the Judge, who was late coming over to the Confederacy.

The British consul here, it seems, has been meddling with matters in Mississippi, the President states, and has had his exequatur revoked.

Gen. D. H. Hill recommends the abandonment of the line of the Blackwater, for Gen. Martin informs him that the enemy are preparing their expeditions to cut our railroads in North Carolina. Gen. Hill fears if the present line be held we are in danger of a great disaster, from the inability to transport troops from so remote a point, in the event of a sudden emergency. Gen. Lee refuses to let him have Ranseur's brigade.

There are rumors of picket fighting near Fredericksburg, and Davis's (the President's nephew) brigade, just from North Carolina, proceeded through the city to-day in that direction. Shall we have *another* great battle on the Rappahannock? I think it a ruse.

JUNE 7TH.—I saw yesterday a specimen of the President's elaborate attention to the matter of appointments. Lieut.-Gen. A. P. Hill having asked for a military court to his corps, and having recommended the officers, the President, with his own hand, laid down the rule of selection for the guidance of the Secretary, viz.: the State which had the greatest number of regiments would be entitled to the choice of positions, to be taken from the candidates of its citizens according to qualifications, recommendations, etc. It appeared that North Carolina stood first on the list, Virginia next, Georgia next, and so on.

Oh that we could get something decisive from Vicksburg! If Grant's and Banks's armies should be destroyed, I think there would be some prospect of peace at an early day. For, if Lincoln should persist in a prolongation of the war, the probabilities would be the expulsion of the enemy from the Mississippi Valley and the recovery of New Orleans. After the fifteenth of this month, operations must cease on the Carolina and Georgia coasts—Charleston and Wilmington being still in our possession. But we should not be idle. Lee, in disdaining the sheltered army of the invaders, would be likely to invade in turn; and the public demand of retaliation for the cruelties and destruction of private property perpetrated by the enemy could not be resisted. His men would probably apply the torch to the towns and cities of the Yankees, destroying their crops, farming utensils, etc., as the invaders have done in Virginia and elsewhere.

To avoid these calamities, it is possible Lincoln would make peace. Therefore we are so anxious to hear from Vicksburg, the turning-point of the war.

Besides, we shall not please England by our treatment of her consuls; and this may stimulate the United States to concentrate its wrath upon its ancient foe.

JUNE 8TH.—Well, the enemy have thrown another column over the Rappahannock, below Fredericksburg. This is probably a manœuvre to arrest Lee's advance in Culpepper County. But it won't do—Lee's plans cannot be changed—and this demonstration was in his calculations. If they think Richmond can be taken now, without Lee's army to defend it, they may find their mistake.

The clerks and employees in the departments are organizing to man the fortifications, should their aid be needed.

Hon. M. R. H. Garnett writes from Essex County that the enemy have had Lawrence Washington, arrested in Westmoreland County, confined in a prison-ship in the Potomac, until his health gave way. He is now in Washington, on parole not to escape.

About 140,000 bushels of corn have been sent to Lee's army in May, which, allowing ten pounds per day to each horse, shows that there are over 20,000 horses in this army. But the report says not more than 120,000 bushels can be forwarded this month.

The press everywhere is opening its batteries on the blockade-runners, who bring in nothing essential to the people, and nothing necessary for the war.

The arrivals and departures of steamers amount to one per day, and most of the goods imported are of Yankee manufacture. Many cargoes (unsold) are now held in Charleston—and yet the prices do not give way.

JUNE 9TH.—There is rumor that the President has received bad news from the West. This may be without foundation; but it is a little strange that we are not in receipt of authentic accounts of transactions there. Time, however, will reveal all things.

Lee is "marching on," Northward, utterly regardless of the demonstrations of Hooker on the Lower Rappahannock. This is a good omen; for no doubt the demonstrations are designed merely to arrest his advance. Lee has, perhaps, 70,000 fighting men with him—leaving some 15,000 behind to defend Richmond.

The people in the "Northern Neck" have been much harassed by the incursions of the invaders. I clip the following account from the *Whig* of this date:

"Nearly every house was visited, and by deceptive artifices, such as disguising themselves in Confederate gray clothes, stolen, or otherwise surreptitiously obtained, they imposed themselves upon our credulous and unsuspecting people; excited their sympathies by pretending to be wounded Confederate soldiers—won their confidence, and offered to hide their horses and take care of them for them, to prevent the Yankees from taking them, who, they said, were coming on. They thus succeeded in making many of our people an easy prey to their rapacity and cunning. In this foray, they abducted about 1000 negroes, captured from 500 to 700 horses and mules, a large number of oxen, carriages, buggies and wagons—stole meat, destroyed grain, and robbed gentlemen, in the public road, of gold watches and other property. There are some instances related of personal indignity and violence. They returned with their spoils to camp, after a week devoted by them in the Northern Neck, among our unhappy people, to the highly civilized, brave, and chivalrous exploits of theft, robbery, and almost every species of felony committed upon a defenseless, unarmed, and helpless population—chiefly consisting of women and children! It was an easy achievement—a proud conquest—the more glorious to the noble and heroic Yankee, because stained with crime and won without danger to his beastly carcass."

This is but a fair specimen of their conduct whenever they have been permitted to devastate the country with impunity.

A few days ago I addressed a letter to the Secretary of War, suggesting that the department encourage voluntary organizations of non-conscripts for local defense, and that they be armed with every superfluous musket that the government may possess. If this be done, the army will not be so much embarrassed by vehement calls to protect the people from raids everywhere; and in the event of serious disaster, the people would still make resistance. But an unarmed people would have no alternative but submission. This plan would also effectually prevent servile insurrections, etc.

To-day I received the reply, saying it would be done. But will the *arms* be distributed among them?

JUNE 10TH.—We have news of a fight on the Rappahannock yesterday, above Fredericksburg, the enemy having crossed again. They were driven back.

There are also reports from Vicksburg, which still holds out. Accounts say that Grant has lost 40,000 men so far. Where Johnston is, we have no knowledge; but in one of his recent letters he intimated that the fall of Vicksburg was a matter of time.

JUNE 11TH.—It appears that the enemy design to attack us. The following is Lee's dispatch:

"CULPEPPER, June 9th, 1863.

"TO GENERAL S. COOPER.

"The enemy crossed the Rappahannock this morning at five o'clock A.M., at the various fords from Beverly to Kelly's, with a large force of cavalry, accompanied by infantry and artillery. After a severe contest till five P.M., Gen. Stuart drove them across the river. R. E. LEE."

We have not received the details of this combat, further than that it was a surprise, not creditable to our officers in command, by which a portion of ten regiments and 600 horses were taken by the enemy. We lost, killed, also a number of cavalry colonels. We, too, captured several hundred prisoners, which have arrived in the city. Of the killed and wounded, I have yet obtained no information—but it is supposed several hundred fell on both sides.

Still I do not think it probable this affair, coupled with the fact that the enemy have effected a lodgment on this side of the Rappahannock below Fredericksburg, and are still crossing, will frustrate any plan conceived by Lee to invade their country. If, however, Lincoln concentrates all his forces in the East for another attempt to capture Richmond, and should bring 300,000 men against us—we shall have near 200,000 to oppose them.

The Northern Democratic papers are filled with the proceedings of indignation meetings, denouncing the Republican Administration and advocating peace.

JUNE 12TH.—A beautiful, bright warm summer day—and yet a little somber.

The surprise of Stuart, on the Rappahannock, has chilled every heart, notwithstanding it does not appear that we lost more than the enemy in the encounter. The question is on every tongue—have our generals relaxed in vigilance? If so, sad is the prospect!

But Vicksburg is the point of intensest interest and anxieties. Gen. Johnston writes from Canton, Mississippi, on the 5th inst., in reply to the Secretary, that he regrets such confidence is reposed in his ability to save Vicksburg, and fears that such expectations will be disappointed. Grant is receiving reinforcements daily—while he (Johnston) is not to have more troops. He does not state the number he has, but he says it seems to him that the relief of Vicksburg is *impossible.* Pemberton will hold out as long as he can; but if Grant's line be not broken, the fall of Vicksburg is only a question of time. Grant's force (he continues) is more than treble his; and Grant has constructed lines of circumvallation, and blocked up all the roads leading to his position. To force his lines would be difficult with an army twice as numerous as the one he (Johnston) commands. He will try to do something in aid of the besieged—but it seems a *desperate case.* He has not wagons and provisions enough to leave the railroads more than four days. The track to Vicksburg is destroyed. It was his intention at first to unite all the troops in his command—but it was impracticable. So much for these lugubrious tidings. Nothing but a miracle can save Vicksburg!

The Governors of Alabama and Mississippi unite in urging the government to suppress both the foreign and border traffic. I fear it is too late!

There is a street rumor that the enemy have appeared on the Chickahominy, and on the James River. If this be so, it may be to embarrass Lee; or it may be a determined and desperate assault on this city. We shall know very soon. But never before were we in such doubt as to the designs of the enemy; and never before have they evinced such apparent vigor and intrepidity. Yet, they know not what Lee is doing to call them *home.*

JUNE 13TH.—Col. Baylor, of Arizona, has been heard from again. He confesses that he issued the order to slaughter the Apaches in cold blood, and says it is the only mode of dealing with such savages. The President indorses on it that it is "a confession of an infamous crime."

Yesterday the enemy appeared on the Peninsula, in what numbers we know not yet; but just when Gen. Wise was about to attack, with every prospect of success, an order was received from Gen. Arnold Elzey to fall back toward the city, pickets and all.

A letter from Gen. Holmes, containing an account from one of his scouts, shows that the enemy's militia in Arkansas and Missouri are putting to death all the men, young or old, having favored the Confederate cause, who fall into their hands. These acts are perpetrated by order of Gen. Prentiss. The President suggests that they be published, both at home and abroad.

Mr. L. Heyliger, our agent at Nassau, sends an account of the firing into and disabling the British steamer Margaret and Jessee by the United States steamer Rhode Island, within a half mile of shore. Several British subjects were wounded. This may make trouble.

Mr. J. S. Lemmon applied by letter to-day for permission to leave a Confederate port for Europe. Major-Gen. Arnold Elzey indorsed on it: "This young man, being a native of Maryland, is not liable to military service in the Confederate States." Well, Arnold Elzey is also a native of Maryland.

JUNE 14TH.—W——ll, one of the Winder *detectives* that fled to Washington last year, is back again. But the Mayor has arrested him as a spy, and it is said a lady in the city can prove his guilt. Gen. Winder wanted to bail him; but the Mayor was inexorable, and so W——ll is in the jail, awaiting his trial. Two others, of Winder's police, have likewise been arrested by the city authorities for some harsh treatment of a citizen supposed to have a barrel of whisky in his house. The justification offered is the jurisdiction of martial law, which Gen. Winder still thinks exists, although annulled by Congress.

The company (of 104) organized in the War Department as independent volunteers for local defense, being objected to by Gen. Elzey, because they would not be subject to his command, was rejected by the President, who insisted that the officers of the departments (civil) should be mustered into the service under the act of August 21st, 1861, and are subject to *his* control, and liable to be attached to battalions, regiments, etc., he appointing the field and staff officers. This was communicated to the lieutenant of the company by the Secretary of War, who stated also that the President required the names of all refusing to reorganize on that basis *to be reported to him.*

There is an indefinable dread of conspiracy, and the President is right, perhaps, to frown upon all military organizations not subject to his orders. Mr. Randolph, late Secretary of War, has been very busy organizing the second class militia of the city for "local defense," under the supposition that he would command them; but the President has made a requisition for 8000 of this class of men, for the same purpose, which will put them under Confederate orders, perhaps. A jealousy, I fear, is growing up between Confederate and State authority. This when the common enemy is thundering at all our gates!

JUNE 15TH.—The enemy have abandoned the vicinity of Fredericksburg, falling back across the river, and probably retiring toward Alexandria, or else they have taken to their transports, and intend making another effort to capture Richmond. It is rumored that Gen. Ewell has taken Winchester; but this, I think, is at least premature.

Certainly the government is taking steps to guard against a blow at Richmond. All the civil officers (subordinates, only, of course) are being mustered into the service for "local defense or special duty;" but Gen. Elzey, the Marylander, it is reported, has said the "d——d clerks have given me so much trouble, that I intend to keep them on duty in such a way that they cannot perform their functions in the departments, and so others must be appointed in their places." This would be in violation both of the Constitution and several acts of Congress. Yet they are to be mustered in this evening "for three years, or the war." And the Secretary of the Treasury has announced that all who refuse to volunteer are to be reported, by the President's command, and will be removed. The President has intimated no such thing. Of course they will *volunteer*. There is much censure of the President for "bad faith"—most of the clerks being refugees, with families to support.

Mayor Mayo has refused to admit Gen. Winder's three policemen (all imported) to bail, and they remain in prison; and Judge Meredith has refused to discharge them on a writ of *habeas corpus*—resolving first to test the validity of the martial law set up for them in their defense.

I believe the government is acting on my suggestion to Col. Johnston, A. D. C., in regard to searching blockade-runners, caught in the lines, bearing sealed letters to the North. To-day the Attorney-General sent to the department, for Mr. Seddon's approval, instructions to Confederate Attorneys and Marshals to aid and co-operate with *M. Greenwood*, a detective agent of the government. I think about the first men he detects in treasonable practices will be Gen. Elzey and Gen. Winder's detectives.

Mr. Vallandigham has been nominated for Governor of Ohio.

The following are the conditions upon which women and children can come to the South, or go to the North, published in Washington and Baltimore :

"*First.*—All applications for passes to go South must be made in writing and verified by oath, addressed to Major L. C. Turner, Judge Advocate, Washington, D. C., as follows :

"I, A—— B——, applicant for a pass to go to City Point, Virginia, and now residing at ——, do solemnly swear that, if said pass be granted, I will not take any property excepting my wearing apparel, and that all the articles to be taken with me are contained in the trunk or package delivered or to be delivered to the quartermaster on the transport steamer on which I am to go to City Point. That I have not been in any insurgent State, nor beyond the military lines of the United States, within thirty days last past. That I will not return within the military lines of the United States during the present war, and that I have not in my trunk nor on my person any papers or writings whatsoever, nor any contraband articles.

"No person will be allowed to take more than one trunk or package of female wearing apparel, weighing not over one hundred pounds, and subject to inspection ; and if anything contraband be found in the trunk or on the person, the property will be forfeited and the pass revoked.

"*Second.*—A passenger boat will leave Annapolis, Md., on the first day of July next, to deliver those permitted to go South at City Point, and the baggage of each applicant must be delivered to the quartermaster on said boat, at least twenty-four hours previous to the day of departure for inspection.

"*Third.*—Children will be allowed to accompany their mothers and relatives, and take their usual wearing apparel ; but the name and age of each child must be given in the application.

"*Fourth.*—Ladies and children desiring to come North will be received on the boat at City Point and taken to Annapolis, and every adult person coming North will be required to take and subscribe to the oath of allegiance to the Government of the United States before the boat leaves Fortress Monroe.

"L. C. TURNER, *Judge Advocate.*"

JUNE 16TH.—We have nothing from the West to-day. But it is believed that Hooker is retiring toward Manassas—that fatal field—where another (and the third) battle may be fought. Lee's army is certainly on the march, and a collision of arms cannot be averted many days. It is believed Gen. Ewell, successor of Jackson, has beaten Milroy at Winchester.

But, while terrible events are daily anticipated in the field, all the civilians seem to have gone wild with speculation, and official corruption runs riot throughout the land. J. M. Seixas, agent of the War Department, writes from Wilmington that while the government steamers can get no cotton to exchange abroad for ordnance stores, the steamers of individuals are laden, and depart almost daily. This is said to be partly the work of the "Southern Express Company," believed to be Yankees (a portion of them), which contracts to deliver freight, and bribes the railroads and monopolizes transportation. *This* is the company on whose application Judge Campbell, Assistant Secretary of War, granted so many exemptions and details! It takes a great number of able-bodied men from the army, and then, by a peculiar process, absolutely embarrasses, as Gen. Whiting says, the conduct of the war.

Judge Dargan, of Alabama, writes that private blockade-runners are ruining the country—supplying the enemy with cotton, and bringing in liquors and useless gew-gaws.

JUNE 17TH.—The city has been gladdened by the reception of this dispatch from Gen. Lee:

"JUNE 15th, 1863.

"HIS EXCELLENCY, JEFFERSON DAVIS.

"God has again crowned the valor of our troops with success. Early's division stormed the enemy's intrenchments at Winchester, capturing their artillery, etc.

"(Signed) R. E. LEE, *General.*"

Subsequent reports to the press state that we captured some 6000 prisoners, Gen. Milroy among them, 50 guns, and a large amount of stores. If we caught Milroy, the impression prevails that he was hung immediately, in accordance with the President's order some time since, as a just punishment for the outrages inflicted by him on our helpless old men, women, and children.

A sealed envelope came in to-day, addressed by the President to the Secretary of War, marked "Highly important and confidential," which, of course, I sent to the Secretary immediately without breaking the seal, as it is my duty to do to all letters not private or confidential. I can as yet only conjecture what it referred to. It may be of good, and it may be of bad import. It may relate to affairs in the West; or it may be a communication from abroad, several steamers having just arrived. *Can* it be from the Government at Washington? I care not what it is, if we hold Vicksburg.

The Commissary-General reports that he has some 8,000,000 pounds of bacon, and quite as much salt and fresh beef at the various depots, besides some 11,000 head of cattle. This is not a large amount for such armies as we have in the field; but in the fall we shall have 10 per cent. of all the products in the Confederate States as tax in kind. The Commissary-General, however, recommends the following reduction of rations: for men in garrison or batteries, a quarter pound of bacon per day; in camp, one-third of a pound; and marching, half a pound.

Mr. James Spence, our financial agent in England, gives a somewhat cheering account of money matters. He recommends the shipping of $1,000,000 worth of cotton per week, which appears to be practicable. He also advises the shipment of the few millions of gold the government holds in this country to England; and Mr. Memminger approves it—in boxes weekly, containing $75,000. If this were known, it could hardly be accomplished, for such is the distrust of several members of the cabinet that the people would revolt. They would believe the cabinet meant soon to follow the gold. And some of our military commanders have no better opinion of them than the people. Beauregard once stopped some bullion ordered away by Mr. Memminger.

There is a rumor that Gen. Wise had a combat yesterday on the Peninsula. But the operations beyond the Rappahannock, and approaching the capital of the United States, must relieve Richmond of all immediate danger.

Mr. Lincoln says he is "making history;" forgetful of the execrable figure he is likely to be in it. Our papers to-day contain the following:

"*Yankee Cruelty; Forty-three Negroes Drowned.*—One of

the most atrocious incidents of the whole war was yesterday related to us by a gentleman of this city, who obtained the facts from Capt. Jas. G. White, of King William County, who vouches for the accuracy of the statement. Some days ago, when the Yankees made their raid to Aylett's, they visited the place of Dr. Gregg, living in the neighborhood, and took from their comfortable homes forty-three negroes, who were hurried off to York River and placed on board a vessel bound Northward. Along with these negroes, as a prisoner, was a gentleman named Lee, a resident and highly respectable citizen of King William, who has since been released and allowed to return to his home. He states that when the vessel arrived in Chesapeake Bay, the small-pox made its appearance among the negroes, that disease having existed to some extent among the same family before they were dragged from their homes in King William. The captain of the Yankee vessel and his crew were greatly alarmed at the appearance of the disease on board, and very soon determined to rid the vessel of the presence of the negroes. Without attempting to make the shore, and not considering for an instant the inhumanity of the cruel deed, the whole negro cargo was thrown into the bay, and every one left to perish by drowning. Not one, perhaps, escaped the cruel fate visited upon them by those who profess to be their earnest friends and warmest sympathizers."

JUNE 18TH.—From Winchester we have many accounts, in the absence of official reports (Gen. Lee being too busy in the saddle to write), which have exalted our spirits most wonderfully. The number of prisoners taken, by the lowest estimate is 5000,—the others say 9000,—besides 50 guns, and an immense amount of stores. Our own loss in storming the fortifications was only 100 killed and wounded! Milroy, they say, escaped by flight—but may not have gotten off very far, as it seems certain that our one-legged Lieut.-Gen. Ewell (fit successor of Jackson) pushed on to the Potomac and surrounded, if he has not taken, Harper's Ferry, where there is another large depot of supplies. The whole valley is doubtless in our possession—the Baltimore and Ohio Railroad—and the way is open into Maryland and Pennsylvania. It is believed Hooker's army is utterly demoralized, and that Lee is *going on*. This time, perhaps, no Sharpsburg will embarrass his progress, and the long longed-for day of retributive invasion may come at last.

Col. Gorgas, Chief of Ordnance (Northern born), recommends that the habit of issuing twenty cartridges extra to each of our men be discontinued, and suggests that they be given three cartridges per month, and all over that to be issued upon requisition of the commanding general, on the eve of battle. But might they not, if this were adopted, be liable to be caught sometimes without enough ammunition? He says there is a deficiency of lead.

There is a rumor that the Secretary of the Navy sent an iron-clad out yesterday, at Savannah, to fight two of the enemy's blockading squadron, and that after an engagement of thirty minutes, our ship struck her colors. If this be so, the people will wish that the Secretary had been on the boat that surrendered.

A man by the name of Jackson a short time since obtained a passport through our lines from Judge Campbell, and when a negro was rowing him across the Potomac, drew a pistol and made him take him to a Federal gun-boat in sight. He was heartily received, and gave such information to the enemy as induced them to engage in a raid on the Northern Neck, resulting in the devastation of several counties. These facts I got from the President's special detective, Craddock. Craddock also informs me that my communication to Col. Johnston was laid before the President, who called in the Secretary of State and the Secretary of War, to consult on some means of regulating the passport business, etc. He says prompt measures will be adopted immediately.

Craddock also informs me that a Jew named Cohen, in this city, has been co-operating with his brother living in the North, obtaining passports both ways for bribes—and bribing the officials that granted them, much to our detriment. This, perhaps, has alarmed the President; but if the business of selling passports be lucrative, I despair of his being able to put an end to it.

I see the enemy have destroyed the President's house, furniture, etc., in Mississippi.

I have good reason to suppose that the package marked "important," etc., sent from the President's office yesterday to the Secretary of War, was the substance of a conversation which took place between Mr. Ould and Mr. Vallandigham. What Mr. V. revealed to Mr. O., perhaps supposing the latter, although employed here, friendly to ultimate reconstruction, there is no means of conjecturing. But it was deemed "highly important."

JUNE 19TH.—Gen. Lee telegraphs from *Culpepper Court House* yesterday, that Gen. Rhodes captured Martinsburg, Sunday, 14th inst., taking several guns, over 200 prisoners, and a supply of ammunition and grain. Our loss was only one killed and two wounded.

The Secretary of the Navy is in bad odor for ordering out the Atlanta at Savannah to fight *two* Federal steamers, to whom she surrendered.

There is nothing more definite or authentic from Winchester, except that we certainly captured Milroy's army of not less than 5000 men.

To-day the government issued musket and ball-cartridges (forty to each) to the volunteer companies raised in the departments for home defense. If this does not signify apprehension of an immediate attack, it proves at all events that Lee's army is not to be around the city as it was a year ago—and that signifies his purpose to advance.

JUNE 20TH.—It has got out that the President intends to dispense with the services of Mr. Myers, the Jew Quartermaster-General, and Mr. Miles, member of Congress from South Carolina, who happens to be his friend, is characteristically doing the part of a friend for his retention. But he gives the President some severe raps for alleged contempt of the wishes of Congress, that body having passed a bill (vetoed by the President) conferring on Col. M. the rank and pay of brigadier-general.

The operations of Gen. Lee have relieved the depot here, which was nearly empty. Since the capture of Winchester and Martinsburg, only about 1500 bushels of corn are sent to the army daily, whereas 5000 were sent before, and there were rarely more than a day's supply on hand.

To-day, about one o'clock, the city was thrown into a state of joyful excitement, by the reception of news from the North. From this source it was ascertained, what had hitherto been only a matter of conjecture, that a portion of our forces, the same that captured Winchester and Martinsburg, were in Pennsylvania! Gen. Jenkins, with his cavalry, had taken Chambersburg on the 16th inst. —and the North, from the line of Pennsylvania to the lakes, and from the seaboard to the western prairies, was stricken with consternation. These are some of the dispatches, as copied from Northern papers :

"The Governor of Ohio calls for 30,000 troops. The Governor of Pennsylvania calls for 50,000, to prevent the invasion of each State.

"WASHINGTON, June 15th.—Lincoln has issued a proclamation for 100,000 men, to repel the invasion of Maryland, Northern Virginia, Pennsylvania, and Ohio.

"HARRISBURG, June 15th.—Dispatches from Chambersburg and Hagerstown state that the rebel cavalry are at Berryville and Martinsburg. A dispatch dated 14th, says that hard fighting is going on. The rebels had driven Reynolds from Berryville, and were advancing on the capital. The towns and cities throughout Pennsylvania are in danger.

"LATER.—Private dispatches state that on the 16th the rebels were at Chambersburg in force. The Federals were removing the railroad machinery, stock, and stores. Great excitement and alarm pervaded the entire country."

In the "hard fighting," Gen. Lee reports our loss as "one killed and two wounded." Here's the second dispatch:

"SHELBYVILLE, TENN., June 18th.—Nashville papers of the 17th inst. have been received here. They contain Lincoln's proclamation, calling for 100,000 militia, for six months' service, and the following highly interesting telegrams:

"LOUDON, PA., June 16th.—The rebels are in heavy force in the Cumberland Valley.

"BEDFORD, PA., June 16th.—Scouts report 6000 rebels at Cumberland, Maryland. The inhabitants are flying for safety from Harper's Ferry.

"HARRISBURG, June 16th.—Business is suspended here. All the important documents have been removed from the capital.

"Milroy telegraphs officially his repulse from the fortifications at Winchester by 15,000 rebels, with the loss of 2900 men.

"Governor Curtin calls upon the people of Pennsylvania to defend the State, saying that Philadelphia has not responded, while the enemy are in Chambersburg. He reproaches Pennsylvania for sniffling about the length of service when the exigency exists.

"Dispatches state that everything looks gloomy, and there is no saving the country south of the Susquehanna.

"BALTIMORE, June 16th.—Governor Bradford calls on the people to rally to the defense of Maryland.

"PROVIDENCE, R. I., June 16th.—Governor Smith convenes the Legislature on Thursday for the purpose of raising troops.

"PHILADELPHIA, June 16th.—The Mayor has issued a proclamation closing the stores in order that the occupants may join military organizations to defend the city.

"NEW YORK, June 16th.—All the regiments are getting ready under arms. The Brooklyn bells were rung at midnight, summoning the men to the regiments, which were to leave immediately for Philadelphia.

"Governor Andrews, of Massachusetts, tenders Lincoln all the available force of militia from that State."

Milroy's statement in relation to the number of prisoners taken by us is pretty fair, when compared with Hooker's official statements on similar occasions. Some of the prisoners will probably arrive in Richmond to-day—and the Agent of Exchange has been notified that 7000 would be sent on. So Gen. Milroy told nearly *half* the truth.

Again:

THIRD DISPATCH.

"SHELBYVILLE, June 19th.—Other dispatches in the Nashville papers say that the rebels advanced six miles beyond Chambersburg. On the 16th Gen. Taylor telegraphs officially his retreat, and the capture of the Federal forces at Winchester."

Later in the day the New York *Herald* of the 17th inst. was received by the flag of truce boat. I now quote from it:

"Fortifications are being rapidly erected all along the north bank of the Susquehanna, and Gen. McClellan or Gen. Franklin has been called for to head the State troops.

REPORTS FROM HARRISBURG.

"HARRISBURG, PA., June 16th.—Midnight.—Rebel cavalry today occupied Littletown, eleven miles from Gettysburg, but at last accounts had not advanced beyond that point.

"The rebel officers at Chambersburg stated that they were only waiting for infantry to move forward. The authorities are inclined to believe, however, that they will not move farther North.

"The farmers in the valley are sending their horses and cattle into the mountains.

"The rebels are gathering up all the negroes that can be found.

"Private property has been respected.

"They burned the railroad bridge across Scotland Creek, six miles this side of Chambersburg.

HARPER'S FERRY INVESTED.

"BALTIMORE, June 16th.—Fugitives from Hagerstown report the rebels picketing all the roads and not permitting any one to pass.

"The force that passed through were all cavalry, under Jenkins and Imboden, and did not exceed 2500.

"All was quiet at Frederick up to five o'clock this evening, though the people were greatly excited and hundreds were leaving.

"HARRISBURG, June 17th.—The aspect of affairs, so far as can be judged by the reports from the border, seems to be this:

"The rebel force occupy Hagerstown and such other points as leave them free to operate either against Harrisburg or Baltimore.

"Apprehensions are entertained by the people of Altoona and other points on the line of the Pennsylvania Railroad, that the rebels will strike for the West, and then go back to their own soil by way of Pittsburg and Wheeling.

"The fortifications constructed on the hills opposite Harrisburg are considered sufficient protection for the city, and an offensive movement on our part is not unlikely."

JUNE 21ST.—To-day we have an account of the burning of Darien, Ga. The temptation is strong for our army to retaliate on the soil of Pennsylvania.

JUNE 22D.—To-day I saw the memorandum of Mr. Ould, of the conversation held with Mr. Vallandigham, for file in the archives. He says if we *can only hold out* this year that the peace party of the North would sweep the Lincoln dynasty out of political existence. He seems to have thought that our cause was sinking, and feared we would submit, which would, of course, be ruinous to his party! But he advises strongly against any invasion of Pennsylvania, for that would unite all parties at the North, and so strengthen Lincoln's hands that he would be able to crush all opposition, and trample upon the constitutional rights of the people.

Mr. V. said nothing to indicate that either he or the party had any other idea than that the Union would be reconstructed under Democratic rule. The President indorsed, with his own pen, on this document, that, in regard to invasion of the North, experience proved the contrary of what Mr. V. asserted. But Mr. V. is for restoring the Union, amicably, of course, and if it cannot be so done, then possibly he is in favor of recognizing our independence. He says any reconstruction which is not voluntary on our part, would soon be followed by another separation, and a worse war than the present one.

The President received a dispatch to-day from Gen. Johnston, stating that Lt.-Gen. Kirby Smith had taken Milliken's Bend. This is important, for it interferes with Grant's communications.

Gov. Shorter writes that a company near Montgomery, Ala., have invented a mode of manufacturing cotton and woolen hand-cards, themselves making the steel and wire, and in a few weeks will be turning out from 800 to 1000 pairs of cards per week. This will be a great convenience to the people.

Gen. Whiting writes that the river at Wilmington is so filled with the ships of private blockade-runners that the defense of the harbor is interfered with. These steamers are mostly filled with Yankee goods, for which they take them cotton, in the teeth of the law. He pronounces this business most execrable, as well as injurious to the cause. He desires the President to see his letter, and hopes he may be instructed to seize the steamers and cargoes arriving belonging to Yankees and freighted with Yankee goods.

It is a difficult matter to subsist in this city now. Beef is $1 and bacon $1.65 per pound, and just at this time there are but few vegetables. Old potatoes are gone, and the new have not yet come. A single cabbage, merely the leaves, no head, sells for a dollar, and this suffices not for a dinner for my family.

My little garden has produced nothing yet, in consequence of the protracted dry weather. But we have, at last, abundant rains. To-day I found several long pieces of rusty wire, and these I have affixed horizontally to the wood-house and to the fence, intending to lead the lima beans up to them by strings, which I will fasten to switches stuck between the plants. My beets will soon be fit to eat, and so will the squashes. But the potatoes do not yet afford a cheering prospect. The tomatoes, however, are coming on finely, and the cherries are nearly ripe. A lady has sent me 50 cabbage plants to set out, and two dozen red peppers. Every foot of my ground is occupied, and there is enough to afford me some exercise every afternoon.

JUNE 23D.—From the army on the Potomac we have a dispatch from Lee, saying there have been several cavalry engagements during the last week, wherein our arms were successful. Lee will soon electrify us with another movement of his grand army,—such is the general belief.

From the West we learn that on Saturday last, Grant, no doubt driven to desperation by our occupation of Milliken's Bend cutting off his supplies and reinforcements, made a more furious attempt than ever to take Vicksburg by assault, and was repulsed disastrously. His loss is estimated at between 7000 and 10,000 men. Pemberton is now greatly praised by many people, while some of our officers shake their heads and say he is fighting with the halter around his neck, and that if he were *not* to fight and hold out to the last, his own men would hang him.

Notwithstanding the immense amount of goods brought in daily, the prices keep high.

JUNE 24TH.—We have nothing additional from Vicksburg or from the Potomac, but there is a rumor of fighting near Leesburg.

The first installment of Winchester prisoners reached the city yesterday, 1600 in number, and there are over 4000 more on the way. So much for Milroy's 2000 or 3000!

To-day the President desired the Secretary of War to send him all the correspondence with Gen. Johnston, as he intends to write him a confidential letter touching reinforcements, and he wishes to inform him of the military situation of affairs everywhere.

This afternoon some excitement prevails in the city, caused by a notification of the Governor placarded at the corner of the streets, calling on the citizens to assemble at the Capitol Square at 7 o'clock P.M., and announcing that reliable information has been received of the landing of the enemy (how many is not stated) at Brandon, on the James River, and at the White House, on the York, some thirty-five miles below. There was also a meeting of the clerks of the departments, and it was agreed that at the sounding of the tocsin they should assemble (day or night) with arms at their respective offices.

This may be another Pawnee alarm of the government, and it may be the wolf. If some 30,000 of the enemy's troops make a dash at Richmond now, they may take it. But it will, of course, be defended with what means we have, to the last extremity.

Still, I think it nothing more than a strategical movement to save Washington or to embarrass Lee's operations, and it will fail to retard his movement. We shall soon see what it is

JUNE 25TH.—The excitement has subsided. No doubt small detachments of the enemy were seen at the places indicated, and Gen. Elzey (who some say had been drinking) alarmed the Governor with a tale of horror. The reports came through Gen. Winder's detectives, one-half of whom would rather see the enemy here than not, and will serve the side that pays most. Yet, we should be prepared.

I saw an indorsement by the President to-day, that foreigners should give guarantees of neutrality or be sent out of the city.

Nothing from Lee.

JUNE 27TH.—An officer of the Signal Corps reported, yesterday, the force of Gen. Keyes, on the Peninsula, at 6000. To-day we learn that the enemy is in possession of Hanover Junction, cutting off communication with both Fredericksburg and Gordonsville. A train was coming down the Central Road with another installment of the Winchester peisoners (some 4000 having already arrived, now confined on Belle Island, opposite the city), but was stopped in time, and sent back.

Gen. Elzey had just ordered away a brigade from Hanover Junction to Gordonsville, upon which it was alleged another raid was projected. What admirable manœuvring for the benefit of the enemy!

Gen. D. H. Hill wrote, yesterday, that we had no troops on the Blackwater except cavalry. I hope he will come here and take command.

Gen. Whiting has arrested the Yankee crew of the Arabian, at Wilmington. It appears that she is owned by New Yorkers, sailed from New York, and has a Yankee cargo!

Capt. Maury writes from London that R. J. Walker, once a

fire-and-fury Mississippi Senator (but Yankee-born), is in Europe trying to borrow £50,000,000 for the United States. Capt. Maury says the British Government will not willingly let us have another "Alabama;" but that it is also offended at the United States for the atrocities of Wilkes, and this may lead to war. The war, however, would not be intended as a diversion in our behalf.

Nothing is heard to-day from Lee, except what appears in Northern papers several days old, when our troops were occupying Hagerstown, Cumberland, etc., in Maryland, and foraging pretty extensively in Pennsylvania.

Nothing from Vicksburg.

Just as I apprehended! The brigade ordered away from Hanover to Gordonsville, upon a wild-goose chase, had not been gone many hours before some 1200 of the enemy's cavalry appeared there, and burnt the bridges which the brigade had been guarding! This is sottishness, rather than generalship, in our local commanders.

A regiment was sent up when firing was heard (the annihilation of our weak guard left at the bridges) and arrived just two hours too late. The enemy rode back, with a hundred mules they had captured, getting under cover of their gun-boats.

To-day, it is said, Gen. Elzey is relieved, and Gen. Ransom, of North Carolina, put in command; also, that Custis Lee (son of Gen. R. E. Lee) has superseded Gen. Winder. I hope this has been done. Young Lee has certainly been commissioned a brigadier-general. His brother, Brig.-Gen. W. H. F. Lee, wounded in a late cavalry fight, was taken yesterday by the enemy at Hanover Court House.

Gen. Whiting's letter about the "Arabian" came back from the President, to-day, indorsed that, as Congress did not prohibit private blockade-running, he wouldn't interfere. So, this is to be the settled policy of the government.

This morning the President sent a letter to the Secretary of War, requesting him to direct all mounted officers—some fifty A. A. G.'s and A. D.'s—to report to him for duty around the city. Good! These gentlemen ought to be in the saddle instead of being sheltered from danger in the bureaus.

3 O'CLOCK P.M.—Three proclamations have just been issued! One (a joint one) from the President and the Governor, calling

upon everybody to organize themselves into companies, battalions, and regiments, when they will be armed. They say "no time is to be lost, the danger is great." The Mayor, in his document, warns the people in time to avoid the fate of New Orleans. He says the enemy is advancing on the city, and may assail it before Monday morning. This is Saturday. The third proclamation is by E. B. Robinson, one of my printers, twenty years ago, at Washington. He calls upon all natives of Maryland and the District of Columbia to report to him, and he will lead them against the enemy, and redeem them from the imputation of skulking or disloyalty cast upon poor refugees by the flint-hearted Shylocks of Richmond, who have extorted all their money from them.

Besides these inflammatory documents, the militia colonels have out notices for all men under forty-five years of age to meet in Broad Street to-morrow, Sunday.

I learn, however, that there are some 25,000 or 30,000 of the enemy at Yorktown; but if we can get together 12,000 fighting men, in the next twenty-four hours, to man the fortifications, there will not be much use for the militia and the clerks of the departments, more than as an internal police force. But I am not quite sure we can get that number.

June 28th.—By order of Brig.-Gen. G. W. Custis Lee, the department companies were paraded to-day, armed and equipped. These, with the militia in the streets (armed by the government to-day), amounted to several thousand efficient men for the batteries and for guard duty. They are to rendezvous, with blankets, provisions, etc., upon the sounding of the tocsin. I learn that 8000 men in the hospitals within convenient reach of the city, including those in the city, can be available for defense in an emergency. They cannot march, but they can fight. These, with Hill's division, will make over 20,000 men; an ample force to cope with the enemy on the Peninsula. It has been a cool, cloudy day (we have had copious rains recently), else the civilians could not have stood several hours exercise so well. A little practice will habituate them by degrees to the harness of war. No one doubts that they will fight, when the time for blows arrives. Gen. Jenkins has just arrived, with his brigade, from the south side of the James River.

I was in the arsenal to-day, and found an almost unlimited amount of arms.

We get not a word from Gen. Lee. This, I think, augurs well, for bad news flies fast. No doubt we shall soon hear something from the Northern papers. They are already beginning to magnify the ravages of our army on *their* soil: but our men are incapable of retaliating, to the full extent, such atrocities as the following, on the Blackwater, near Suffolk, which I find in the Petersburg *Express:*

"Mr. Smith resided about one mile from the town, a well-to-do farmer, having around him an interesting family, the eldest one a gallant young man in the 16th Virginia Regiment. When Gen. Longstreet invested Suffolk a sharp artillery and infantry skirmish took place near Mr. Smith's residence, and many balls passed through his house. The Yankees finally advanced and fired the houses, forcing the family to leave. Mrs. Smith, with her seven children, the youngest only ten months old, attempted to escape to the woods and into the Confederate lines, when she was fired upon by the Yankee soldiers, and a Minié-ball entering her limb just below the hip, she died in thirty minutes from the loss of blood. The children, frightened, hid themselves in the bushes, while Mr. Smith sat down upon the ground by his wife, to see her breathe her last. After she had been dead for some time, the Yankee commander permitted him to take a cart, and, with no assistance except one of his children, he put the dead body in the cart and carried it into the town. On his arrival in town, he was not permitted to take the remains of his wife to her brother's residence until he had first gone through the town to the Provost Marshal's office and obtained permission. On his arrival at the Provost Marshal's office, he was gruffly told to take his wife to the graveyard and bury her. He carried her to her brother's, John R. Kilby, Esq., and a few friends prepared her for burial; Mr. Kilby not being allowed to leave the house, or to attend the remains of his sister to the graveyard.

"Nor did the cruelty of the fiends stop here. Mr. Smith was denied the privilege of going in search of his little children, and for four days and nights they wandered in the woods and among the soldiers without anything to eat or any place to sleep. The baby was taken up by a colored woman and nursed until some private in the Yankee army, with a little better heart than his associates, took it on his horse and carried it to town. Mr. Smith is still in the lines of the enemy, his house and everything else he had destroyed, and his little children cared for by his friends.

"Will not the Confederate soldiers now in Pennsylvania remember such acts of cruelty and barbarism? Will not the Nansemond companies remember it? And will not that gallant boy in the 16th Regiment remember his mother's fate, and take vengeance on the enemy? Will not such a cruel race of people eventually reap the fruit of their doings? God grant that they may."

SUNDAY AFTERNOON.—There are two reports of important events current in the streets: first, that Lee's army has taken and destroyed Harrisburg, Pennsylvania; and second, that Vicksburg has fallen. I am not prepared to credit either, although the first is said to be true by no less a person than Gov. Letcher. And yet one or both may be confirmed to-morrow; and if so, that is, if Vicksburg has fallen, and Lee should retire, as he must sooner or later, there will be a dark and desponding season in the Confederacy. But the war will go on.

JUNE 29TH.—There is no confirmation of the report of the fall of Vicksburg, but it may be so; nor is it certain that we have advanced to Harrisburg, but it is probable.

Gen. D. H. Hill writes (on Saturday) from Petersburg that 40,000 of the enemy could not take Richmond; but this may be fishing for the command. He says if Gen. Dix comes this way, he would make him a subject of the cartel of exchange which he (Dix) had a hand in negotiating.

J. M. Botts writes, from his farm in Culpepper, that our men are quartered on his premises, and do as much injury as *a* hostile army could. *He* is neutral. They pay him ten cents per day for the grazing of each horse.

The Commissary-General is again recommending the procuring of bacon from within the enemy's lines, in exchange for cotton. Why not get meat from the enemy's country for nothing?

Hon. R. M. T. Hunter writes to the Secretary of War to let the Quartermaster-General alone, that he is popular with Congress, and that his friends are active. It might be dangerous to remove him; the President had better commission him a brigadier-general. He says Judge Campbell wants the President to go to Mississippi; this, Mr. H. is opposed to. Mr. H. is willing to trust Johnston, has not lost confidence in him, etc. And he tells the Secretary to inform the President how much he (H.) esteems him (the President).

The New York *Times* publishes an account of one of their raids on the Peninsula, below this city, as follows:

"Within the past three days a most daring raid has been made into one of the richest portions of the enemy's country, and the success was equal to the boldness of the undertaking.

"The expedition, which was conducted by both land and water, was commanded by Col. Kilpatrick. It started from the headquarters of Gen. Keyes on Wendesday, and returned yesterday. In the interim the Counties of Matthews and Gloucester were scoured. All the warehouses containing grain were sacked, the mills burned, and everything that could in any way aid the rebels were destroyed or captured. Three hundred horses, two hundred and fifty head of cattle, two hundred sheep, and one hundred mules, together with a large number of contrabands, were brought back by the raiders.

"The rebel farmers were all taken by surprise. They had not expected a demonstration of the kind. Not only were they made to surrender everything that could be of the least use to us, but they were compelled to be silent spectators to the destruction of their agricultural implements."

No doubt we shall soon have some account in the Northern papers of *our* operations in this line, in their country.

JUNE 30TH.—Dispatches from the West show that we still held Vicksburg at the last dates; and, moreover, Gen. Taylor (son of Zachary Taylor) had stormed and taken the enemy's fortifications at Berwick's Bay, with the bayonet. We took 1000 prisoners, 10 large cannon, and many stores. Also that we had taken Thibbodauxville, and have thus cut off Banks from New Orleans.

5 O'CLOCK P.M.—The city is now in good humor, but not wild with exultation. We have what seems pretty authentic intelligence of the taking of HARRISBURG, the capital of Pennsylvania, the City of YORK, etc. etc. This comes on the flag of truce boat, and is derived from the enemy themselves. Lee will not descend to the retaliation instigated by petty malice; but proclaim to the inhabitants that all we desire is PEACE, not conquest.

From Vicksburg we have further information that, in springing his mine, Grant destroyed hundreds of his own men, and did us no injury. Also that a battery we have above Vicksburg had fired into some passing transports, doing great damage to life and boats. The troops landed, and failed to take the battery by assault, losing hundreds in addition.

CHAPTER XXVIII.

Enemy threatening Richmond.—The city is safe.—Battle of Gettysburg.—Great excitement.—Yankees in great trouble.—Alas! Vicksburg has fallen.—President is sick.—Grant marching against Johnston at Jackson.—Fighting at that place.—Yankees repulsed at Charleston.—Lee and Meade facing each other.—Pemberton surrenders his whole army.—Fall of Port Hudson.—Second class conscripts called for.—Lee has got back across the Potomac.—Lincoln getting fresh troops.—Lee writes that he cannot be responsible if the soldiers fail for want of food.—Rumors of Grant coming East.—Pemberton in bad odor.—Hon. W. L. Yancey is dead.

JULY 1ST.—The intelligence of the capture of Harrisburg and York, Pa., is so far confirmed as to be admitted by the officers of the Federal flag of truce boat that came up to City Point yesterday.

Of the movements of Hooker's army, we have the following information:

"HEADQUARTERS, CAVALRY DIVISION,
"June 27th, 1863.

"GENERAL:—I took possession of Fairfax C. H. this morning at nine o'clock, together with a large quantity of stores. The main body of Hooker's army has gone toward Leesburg, except the garrison of Alexandria and Washington, which has retreated within the fortifications.

"Very respectfully,
"Your obedient servant,
"J. E. B. STUART, *Major-General.*"

The Northern papers say that our cruiser Tacony, taken from them, has destroyed twenty-two of their vessels since the 12th inst.; but that our men burnt her at last. Her crew then entered Portland, Maine, and cut out the steam cutter Caleb Cushing, which they subsequently blew up, and then were themselves taken prisoner.

The President has decided that the obstructions below the city shall not be opened for the steam iron-clad Richmond to go out, until another iron-clad be in readiness to accompany her.

Capt. Maury, at Mobile, writes that the two iron-clads, Trent and Nashville, now ready for sea, might take New Orleans and *keep it.* The President directs the Secretary of War to consult the Secretary of the Navy, and if they agreed, the attempt should be made without loss of time. So, probably, we shall have news from that quarter soon.

The militia and Department Guard (soon to be called the National Guard, probably) were notified to-day to be in readiness at a minute's warning. It is said positively that Dix is advancing toward the city. Well, let him come.

July 2d.—The President is unwell again; to what extent I have not learned. But the Vice-President is ready, no doubt, to take his place in the event of a fatal result; and some would rejoice at it. Such is the mutability of political affairs!

The Attorney-General Watts, being referred to, sends in a written opinion that foreigners sojourning here, under the protection of the Confederate States, are liable to military duty, in defense of their homes, against any government but the one to which they claim to owe allegiance. This I sent in to the Secretary of War, and I hope he will act on it; but the Assistant Secretary and Mr. Benjamin were busy to-day—perhaps combating the Attorney-General's opinion. Will Mr. Seddon have the nerve to act? It is a trying time, and every man is needed for defense.

The enemy were drawn up in line of battle this morning below the fortifications. The Department Guard (my son Custis among them) were ordered out, and marched away; and so with the second class militia. A battle is looked for to-morrow; and there has been skirmishing to-day. A dispatch from Hanover Court House says the enemy is approaching likewise from the north in large force—and 15 guns. This is his great blunder. He cannot take Richmond, nor draw back Lee, and the detachment of so many of his men may endanger Baltimore and Washington, and perhaps Philadelphia.

JULY 3D.—My son Custis stayed out all night, sleeping on his arms in the farthest intrenchments. A little beyond, there was a skirmish with the enemy. We lost eight in killed and wounded. What the enemy suffered is not known, but he fell back, and ran toward the White House.

This morning, Mr. Ould, agent for exchange of prisoners, reported that "not a Yankee could be found on the face of the earth." And this induced a general belief that the enemy had retired, finally, being perhaps ordered to Washington, where they may be much needed.

The Secretary of War, believing the same thing, intimated to Gen. Elzey (who for some cause is unable to ride, and therefore remains in the city) a desire to send several regiments away to some menaced point at a distance. In response, Elzey writes that none can be spared with safety; that the enemy had apparently divided his force into two bodies, one for Hanover, and the other for the Chickahominy, and both *strong;* and he advised against weakening the forces here He said he had not yet completed the manning of the batteries, the delay being in arming the men—and he hoped "Hill could hold out."

We have 3400 convalescents at Camp Lee, and as many more may be relied on for the defense of the city; so we shall have not less than 22,000 men for the defense of Richmond. The enemy have perhaps 35,000; but it would require 75,000 to storm our batteries. Let this be remembered hereafter, if the 35,000 sent here on a fool's errand might have saved Washington or Baltimore, or have served to protect Pennsylvania—and then let the press of the North bag the administration at Washington! Gen. Lee's course is "right onward," and cannot be affected by events here.

My friend Jacques (clerk) marched out yesterday with the Department Guard; but he had the diarrhœa, and was excused from marching as far as the company. He also got permission to come to town this morning, having slept pretty well, he said, apart from the company. No doubt he did good service in the city today, having his rifle fixed (the ball, I believe, had got down before the powder), and procuring a basket of edibles and a canteen of strong tea, which he promised to share with the mess. He said he saw Custis this morning, looking well, after sleeping on the ground the first time in his life, and without a blanket.

We have nothing further from the North or the West.

JULY 4TH.—The Department Guard (my son with them) were marched last night back to the city, and out to Meadow Bridge, on the Chickahominy, some sixteen miles! The clerks, I understand, complain of bad meat (two or three ounces each) and mouldy bread; and some of them curse the authorities for fraudulent deception, as it was understood they would never be marched beyond the city defenses. But they had no alternative—the Secretaries would report the names of all who did not *volunteer*. Most of the poor fellows have families dependent on their salaries for bread—being refugees from their comfortable homes, for the cause of *independence*. If removed, their wives and little children, or brothers and sisters, must perish. They would be conscribed, and receive only $12 per month.

My friend Jacques did not return to the company yesterday, after all, although I saw him get into an ambulance with a basket of food. He got out again, sending the basket to Mr. K., the young chief of the bureau, and Judge Campbell allowed him to remain.

Mr. Myers the lawyer is much with Judge Campbell, working for his Jew clients, who sometimes, I am told, pay $1000 each to be got out of the army, and as high as $500 for a two months' detail, when battles are to be fought. Mr. M. thinks he has law for all he does.

A letter from Gen. D. H. Hill shows that it was his intention to bring on a battle on the 2d inst., but the enemy fled. It was only a feint below; but we may soon hear news from Hanover County.

Col. Gorgas (ordnance) writes that as his men are marched out to defend the city, he can't send much ammunition to Gen. Lee!

A letter from Lieut.-Gen. E. Kirby Smith, dated June 15th, shows he was at Shreveport, La., at that date.

The poor militia were allowed to return to their homes to-day; but an hour after the tocsin sounded, and they were compelled to assemble and march again. This is the work of the Governor, and the Secretary of War says there was no necessity for it, as Confederate troops here now can defend the city, if attacked.

JULY 5TH.—This morning the wires refused to work, being cut, no doubt, in Hanover County.

The presence of the enemy in this vicinity, I think, since they refuse to fight, is designed to prevent us from sending more troops into Pennsylvania. I trust the President will think of this matter, if he is well enough ; some of his generals here are incapable of thinking at all.

We have just received intelligence of a great battle at Gettysburg, Pennsylvania. I have not heard the day; but the news was brought by flag of truce boat to City Point last night. The Yankee papers, I am told, claim a victory, but acknowledge a loss of five or six generals, among them Meade, commander-in-chief (vice Hooker), mortally wounded. *But we still held the town,* and "actions speak louder than words."

More troops are marching up into Hanover County.

JULY 6TH.—Yesterday evening we received Baltimore and New York papers with accounts (and loose ones) of the battle of Gettysburg. The Governor of Pennsylvania says it was "*indecisive,*" which means, as we read it, that Meade's army was defeated.

The forces (Federal) are withdrawing from the neighborhood of this city, another indication that Lee has gained a victory. Dix has done but little damage. In retreating from Hanover County, he burnt the bridges to retard pursuit.

The "War Department Guard" have returned, my son among them, sun-burnt and covered with dust. They were out five days and four nights, sleeping on the ground, without tents or blankets, and with little or nothing to eat, although the Commissary-General had abundance. The President, however, is better to-day, and able to get out of bed; but his health is apparently gone, and it may be doubtful whether he will ever be quite well again.

The Vice-President went down to the flag of truce boat on Saturday, some say to Fortress Monroe, and others to Washington. It is surmised that he is authorized by the President to have a definitive understanding with the Federal authorities, whether or not private property is to be respected hereafter in the future progress of the war. If not, Gen. Lee will have orders to desolate the Northern States, where he has the power. Some, however, think he goes to Washington, to propose terms of peace, etc.

There is a rumor in the city, generally credited, that another battle was fought in Pennsylvania on Friday, and that the enemy was annihilated; these rumors sometimes assume form and substance, and this one, as if by some sort of magnetism, is credited by many. It is certain that Mr. Morris, superintendent of the telegraph office, has called upon his friends for the largest Confederate flag in the city to hang out of his window. He says nothing more; but he may have sent dispatches to the President, which he is not at liberty to divulge. There may be later news from Lee; or Vicksburg may be relieved; or New Orleans taken; or an armistice; or nothing.

I am glad my son's company were ordered in to-day; for, after a week of fine fair weather, it is now raining furiously. This would have prostrated the *tender* boys with illness.

JULY 7TH.—It appears that the fighting near Gettysburg began on Wednesday, July 1st, continued until Sunday, the 5th, and perhaps longer. Up to Friday the Northern papers claim the advantage.

This morning at 1 P.M. another dispatch was received from the same (unofficial) source, stating that on Sunday the enemy made a stand, and A. P. Hill's corps fell back, followed by the enemy, when Longstreet's and Ewell's corps closed in their rear and captured 40,000 prisoners—who are now guarded by Pickett's division. It states that the prisoners refused to be paroled. This might possibly be true.

This account is credited. Col. Custis Lee, from the President's office, was in my office at half-past two P.M. to-day, and said nothing had been received from his father yet—but he did not deny that such accounts might be substantially true.

The President still keeps his eye on Gen. Beauregard. A paper from the general to Gen. Cooper, and, of course, referred to the President, in relation to the means of defense in his department, and a call for more guns, was sent back to-day, indorsed by the President, that by an examination of the report of Gen. Huger, he thought some discrepancies would appear in the statements of Gen. B. Thus, it would seem, from a repetition of similar imputations, the President has strong doubts of Gen. B.'s accuracy of statements. He is quick to detect discrepancies.

Gen. D. H. Hill sends in a characteristic letter. He says the rivers are all swollen, and he can make no movement to-day in pursuit of Dix's army of the Pamunky—or rather "the monkey army." He says that the Brooke Pike outer defenses are so defective in design, that a force there could be driven off in five minutes by the enemy's sharpshooters. He wants them amended, and a certain grove cut down—and recommends that engineers be put to work, with orders to leave their "kid gloves behind." He thinks more is to be apprehended from an attack on Petersburg than Richmond; and requests that Gen. Wise be ordered to march thither from Chaffin's Bluff, on the first alarm. He had not heard of the reported victory of Lee.

JULY 8TH.—I am glad to copy the following order of Gen. Lee:

"HEADQUARTERS ARMY NORTHERN VIRGINIA,
"CHAMBERSBURG, PA., June 27th, 1863.

"GENERAL ORDERS NO. 73.

"The commanding general has observed with marked satisfaction the conduct of the troops on the march, and confidently anticipates results commensurate with the high spirit they have manifested. No troops could have displayed greater fortitude, or better performed the arduous marches of the past ten days. Their conduct in other respects has, with few exceptions, been in keeping with their character as soldiers, and entitles them to approbation and praise.

"There have, however, been instances of forgetfulness on the part of some, that they have in keeping the yet unsullied reputation of the army, and that the duties exacted of us by civilization and Christianity are not less obligatory in the country of the enemy than in our own.

"The commanding general considers that no greater disgrace could befall the army, and through it, our whole people, than the perpetration of the barbarous outrages upon the innocent and defenseless, and the wanton destruction of private property, that have marked the course of the enemy in our own country. Such proceedings not only disgrace the perpetrators and all connected with them, but are subversive of the discipline and efficiency of the army and destructive of the ends of our present movements. It must be remembered that we make war only upon armed men, and that we cannot take vengeance for the wrongs our people have suffered without lowering ourselves in the eyes of all whose abhorrence has been excited by the atrocities of our enemy, and offending against Him to whom vengeance belongeth, without whose favor and support our efforts must all prove in vain.

"The commanding general, therefore, earnestly exhorts the troops to abstain with most scrupulous care from unnecessary or wanton injury to private property; and he enjoins upon all officers to arrest and bring to summary punishment all who shall in any way offend against the orders on this subject.

"R. E. Lee, *General.*"

We have no additional news from the battle-field, except the following dispatch from Winchester:

"Our loss is estimated at 10,000. Between 3000 and 4000 of our wounded are arriving here to-night. Every preparation is being made to receive them.

"Gens. Scales and Pender have arrived here wounded, this evening. Gens. Armistead, Barksdale, Garnett, and Kemper are reported killed. Gens. Jones, Heth, Anderson, Pettigrew, Jenkins, Hampton, and Hood are reported wounded.

"The Yankees say they had only two corps in the fight on Wednesday, which was open field fighting. The whole of the Yankee force was engaged in the last three days' fighting. The number is estimated at 175,000.

"The hills around Gettysburg are said to be covered with the dead and wounded of the Yankee Army of the Potomac.

"The fighting of these four days is regarded as the severest of the war, and the slaughter unprecedented; especially is this so of the enemy.

"The New York and Pennsylvania papers are reported to have declared for peace."

But the absence of dispatches from Gen. Lee himself is beginning to create distrust, and doubts of decisive success at Gettysburg. His couriers may have been captured, or he may be delaying to announce something else he has in contemplation.

The enemy's flag of truce boat of yesterday refused to let us have a single paper in exchange for ours. This signifies something—I know not what. One of our exchanged officers says he heard a Northern officer say, at Fortress Monroe, that Meade's loss was, altogether, 60,000 men; but this is not, of course, reliable.

Another officer said Lee was retiring, which is simply impossible, now, for the flood.

But, alas! we have sad tidings from the West. Gen. Johnston telegraphs from Jackson, Miss., that Vicksburg capitulated on the 4th inst. This is a terrible blow, and has produced much despondency.

The President, sick as he is, has directed the Secretary of War to send him copies of all the correspondence with Johnston and Bragg, etc., on the subject of the relief of Pemberton.

The Secretary of War has caught the prevailing alarm at the silence of Lee, and posted off to the President for a solution—but got none. If Lee falls back again, it will be the darkest day for the Confederacy we have yet seen.

July 9th.—The sad tidings from Vicksburg have been confirmed by subsequent accounts. The number of men fit for duty on the day of capitulation was only a little upwards of 7000. Flour was selling at $400 per barrel! This betrays the extremity to which they had been reduced.

A dispatch to-day states that Grant, with 100,000 men (supposed), is marching on Jackson, to give Johnston battle. But Johnston will retire—he has not men enough to withstand him, until he leads him farther into the interior. If beaten, Mobile might fall.

We have no particulars yet—no comments of the Southern generals under Pemberton. But the fall of the place has cast a gloom over everything.

The fall of Vicksburg, alone, does not make this the darkest day of the war, as it is undoubtedly. The news from Lee's army is appalling. After the battle of Friday, the accounts from Martinsburg now state, he fell back toward Hagerstown, followed by the enemy, fighting but little on the way. Instead of 40,000 we have only 4000 prisoners. How many we have lost, we know not. The Potomac is, perhaps, too high for him to pass it—and there are probably 15,000 of the enemy immediately in his rear! Such are the gloomy accounts from Martinsburg.

Our telegraph operators are great liars, or else they have been made the dupes of spies and traitors. That the cause has suffered much, and may be ruined by the toleration of disloyal persons within our lines, who have kept the enemy informed of all our movements, there can be no doubt.

The following is Gen. Johnston's dispatch announcing the fall of Vicksburg:

"JACKSON, July 7th, 1863.

"HON. J. A. SEDDON, SECRETARY OF WAR.

"Vicksburg capitulated on the 4th inst. The garrison was paroled, and are to be returned to our lines, the officers retaining their side-arms and personal baggage.

"This intelligence was brought by an officer who left the place on Sunday, the 5th.

"J. E. JOHNSTON, *General.*"

We get nothing from Lee himself. Gen. Cooper, the Secretary of War, and Gen. Hill went to the President's office about one o'clock. They seemed in haste, and excited. The President, too, is sick, and ought not to attend to business. It will kill him, perhaps.

There is serious anxiety now for the fate of Richmond. Will Meade be here in a few weeks? Perhaps so—but, then, Lee may not have quite completed his raid beyond the Potomac.

The *Baltimore American*, no doubt in some trepidation for the quiescence of that city, gets up a most glowing account of "Meade's victory"—if it should, indeed, in the sequel, prove to have been one. That Lee fell back, is true; but how many men were lost on each side in killed, wounded, and prisoners—how many guns were taken, and what may be the result of the operations in Pennsylvania and Maryland—of which we have as yet such imperfect accounts—will soon be known.

JULY 10TH.—This is the day of fate—and, without a cloud in the sky, the red sun, dimly seen through the mist (at noonday), casts a baleful light on the earth. It has been so for several days.

Early this morning a dispatch was received from Gen. Beauregard that the enemy attacked the forts in Charleston harbor, and, subsequently, that they were landing troops on Morris Island. Up to 3 o'clock we have no tidings of the result. But if Charleston falls, the government will be blamed for it—since, notwithstanding the remonstrances of Gen. B., the government, members of Congress, and prominent citizens, some 10,000 of his troops were away to save Vicksburg.

About one o'clock to-day the President sent over to the Secretary of War a dispatch from an officer at Martinsburg, stating that Gen. Lee was still at Hagerstown awaiting his ammunition —(has not Col. Gorgas, Chief of Ordnance, been sufficiently vigilant?)—which, however, had arrived at the Potomac. That all the prisoners (number not stated), except those paroled, were at the river. That *nothing was known of the enemy*—but that cavalry fighting occurred every day. He concluded by saying he did not know whether Lee would advance *or recross the river.* If he does the latter, in my opinion there will be a great revulsion of feeling in the Confederate States and in the United States.

Another dispatch, from Gen. J. E. Johnston, dated yesterday, at Jackson, Miss., stated that Grant's army was then within *four* miles of him, with numbers double his own. But that he would hold the city as long as possible, for its fall would be the loss of the State. I learn a subsequent dispatch announced that fighting had begun. I believe Johnston is intrenched.

To-day Mr. Secretary Seddon requested Attorney-General Watts, if he could do so consistent with duty, to order a *nolle prosequi* in the District Court of Alabama in the case of Ford, Hurd & Co. for trading with the enemy. Gen. Pemberton had made a contract with them, allowing them to ship cotton to New Orleans, and to bring back certain supplies for the army. But Mr. Attorney-General Watts replied that it was not consistent with his duty to comply, and therefore he demurred to it, as the act they were charged with was in violation of the act of Congress of April 19th, 1862.

We lost twelve general officers in the fall of Vicksburg—one lieutenant-general, four major-generals, and seven brigadiers.

Dispatches from Jackson, Miss., say the battle began yesterday, but up to the time of the latest accounts it had not become general. Johnston had destroyed the wells and cisterns, and as there are no running streams in the vicinity, no doubt Grant's army will suffer for water, if the defense be protracted.

From Charleston we learn that we lost in yesterday's combat some 300 men, killed and wounded—the enemy quite as many. This morning the Yankees assaulted the battery on Morris Island, and were repulsed in two minutes, with a loss of 95 killed and 130 wounded, besides prisoners. Our loss was five, killed and wounded. Nothing further was heard up to 7 o'clock P.M.

From Lee we have no news whatever.

A letter from Governor Vance, of North Carolina, complains of an insult offered by Col. Thorburn (of Virginia), and asking that he be removed from the State, and if retained in service, not to be permitted to command North Carolinians. The Governor, by permission of Gen. Whiting, proceeded down the river to a steamer which had just got in (and was aground) from Europe, laden with supplies for the State; but when attempting to return was stopped by Col. T., who said it was against the rules for any one to pass from the steamer to the city until the expiration of the time prescribed for quarantine. The Governor informed him of his special permission from Gen. Whiting and the Board of Navigation—and yet the colonel said he should not pass for fifteen days, "if he *was* Governor Vance or Governor Jesus Christ." The President indorsed on this letter, as one requiring the Secretary's attention, "if the case be as stated."

Again the blockade-runners are at their dirty work, and Judge Campbell is "allowing" them. To-day Col. J. Gorgas, who is daily in receipt of immense amounts of ordnance stores from Europe by government steamers, recommends that passports be given N. H. Rogers and L. S. White to proceed *North* for supplies. This is a small business. It is no time to apply for passports, and no time to grant them.

We now know all about the mission of Vice-President Stephens under flag of truce. It was ill-timed for success. At Washington news had been received of the defeat of Gen. Lee—which may yet prove not to have been "all a defeat."

JULY 12TH.—There is nothing additional this morning from Charleston, Mississippi, or Maryland. Telegraphic communication is still open to Jackson, where all was quiet again at the last accounts; but battle, then, must occur immediately. From Charleston we learn that Beauregard had repulsed every assault of the enemy. It is rumored that Lee's account of the battle of Gettysburg will be published to-morrow, showing that it was the "most brilliant and successful battle of the war." I hope he may say so —for then it will be so.

Our papers are publishing Milroy's papers captured at Winchester.

JULY 13TH.—The *Enquirer* says the President has got a letter from Gen. Lee (why not give it to the people?) stating that his operations in Pennsylvania and Maryland have been successful and satisfactory, and that we have now some 15,000 to 18,000 prisoners, besides the 4000 or 5000 paroled. Nonsense!

Lee and Meade have been facing each other two or three days, drawn up in battle array, and a decisive battle may have occurred ere this. The wires have been cut between Martinsburg and Hagerstown.

Not another word have we from either Charleston or Jackson; but we learn that monitors, gun-boats, and transports are coming up the James River.

Altogether, this is another dark day in our history. It has been officially ascertained that Pemberton surrendered, with Vicksburg, 22,000 men! He has lost, during the year, not less than 40,000! And Lovell (another Northern general) lost Fort Jackson and New Orleans. When *will* the government put "none but Southerners on guard?"

Letters to-day from the Governors of South Carolina, Alabama, and North Carolina show that all are offended at the Confederate government. Judge Campbell's judicial profundity (and he is the department's correspondent) is unfortunate at this crisis, when, not great principles, but quick and successful fighting, alone can serve.

It appears that President Lincoln has made a speech in Washington in exultation over the fall of Vicksburg, and the defeat of an army contending against the principle that all men were created equal. He means the negro—we mean that white men were created equal—that we are equal to Northern white people, and have a right, which we do not deny to them, of living under a government of our own choice.

JULY 14TH.—To day we have tidings of the fall of Port Hudson, on the Mississippi River, our last stronghold there. I suppose some 10,000 or 12,000 of our men had to surrender, unconditionally. Thus the army of Gen. Pemberton, first and last, some 50,000 strong, has been completely destroyed. There is sadness and gloom throughout the land!

The enemy are established on Morris Island, and the fate of Charleston is in doubt.

We have nothing authentic from Gen. Lee; but long trains of the slightly wounded arrived yesterday and to-day.

It has been raining, almost every day, for nearly two weeks.

The President is quite amiable now. The newspaper editors can find easy access, and he welcomes them with smiles.

A letter was received to-day from a Major Jones, saying he was authorized to state that the Messrs. ———, engine-makers in Philadelphia, were willing to remove their machinery to the South, being Southern men. The President indorsed that authority might be given for them to come, etc.

Gen. Beauregard writes for a certain person here skilled in the management of torpedoes—but Secretary Mallory says the enemy's gun-boats are in the James River, and he cannot be sent away. I hope both cities may not fall!

A heavy thunder-storm, accompanied with a deluging rain, prevails this afternoon at 5½ o'clock P.M.

JULY 15TH.—There was a rumor of another battle beyond the Potomac, this morning, but it has not been confirmed.

From Charleston we have no news; but from Jackson there has been considerable fighting, without a general engagement.

The *Enquirer* and *Sentinel* to-day squint at a military dictatorship; but President Davis would hardly attempt such a feat at such a time.

Gen. Samuel Jones, Western Virginia, has delayed 2000 men ordered to Lee, assigning as an excuse the demonstrations of the enemy in the Kanawha Valley. "Off with his head—so much for Buckingham!"

There is some gloom in the community; but the spirits of the people will rebound.

A large crowd of Irish, Dutch, and Jews are daily seen at Gen. Winder's door, asking permission to go North on the flag of truce boat. They fear being forced into the army; they will be compelled to aid in the defense of the city, or be imprisoned. They intend to leave their families behind, to save the property they have accumulated under the protection of the government.

Files of papers from Europe show that Mr. Roebuck and other members of Parliament, as well as the papers, are again agitating the question of recognition. We shall soon ascertain the real intentions of France and England. If they truly desire our success, and apprehend danger from the United States in the event of a reconstruction of the Union, they will manifest their purposes when the news of our recent calamities shall be transported across the ocean. And if such a thing as reconstruction were possible, and were accomplished (in such a manner and on such terms as would not appear degrading to the Southern people), then, indeed, well might both France and England tremble. The United States would have *millions* of soldiers, and the Southern people would not owe either of them a debt of gratitude.

JULY 16TH.—This is another blue day in the calendar. Nothing from Lee, or Johnston, or Bragg; and no news is generally bad news. But from Charleston we learn that the enemy are established on Morris Island, having taken a dozen of our guns and howitzers in the sand hills at the lower end; and that the monitors had passed the bar, and doubtless an engagement by land and by water is imminent, if indeed it has not already taken place. Many regard Charleston as lost. I do not.

Again the *Enquirer*, edited by Mitchel, the Irishman, is urging the President to seize arbitrary power; but the *Examiner* combats the project defiantly.

Mr. Secretary Seddon, who usually wears a sallow and cadaverous look, which, coupled with his emaciation, makes him resemble an exhumed corpse after a month's interment, looks to-day like a galvanized corpse which had been buried two months. The circles round his eyes are absolutely black! And yet he was pacing briskly backward and forward between the President's office and the War Department. He seems much affected by disasters.

The United States agent of exchange has sent a notice to our agent that the negroes we capture from them in battle must be exchanged as other soldiers are, according to the cartel, which said nothing about color; and if the act of Congress in relation to such soldiers be executed, the United States would retaliate to the utmost extremity.

Captains H. W. Sawyer and John Flinn, having been designated by lot for execution in retaliation for two of our captains executed by Gen. Burnside for recruiting in Kentucky, write somewhat lugubriously, in bad grammar and execrable chirography, that, as they never served under Burnside, they should not be made to suffer for his deed. They say we have two of Burnside's captains at Atlanta (and they give their names) who would be the proper victims.

I saw a paper to-day, sent to the department, with a list of the

United States officers at Memphis who are said to have taken bribes; among them is Col. H——r, of Illinois, Provost Marshal General (Grant's staff); Col. A——, Illinois, ex-Provost Marshal; Capt. W——, Illinois, Assistant Provost Marshal; Capt. C—— (Gen. Herbert's staff), and "Dan Ross," citizen of Illinois, *procurer*.

On the 9th instant Gen. D. H. Hill (now lieutenant-general, and assigned to Mississippi) asks if troops are to be sent to cover Lee's *retreat;* and fears, if the enemy establish themselves at Winchester, they will starve Lee to death. Speaking of the raid of the enemy to the North Carolina Railroad, he said they would do the State infinite service by dashing into Raleigh and capturing all the members of the legislature. He also hits at the local newspapers here. Their mention of his name, and the names of other officers in the campaign round Richmond, informed the enemy that we had no troops at Goldsborough and Weldon, and hence the raid. And, after all, he says the enemy were not more numerous than our forces in the recent dash at Richmond. He says it was no feint, but a faint.

To-day an order was issued for the local troops to deliver up their ammunition. What does that mean?

And to-day the President calls for the second class of conscripts, all between eighteen and forty-five years of age. *So our reserves must take the field!*

JULY 17TH.—At last we have the authentic announcement that Gen. Lee has recrossed the Potomac! Thus the armies of the Confederate States are recoiling at all points, and a settled gloom is apparent on many weak faces. The fall of Charleston is anticipated. Subjugation is not apprehended by the government; for, if driven to an interior line of defense, the war may be prolonged indefinitely, or at least until the United States becomes embroiled with some European power.

Meantime we are in a half starving condition. I have lost twenty pounds, and my wife and children are emaciated to some extent. Still, I hear no murmuring.

To-day, for the second time, ten dollars in Confederate notes are given for one in gold; and no doubt, under our recent disasters, the depreciation will increase. Had it not been for the stupidity of our Dutch Secretary of the Treasury, Mr. Memminger, there would have been no financial difficulties. If he had recommended (as he was urged to do) the purchase by the government of all the cotton, it could have been bought at 7 cents per pound; and the *profits* alone would have defrayed the greater portion of the expenses of the war, besides affording immense *diplomatic* facilities and advantages. But red-tape etiquette, never violated by the government, may prove our financial ruin beyond redemption. It costs this government five times as much to support an army as it does the United States; and the call for conscripts is a farce, since the speculators (and who is not one now?) will buy exemptions from the party who, strangely, have the authority to grant them.

The last accounts from Jackson state that Burnside is reinforcing Grant, and that heavy skirmishing is going on daily. But all suppose that Johnston must retreat. And Bragg is in no condition to face Rosecrans.

Whether Lee will come hither or not, no one knows; but some tremble for the fate of Richmond. Lee possibly may cross the Potomac again, however, if Meade detaches a heavy force to capture Richmond.

What our fate would be if we fall into the hands of the invader, may be surmised from the sufferings of the people in New Orleans.

JULY 18TH.—Lee has got over the Potomac with a loss, in crossing, of 1500; and Johnston has abandoned Jackson, Miss.

But we have *awful* good news from New York: an INSURRECTION, the loss of many lives, extensive pillage and burning, with a suspension of the conscription!

Gen. Morgan is in the enemy's country.

JULY 19TH.—We have no news this morning. But a rumor prevails, which cannot be traced to any authentic source, that Texas has put herself under the protection of France. It is significant, because public sentiment seems to acquiesce in such a measure; and I have not met with any who do not express a wish that it may be so. Texas, Louisiana, and Arkansas are now isolated, and no protection or aid can be given them by the government here; and it is natural, after the fall of New Orleans and Vicksburg, for the people to hope that the invaders may be deprived of their prey just at the moment when they anticipated a realization of its enjoyment.

Hon. Wm. Porcher Miles writes that, after consultation, the officers have decided that it would be impracticable to hold Morris Island, even if the enemy were driven from it at the point of the bayonet. Therefore they call loudly for Brooke guns of long range, and guns of large calibre for Sumter, so that the fort may prevent the enemy from erecting batteries in breaching distance. They say, in their appeal, that since the fall of Vicksburg there is no other place (but one) to send them. They are now idle in Richmond. I understand the Secretary of War, etc. are in consultation on the subject, and I hope the President will, at last, yield to Gen. Beauregard's demands.

Gen. Maury also writes for guns and ordnance stores for the defense of Mobile, which may be attacked next. He will get them.

If the insurrection in New York lives, and resistance to conscription should be general in the North, our people will take fresh hope, and make renewed efforts to beat back the mighty armies of the foe—suffering, and more than decimated, as we are.

But if not—if Charleston and Richmond and Mobile should fall, a peace (submission) party will spring up. Nevertheless, the *fighting* population would still resist, retiring into the interior and darting out occasionally, from positions of concentration, at the exposed camps of the enemy.

July 20th.—Nothing from Lee or from Johnston, except that the latter has abandoned Jackson. From Bragg's army, I learn that a certain number of regiments were moving from Chattanooga toward Knoxville—and I suspect their destination is Lee's army.

But we have a dispatch from Beauregard, stating that he has again repulsed an attack of the enemy on the battery on Morris Island with heavy loss—perhaps 1500—while his is trifling.

A thousand of the enemy's forces were in Wytheville yesterday, and were severely handled by 130 of the home guards. They did but little injury to the railroad, and burned a few buildings.

An indignant letter has been received from the Hon. W. Porcher Miles, who had applied for a sub-lieutenancy for Charles Porcher, who had served with merit in the 1st South Carolina Artillery, and was his relative. It seems that the President directed the Secretary to state that the appointment could not be given him because he was not 21 years of age. To this Mr. M. replies that several minors in the same regiment have been appointed. I think not.

Governor Brown writes a long letter, protesting against the decision of the Confederate States Government, that the President shall appoint the colonel for the 51st Georgia Regiment, which the Governor says is contrary to the Confederate States Constitution. He will resist it.

A Mrs. Allen, a lady of wealth here, has been arrested for giving information to the enemy. Her letters were intercepted. She is confined at the asylum *St. Francis de Sales.* The surgeon who attends there reports to-day that her mental excitement will probably drive her to madness. Her great fear seems to be that she will be soon sent to a common prison. There is much indignation that she should be assigned to such comfortable quarters—and I believe the Bishop (McGill) protests against having criminals imprisoned in his religious edifices. It is said she has long been sending treasonable letters to Baltimore—but the authorities do not have the names of her letter-carriers published. No doubt they had passports.

A letter from Lee's army says we lost 10,000 in the recent battle, killed, wounded, and prisoners. We took 11,000 prisoners and 11 guns.

Thank Heaven! we have fine weather after nearly a month's rain. It may be that we shall have better fortune in the field now.

Some of the bankers had an interview with the government today. Unless we can achieve some brilliant success, they cannot longer keep our government notes from depreciating, down to five cents on the dollar. They are selling for only ten cents now, in gold. In vain will be the sale of a million of government gold in the effort to keep it up.

Gen. Morgan, like a comet, has shot out of the beaten track of the army, and after dashing deeply into Indiana, the last heard of him he was in Ohio, *near Cincinnati.* He was playing havoc with steam-boats, and capturing fine horses. He has some 3000 men we cannot afford to lose—but I fear they will be lost.

JULY 21ST.—We have intelligence to-day, derived from a New York paper of the 18th inst., that the "insurrection" in New York had subsided, under the menacing attitude of the military authority, and that Lincoln had ordered the conscription law to be enforced. This gives promise of a long war.

Mr. Mallory sent a note to the Secretary of War to-day (which of course the Secretary did not see, and will never hear of) by a young man named Juan Boyle, asking permission for B. to pass into Maryland as an agent of the Navy Department. Judge Campbell indorsed on the back of it (to Brig.-Gen. Winder) that permission was "allowed" by "order." But what is this "agent" to procure in the United States which could not be had by our steamers plying regularly between Wilmington and Europe?

JULY 22D.—Col. Northrop, Commissary-General, sends in a paper to-day saying that only a quarter of a pound of meat per day can be given the soldiers, except when marching, and then only half a pound. He says no more can be derived from the trans-Mississippi country, nor from the State of Mississippi, or Tennessee, and parts of Georgia and Alabama; and if more than the amount he receives be given the soldiers, the negroes will have to go without any. He adds, however, that the peasants of Europe rarely have any meat, and in Hindostan, never.

Col. Bradley T. Johnson, who commanded a brigade at Gettysburg, writes that on the first day we carried everything before us, capturing 8000 prisoners and losing but few men; the error was in not following up the attack with all our forces immediately, and in not having sufficient ammunition on the field.

The newspapers to-day contain pretty accurate accounts of the battle.

JULY 23D.—We have the following dispatch from Gen. Beauregard, which is really refreshing in this season of disasters:

"CHARLESTON, July 22d, 1863.

"The enemy recommenced shelling again yesterday, with but few casualties on our part. We had, in the battle of the 18th inst., about 150 killed and wounded. The enemy's loss, including prisoners, was about 2000. Nearly 800 were buried under a flag of truce.

"Col. Putnam, acting brigadier-general, and Col. Shaw, commanding the negro regiment, were killed.

"(Signed) G. T. BEAUREGARD, *General.*"

It is said the *raiders* that dashed into Wytheville have been taken; but not so with the raiders that have been playing havoc with the railroad in North Carolina.

Another letter from J. M. Botts, Culpepper County, complains of the pasturing of army horses in his fields before the Gettysburg campaign, and asks if his fields are to be again subject to the use of the commander of the army, *now returning to his vicinity.* If *he* knows that Gen. Lee is fallen back thither, it is more than any one here seems to know. We shall see how accurate Mr. B. is in his conjecture.

A letter from Mr. Goodman, president of Mobile and Charleston Railroad, says military orders have been issued to destroy, by fire, railroad equipments to the value of $5,000,000; and one-third of this amount of destruction would defeat the purpose of the enemy for a long time. The President orders efforts to be made to bring away the equipments by sending them down the road.

Col. Preston, commandant of conscripts for South Carolina, has been appointed Chief of the Bureau of Conscription; he has accepted the appointment, and will be here August 1st. The law will now be honestly executed—if he be not too indolent, sick, etc.

Archbishop Hughes has made a speech in New York to keep down the Irish.

JULY 24TH.—Nothing from Lee, or Johnston, or Beauregard, or Bragg—but ill luck is fated for them all. Our ladies, at least, would not despair. But a day may change the aspect; a brilliant success would have a marvelous effect upon a people who have so long suffered and bled for freedom.

They are getting on more comfortably, I learn, on the Eastern Shore of Virginia. Only about 25 of the enemy's troops are said to be there, merely to guard the wires. In the Revolutionary war, and in the war of 1812, that peninsula escaped the horrors of war, being deemed then, as now, too insignificant to attract the cupidity of the invaders.

The Secretary of the Treasury sent an agent a few weeks ago with some $12,000,000 for disbursement in the trans-Mississippi country, but he has returned to this city, being unable to get through. He will now go to Havana, and thence to Texas; and hereafter money (if money it can be called) will be manufactured at Houston, where a paper treasury will be established.

Gen. Jos. E. Johnston has recently drawn for $20,000 in gold.

A letter from the Commissary-General to Gen. Lee states that we have but 1,800,000 pounds of bacon at Atlanta, and 500,000 pounds in this city, which is less than 30 days' rations for Bragg's and Lee's armies. He says all attempts to get bacon from Europe have failed, and he fears they will fail, and hence, if the ration be not reduced to $\frac{1}{4}$ pound we shall soon have no meat on hand. Gen. Lee says he cannot be responsible if the soldiers fail for want of food.

JULY 25TH.—Gen. Beauregard telegraphs that preparations should be made to withstand a bombardment at Savannah, and authority is asked, at the instance of Gov. Brown, to impress a sufficient number of slaves for the purpose.

Gen. Jos. E. Johnston telegraphs the President that Grant has fallen back to Vicksburg, and, from information in his possession, will not stay there a day, *but will proceed up the river.* Gen. Johnston asks if this eccentric movement does not indicate a purpose to concentrate the enemy's forces for the reduction of Richmond.

Grant's men, no doubt, objected to longer service at this season in the Southwest; perhaps Lincoln thinks Grant is the only general who can take Richmond, or it may be necessary for the presence of the army in the North to enforce the draft, to overawe conspirators against the administration, etc. We shall soon know more about it.

Misfortunes come in clusters. We have a report to-day that Gen. Morgan's command has been mostly captured in Ohio. The recent rains made the river unfordable.

It appears that Gen. Pemberton had but 15 days' rations to last 48 days, that the people offered him a year's supply for nothing if he would have it, and this he would not take, red tape requiring it to be delivered and paid for, so it fell into the hands of the enemy. He had a six months' supply of ammunition when he surrendered, and often during the siege would not let his men reply to the enemy's guns.

Advertisers in the papers offer $4000 for substitutes. One offers a farm in Hanover County, on the Central Railroad, of 230 acres, for a substitute. There is something significant in this. It was so in France when Napoleon had greatly exhausted the male population.

July 26th.—Letters were received to-day from Gens. Beauregard, Mercer, Whitney, and S. Jones.

It appears that Beauregard has some 6000 men of all arms, and that the enemy's force is estimated to be, or to have been (before losing some 3000), about 10,000. It is true the enemy has the benefit of his floating batteries, but we have our stationary ones. I think Charleston safe.

Gen. Mercer *squeaks* for the fate of Savannah, unless the government impresses slaves to work on the fortifications. All our generals *squeak* when an attack is apprehended, for the purpose of alarming the government, and procuring more men and material, so as to make success doubly sure.

And Gen. Whiting is squeaking loudly for the impressment of a thousand slaves, to complete his preparations for defense; and if he does not get them, he thinks the fall of Wilmington a pretty sure thing.

And Gen. Jones squeaks from the West, asking that the 3000 infantry he was at last compelled to send to Gen. Lee, near Winchester, be returned to him to oppose the enemy's raids. But what were they sent to Lee for, unless he meant to give battle? Such may be his intention, and a victory now is demanded of him to place him *rectus in curio.*

Beauregard says Fort Wagner, which has made such a successful defense on Morris Island, was located by Gen. Pemberton, and this is evidence of some military skill. But all the waters of Lethe will not obliterate the conviction of the people that he gave his army in the West to the enemy. If he had not been Northern born, they would have deemed him merely incompetent. Hence the impolicy of the government elevating Northern over Southern generals. All generals are judged by the degree of success they achieve, for success alone is considered the proof of merit, and one disaster may obliterate the memory of a dozen victories. Even Lee's great name is dimmed somewhat in the estimation of fools. He must beat Meade before Grant comes up, or suffer in reputation.

Gov. Bonham has demanded the free negroes taken on Morris Island, to be punished (death) according to the State law.

July 27th.—Nothing but disasters to chronicle now. Natchez and Yazoo City, all gone the way of Vicksburg, involving a heavy loss of boats, guns, and ordnance stores; besides, the enemy have got some twenty locomotives in Mississippi.

Lee has retreated as far as Culpepper Court House.

The President publishes another proclamation, fixing a day for the people to unite in prayer.

The weather is bad. With the exception of one or two bright days, it has been raining nearly a month. Superadded to the calamities crowding upon us, we have a rumor to-day that Gen. Lee has tendered his resignation. This is false. But it is said he is opposed to the retaliatory executions ordered by the President, which, if persisted in, must involve the life of his son, now in the hands of the enemy. Our officers executed by Burnside were certainly recruiting in Kentucky within the lines of the enemy, and Gen. Lee may differ with the President in the equity of executing officers taken by us in battle in retaliation.

JULY 28TH.—The rumor that Gen. Lee had resigned was simply a fabrication. His headquarters, a few days ago, were at Culpepper C. H., and may be soon this side of the Rappahannock. A battle and a victory may take place there.

Col. J. Gorgas, I presume, is no friend of Pemberton; it is not often that Northern men in our service are exempt from jealousies and envyings. He sends to the Secretary of War to-day a remarkable statement of Eugene Hill, an ordnance messenger, for whom he vouches, in relation to the siege and surrender of Vicksburg. It appears that Hill had been sent here by Lieut.-Gen. Holmes for ammunition, and on his way back to the trans-Mississippi country, was caught at Vicksburg, where he was detained until after the capitulation. He declares that the enemy's mines did our works no more injury than our mines did theirs; that when the surrender took place, there were an abundance of caps, and of all kinds of ordnance stores; that there were 90,000 pounds of bacon or salt meat unconsumed, besides a number of cows, and 400 mules, grazing within the fortifications; and that but few of the men even thought of such a contingency as a surrender, and did not know it had taken place until the next day (5th of July), when they were ordered to march out and lay down their arms. He adds that Gen. Pemberton kept himself very close, and was rarely seen by the troops, and was never known to go out to the works until he went out to surrender.

Major-Gen. D. Maury writes from Mobile, to the President, that he apprehends an attack from Banks, and asks instructions relative to the removal of 15,000 non-combatants from the city. He says Forts Gaines and Morgan are provisioned for six months, and that the land fortifications are numerous and formidable. He asks for 20,000 men to garrison them. The President instructs the Secretary, that when the purpose of the enemy is positively known, it will be time enough to remove the women, children, etc.; but that the defenses should be completed, and everything in readiness. But where the 20,000 men are to come from is not stated—perhaps from Johnston.

JULY 29TH.—Still raining! The great fear is that the crops will be ruined, and famine, which we have long been verging upon, will be complete. Is Providence frowning upon us for our sins, or upon our cause?

Another battle between Lee and Meade is looked for on the Upper Rappahannock.

Gov. Harris, in response to the President's call for 6000 men, says Western and Middle Tennessee are in the hands of the enemy, and that about half the people in East Tennessee sympathize with the North!

Some two or three hundred of Morgan's men have reached Lynchburg, and they believe Morgan himself will get off, with many more of his men.

The New York *Herald's* correspondent, writing from Washington on the 24th inst., says the United States ministers in England and France have informed the government of the intention of those powers to intervene immediately in our behalf; and that they will send iron-clad fleets to this country without delay. Whereupon the *Herald* says Mr. Seward is in favor of making peace with us, and reconstructing the Union—pardoning us—but keeping the slaves captured, etc. It is a cock-and-bull story, perhaps, without foundation.

JULY 30TH.—Raining still! Lee's and Meade's armies are manœuvring and facing each other still; but probably there will be no battle until the weather becomes fair, and the gushing waters in the vales of Culpepper subside.

From Charleston we learn that a furious bombardment is going on, the enemy not having yet abandoned the purpose of reducing the forts and capturing the city. Mr. Miles calls loudly for reinforcements and heavy cannon, and says the enemy was reinforced a few days since.

An indignant letter was received from Gov. Vance to-day, in response to the refusal of the government and Gen. Lee to permit him to send with the army a newspaper correspondent to see that justice was done the North Carolina troops. He withdraws the application, and appeals to history for the justice which (he says) will never be done North Carolina troops in Virginia by their associates. He asserts also that Gen. Lee refused furloughs to the wounded North Carolinians at the battle of Chancellorville (one-half the dead and wounded being from North Carolina), for fear they would not return to their colors when fit for duty!

Hon. Wm. L. Yancey is dead—of disease of the kidney. The *Examiner*, to-day, in praising him, made a bitter assault on the President, saying he was unfortunately and hastily *inflicted* on the Confederacy at Montgomery, and when fixed in position, banished from his presence the heart and brain of the South—denying all participation in the affairs of government to the great men who were the authors of secession, etc.

July 31st.—Hon. E. S. Dargan, member of Congress, writes from Mobile that Mississippi is nearly subdued, and Alabama is almost exhausted. He says our recent disasters, and Lee's failure in Pennsylvania, have nearly ruined us, and the destruction must be complete unless France and England can be induced to interfere in our behalf. He never believed they would intervene unless we agreed to abolish slavery; and he would embrace even that alternative to obtain their aid. He says the people are fast losing all hope of achieving their independence; and a slight change of policy on the part of Lincoln (pretermitting confiscation, I suppose) would put an end to the revolution and the Confederate States Government. Mr. D. has an unhappy disposition.

Mr. L. Q. Washington recommends Gen. Winder to permit Mr. Wm. Matthews, just from California, to leave the country. Gen. W. sends the letter to the Assistant Secretary of War, Judge Campbell, who "allows" it; and the passport is given, without the knowledge of the President or the Secretary of War.

The news from Mexico (by the Northern papers) is refreshing to our people. The "notables" of the new government, under the auspices of the French General, Forey, have proclaimed the States an Empire, and offered the throne to Maximilian of Austria; and if he will not accept, they "implore" the Emperor of France to designate the one who shall be their Emperor. Our people, very many of them, just at this time, would not object to being included in the same Empire.

The President is still scrutinizing Beauregard. The paper read from the general a few days since giving a statement of his forces, and the number of the enemy, being sent to the President by the Secretary of War, was returned to-day with the indorsement, that he hoped "a clearer comprehension of the cause," in the promised further report of the general, would be given "why the enemy approached Morris Island before being observed." So, omitting all notice of the defense (so far) of the batteries, etc., the attention of the President seems fixed on what the general omitted to do; or what he might, could, or should have done.

END OF VOL. I.